1990

Science Year

The World Book Annual Science Supplement

A review of Science and Technology
During the 1989 School Year

World Book, Inc.

a Scott Fetzer company

Chicago London Sydney Toronto

Staff

Publisher
William H. Nault

Editor in Chief
Robert O. Zeleny

Editorial
Executive Editor
A. Richard Harmet

Managing Editor
Wayne Wille

Associate Editor
Darlene R. Stille

Senior Editors
David L. Dreier
Robin Goldman
Jinger Hoop
Mary A. Krier
Barbara A. Mayes
Jay Myers
Rod Such

Contributing Editors
Sara Dreyfuss
Joan Stephenson

Index Editor
Beatrice Bertucci

Cartographic Services
H. George Stoll, Head
Wayne K. Pichler

Editorial Assistant
Ethel Matthews

Art
Art Director
Alfred de Simone

Senior Artist, Science Year
Lucy Smith

Senior Artists
Nikki Conner
Melanie J. Lawson

Contributing Artists
Alice Gardner
Brenda Tropinski
Deirdre Wroblewski

Photographs
Photography Director
John S. Marshall

Senior Photographs Editor
Sandra M. Ozanick

Photographs Editor
Geralyn Swietek

Research Services
Director
Mary Norton

Library Services
Mary Kayaian, Head

Product Production
Executive Director
Peter Mollman

Director of Manufacturing
Henry Koval

Manufacturing, Manager
Sandra Van den Broucke

Pre-Press Services
Jerry Stack, Director
Madelyn Krzak
Randi Park
Barbara Podczerwinski

Proofreaders
Anne Dillon
Marguerite Hoye
Daniel Marotta

ISBN 0-7166-0590-2

ISSN 0080-7621
Library of Congress Catalog Number: 65-21776
Printed in the United States of America.

Editorial Advisory Board

Contents

See page 10.

See page 68.

See page 92.

See page 115.

See page 181.

Contributors

Adelman, George, M.S.
Editorial Director and Editor,
Encyclopedia of Neuroscience.
[*Neuroscience*]

Andrews, Peter J., M.S.
Free-Lance Writer, Chemist.
[*Chemistry; Science You Can Use: Taking the Caffeine Out of Coffee*]

Barone, Jeanine, M.S.
Nutritionist/Exercise Physiologist,
American Health Foundation.
[*Nutrition*]

Booth, Stephen A., B.A.
Electronics and Photography Editor,
Popular Mechanics Magazine.
[*Electronics*]

Brett, Carlton E., Ph.D.
Associate Professor,
Department of Geological Sciences,
University of Rochester.
[*Paleontology*]

Brower, Lincoln Pierson, Ph.D.
Professor of Zoology,
University of Florida.
[*Special Report, Practicing to Deceive*]

Cain, Steve, B.S.
News Coordinator,
Purdue University.
[*Agriculture*]

Camper, John, B.A.
Reporter,
Chicago Tribune.
[*People in Science, Walter E. Massey*]

Chazdon, Robin L., Ph.D.
Assistant Professor,
University of Connecticut, Storrs.
[*Special Report, The Organization for Tropical Studies*]

Christensen, Jennifer, B.A.
Research Analyst,
Cambridge Communications.
[*Science You Can Use: The Facts About Fax*]

Colwell, Robert K., Ph.D.
Professor of Zoology,
University of Connecticut, Storrs.
[*Special Report, The Organization for Tropical Studies*]

Covault, Craig P., B.S.
Senior Space Editor,
Aviation Week Magazine.
[*Space Technology*]

Dennett, Joann Temple, Ph.D
Lecturer,
University of Colorado.
[*Special Report, Who (or What) Killed the Giant Mammals?*]

Donnan, Christopher B., Ph.D.
Professor of Anthropology,
University of California, Los Angeles.
[*Archaeology, New World* (Close-Up)]

Ferrell, Keith
Features Editor,
Compute! Publications.
[*Computer Hardware; Computer Software*]

Fisher, Arthur, B.A.
Science and Technology Editor,
Popular Science.
[*Special Report, Is Earth Overheating?*]

Franklin, Jerry F., Ph.D.
Bloedel Professor of Ecosystem
Analysis,
University of Washington.
[*Special Report, A Mountain Bounces Back*]

Gannon, Robert
Associate Professor,
Pennsylvania State University.
[*Materials Science* (Close-Up)]

Goldhaber, Paul, D.D.S.
Dean and Professor of
Periodontology,
Harvard School of Dental Medicine.
[*Dentistry*]

Goodman, Richard A., M.D.
Assistant Professor,
Division of Public Health,
Emory University.
[*Public Health*]

Gove, Harry E., Ph.D.
Professor of Physics,
University of Rochester.
[*Archaeology, Old World* (Close-Up)]

Hall, Charles A. S., Ph.D.
Associate Professor of Ecology and
Systematics,
State University of New York,
College of Environmental Sciences
and Forestry.
[*World Book Supplement: Ecology*]

Hawkins, William J.
Senior Editor—Electronics,
Popular Science.
[*Special Report, The Endless Quest for a Better TV Picture; Science You Can Use: Cooking with Microwaves*]

Hay, William W., Ph.D.
Director, University of Colorado
Museum,
University of Colorado at Boulder.
[*Geology*]

Haymer, David S., Ph.D.
Department of Genetics,
University of Hawaii.
[*Genetic Science*]

Hellemans, Alexander, B.S.
Senior Editor,
World Book International.
[*Physics, Fluids and Solids*]

Hester, Thomas R., Ph.D.
Professor of Anthropology and
Director,
Texas Archaeological Research
Laboratory,
University of Texas at Austin.
[*Archaeology, New World*]

Hohlfelder, Robert L., Ph.D.
Professor of History,
University of Colorado at Boulder.
[*Special Report, Excavating Herod's Dream*]

Jones, William G., A.M.L.S.
Assistant University Librarian and
Associate Professor,
University of Illinois at Chicago.
[*Books of Science*]

Katz, Paul, M.D.
Associate Professor and Vice
Chairman, Department of Medicine,
Georgetown University School of
Medicine.
[*Immunology*]

King, Lauriston R., Ph.D.
Deputy Director,
Office of University Research,
Texas A&M University.
[*Oceanography*]

Lechtenberg, V. L., Ph.D.
Associate Director,
Agricultural Research,
Purdue University.
[*Agriculture*]

Lewin, Roger, Ph.D.
Editor, Research News,
Science Magazine.
[*Environment* (Close-Up)]

Limburg, Peter R., M.A.
Author and Free-Lance Writer.
[*People in Science, James D. Watson*]

Lunine, Jonathan I., Ph.D.
Assistant Professor,
Lunar Planetary Lab,
University of Arizona.
[*Astronomy, Solar System*]

Maran, Stephen P., Ph.D.
Senior Staff Scientist,
NASA-Goddard Space Flight Center.
[*Special Report, New Eyes on the Sky*]

March, Robert H., Ph.D.
Professor of Physics,
University of Wisconsin.
[*Physics, Subatomic*]

Merbs, Charles F., Ph.D.
Professor, Department of
Anthropology,
Arizona State University.
[*Anthropology*]

Merz, Beverly, A.B.
Associate Editor,
Journal of the American Medical Association.
[*Medical Research*]

Meyer, B. Robert, M.D.
Chief, Division of Clinical
Pharmacology,
North Shore University Hospital.
[*Drugs*]

Moores, Eldridge M., Ph.D.
Professor and Chairman,
Department of Geology,
University of California at Davis.
[*Geology* (Close-Up)]

Murray, Stephen S., Ph.D.
Astrophysicist,
Harvard/Smithsonian Center for
Astrophysics.
[*Astronomy, Extragalactic*]

Olson, Judy M., Ph.D.
Professor,
Department of Geography,
Michigan State University.
[*World Book Supplement: Map*]

Patrusky, Ben, B.E.E.
Free-Lance Science Writer.
[*Special Report, "Magic Bullets" Against Disease*]

Pennisi, Elizabeth, M.S.
Free-Lance Science Writer.
[*Zoology*]

Primack, Joel R., Ph.D.
Professor of Physics,
University of California at Santa Cruz.
[*Special Report, The Case of the Dark Matter*]

Raloff, Janet, M.S.J.
Environment/Policy Editor,
Science News Magazine.
[*Special Report, The Growing Garbage Mess; Environment*]

Rensberger, Boyce, M.S.
Science Editor,
The Washington Post.
[*Special Report, Creating the Ultimate Map of Our Genes*]

Salisbury, Frank B., Ph.D.
Professor of Plant Physiology,
Utah State University.
[*Botany; Botany* (Close-Up)]

Snow, John T., Ph.D.
Associate Professor,
Purdue University.
[*Meteorology*]

Snow, Theodore P., Ph.D.
Professor of Astrophysics,
University of Colorado at Boulder.
[*Astronomy, Galactic*]

Somerville, Diana, B.A.
Free-Lance Science Writer.
[*Special Report, Science Versus Wind Shear*]

Stanley, Steven M., Ph.D.
Professor and Chairman,
Earth and Planetary Sciences,
The Johns Hopkins University.
[*World Book Supplement: Fossil*]

Swanton, Donald W., Ph.D.
Chairman, Department of Finance,
Roosevelt University.
[*Science You Can Use: Sorting Out the Averages*]

Tamarin, Robert H., Ph.D.
Professor of Biology,
Boston University.
[*Ecology*]

Tobin, Thomas R., Ph.D.
Assistant Professor,
ARL Division of Neurobiology,
University of Arizona.
[*Zoology*]

Trotter, Robert J., B.S.
Free-Lance Science Writer.
[*Psychology*]

Visich, Marian, Jr., Ph.D.
Associate Dean of Engineering,
State University of New York.
[*Energy*]

Wallace, Joseph, B.A.
Free-Lance Writer.
[*Special Report, Mysteries of the Ocean's Midwater*]

Wenke, Robert J., Ph.D.
Associate Professor,
Department of Anthropology,
University of Washington.
[*Archaeology, Old World*]

Wolff, Barbara, M.A.T.
Physics Teacher,
Livingston High School,
Livingston, N.J.
[*Physics, Fluids and Solids* (Close-Up)]

Woods, Michael, B.S.
Science Editor,
The Toledo Blade.
[*Science You Can Use: Getting a Reading on Blood Pressure Devices*]

Yager, Robert E., Ph.D.
Professor of Science Education,
University of Iowa.
[*Science Education*]

Special Reports

Fourteen articles give in-depth treatment to significant and timely subjects in science and technology.

Scientists may never know for certain
whether a climate change or human
hunters caused widespread extinctions
of large mammals at the end of
the last Ice Age.

Who (or What) Killed the Giant Mammals?

BY JOANN TEMPLE DENNETT

Thirty thousand years ago, during the Ice Age epoch known as the Pleistocene, the world was a land of giants. In North America, it was the time of the elephantlike mastodon and the woolly mammoth, the saber-toothed cats and the Florida cave bear. In the area that is now Europe, there were deer with tree-sized antlers. Predators such as cave lions, cheetahs, and jaguars found good hunting among large herds of browsing and grazing animals in North America, Europe, and Asia.

In North America, mastodons fed in the jack pine and spruce forests of the east, while beavers the size of modern bears felled large trees to build their dams. In the regions that are now Mexico and the southeastern United States, llamas, Florida cave bears, giant tortoises, and glyptodons—armadillolike creatures as big as lions—lived in deciduous forests and tropical evergreen groves. On the grassy plains in the western part of the continent browsed ground sloths as massive as small elephants. They shared the landscape with herds of grazing animals—shaggy horses, giant bison, mule deer, and even camels. In the far northwest, woolly mammoths, yaks, stag moose, and antelope lived on a vast grassland. At high elevations, musk oxen and caribou lived in a tundra environment much like the fragile, frozen permafrost of today's Alaska.

Unlike the dinosaurs that had roamed Earth until 65 million years ago, these giants were mammals. But like the dinosaurs, many of these large mammals—browsers, grazers, and predators—became extinct. In the space of a few thousand years, a very short time in the geologic history of the world, 33 *genera* (groups of related species) of large mammals died out completely. Mammoths and mastodons were extinct; ground sloths and giant beavers were gone; saber-toothed cats had vanished. Other large mammals, such as the camel and the horse, died out in North America though they survived on other continents. The number of species of smaller animals, however, experienced little change.

Scientists have long wondered what happened to the giant mammals—especially those in North America, where the most extensive extinctions occurred all at about the same time. Like detectives puzzling over a crime committed long-ago, researchers are faced with a scarcity of clues.

The bits of evidence they do have—plant and bone fossils, stone spearpoints, samples of rock on land and sediment from the bottom of the sea—have led many scientists to conclude that a worldwide climate change—from cold to warmer—killed the mammals. But the very same clues have convinced others that human hunters caused the extinctions. Although we may never find enough evidence to confirm either theory, learning about them gives us information about a fascinating time in Earth's history—and a look at the way scientists and researchers proceed when they are faced with incomplete information.

What do scientists know for certain about the mysterious extinctions? To start with the most basic point, they say with great

The author:
Joann Temple Dennett is a free-lance science writer and a lecturer at the University of Colorado in Boulder.

assurance that the huge mammals once lived. One proof of this is the existence of the animals' fossilized bones. *Paleontologists*, who study fossils, have found mammoth bones in at least 1,400 different locations, and bones of other Pleistocene animals are almost as abundant.

If this evidence were not convincing enough, entire mummified Pleistocene animals occasionally have been found frozen in icy regions. Many frozen mammoth remains have been discovered in Siberia alone.

Yet another type of evidence is the depiction of these creatures in cave art. Unlike the dinosaurs, the giant mammals lived when Earth was populated by humans. Although these prehistoric people had no written language, they left a record in the form of paintings, drawings, carvings, and sculpture—much of it found in caves in France and Spain. Since the late 1800's, nearly 200 caves decorated by prehistoric people have been discovered. Depictions of bison, horses, mammoths, reindeer, and sometimes cave lions and bears appear on the walls of these caves.

The bones of the giants

We know that the giant mammals lived in North America because paleontologists have discovered more than 150 fossil sites in the United States and Canada. The skeletons of more than 1 million Pleistocene animals have been discovered in the La Brea pits, an ancient asphalt bog in Hancock Park in Los Angeles. Paleontologists have unearthed skeletons of camels, ground sloths, horses, llamas, saber-toothed cats, and other Pleistocene animals that became trapped in the sticky bog.

Another site, in Hot Springs, S. Dak., yielded the bones of 30 mammoths who were apparently attracted to an ancient warm spring in a steep, slippery-sided sinkhole. They drowned there, leaving tracks showing their death struggles in sediment that later solidified into rock.

In north-central Wyoming, near the Montana border, the bones of more than 30,000 Pleistocene animals rest in Natural Trap Cave, a sinkhole 24 meters (85 feet) deep. This bell-shaped pit, hidden by the landscape and surrounded by slippery limestone, was a death trap for animals for at least 75,000 years, until scientists placed a steel grate over the large opening in the 1950's.

Finally, scientists have a rough idea of when these animals became extinct. Using a technique called *radiocarbon dating*, which measures the ratio of different forms of the element carbon in fossilized bones, paleontologists are able to estimate a bone's age with a fair degree of accuracy. Radiocarbon dating of the bones of North America's now-extinct large mammals indicates that most died out between 10,000 and 12,000 years ago.

Scientists also have firm evidence that the world's climate changed drastically at about the time of the extinctions. Scientific examination of samples of sediment from the ocean floor, along with soil and rock samples, show that vast regions of the world were covered with ice throughout the Pleistocene (which lasted from about 2 million years ago to about 10,000 years ago).

World of ice

When the giant mammals lived, glaciers—great sheets of ice formed from snow—covered much of Earth. In North America, the glaciers spread out from the Hudson Bay region of Canada to cover much of the Northern Hemisphere, at times extending as far south as southern Illinois. Over Hudson Bay, the ice may have reached depths of 3,000 meters (10,000 feet). In Europe, glaciers covered what is now northern England, Denmark, and Germany.

As many as 18 times during the Pleistocene, however, Earth's climate warmed—melting the great glaciers of Europe and North America—and then cooled off again. No one knows the reason for this fluctuation in climate, but many scientists think it may have been caused by the fact that Earth wobbled a bit on its axis. This event might have changed the amount of sunshine reaching Earth, causing a worldwide temperature change (in the Special Reports section, see Is EARTH OVERHEATING?).

The glaciers reached their largest extent about 18,000 years ago. Then, some 13,000 and 11,000 years ago—about the same time that the large mammals became extinct—Earth's climate underwent its most recent long-term warmings. The glaciers began to melt, and water newly unlocked from the ice swelled rivers and lakes, raised sea levels, and flooded coastal plains throughout the world. The melting ice provided more water than could evaporate into the atmosphere, producing more rain and snow.

The impact on North America's climate was dramatic. Although the central plains of North America were frigid before the glaciers melted, the towering glaciers acted like a mountain range and blocked winter's cold Arctic winds. This resulted in a relatively constant year-round temperature. After the glaciers melted, the plains experienced extreme fluctuations in temperature, with hotter summers and colder winters.

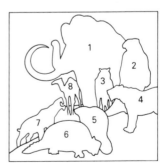

Portrait of the Victims

Animals that became extinct in North America at the end of the last Ice Age 10,000 years ago include: 1. mammoth; 2. pin-headed sloth; 3. native horse; 4. cave lion; 5. giant beaver; 6. glyptodon; 7. saber-toothed cat; 8. native camel.

Firm Evidence of Mass Extinctions

Scientists know that giant mammals once existed because they have found fossils of the animals, frozen carcasses, and pictures of them drawn by pre-historic artists. Scientists also know that North America lost almost half of its large-mammal species, while smaller animals survived.

A researcher in the early 1900's sorts some of the thousands of fossil bones, *above,* excavated from the La Brea pits in Los Angeles. The saber-toothed cat, *right,* is one of the many species of Pleistocene animals whose fossils have been found at La Brea and other sites in North America.

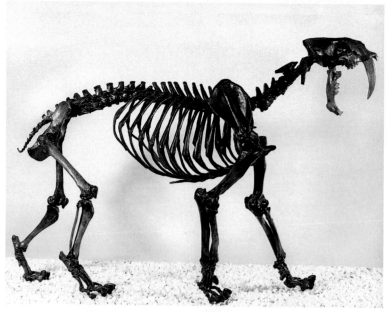

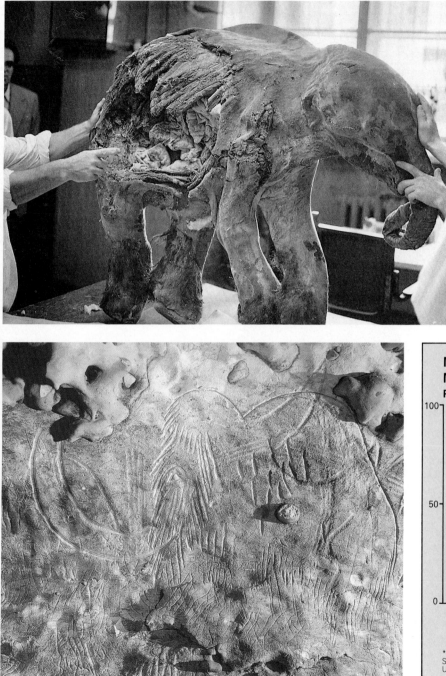

Soviet scientists examine the carcass of a baby woolly mammoth, *left.* Many mammoth carcasses, frozen for 10,000 years, have been discovered in the Siberian ice sheet.

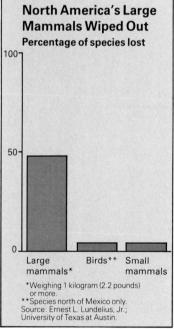

North America's Large Mammals Wiped Out
Percentage of species lost

*Weighing 1 kilogram (2.2 pounds) or more.
**Species north of Mexico only.
Source: Ernest L. Lundelius, Jr.; University of Texas at Austin.

Etched by an Ice Age artist in a cave in France, a depiction of a woolly mammoth gives scientists clues about the appearance of the now-extinct mammal.

Whatever caused the extinctions most severely affected large mammals. Almost half of these species were wiped out, while the number of species of smaller animals changed little.

17

Was a Changing Climate the Culprit?

Many scientists believe that global warmings occurring 13,000 and 11,000 years ago led to the mass extinctions. The warmings partially melted the glaciers that once dominated Earth, *below,* drastically changing the mammals' habitats, *opposite page.*

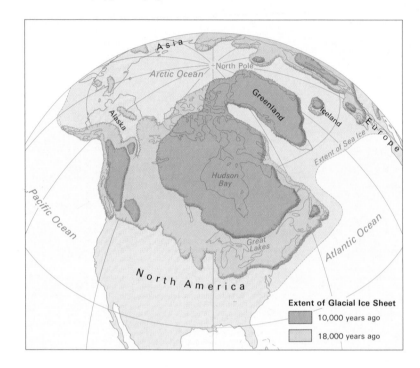

Extent of Glacial Ice Sheet
- 10,000 years ago
- 18,000 years ago

Did climate do it?

Around 1800, scientists first proposed that the extinctions of the giant mammals were linked to the climate change. Today, scientists from a diverse range of disciplines speculate that the climate change had severe, wide-ranging effects on North American mammals, destroying the animals' habitats, decreasing their food sources, and forcing them to migrate north. The climate change might have even killed outright many newborn animals, who are more vulnerable to inclement weather than are adults.

The basis of this theory is the effect of climate change on animals' habitats, according to two of its prominent proponents, geologist Ernest L. Lundelius, Jr., of the University of Texas at Austin and paleontologist Russell W. Graham of the Illinois State Museum in Springfield. If the temperature changes were rapid enough, plants—which are important for both food and shelter—would have been hard-hit. Since plants cannot move quickly to a more suitable climate, many plant species might have died, with different varieties springing up to take their place. Animals who could not thrive on the new mixture of plants would have been forced to migrate. Then

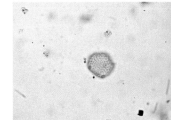

Analysis of fossil pollen from the Pleistocene Epoch, *above,* shows that southern Illinois, *left,* just one of many areas altered by the global warmings, was once dominated by forests of spruce, the mastodon's favorite food source.

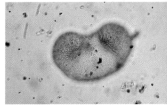

Fossil pollen from after the warmings, *above,* indicates that southern Illinois changed to a dense forest of elms, *left,* unsuitable for mastodons but ideal for smaller animals such as deer and muskrats.

predatory animals, such as the saber-toothed cat, that depended on the plant-eaters for food would also have had to migrate. For example, in North America, the mastodons, who ate needles from spruce trees, might have found their environment changing quickly as the climate warmed and the spruce died off and were replaced by forests of leafy deciduous trees. The mastodons living in spruce forests near what is now St. Louis, Mo., might have had to migrate toward what is now New England to find another suitable habitat.

The need to migrate might have caused many problems. Species that once shared a habitat could have moved in different directions, for example. If one species had previously depended on another for food, they might have found it difficult, if not impossible, to survive in a new region without their previous prey. Conversely, two or more species that had never before come in contact might have been forced to share a habitat. Such a situation could have exposed the animals to diseases carried by another species—infectious diseases they had never encountered before and to which they might have been especially vulnerable.

Proponents of this theory explain that large mammals would have been most affected by the climate change for several reasons. Large animals tend to need more food, more often, than smaller animals do, and so would have been more severely affected by a changing habitat. And adverse weather changes during the breeding season could seriously affect large animals because their pregnancies last longer than those of smaller animals.

Scientists who favor the climate-change theory cite evidence that shows sudden changes in the plant growth in various regions of North America. One type of evidence is fossil pollen, which is found by using a microscope to examine sediment that has been treated with strong chemicals to eliminate extraneous material. Fossil animal dung (*coprolites*) is studied to determine the kind of plants eaten by now-extinct animals.

Scientists also cite evidence that some species of animals living during the Pleistocene shifted their ranges after the climate change. Musk oxen and caribou now live only on the northern tundra. Horses disappeared from the plains of North America but lived on in Eurasia.

Flaws in the climate-change theory

Although the climate-change theory is popular, it is not without detractors, who cite several flaws. First, the global warmings that coincided with the extinctions were only the latest in a long series of warmings. Why should these climate changes wipe out species that had survived many others? What is needed is proof that the last climate changes were more severe than previous ones, and such evidence has not been found.

A second problem with the theory is that it does not explain why extinctions did not occur at the same rate around the world. North

America and Australia lost a greater percentage of their large mammal species than did Asia and Africa. Since the climate changes affected the entire planet, why did far fewer species in Africa and Asia become extinct?

Finally, proponents of the climate-change theory have not yet amassed enough evidence to conclusively explain why some animals became extinct even though their habitat apparently remained suitable. The native horse, for example, died out in North America during the Pleistocene, but similar horse species flourished in the same area after being reintroduced by Europeans thousands of years later. The huge Shasta ground sloth also became extinct, yet analysis of its coprolites from Rampart Cave at the western end of the Grand Canyon in Arizona shows that the sloth lived 11,000 years ago on plant species still growing today in its former habitat.

Did people do it?

Some scientists think that the extinction of the giant mammals may have coincided with another event—the arrival of human beings in North America. Archaeologists, who study the customs and life of ancient people, have unearthed evidence that the population of a prehistoric people reached its peak in the American southwest about 11,500 years ago. Archaeologists use the name *Clovis* to refer to this culture because the distinctive stone spearpoints—flat, two-faced points with a groove so that they could be bound to a shaft—made by these people were first discovered at an excavation site near Clovis, N. Mex., in 1934.

The discovery that people may have first appeared in the Americas at about the same time that the early mammals became extinct forms the basis for the second major theory about the Pleistocene extinctions: that people hunted the large mammals to extinction. In 1967, ecologist Paul S. Martin at the University of Arizona in Tucson proposed that humans decimated North America's large-mammal populations within a few thousand years.

Central to this "overkill" theory is Martin's belief that people first arrived in the Americas only about 12,000 years ago, crossing the Bering Strait on a land bridge that linked Asia and North America. During this time, the glaciers had melted enough to open an ice-free passageway between what is now Alaska and the western United States but had not melted enough to cause rising seas to flood the land bridge.

Martin believes that these early people were skilled hunters who found vast herds of large mammals that—having never seen human beings before—were unafraid of people and thus were easily approached and killed. Martin proposed that the Clovis population increased so quickly that the populations of the animals they hunted did not have time to recover. According to this theory, when the hunters killed off the large mammals in one area, the early people then moved to new hunting grounds. Eventually, people spread

Did Hunters Wipe Out the Large Mammals?

The theory that early people hunted the mammals to extinction has garnered support from many scientists since it was proposed in 1967. The most important evidence supporting this theory is the discovery of stone spearpoints among the fossil bones of some of the now-extinct animals.

Researchers unearth the bones of 12 mammoths at the base of a bluff near Denver, *left,* in the 1930's. Stray boulders and spearpoints among these fossils led scientists to speculate that prehistoric hunters stampeded the mammoths, forced them over the bluff, then speared and stoned the injured beasts to death.

A stone spearpoint, *above,* rests near bison bones at a Colorado excavation site, indicating that the bison may have been killed by a prehistoric hunter.

New high-tech research submarines are allowing scientists to study the strange animals that live in the midwater, the largest environment on Earth.

Mysteries of the Ocean's Midwater

BY JOSEPH WALLACE

About a thousand meters below the sunny surface of California's Monterey Bay, a robot vessel hovers quietly in the inky darkness. Spotlights mounted on the front of the vessel create a pool of light in which thousands of creatures swim. On-board cameras record a passing school of fish with small glowing lights like the headlamps on an old-fashioned car. Suddenly, a group of tiny octopuses speed past. Dominating the scene are swarms of "jellies"—jellyfish and other *coelenterates* or *cnidarians* (jellylike marine animals). Some are tiny creatures so delicate that they look as though the slightest touch would shatter them. Others, linked in chains meters long, float by like silent supertankers.

The robot vessel is a computerized *submersible* (a deep-sea exploration device) called a Remotely Operated Vehicle (ROV). It is helping scientists at the Monterey Bay Aquarium Research Institute (MBARI) in Pacific Grove, Calif., explore and study one of the most mysterious environments on Earth—the ocean's midwater. Despite hundreds of years of oceanographic research, scientists know remarkably little about this watery territory, which is, in fact, the largest environment on Earth. Only in the past 10 years have they discovered how abundant and complex life in the midwater really is.

Put simply, the midwater encompasses most of the ocean. It begins about 10 meters (33 feet) below the surface, just beneath the so-called

Opposite page: A visit from a curious giant starfish surprises a scientist in *Deep Rover* during a dive to study the midwater.

mixed layer where the wind churns the water. The midwater is like a layer cake, with horizontal zones of varying temperature, chemical composition, and depth. The thickness of these layers varies, depending on currents in the ocean.

Oceanographers recognize four major zones in the midwater. The *epipelagic zone* is the uppermost region and contains most of the familiar animals that live in the open sea. Next, at depths from about 250 to 1,000 meters (820 to 3,300 feet), is the *mesopelagic zone*. Many animals in this zone are *bioluminescent* (give off their own light) and rise to the surface to feed at night. The cold, dark *bathypelagic zone* extends from about 1,000 meters below the surface to about 50 meters (160 feet) above the sea floor. It is one of the strangest environments on Earth—and one of the most difficult to study. The lowest zone of the midwater is the *benthopelagic*, which begins about 50 meters above the sea floor. Here live strange, streamlined creatures specially adapted to the eternal darkness and tremendous pressure of the ocean depths.

The midwater ends about 10 meters (33 feet) above the sea floor. Between the midwater and the sea floor is a layer called the *benthic boundary layer*. This zone contains suspended sediment made up of plant, animal, and mineral debris that has settled from above.

The sheer quantity of ocean included in the midwater is hard even to imagine. The ocean covers 360 million square kilometers (140 million square miles), about 70 per cent of Earth's surface. In a few places it is more than 10,000 meters (33,000 feet) deep, with an overall average depth of 4,000 meters (13,000 feet).

The midwater environment also varies greatly from place to place. Just as different types of animals live in humid tropical swamps and on frigid, barren mountaintops, different kinds of animals live in different parts of the midwater. Temperature, light conditions, pressure, and ocean currents all help determine the type and relative number of animals inhabiting a specific area.

The upper midwater includes regions of murky twilight traveled by whales, sharks, and other familiar marine animals. Most of the

The author:
Joseph Wallace is a free-lance science writer.

midwater, however, is a realm of bitter cold and crushing pressure. By about 600 meters (2,000 feet) down, nearly all light has disappeared, leaving a region of perpetual darkness pierced only by the cold illumination given off by bizarre-looking creatures, many of which scientists are just starting to identify. "The midwater is the home of the largest communities of animals on Earth—communities that until recently we had barely explored," says marine biologist Bruce Robison, a leader of MBARI's ROV project.

Why is the midwater so little known? One reason is the region's vastness. Another is that it is difficult for scientists to reach and stay suspended in the various layers of the midwater. With scuba gear, divers can descend to about 40 meters (130 feet). But even at 40 meters, a diver has barely penetrated the midwater.

In the early 1930's, two men in a spherical container with thick windows called a *bathysphere* caught the first bewitching views of the deeper midwater and its eerie menagerie. Explorer and naturalist William Beebe of the New York Zoological Society and businessman and inventor Otis Barton, who designed and built the bathysphere, made more than two dozen dives near Bermuda, journeying to a depth of 900 meters (3,000 feet).

It would be logical to think that Beebe and Barton's exploits sent dozens of biologists hurrying to explore the midwater. But they didn't. The bathysphere was dangerous to use and expensive to build, and so little was known about the ocean that marine researchers could easily focus on less risky and less costly areas of study. Then, when better diving technology permitted safer exploration of the ocean depths, scientists turned their attention not to the midwater but to the ocean floor.

During the past 25 years, submersibles such as *Alvin*, which explored the wreck of the *Titanic* in 1986, have been designed to sink quickly to the bottom, not to tarry in the midwater. At best, they might provide only a fleeting glimpse of what lies between the surface and the ocean floor.

As a result, scientists studying the midwater have been forced to

Finding vehicles that could hover quietly in the midwater was a major research problem. The *WASP Atmospheric Diving Suit, opposite page,* used for midwater research in 1982, had a limited air supply and was awkward to maneuver. *Deep Rover, above left,* a one-person submersible equipped with sensitive cameras and specimen-collecting equipment, was first used for midwater research in 1985. The latest advance is the *Remotely Operated Vehicle, above right,* a robot submersible that can study the midwater for days at a time.

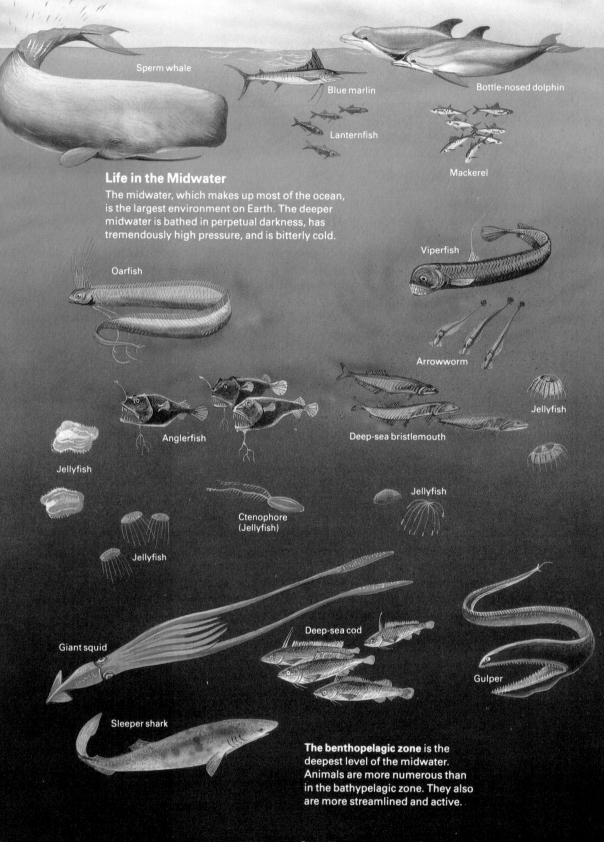

Sperm whale

Blue marlin

Bottle-nosed dolphin

Lanternfish

Mackerel

Life in the Midwater

The midwater, which makes up most of the ocean, is the largest environment on Earth. The deeper midwater is bathed in perpetual darkness, has tremendously high pressure, and is bitterly cold.

Viperfish

Oarfish

Arrowworm

Jellyfish

Anglerfish

Deep-sea bristlemouth

Jellyfish

Jellyfish

Ctenophore (Jellyfish)

Jellyfish

Jellyfish

Deep-sea cod

Giant squid

Gulper

Sleeper shark

The benthopelagic zone is the deepest level of the midwater. Animals are more numerous than in the bathypelagic zone. They also are more streamlined and active.

Sea spider

The animals shown here are not drawn to scale.

White shark

Tuna

Krill

Copepods

The epipelagic zone is home to most of the familiar animals of the open ocean. Because it is the only zone that receives much sunlight, it is the only zone in which plants grow—microscopic phytoplankton, the base of the ocean's food chain.

Midwater begins about 10 meters (33 feet) down

Epipelagic zone down to about 250 meters (820 feet)

The mesopelagic zone receives only faint sunlight. Below about 600 meters (2,000 feet), no light penetrates. Most mesopelagic animals are *bioluminescent* (give off their own light), and many rise to the surface at night to feed.

Mesopelagic zone about 250 to 1,000 meters (820 to 3,300 feet)

Lancet fish

Jellyfish

Hatchet fish

Dragonfish

Devilfish

Bathypelagic zone about 1,000 meters below the surface to about 50 meters (160 feet) above the sea floor

Siphonophore (Jellyfish)

Jellyfish

The bathypelagic zone, one of the most mysterious environments on Earth, is very cold and completely dark except for the light given off by its bioluminescent creatures. Some drift with the currents, capturing prey by lying in ambush.

Jellyfish

Polyacanthonotus

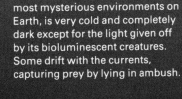
Skate

Benthopelagic zone up to about 50 meters above the sea floor

Ratfish

Midwater ends about 10 meters above sea floor

Rat-tailed fish

depend on extremely primitive techniques. "The most commonly used research method is very simple," Robison explains. "All you do is drag a large net behind a ship, then pull the net up and see what you've caught."

This technique, called trawling, has some serious drawbacks. Many other midwater creatures can avoid the net, and the animals that are caught usually die or become a huge mass of jelly, impossible even to identify. Trying to understand the feeding habits, migration patterns, and reproductive behavior of midwater animals by looking at these specimens is hopeless.

Nevertheless, marine scientists probing the midwater by trawling at various depths came to a few conclusions. They learned that certain midwater creatures seemed to live permanently at specific depths. Others, such as tuna, marlin, and swordfish, just pass through the midwater. They also found that although fish and jellies live throughout the midwater, most of the animals are concentrated in the upper 1,000 meters (3,300 feet) and bottom 100 meters (330 feet)—because that's where most of the food is. But they still knew almost nothing about the behavior of the midwater creatures they pulled up, and they had not been able to identify most of the midwater jellies.

In the mid-1970's, midwater studies took a giant leap forward when scientists began using submersibles called *Johnson-Sea-Link*. The first *Sea-Link* had been launched in 1971 and a second in 1975. Nearly 7 meters (22 feet) long, boasting video and still cameras and hydraulic arms extending 2.4 meters (8 feet), these subs could descend more than 760 meters (2,500 feet) below the surface. Even more important, they could hover in the midwater.

The *Sea-Links* were used by a number of scientists to study the midwater. One of these was marine biologist Richard Harbison, then at the Woods Hole Oceanographic Institution on Cape Cod, Mass. "In a single series of dives near the Bahamas in October and November 1984," Harbison says, "we brought up more than 30 species of siphonophores, a type of jelly. About half of these were previously unstudied or even unnamed."

Although capable of hovering in the midwater, *Sea-Link* suffered from some of the same disadvantages that affect vessels that explore the ocean bottom. It was large, obtrusive, and costly to operate. So scientists continued to search for a better vehicle. In 1982, Robison, then at the University of California in Santa Barbara, led five other scientists on a pioneering series of dives in a device called the WASP Atmospheric Diving Suit. (The yellow and black suit was called WASP because it resembled a yellow jacket, a type of wasp.) A diver in the WASP could descend nearly 600 meters (2,000 feet) below the ocean surface.

Robison and his team made 33 day and night dives in the WASP in the Santa Barbara Basin, a relatively shallow sea floor basin—less than 600 meters deep—off the southern coast of California. Almost at once, the researchers began to realize that they had to abandon nearly all their earlier ideas about life in the midwater. "For example, the abundance of many creatures—particularly fish and jellies—was far greater than we ever found in nets," Robison recalls. "Equally surprising was the great diversity of gelatinous animals, including previously unknown ctenophores [small transparent animals] and ostracods [very small shellfish]. Previously, many of these animals had appeared only as a jellylike mass in the bottom of a net."

Another surprising find was the huge number of *copepods*, tiny relatives of the shrimp, that make up part of the *plankton*, microscopic plant and animal life that drifts through the ocean and serves as an important source of food for larger creatures. The scientists estimated that there were from 2 million to 4 million of these animals per cubic meter (1.3 cubic yards) of water.

Although the WASP provided the scientists with tantalizing glimpses of an unknown world, the suit also had a number of shortcomings for exploring the midwater. The WASP's air supply lasted only four to six hours. It was awkward to move forward or backward, and the diver could carry only a limited number of collecting and recording devices. Also, the suit's cameras weren't advanced enough to produce clear photographs.

So Robison set out to find a submersible designed specifically for midwater research. His search led him to *Deep Rover*, a one-person submersible that was originally built for commercial purposes, such as inspecting and repairing undersea oil platforms. Just 220 centimeters (7 feet 4 inches) high and 310 centimeters (10 feet) long, *Deep Rover* is small enough not to disturb the midwater creatures Robison wanted to observe. Even more important, *Deep Rover* can dive far deeper than the WASP. Its quiet engines can keep it hovering at any depth up to 900 meters (3,000 feet), and it can be maneuvered easily in any direction. Best of all, *Deep Rover* could be equipped with far more—and far more sophisticated—scientific instruments than a diver in the WASP could carry.

In 1985, Robison leased the submersible and equipped it with powerful still and video cameras—with telephoto lenses—that provided clear photographs even under low-light conditions. Also attached to the submersible were collection devices that could catch fragile midwater creatures and place them in bottles without harming them.

Finally, *Deep Rover* was fitted with red spotlights. "Since the only natural light that reaches the midwater falls in the blue-green part of the spectrum, we theorized that midwater animals can see only blue-green light and so wouldn't be disturbed by red light," Robison explains. "On midwater expeditions in the *Johnson-Sea-Link* and WASP, we found that this was true."

As the site for his dives, Robison chose Monterey Canyon. This vast trench in the sea floor, as deep and dramatic as the Grand Canyon, sits about 17 kilometers (10 miles) off the California coast. Trawling and other observations had shown that the cold, nutrient-rich waters of Monterey Canyon teem with an abundance of sea life rivaling that in any other body of water on Earth. The creatures range from sea otters, seals, and sea lions to commercial fish and countless smaller marine animals. In addition to Robison, the team assembled to work in *Deep Rover* included Harbison, chosen for his knowledge of jellies, and biologist Edie Widder of Santa Barbara, an expert in bioluminescence. During the summer of 1985, the three scientists embarked on a series of dives in *Deep Rover* that took them 900 meters (3,000 feet) below the ocean surface.

"We saw dozens of fish and jellies that we'd never seen before," Robison recalls. They also discovered a species of tiny creatures called *larvaceans* that build large structures of mucus. These structures, up to 3 meters (10 feet) long, are used to filter food particles out of the water. "It's been four years since we went down there," Robison says, "and we're still studying the specimens, photographs, and other information we brought to the surface." As in the Santa Barbara Basin, the most striking sight during the *Deep Rover* dives was the seemingly endless variety of beautiful, delicate jellies. Some, such as salps—small, barrel-shaped, transparent animals—were already well known. But others had never been seen before.

The scientists also got a closer look at the siphonophores. These creatures, long known to scientists but little studied, are the jelly superstars of the midwater. Siphonophores live in huge colonies up to 30 meters (100 feet) in length. In such a colony, each siphonophore performs a specific function. Some of the individuals help propel the chain. Others develop stinging tentacles to trap food. Still others digest the food. The Monterey Bay siphonophores not only were bigger than those observed elsewhere but they also represented a number of previously unknown species.

One of the most interesting things Robison observed about siphonophores in Monterey Bay is their relationship with midwater fish. He saw shrimp and at least two species of larger fish living in the company of a siphonophore called *Apolemia*. One type of fish, called *Leuroglossus stilbius*, actually nestles amid the jelly's stinging tentacles—apparently unharmed. The fish-siphonophore relationship first discovered by Robison while diving in the WASP, was confirmed by the *Deep Rover* team. But it has not yet been observed outside California waters. In both the Santa Barbara Basin and Monterey Canyon, Robison found that 75 per cent or more of the fish he observed 600 meters below the surface were congregated around the siphonophores.

Food may be the attraction. Often, the siphonophore's tentacles are thick with the shrimp and other tiny crustaceans that are its prey. Robison has observed the fish stealing food caught by the siphono-

Delicate Midwater Beauties

During their dives, scientists have found that an astounding number and variety of jellyfish inhabit the midwater. Many species had never been seen before. Although there is tremendous pressure in the deeper parts of the midwater, it does not crush these delicate-looking animals because their bodies consist mainly of water, which, since water cannot be compressed, is at the same pressure as the surrounding sea.

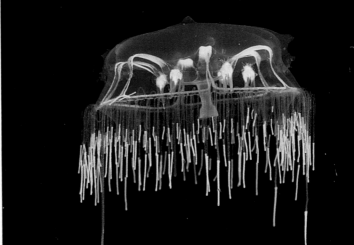

Bathocyroe fosteri

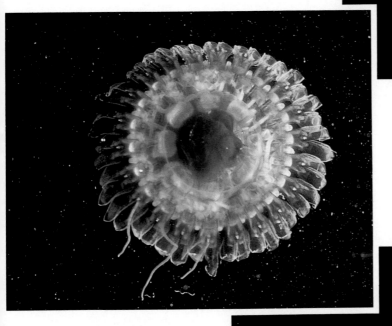

Atolla wyuillei

Halicreas minimum

phore's tentacles. The feeding connection is supported by the scientists' observation that when the siphonophore's tentacles are retracted—meaning that the animal is not feeding—the fish frequently disappear.

Siphonophores may also provide fish with a place to hide. In every other environment on Earth—from forests to sea floor—animals are able to find caves, hollows, and other secluded spots where they can give birth, raise their young, and hide from predators. Only the midwater, at first glance, appears to be devoid of such features. But siphonophores may actually serve as one of the midwater's chief physical features.

They may also help midwater creatures orient themselves. In the midwater, there are no trees, rocks, mountains, or other solid objects to serve as reference points. So siphonophores and other jellies may serve that function. Scientists still don't know, however, how midwater creatures orient themselves when these reference points are constantly moving or temporary.

New information about siphonophores was not the only valuable discovery made by the *Deep Rover* team. "The most important thing we learned—far more crucial than the fish-siphonophore relationship—was the pattern of interaction in the midwater," Robison explains. "At first, we were surprised at how little most of the animals moved. But then we saw that they were *poised*, that there was a constant level of tension, as if each animal was waiting for another to make the first move."

The animals' activity came in flurries and was accompanied by bursts of light. For example, a copepod would suddenly jostle its neighbor, a group of salps would luminesce, a predatory fish would snap up a tiny shrimp. There would be movement, life, bioluminescence everywhere—and then, just as suddenly, nothing but stillness again. Why this happens is still a midwater mystery.

The *Deep Rover* missions provided a wealth of new information about bioluminescence, an adaptation to an environment of total darkness. Bioluminescent light, which is produced without heat, is the result of chemical activity in the tissues of the animal. About 90 per cent of all marine creatures living at depths of 100 to 1,000 meters can give off a bioluminescent glow.

Fish use bioluminescence for a variety of reasons, such as attracting prey or finding a mate. Widder found that some jellyfish have developed a clever method of using bioluminescence to discourage predatory fish. "At the last instant, just as it's about to be eaten, the jellyfish will light up, illuminating not only itself but its attacker," she explains. "During the *Deep Rover* dives, we saw larger fish—which have no interest in the jelly—attack the spotlighted predator. This maneuver may discourage predators from hunting the jelly," she says.

During the *Deep Rover* dives, Widder also answered a long-standing

Opposite page: One of the major discoveries about midwater life in the Pacific Ocean was fish feeding around long colonies of jellies called *siphonophores.* Stretching up to 30 meters (100 feet), these structures might act as floating islands used by other creatures to orient themselves in this dark and featureless environment. This and other mysteries of the midwater are still waiting to be resolved by scientists on future dives.

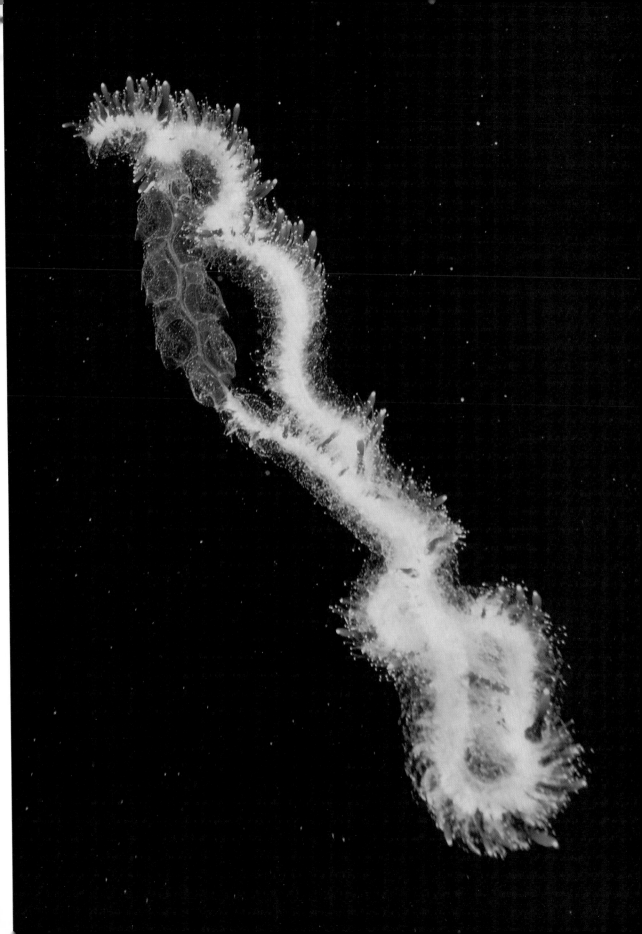

question about midwater bioluminescence: Is the midwater usually dark or does it usually resemble the night sky, with the light from bioluminescent creatures appearing like twinkling stars slowly flashing on and off. Widder found that the midwater is usually bathed in an impenetrable darkness and that nearly all bioluminescent midwater creatures light up only when they're touched by another animal or ruffled by a passing piece of debris or sudden current.

In 1986, shortly after the *Deep Rover* dives, Widder began focusing her attention on the development of an instrument that would allow scientists to measure more precisely the type and amount of light given off by bioluminescent creatures. "Until now, we've measured bioluminescence with primitive systems that pumped a small quantity of ocean water [containing bioluminescent creatures] past a single light detector—a frustratingly inaccurate method," Widder said. "We knew we had to design a more powerful device if we were to learn about midwater bioluminescence."

The resulting instrument is a tube 120 centimeters (48 inches) long and 13 centimeters (5 inches) in diameter set inside a sturdy cage. The instrument, named HIDEX (*High-Intake Defined EXcitation* bioluminescence profiler), can be dangled over the edge of a surface ship or carried into the deep by a submersible. The tube takes in large quantities of water—up to 40 liters (10½ gallons) per second—along with any animals in the water. The water passes over a grid, which disturbs the bioluminescent organisms, causing them to light up. (The grid is not electrified. The mere fact that the animals are carried past an unusual obstruction is enough to make them flash their light.) Within the tube are light-sensitive electrodes and a system that can measure both the wavelength and intensity of light emitted by the organisms.

"By studying the midwater with this system, we can measure the overall level of bioluminescence in an area," Widder points out. "Most exciting of all, we will be able to create the first accurate map of populations of bioluminescent organisms—where they are abundant, where there are few or none."

Since the *Deep Rover* dives, Harbison, now at the Harbor Branch Oceanographic Institute in Fort Pierce, Fla., and Robison have continued to probe the midwater. Harbison uses a more advanced model of the *Johnson-Sea-Link*. Its improved catching nets and suction devices enable scientists to capture a far greater number of midwater fish.

Since 1987, Harbison and a team of Harbor Branch scientists have been studying midwater life off Massachusetts and the Florida Keys. Harbison is particularly interested in the relationships between fish and jellies. "For example," he reports, "we've found a species of fish that actually mimics the siphonophores. It has long fins that resemble the siphonophore's stinging tentacles." Harbison thinks the mimicry may help the fish avoid predators that have no interest in tangling with a creature they believe will sting. In the Special Reports section, see PRACTICING TO DECEIVE.

Robison continues to focus on Monterey Canyon and its teeming undersea life. In 1988, the aquarium's research institute launched a specially equiped ROV. Only 2 meters (6 feet 6 inches) long and 1.5 meters (5 feet) high, this ROV can move quietly and gently through water up to 1,800 meters (6,000 feet) deep. And because it needs no on-board human pilot, the ROV can remain underwater for hours—or even days—at a time.

But perhaps most important, the cable that carries commands from the surface to the ROV's on-board computers is made of hair-thin glass optical fibers. They can transmit huge quantities of information ranging from sound to visual images to computer data as coded pulses of light. Powerful computers decode the signals. The result is immediate, crystal-clear transmission of all information and images recorded by the ROV instruments, even from 1.6 kilometers (1 mile) beneath the surface of Monterey Bay.

Using optical fibers, Robison and his colleagues were able to pack the ROV with a greater array of sophisticated instruments than *Deep Rover* could carry. These include sonar, temperature and dissolved-oxygen meters, and a variety of devices for collecting specimens. But the sub's crowning glory is its cameras, which include a high-quality color-video camera, a camera capable of filming in dim light, and four side-view cameras that provide a panoramic view.

Using the ROV, Robison and his colleagues not only have discovered new species of fish and jellies but also have found that midwater communities are more abundant and complex than previously suspected. They are beginning to study the relationships between community members, such as that between prey and predators or between species that benefit each other. In some cases, scientists were unaware that such relationships between these animals existed.

Robison hopes the robot sub will provide answers to some of the many questions remaining about the midwater. For example, researchers want to know why some midwater animals that have the ability to bioluminesce apparently almost never do so. Many questions also remain about the relationship between those animals that live their entire lives in the midwater—such as most jellies—and large fish, such as tuna and swordfish, that just pass through. The midwater remains one of Earth's last frontiers, with many mysteries still hidden in its vast depths.

For further reading:

Beebe, William. *Half mile down*. Duell, Sloan and Pearce, 1951.
Cousteau, Jacques. *The Ocean World*. Abrams, 1979.
Jordan, Bernard L., ed. *Man and the Sea: Classic Accounts of Marine Exploration*. The Natural History Press, 1970.

BY ROBERT L. HOHLFELDER

Excavating Herod's Dream

Built by Herod the Great 2,000 years ago,
Caesarea until 1291 was a major Mideastern
city. Archaeologists digging through its ruins
are now bringing the city's past to light.

The first rays of the brilliant Mediterranean sun rake the sand dunes as two small inflatable boats push into the Mediterranean Sea off the coast of Israel. The roar of their outboard motors breaks the tranquil silence of the early morning. The boats, carrying scuba divers and a support crew, head for a small diving barge gently bobbing at anchor 180 meters (600 feet) offshore. The barge—made of oil barrels topped with plywood sheets—is not the most impressive oceanographic research vessel. But it serves adequately as the nerve center for our ongoing explorations of the ruins of the harbor at Caesarea Maritima (Caesarea by the Sea). This magnificent city was constructed 2,000 years ago by Herod the Great of Judaea (also spelled Judea), a region in what is now the state of Israel. After getting last-minute instructions and gathering their gear—collection bags and baskets, tape measures and plastic writing slates—the divers slip into the murky water. Their trails of bubbles are the only evidence of the exciting work going on below. Another day of research has begun.

Diving at Caesarea is an intoxicating experience. Nowhere else in the Mediterranean is there a submerged archaeological site as large as the harbor ruins of this ancient city about halfway between Tel Aviv and Haifa. The harbors and anchorages that made up the harbor complex, collectively called Sebastos, represented a triumph of ancient engineering. The main harbor consisted of two huge breakwaters. The south breakwater, which was about 800 meters (2,600 feet) long, extended west from the shore and then turned north, forming a "J." The north breakwater stretched due west about 280 meters (920 feet). It was a sizable harbor even by modern standards, covering 200,000 square meters (240,000 square yards). The main harbor was also the first large-scale harbor ever built into the open sea. Sebastos also included a smaller harbor carved into the shore, which we call the inner harbor. Outside the breakwater to the north and south were two small, unprotected anchorages usable only in fair weather.

The harbor was built in little more than a decade—between 22 and 10 or 9 B.C.—along a treacherous stretch of shoreline that is buffeted by storms for most of the year. According to the ancient Jewish historian Flavius Josephus, Herod conquered nature itself to build Caesarea and its magnificent harbor complex.

The author:
Robert L. Hohlfelder is professor of history at the University of Colorado in Boulder and a leader of the underwater excavations at Caesarea's harbor.

Caesarea immediately became one of the busiest and most important seaports of the ancient world. Excavations in the harbor area have found porcelain from China and fish-sauce containers from Spain, as well as other trade goods from England and what is now the southern Soviet Union. According to the Bible, Saint Peter converted the first non-Jew to Christianity at Caesarea, and until about A.D. 400, Caesarea was the most important Christian city in Palestine—even more important than Jerusalem.

Caesarea was occupied by Romans, Byzantines, Muslims, and European crusaders in succession until 1291, when Muslims finally destroyed it. In the centuries that followed, the forces of wind and water reclaimed the city and its harbor. Today, however, artifact by artifact, Caesarea's story is emerging from sand and sea.

My part in the fascinating story of Caesarea began in 1978, when I left Greece—where I had been exploring ancient harbors—to accept an invitation from American archaeologist Robert Bull to survey the harbor ruins at Caesarea. In 1971, Bull and scientists from 22 United States and Canadian universities formed the Joint Expedition to Caesarea Maritima to excavate selected areas of the city. On my arrival, I quickly headed for the highest point along that part of the coast, a balcony atop a restaurant. Looking west, I could make out beneath the water the dark ruins of the harbor complex, sunk by earthquakes and centuries of assault by the turbulent sea.

Caesarea was the most daring and spectacular of the many magnificent projects built by Herod, the ruler of Judaea from 40 to 4 B.C. Herod is infamous today because of the account in the Gospel of Matthew, which states that he ordered the slaughter of infant boys in and around Bethlehem in an attempt to kill the infant Jesus. But Herod was known chiefly then as a shrewd and ruthless politician. Herod built Caesarea Maritima to honor Caesar Augustus, his patron and the man who in 27 B.C. became Rome's first emperor. The decision to build Caesarea at such an unlikely location was mainly a political one. Caesar Augustus had given Herod that part of Judaea in 30 B.C., and Herod wanted to establish his authority over it. In addition, Caesarea was intended as a monument to Herod's own power and to ensure his place in history. But Herod also built Caesarea to make money on maritime trade, a bold gamble that repaid his investment many times over.

Caesarea, stretching 2.4 kilometers (1½ miles) along the shore, rose on the ruins of a small settlement known as Strato's Tower, built in the 300's B.C. Only a small percentage of the city's estimated 50,000 inhabitants were Jews. Herod, a Jew who was enamored of all things Roman, built Caesarea in the classical Greek and Roman style, complete with temples and baths. The city's white marble palaces and villas reflected the wealth of its inhabitants. In Caesarea's bustling markets, merchants displayed an international array of goods. Extensive farm fields to the north, south, and east supplied the city with food. Water was piped through an aqueduct from springs in the foothills of Mount Carmel 14.5 kilometers (9 miles) to the northeast.

Today, a luxury hotel and its adjacent golf course cover what once was one of Caesarea's suburbs. Just south of the city is Kibbutz Sdot Yam, a prosperous agricultural settlement of about 600 people. One of their barley fields surrounds the ruins of Herod's amphitheater. In Caesarea itself, modern shops made of stones first used by ancient builders often stand where shops and warehouses stood almost 2,000 years ago.

Luckily for archaeologists, Caesarea, though abandoned, was never lost or forgotten. Archaeologists have been excavating at

Caesarea since the state of Israel was founded in 1948. In addition to sponsoring its own archaeologists, Israel has permitted scientists from many other countries to conduct excavations. For example, in the 1960's, Israeli archaeologists excavated and restored the fortifications built by the crusaders in the mid-1200's. Also in the 1960's, a team of Italian archaeologists excavated and restored the theater Herod built on the shore in the southern part of the city. Marine archaeologist Edwin A. Link, an American, first explored the underwater site of the harbor in 1960. Yet after 40 years of explorations, less than 10 per cent of the ancient city has been excavated. Only about 1 per cent of Herod's Caesarea has been studied; most of it still lies more than 6 meters (20 feet) below the sand.

A year after my arrival, several other marine archaeologists and I formed the Caesarea Ancient Harbour Excavation Project (CAHEP) to conduct large-scale excavations of the harbor. Our group included John Oleson of the University of Victoria in Canada and various Israeli teams, including one from the University of Haifa under the direction of Avner Raban and Elisha Linder. Some of CAHEP's workers are professional archaeologists. But most are volunteers from many countries who pay their own expenses to participate in this research project. In the past 10 years, we have begun to unlock some of the harbor's undersea mysteries.

Our guide to the harbor excavations at Caesarea has been Flavius Josephus, who died about A.D. 100. In his history, *Jewish Antiquities*, written several decades after Caesarea was completed, Josephus wrote extravagantly about the construction of a harbor he called *Sebastos*, the Greek equivalent of the name Augustus.

Josephus relates how Herod's workers lowered huge stone blocks measuring 15 meters (50 feet) long, 5.5 meters (18 feet) wide, and 2.7 meters (9 feet) high into the open sea to construct a huge breakwater almost 800 meters (2,600 feet) long and some 60 meters (200 feet) wide. On the breakwater, according to Josephus, Herod erected a sea wall topped by large towers. On the inner side of the sea wall were warehouses, a walkway, and loading quays.

The entrance to the harbor faced north, because the most severe winter storms arrived from the southwest. It was decorated with six colossal statues, which, we think, probably represented members of Augustus' family. Finally, on a platform adjacent to the harbor, Herod built a huge temple to Augustus and to the goddess Roma, the personification of the Roman Empire. According to Josephus, the temple was a landmark for incoming ships. Josephus' account seemed so fantastic that many historians accused him of "grandiloquent hyperbole," a polite way of saying that he had lied.

We wanted to determine just how accurate Josephus was. To date, underwater explorations have uncovered only a small portion of Caesarea's maritime past. But now we know Josephus could have

The site of ancient Caesarea lies on the Mediterranean coast of what is now the state of Israel, *right.* The outline, *above,* shows how far the harbor's breakwaters once extended into the open sea. At the height of its glory, Caesarea was an international port, a major trading center, and a monument to the power of the Roman Empire.

been even more grandiloquent in his praise of Caesarea's harbor complex.

Before Caesarea, most harbors were built to take advantage of the natural features of a coastline, such as bays or inlets. Sometimes, harbors were built by excavating a basin inland and then flooding it. Nowhere had anyone attempted to build a completely artificial harbor on such a storm-swept coast. At Caesarea, waves 2.4 to 3 meters (8 to 10 feet) high frequently roll in during the summer. In winter, the seas are much higher. In addition, a strong offshore current running from south to north parallel to the coast carries great quantities of sand from the Nile Delta and the Sinai. Silt from these areas still plagues Israeli harbors today. These obstacles must have given Herod's engineers nightmares. But Herod had chosen this unlikely location to please his emperor, not his engineers.

During my first excavation season at Caesarea, my colleagues and

I examined and photographed nearly all the harbor's submerged ruins. We found, as Josephus had written, that huge blocks had indeed been used to construct the breakwaters. In some places, the blocks seem almost intact. Most of them, however, have been damaged or eroded by centuries of storms and currents. Many are partially or completely buried in sand. To our amazement, we also discovered that most of the blocks were not stone but concrete.

How had they gotten there? There were two possibilities, both of which staggered the imagination. Herod's engineers could have poured the huge blocks on land, moved them out into the sea, then lowered them precisely onto the seabed. Or Herod's engineers could have poured *hydraulic concrete* (concrete that hardens underwater) into wooden frames sunk at specified points.

The Romans invented hydraulic concrete, stone rubble bonded together by a mortar made of lime and volcanic ash. The ash was the key ingredient, because it hardened on contact with water. (In modern hydraulic concrete, the hardening element is portland cement.) The Romans had experimented with hydraulic concrete as early as 100 B.C. at a small harbor in Italy. In addition, a Roman engineer had written a tract about hydraulic concrete. But archaeologists had never found evidence of its use on a large scale.

Oleson, one of the world's leading authorities on ancient technology, convinced us that the Romans lacked the technical expertise to move massive concrete blocks and then lower them with great precision onto the sea floor. Therefore, it seemed more likely that the blocks were poured in place—but it was still unbelievable.

Then in May 1982, we found the evidence we needed to confirm our "unbelievable" theory. We were excavating along the northern edge of the north breakwater when the crew on the diving barge radioed that divers using an airlift (a suction device that lifts sand from the sea floor) had uncovered two large wooden beams joined at the corner of a concrete block. The divers had also found the remains of two parallel wooden walls rising vertically along the face of the block.

Of all my hundreds of dives at Caesarea, the one I made following this discovery was the most exciting. I saw the beams, protected from decay and destruction in their sandy tomb, looking as if they had been placed there yesterday. Their undisturbed appearance strongly indicated that they dated from the original period of construction. If the blocks had been poured on shore, the support frame would surely have been removed for reuse before the blocks were lowered into the water. Viewing the beams and the remains of the wooden walls, I realized we had sound evidence that the concrete for the blocks had been poured into the open sea.

Later, a laboratory technique called *radiocarbon dating* revealed through analysis of types of carbon atoms in the wood that the beams were about 1,970 years old. An analysis of the beams' tree rings—

Caesarea Through Time

The excavations at Caesarea have allowed archaeologists to travel backward in time through the city's 1,200-year history. The various layers, *below left,* representing different periods of occupation, have yielded artifacts, skeletons, and the remains of buildings. Such evidence has provided archaeologists with information about how Caesarea looked as well as the activities and life styles of its inhabitants over time.

Modern Period
Muslims capture Caesarea in 1291 and destroy it to deny crusaders any Middle Eastern foothold. Today a resort and agricultural settlement stand on the site of the ancient city.

Crusader Period
Crusaders from Europe capture Caesarea in 1101. They build a small settlement and military fortifications on ruins of the south breakwater.

Islamic Period
Muslims capture Caesarea in 640, and it shrinks to an agricultural town. Stones from ruins are used for new buildings, such as a great mosque.

Byzantine Period
Caesarea expands rapidly in the early 300's as the Roman Empire becomes Christianized. After a brief period of strife and economic decline, the harbor is restored in the 500's. The city grows to its peak of population and prosperity.

Roman Period
Judea becomes a Roman province in A.D. 6, with Caesarea its capital. Now a major trading center, it is the most important city in Palestine.

Herodian Period
Herod the Great, King of Judea, builds Caesarea between 22 B.C. and 9 or 10 B.C. The city soon becomes one of the most important seaports in the ancient world.

Uncovering the Harbor's Past

Underwater archaeologists working on the bottom of the harbor have uncovered clues to how the breakwaters were built as well as the extent of the ancient city's trade. A diver, *right,* suctions silt from a 2,000-year-old beam, part of the framework used to form the breakwater's massive concrete blocks.

Artifacts from all periods of Caesarea's history washed out of the harbor and piled up at its entrance. There, archaeologists carefully lift out pieces of pottery, such as this large storage jar, *above,* which was used to transport goods. An expert at the nearby University of Haifa, *right,* catalogs the finds and tries to determine which era each piece belongs to.

which grow annually and so can be used to date wooden structures—confirmed this date.

The laboratory analysis of the beams and the concrete used to construct the blocks revealed more interesting information. The beams had been hewn not from local trees but from varieties of spruce, poplar, and other trees that grow only in central Europe. The chemical composition of the volcanic ash used for the concrete was identical to that of ash found at Mount Vesuvius near Naples, Italy. Josephus, who had written that Herod had imported much of his building material, was right once again.

It may seem odd or inefficient to us to import timber and ash when local supplies were available. But the men who built the harbor were executing what was probably the most important commission of their lives for an eccentric and ruthless client. Herod would not accept mistakes lightly. The engineers used things they knew worked. Moreover, transporting materials hundreds of kilometers by sea may have been quicker and less expensive than carting the materials overland from even 80 kilometers (50 miles) away.

Excavation at other sites along the breakwaters revealed more about the meticulous engineering that went into Herod's harbor. Under the concrete blocks at a number of places, we found a layer of stone rubble and pebbles from 0.3 to 1 meter (1 to 3 feet) high. This layer provided a stable foundation for the breakwater, preventing waves and currents from undermining the structure.

No written records, not even Josephus' accounts, exist to tell us how Sebastos was actually constructed. But the discovery of the wooden forms and the rubble foundation—and our knowledge of Roman construction techniques—has enabled CAHEP's archaeologists to devise a scenario that may explain how Herod's engineers built this magnificent complex.

First, the sea floor was cleared of large rocks by divers, whose only equipment was good lungs, a safety rope, and a large weight to speed their descent. According to ancient texts, the divers could work in water more than 27 meters (90 feet) deep, so diving at Caesarea, where the water was about 3 to 5 meters (10 to 11½ feet) deep in most places, must have seemed easy. Then men in small boats dropped rubble onto the sea floor to create the platform.

Meanwhile, on shore, carpenters were building the wooden frames. The rectangular base of the frames consisted of four large wooden beams, the two longest about 15 meters (50 feet) in length. On each of the four beams, the carpenters built two parallel walls about 2 meters (6½ feet) tall. The result was a large, wooden box with no floor and hollow, double-walled sides.

Sailors rowing small boats floated the frames into position over the rubble platform. Once a frame was over its site, other construction workers packed the hollow double walls with mortar made of volcanic ash to provide enough weight to sink the frame.

Herod's Engineering Triumph

The main harbor at Caesarea was the first large-scale harbor built into the open sea away from a bay or other natural protective feature. Thousands of divers, carpenters, and other workers toiled for almost 12 years to complete the harbor's two huge breakwaters. Each consisted of a rubble platform on the sea floor on which were set two rows of concrete blocks, finally capped with a paving stone platform. This platform held a tall sea wall, warehouses, and areas for loading and unloading ships.

1. The platform on which each breakwater rested was made of stone rubble and pebbles dumped onto the sea floor by men in small boats. The rubble platform, which was more than 60 meters (200 feet) wide and from 0.3 to 1 meter (1 to 3 feet) high, provided a more stable base than the sandy bottom.

3. Workers in small boats floated the frames into position over the rubble platform, then poured mortar between the parallel walls to sink the frames. After dumping rubble against the base of the submerged frames to stabilize them, workers poured concrete into the center of each frame and raked it smooth. When the concrete reached nearly to the surface of the water, it was left to harden.

2. On shore, carpenters built boxlike rectangular wooden frames, up to 15 meters (50 feet) long, that were open at the top and bottom. Each side consisted of two parallel walls about 2 meters (6.5 feet) high, with a space of 20 to 30 centimeters (8 to 12 inches) between these walls.

4. The space between the rows of blocks was filled with more concrete or with sand deposited by waves breaking over the blocks. Workers capped the blocks and spaces between them with rubble and paving stones. A protective sea wall was then built. A rubble *berm* (sloping barrier) built against the outer side of each breakwater helped reduce the force of waves striking the breakwaters. On the inner side of each breakwater, workers constructed warehouses, loading areas, and a walkway. The harbor was shallow because the round-bottomed ships did not need deep water, and the tides rose and fell very little.

**Sailing into
a Safe Harbor**

Ancient mariners
approaching Caesarea
were guided in by the
light of fires burning in a
tower near the harbor
entrance. They sailed
past massive statues
"guarding" the entrance,
and anchored safely in-
side. There, the waters
were calm, protected
from waves rolling in
from the south and
breaking against the
massive structures that
formed the world's first
totally artificial harbor.

When the wooden frame was in place on the ocean floor, workers in small boats dumped rubble around its base to stabilize it. The frame was then ready for the liquid concrete, which was mixed either onshore or on finished sections of the breakwater. Workers, standing on the submerged frames, poured the concrete from baskets and then smoothed it with long-handled rakes. When the concrete reached almost to the surface of the water, it was left to harden.

We discovered that each breakwater actually consisted of two parallel rows of concrete blocks laid at least 6 meters (20 feet) apart. In some places, the space between the two rows was filled with more concrete. In other places, the space was filled with sand, and this created quite a puzzle for us. We uncovered the first of these sand-filled pockets in 1984. What purpose had they served? In summer 1988, we uncovered yet another of the sand-filled pockets, but this one was different. It had a rubble covering.

We believe this discovery is evidence that Herod's engineers not only conquered nature to build his great harbor but actually used the heavy seas that pound this area of the Mediterranean to do some of their work. We think they discovered that the hollow space between the two rows of concrete blocks would fill quickly with sand as the waves washed over the first line of blocks. When the sand in the hollows had accumulated to near sea level, workers dumped rubble on top to cap and seal them. We believe this process, which, as far as we know, had not been used previously, also helps explain how the harbor could have been constructed so quickly along a coast where work in the open sea would have been limited by weather to only a few months a year. Workers then placed paving stones over both the concrete blocks and rubble-capped sand deposits. The stones created a platform at least 18 to 21 meters (60 to 70 feet) wide.

For a description of the above-water parts of the breakwater, we

must rely chiefly on Josephus. He reported that a great stone sea wall, perhaps 9 meters (30 feet) high and 2 meters (6 feet) wide, stood on the breakwaters. We have not yet found any evidence of the sea wall. But at intervals along the base of the breakwaters, we have uncovered piles of rubble that may be the remains of the towers Josephus says adorned the sea wall. Against the outer side of the breakwaters, facing the sea, workers created a *berm*, a sloping barrier of rubble that ran from the base of the breakwater to the sea floor to reduce the force of the waves.

While work proceeded on the berm, other builders constructed the inner side of the breakwater, finishing the walkway as well as the warehouses that backed against the inner face of the sea wall. Thanks to the protection provided by the sea wall and the berm, this construction went on in a safer and more leisurely way.

In 1981 and 1982, we found an unusual innovation about 4.5 meters (15 feet) south of the south breakwater. There, Herod's engineers built an unconnected series of rubble *islets* (tiny islands) parallel to the breakwater. These islets, which probably came only to sea level in ancient times, may have served as the first line of defense against winter storms. They not only reduced the force of incoming waves but also cut down on the amount of spray washing over the sea wall and spilling onto the warehouses.

With its several lines of defense against winter storms, Herod's harbor provided a secure haven for the months of October through March, when ancient mariners normally did not sail. During these months, merchant ships moored at Caesarea to wait out the winter could be loaded in relative safety from the elements. When good seas returned, the ships would make an early dash to Rome and other western markets.

Over the centuries, the harbor's fortune ebbed and flowed with that of Caesarea. The city retained its place as a major trading center in the Roman Empire through the A.D. 300's. During the 300's, Christianity gradually became the official religion of the Roman Empire, whose capital moved from Rome to Byzantium (now Istanbul) in Turkey. Although historians of ancient Palestine call the period from 324 to 640 the *Byzantine Period*, the inhabitants of Caesarea during that time still called themselves Romans.

In the 400's, Byzantine Caesarea was beset by tensions between Christians and Jews, political uprisings, and an extended drought. Trade fell off, and the harbor—neglected and assaulted by the sea—became useless. In the early 500's, the Byzantine Emperor Anastasius restored the harbor, and the city began to flourish once more. Caesarea may have reached its peak of prosperity and population—about 150,000 people—in the mid-500's and was the most important port on the eastern Mediterranean coast.

In the 630's, Muslims stormed out of the Arabian Peninsula and began to conquer Byzantine territories in the Middle East. They took over Caesarea in 640 or 641. Under Arab control from then until 1101, Caesarea ceased to be a major international seaport and became a coastal guard station for local trade and an agricultural town of considerable prosperity. The city, now a frontier settlement on the borders of a desert empire, looked to the east, not across the Mediterranean Sea to the west. The artificial harbor that Herod had built was quickly reclaimed by the sea. Natural forces, including several earthquakes, ravaged the site. The warehouses and sea wall slipped into ruins, and portions of the breakwaters gradually slumped into the sea.

By the time the crusaders conquered Caesarea in 1101, little of the harbor remained above the sea. The crusader knights, using stones from the ancient city, constructed a fortified settlement and built a small harbor for military craft near the ruins of the south breakwater. One writer of that time reported that the harbor was large enough for only one ship. How things had changed from Herod's days, when 100 large merchant ships stood at anchor in the outer harbor alone.

When the last knights departed from Palestine in 1291, the Muslims destroyed Caesarea—along with other coastal fortresses— to deny any future crusades an easy foothold in the Middle East. Urban life at Caesarea ended.

Not until 1882, when a small group of Muslims settled among the ruins, did people begin to live in Herod's city again. Kibbutz Sdot Yam was founded on the site in 1940. Today, villas again are being built north of the city walls where their ancient counterparts once stood. Tourists from around the world now flock to Caesarea's ruins, making it the third most popular attraction in Israel, after Jerusalem and Masada, the historic Jewish mountaintop fortress also built by Herod. The king who wanted to achieve immortality through his buildings was remarkably successful.

Early in July 1988, as we finished breaking camp at the end of another season of excavations, I sat with Avner Raban, watching another magnificent Caesarea sunset—a bright orange ball sliding into the sea. "What's left to find?" I asked Avner.

"We have only scratched the surface," he replied. "The discovery of most of Caesarea's secrets lies ahead." All archaeologists are incurable optimists, and my friend's comments certainly mirrored this attitude. But somehow I think he may be correct.

For further reading:

Holum, Kenneth; Hohlfelder, Robert; Bull, Robert; and Raban, Avner. *King Herod's Dream: Caesarea on the Sea.* Norton, 1988.
Raban, Avner. "Herod's Great Harbor." *The Courier*, November 1987.

While the United States is generating ever more garbage, local opposition to landfills and incinerators is straining society's ability to deal with its trash.

The Growing Garbage Mess

BY JANET RALOFF

Illegally dumped medical wastes washed ashore from Maine to Florida in the summer of 1988, forcing health officers to close beaches. The refuse included used hypodermic needles and bandages—even vials of blood contaminated with the virus that causes AIDS. About the same time, boats loaded down with incinerator ash left over from garbage that had been burned in the United States steamed between foreign ports, searching for a country that would accept their cargo.

These incidents were dramatic evidence of the United States struggle to cope with a growing mountain of wastes. Compounding the problem is growing public opposition to the construction of new waste-disposal facilities—the so-called not-in-my-backyard resistance.

This trash crisis is not unique to America. Although the United States is the world leader in the production of waste per person, other industrial nations are also piling up ever-increasing amounts of trash—from household and institutional garbage to toxic industrial chemicals and radioactive wastes from atomic power plants, nuclear-medicine facilities, and weapons factories.

In many countries, strict rules regulate the disposal of the most poisonous of this trash, such as medical, radioactive, and toxic industrial wastes. Most of the waste, however, is commercial and residential trash, which is not subject to such laws.

The United States generated 143.0 million metric tons (157.7 million short tons) of such garbage in 1986, according to the U.S. Environmental Protection Agency (EPA)—a big increase over the 109.3 million metric tons (120.5 million short tons) in 1970. Paper and paperboard made up 41 per cent of the 1986 trash heap. Yard wastes, such as grass clippings and leaves, accounted for 18 per cent. The remaining 41 per cent was divided almost equally into five categories—metals, food wastes, glass, plastics, and various items made of rubber, leather, textiles, and wood. But worse is yet to come. The EPA predicts that the total garbage output will reach almost 175 million metric tons (193 million short tons) by the year 2000.

Humanity's oldest and most common means of waste disposal has been the garbage dump—a pit, ravine, or field outside a city or town. Open dumping, however, has been declared illegal in most parts of the world, because wastes pitched in open dumps harbor disease-carrying vermin such as flies and rats—to say nothing of the foul odors generated by decomposing garbage. Today, the town dump has been replaced by the sanitary landfill, where dirt is spread to contain the most recently dumped waste.

Landfills vary in size from a few hectares to several hundred hectares and consist of a series of individual sections called cells, which are put into use one at a time. A typical cell measures about 30 meters long, 90 meters wide, and 6 meters deep (100 feet by 300 feet by 20 feet), and may take months or years to fill.

Another favorite old method of waste disposal was the burning of paper trash, leaves, and branches in curbside or backyard bonfires. By the 1970's, however, most U.S. communities had outlawed such burning because it pollutes the air.

Today, a few communities burn garbage in large incinerators—either *mass-burn plants* or *processing plants*. A mass-burn plant is essentially a large furnace in which all the garbage collected is burned. At a processing plant, by contrast, people and machines first extract from the waste certain materials such as metals that can be reused and leaves and garden scraps, which can be composed. Mechanical presses convert the remainder of the waste to pellets called *refuse-derived fuel*, which is burned at the plant or sold.

During the 1970's, as people became more concerned about the environment, the idea of *recycling* came into vogue. Recycling involves separating trash items according to the substances of which they are made—such as aluminum, paper, and glass—then shipping

The author:
Janet Raloff is environ-ment/policy editor of *Science News* magazine.

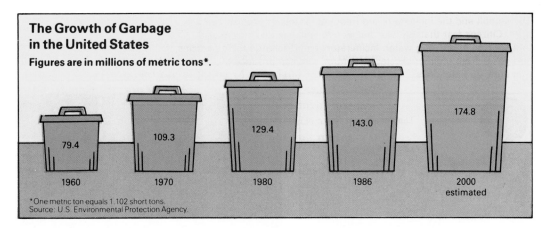

The Growth of Garbage in the United States

Figures are in millions of metric tons*.

79.4	109.3	129.4	143.0	174.8
1960	1970	1980	1986	2000 estimated

*One metric ton equals 1.102 short tons.
Source: U.S. Environmental Protection Agency.

them to companies that recover valuable materials from them. Eventually, these materials are made into useful products.

Each of the three methods of waste management—landfilling, incineration, and recycling—has its advantages and disadvantages, some technical, some economic, and some political. The main advantages of landfilling are that it is cheap and that most U.S. communities have experience in disposing of garbage this way. Most communities routinely used landfills as their main method of disposal until the 1970's.

By then, studies were uncovering a previously hidden cost of landfills—extensive pollution of ground water, soil, and air. Even ordinary household trash contains dangerous chemicals and metals that can *leach out* of landfills, for example. In this process, rain water or water trapped in food wastes filters through a landfill, dissolves chemicals, and carries the chemicals into the ground, where they contaminate water. Leaching is especially worrisome because ground water provides about half the nation's drinking water.

The National Solid Wastes Management Association (NSWMA), an organization of businesses that collect, dispose of, and recycle trash, acknowledges that by 1990 a mere 10 per cent of existing landfills "are likely to provide adequate environmental safeguards." Nevertheless, about 83 per cent of U.S. garbage ends up in landfills.

But another disadvantage may lower this percentage sharply in the near future: Landfilling cannot reduce the ever-growing volume of trash.

The Creation of a Garbage Crisis

The amount of residential and commercial waste generated in the United States has been rising steadily, *above,* and may well increase for the remainder of the century, straining society's ability to dispose of it safely. Paper and paperboard makes up the largest category of trash, *below.* Plastics make up only 6.5 per cent of all garbage, but they are difficult to dispose of because they do not decay naturally.

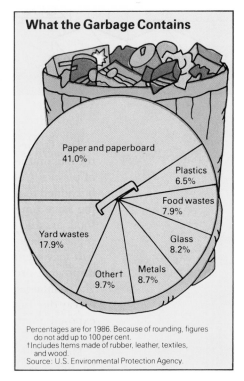

What the Garbage Contains

Paper and paperboard 41.0%
Plastics 6.5%
Food wastes 7.9%
Glass 8.2%
Metals 8.7%
Other† 9.7%
Yard wastes 17.9%

Percentages are for 1986. Because of rounding, figures do not add up to 100 per cent.
†Includes items made of rubber, leather, textiles, and wood.
Source: U.S. Environmental Protection Agency.

Changing Trends in Trash Disposal
Weights are in millions of metric tons*

	1960 Weight	1960 Per cent	1970 Weight	1970 Per cent	1986 Weight	1986 Per cent	2000 (estimated) Weight	2000 (estimated) Per cent
Landfills	74.1	93	101.7	93	119.0	83	124.1	71
Incineration	0.0	0	0.4	0	8.7	6	29.0	17
Recycling	5.3	7	7.2	7	15.3	11	21.7	12
Total	79.4	100	109.3	100	143.0	100	174.8	100

*One metric ton equals 1.102 short tons.
Source: U.S. Environmental Protection Agency.

Since 1960, there have been major changes in the way garbage is handled. As pollution problems involving landfills grew worse, incineration became more common, because it sharply reduces the volume of trash that must be buried. Burning garbage can also be used to produce steam and electricity. As the U.S. trash heap grows, landfills likely will continue to receive a declining percentage of garbage, while recycling programs gain a larger percentage of the nation's trash.

result, there will be a greater risk that unacceptable amounts of heavy metals will leach out of landfills where incinerator ash is buried and contaminate ground water.

The new pollution-control systems required on incinerators are a major reason for the soaring cost of incineration. Furthermore, as the metal content of incinerator ash increases, the cost of burying this toxic waste safely threatens to spiral out of sight.

The cost of dumping waste at an ordinary landfill ranges from about $20 to $75 per ton. If the incinerator ash is contaminated enough to be classified as hazardous waste, it must be buried in a specially designed landfill lined with layers of compacted clay and plastic sheeting to prevent leaching. To dump waste at one of these landfills now costs more than $200 per ton.

As the problems of incineration and landfills grow, recycling becomes more attractive. The Institute for Local Self-Reliance (ILSR), a private organization that deals mostly with relationships between urban neighborhoods and government agencies, compared the costs of incineration with the costs of recycling and found that before 1982, it was more expensive to recycle than to burn. "Now it's just the opposite," says Neil Seldman, a codirector of the Institute.

Although the cost of waste disposal varies greatly from one community to another, depending on such factors as salaries, the ILSR found in January 1989 that incineration on the average costs about 50 per cent more than recycling. Moreover, notes Seldman, recycling is becoming less expensive year by year because manufacturers are paying more for recycled materials.

The EPA in September 1988 announced a goal of recycling 25 per cent of the nation's municipal solid waste—more than twice as much as currently—by 1992. Many communities throughout the world's industrialized countries already recycle more than this. In fact, INFORM, an environmental research organization based in New York City, in October 1987 said it was likely that about 50 per cent of

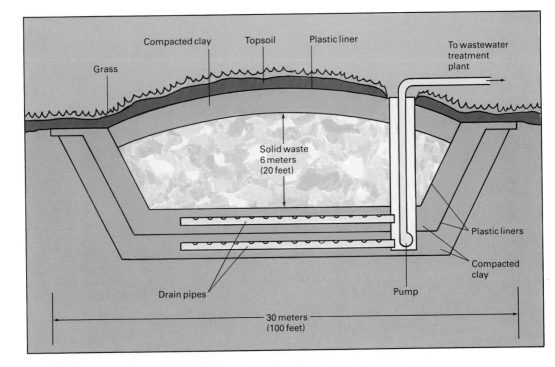

Grass   Compacted clay   Topsoil   Plastic liner

To wastewater treatment plant

Solid waste
6 meters
(20 feet)

Plastic liners

Compacted clay

Drain pipes

Pump

30 meters
(100 feet)

Solving the Landfill Problem

A modern landfill being constructed for ordinary garbage, *left,* uses a plastic liner and layers of compacted clay to minimize the leakage of toxic chemicals dissolved in water that enters the landfill as rain. In a landfill designed to accept hazardous wastes, *above,* contaminated water drains into pipes embedded in two layers of clay at the bottom of the landfill. A pump sends this water to a plant where the toxic substances are removed.

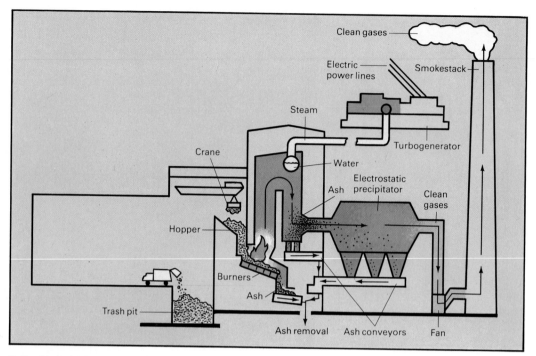

Clean gases

Electric power lines

Smokestack

Steam

Crane

Turbogenerator

Water

Electrostatic precipitator

Ash

Clean gases

Hopper

Burners

Ash

Trash pit

Ash removal   Ash conveyors   Fan

Safer Incinerators

Incinerators can be built not only to reduce the amount of waste that must be buried in landfills but also to generate electricity. At Baltimore's incinerator, *opposite page, below,* transfers trash from a pit to a hopper leading to a row of burners, *above.* The heat produces steam that drives a turbogenerator. Gases and ash flow through an *electrostatic precipitator,* a device that removes the toxic ash.

all municipal wastes in Japan are recycled—the highest recycling rate in the world. By contrast, the ILSR reported in February 1989 that only 20 U.S. communities—from small towns to big cities—were recycling 30 per cent or more of their municipal wastes.

Yet recycling has a tremendous potential in the United States. In January 1989, researchers at Queens College in New York City reported on a 10-week trash-disposal experiment and concluded that "recycling appears to be a viable alternative to incineration." During the 10 weeks, researchers removed items that could be recycled from trash discarded by 100 households in East Hampton, N.Y. They found that 84 per cent of the garbage was recyclable.

The biggest obstacle to recycling for most communities is inexperience. A municipality making a switch to recycling from landfilling or incineration must begin with an education campaign to inform consumers how and where to save recycled goods for collection. Such campaigns can be costly.

Each participating household or business then must get used to new ways of separating and storing trash. Some cities require consumers to maintain four trash bins—one for glass, one for metals, one for paper goods, and one for everything else.

Recycling can put a financial strain on communities that collect trash at the curb, especially municipalities that recycle several kinds of wastes. They either must modify their garbage trucks to keep the various kinds of trash separated or must separate a hodgepodge of recyclable garbage at a collection depot.

At some depots, workers sort the waste by hand. At many of the newer depots, however, machines sort at least some of the recyclable items. An automatic sorting operation might begin with all recyclables except newspapers moving along on a conveyor belt. An arm carrying an electromagnet sweeps over the belt, collecting tin cans and other wastes containing iron. A similar process collects aluminum from the belt. What remains is mostly glass, which is crushed in a large, rotating bin at the end of the belt. Regardless of the method of separation, the community must buy equipment for such jobs as baling paper and crushing glass.

Finally, the community must try to find buyers for the separated materials. This is not always easy. Even when new and used materials cost the same, companies often choose the new materials.

Another obstacle on the path to recycling involves the rich variety of plastics. Although many plastics look much the same, 46 different plastic substances called *resins* are commonly used in consumer products. When two or more resins are recycled together, the end product is a lower-grade—and therefore less valuable—plastic. There are machines that will separate resins from each other, but they can handle no more than three resins at the same time.

Researchers are trying to transform discarded plastics into a valuable commodity. One notable example is a project carried out at the Center for Plastics Recycling Research at Rutgers the State University of New Jersey in Piscataway. The research center built and operates a plant to demonstrate how industry could recycle plastics.

The Recycling Solution

Because recycling reduces the amount of trash to dispose of, this technique promises to play a major role in future garbage-collection programs. Householders would separate their trash for recycling and place it in containers according to category, such as paper or glass. A truck would carry this waste in separate compartments. Only garbage that could not be recycled would be buried in landfills or burned in incinerators. Recycling could be teamed with waste-to-energy incineration, which produces electrical power while further reducing the amount of trash that needs to be buried.

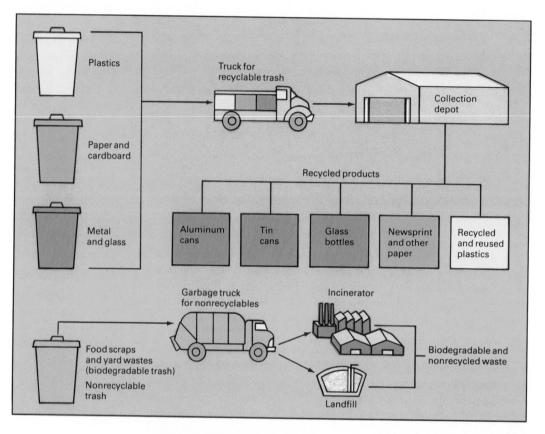

A worker in Seattle's recycling program, *right,* picks up trash placed in boxes that are color-coded according to categories of waste. To keep the trash separated, the garbage truck has a separate compartment for each category.

The plant recycles containers such as milk jugs and soft-drink bottles. Machines at the plant shred the containers and grind them into chips, remove bits of labels from the chips, and separate the chips according to the type of resin. The plastic chips sell for about half the cost of newly made resins.

Because some municipal wastes will continue to be landfilled for years to come, several researchers are exploring technologies to make burial safer. At Kansas State University in Manhattan, for example, chemists are developing sensors to detect toxic gases in the air above landfills. Such sensors would provide evidence that government officials could use to enforce clean-air standards.

And a team of researchers at State University of New York in Stony Brook may have found a way to transform incinerator ash from a toxic waste into a construction material. By mixing this ash with portland cement, they are making such products as cement blocks for construction. Initial studies indicate that the process prevents toxic metals from escaping into the environment.

While the world struggles with ways to dispose of its growing trash heap, some communities are looking at the other side of the problem—stopping waste build-up before it starts. One proven strategy is to require deposits on beverage bottles and cans—making it literally pay for consumers to keep these products out of the waste stream. Nine states already require such deposits.

Another strategy is to ban products that otherwise would become unmanageable wastes. This strategy is gaining favor in many areas overwhelmed by nonrecycled plastics.

A third strategy is to develop plastics that biodegrade rapidly and so could be dumped into a landfill to decay. Researchers already have produced plastics that decay in periods ranging from only 15 months to 5 years.

Today's waste problem has many causes, including a glut of packaging materials used once and thrown away by a consumer society, the introduction of products made of hard-to-recycle plastics, tougher air- and water-pollution laws, local opposition to landfills and incinerators, and—perhaps the most important cause—the discarding of materials with little regard for their value as a resource. Many resource analysts say that our society's environmental and economic health may one day depend upon how effectively we deal with our garbage. Considering the growing size of the world's trash heap, that day may be rapidly approaching.

For further reading:

Cook, James. "Not in Anybody's Backyard." *Forbes*, Nov. 28, 1988.
Hershkowitz, Allen; De Kadt, Maarten; and Underwood, Joanna. *Garbage: Practices, Problems & Remedies*. INFORM, 1988.
Langone, John. "A Stinking Mess." *Time*, Jan. 2, 1989.
Waters, Tom. "The Plastics Problem." *Discover*, February 1989.

By mimicking things they are not, some animals and plants gain an edge in the struggle to survive and reproduce.

Practicing to Deceive

BY LINCOLN PIERSON BROWER

The Greek philosopher and scientist Aristotle, who lived in the 300's B.C., described a bizarre creature that lived among seaweed on the shores of the Aegean Sea. He called it the angler fish because the first fin on its back resembled a baited fishing line. It consisted of a "rod" on the end of which was a wormlike structure. As a smaller fish dived toward the false bait, the angler fish flicked its fin toward its mouth and gulped down the unsuspecting prey.

More than 2,200 years later, as a young naturalist in New Jersey walking through lush summer fields, I witnessed a drama of deceit similar to the one described by Aristotle. A butterfly I thought was drinking nectar from a daisy seemed stuck in the petals. When I looked more closely, I saw that

A crab spider attacks a honey bee that came to feed on nectar and was fooled by the spider's ability to mimic the flower's color.

the butterfly was held in the jaws of a hungry crab spider. To my amazement, the spider was almost the exact color as the daisy petals. Subsequently, I learned that crab spiders can actually change their color to match the flower on which they sit and wait for unsuspecting prey.

The angler fish and the crab spider are examples of *mimicry* in nature—living things that appear to be something they are not. There are many forms of mimicry, found among all types of creatures—insects, fish, birds, clams, even plants. And there are various reasons for mimicry.

There are animals that appear to be something they are not in order to avoid being eaten. For example, some small leaf-feeding beetles look like raindrops glistening in the sun. This is because their wing covers reflect sunlight in the same way as a drop of water on a leaf. Deeper in the jungle, where sunlight filters down through tree leaves to make a beautifully dappled mosaic of light and shade, the *chrysalids* (hard shells) of some butterfly caterpillars resemble gold or silver mirrors that baffle predators. Some colorful bugs congregate on stems and arrange themselves as if they are the flowers or seeds of the plant. Similar disguise has been successful for certain plants in South Africa. Growing on barren deserts, these plants resemble rocks and pebbles except for a brief period when they bloom. All of these kinds of imitations involve plants or animals that look like, or mimic, common background objects and so greatly increase their chances of being overlooked by predators.

In another form of mimicry, animals avoid being eaten by appearing to be an enemy of their own predators. The caterpillars of a group of moths known as *sphingids* are particularly good at this form of mimicry. While doing research in Central and South America where poisonous vipers are common, I encountered the caterpillar of the moth *Eumorpha labruscae*, which is astoundingly snakelike in appearance. I watched as the caterpillar's front end swelled. Spots on the caterpillar grew into large fake eyes, beneath which false scales perfectly mimicked the scales of a snake. Colored lines on its head suggested a forked tongue, and to enhance the caterpillar's ferocious appearance, the back end of its body had a glossy disk that winked like an evil eye. This caterpillar was totally harmless, but to birds that eat caterpillars, it must have looked like one of the bird's own predators.

Another sphingid moth I encountered on the tropical island of Trinidad near South America occurs in green, yellow, or brown forms, as do the small vipers in that part of the world. When I touched one caterpillar, it performed an incredible display. It swung its front end to the side, swelled up to open huge false eyes, and struck repeatedly against my thumb. Such behavior and coloration must be extremely successful in scaring off birds that would otherwise eat the caterpillar.

The author:
Lincoln Pierson Brower is distinguished professor of zoology at the University of Florida in Gainesville.

Imitative Insect
Some plants and many animals mimic the characteristics of other species, usually to avoid being eaten. The long, slender walking stick—which looks like a twig—is an example of an edible insect that mimics background objects to hide from its enemies.

Then there are animals that appear to be something they are not in order to eat other animals. They act, in effect, like a wolf in sheep's clothing and are involved in a prey-predator interaction that scientists call *aggressive mimicry*. For example, while doing research in Trinidad, I discovered a praying mantis disguised as a dead leaf. The mantis surprised and ate unsuspecting insects that failed to detect the disguise. So-called assassin bugs behave similarly and improve their deception by attaching small bits of vegetation to their bodies.

This type of deceit also occurs on coral reefs, where tiny cleaner fish nibble parasites and damaged skin from larger fish that swim up to them. But lurking nearby are other small fish similar to the cleaners in size, shape, and color. Seemingly innocent, these mimics swim up to the larger fish and then suddenly bite pieces out of them instead of joining in the cleaning.

The first studies of mimicry in nature were made in the 1800's by English naturalist Henry W. Bates. In 1849, Bates traveled into the heart of the largest and most complex rain forest in the world, the Amazon in South America. Wanting to understand how species of plants and animals originated, Bates planned to record scientific facts about as many new species as he could study. Over a period of 11 enormously difficult years, Bates encountered the largest diversity of butterfly species anywhere on Earth. Some were dull and inconspicuous. Others were brilliantly colored on one surface of their wings and almost invisibly camouflaged on the other. Still others were brightly colored in every conceivable respect.

An Aggressive Angler
Some animals use mimicry to catch prey. The angler fish is an example of this *aggressive mimicry.* It has a fin on its back, *top,* that looks like a fishing rod with a worm on its end. When a smaller fish approaches the "bait," the angler fish attacks and eats it, *above.*

Most of the inconspicuous butterflies darted furtively among the dense vegetation, apparently to avoid being seen by predators such as birds and lizards. The brightly colored species, however, flew slowly in sunny patches, apparently open to attack by predators. Pondering this difference in appearance and behavior, Bates theorized that he was dealing with two very different ways of life among butterflies. The inconspicuous ones must be *palatable* (tasty and nutritious), he decided, and had evolved to conceal their presence from birds and lizards. On the other hand, the brightly colored species flaunted their colors in the face of these predators without danger of attack. With great insight, Bates reasoned that these must be *unpalatable* (foul-tasting or sickening) and that their distinctive colors were, in effect, a warning to predators to stay away. Scientists today call this *warning coloration.*

We now know that many insect species gain protection by being foul-tasting or poisonous. Brightly colored monarch butterflies, for example, contain poisons that cause birds to vomit a few minutes after they eat one. As Bates had predicted, a single nauseating experience is enough to teach the bird to avoid monarchs in future encounters on sight alone. Over the past 20 years, the enormous strides made in understanding the chemistry of insect defense have proven Bates's remarkable insights. While some chemicals, such as those in the monarch, cause vomiting, others are foul-tasting, and still others cause internal pain and suffering when eaten.

While classifying these new butterfly species, Bates was baffled by a few rare species that had bright color patterns though all their other characteristics—the pattern of veins in their wings and other anatomical features—indicated they belonged to the family of palatable inconspicuous butterflies. Why should these palatable butterflies advertise their presence to predators? Bates reasoned that they had come to look like, or *mimic,* the unpalatable species and so were able to deceive their predators into thinking that they, too, were unpalatable. He called the palatable species the *mimic,* and the unpalatable species that it mimicked the *model.*

How had this nearly exact resemblance, or mimicry, evolved? Bates reasoned that anytime an individual butterfly of a palatable species inherited a variation in color pattern that made it look more like the butterfly of an unpalatable species, this resemblance would tend to dupe the birds and lizards into leaving it alone. In other words, it would have a better chance of surviving and producing offspring. Its offspring would inherit the altered color pattern, and they, too, would survive better and reproduce more individuals. Over hundreds of generations, new variations would occur to make the mimics look ever more like the model, until eventually even scientists would have difficulty telling them apart.

Bates reported his discovery of mimicry among butterflies in 1862, three years after the English naturalist Charles R. Darwin published his theory of natural selection in *On the Origin of Species by Means of Natural Selection, or the Preservation of Favoured Races in the Struggle for Life*. Darwin wrote Bates that the report on mimicry was the first really convincing evidence supporting the theory of natural selection.

Darwin's theory explained how evolution occurred. Darwin argued that living things commonly give birth to more offspring than are needed to replace themselves. The amount of food needed for survival is limited, however, so new individuals in each generation must compete with each other for the limited resources in a struggle

The Sneaky Saber Tooth

The saber tooth blenny, *above,* mimics the harmless cleaner fish. The cleaner fish eats parasites off the body of a larger fish known as the wrasse, *left,* but the blenny prefers to eat pieces of the wrasse. By resembling the cleaner fish, and behaving like one, the saber tooth blenny can sneak up on the wrasse and take a bite out of it.

Mimicking the Menacing Moray

A harmless spotted ocean fish, *top,* has one spot on its side that looks like the eye of a moray eel, *middle.* The spotted fish is preyed upon by larger fish, which are in turn preyed on by morays. When in danger, the spotted fish hides in rocks with only its "eye" showing, *bottom,* to scare off predators.

for existence. They also compete with each other to avoid being found and eaten by predators. Darwin suggested that those individuals that inherit variations which enable them to compete more effectively are more likely to survive. These survivors will then pass the variations on to their offspring. Through the successive accumulation of beneficial variations, their competitive ability is sharpened, thereby resulting in the long-term survival of the species. Darwin termed this process *natural selection* and reasoned that its continuous operation over hundreds of millions of years—the accumulation of small inherited changes—resulted in the origin of new species.

Following Bates's report, other scientists reported discovering instances of mimicry in Africa, Australia, and Malaysia. One of the most famous cases of all was described in North America, where the palatable viceroy butterfly was discovered to be a nearly perfect mimic of the unpalatable monarch. But butterflies were not the only insect mimics. Flies were discovered that resembled bees or wasps, unpalatable or dangerous because of their stings. Today, hundreds of examples are known of what *entomologists* (scientists who study insects) call *Batesian mimicry,* in which a palatable insect species mimics an unpalatable model.

In spite of Bates's great knowledge of insects, even he was partially deceived by another type of mimicry. Bates noticed that two large groups of Amazonian butterflies—the *Heliconiines* and *Ithomiines*—closely resembled each other, but both were inedible. He could not explain why two unpalatable species would have the same warning coloration patterns. In 1878, German naturalist Fritz Müller suggested that the two species had started out with completely different warning coloration patterns. As a result, predators had to kill a few of each to learn to avoid both. Müller theorized further that if they developed inheritable variations that made one species look like the other, then predators would only have to learn to avoid the single shared color patterns. As a result, fewer individuals of both species would be killed. This new extension of mimicry theory came to be known as *Müllerian mimicry.*

The theories of Batesian and Müllerian mimicry

A Convertible Caterpillar

A moth caterpillar found in Central and South America, *right,* warns away predators by mimicking the ferocious appearance of a viper. The caterpillar swells up to display large fake eyes, *below.*

A Terrible-Tasting Trio

Two wasps, *above left* and *middle,* and a bee, *above right,* have almost identical color patterns. All three also taste bad to predators. By mimicking each other's appearance, all three benefit from their predators' bad experiences. After a few such experiences while sampling an individual from any one of the three species, a predator learns to avoid any insect that looks like this. As a result, fewer individuals of any one of these species need to be sacrificed before a predator learns to leave all three alone. This is called *Müllerian mimicry.*

formed a rational explanation of the diverse examples of mimicry observed by naturalists in the late 1800's and the early 1900's. Until the 1950's, however, no adequately controlled experiments to test the theories had ever been carried out. Then, Jane Van Zandt Brower, a graduate student at Yale University in New Haven, Conn., conducted a series of experiments involving birds and butterflies. The butterflies were the monarch and its famous mimic, the viceroy, along with the tiger swallowtail, which looked like neither the monarch nor the viceroy. She offered caged Florida scrub jays a diet of bad-tasting monarchs and good-tasting tiger swallowtail butterflies. The birds in these experiments almost always refused to eat more monarchs after having become sick after eating a few. But they consistently ate the swallowtails. After about 50 trial feedings, Brower then offered viceroys to the scrub jays. All but one bird clearly mistook the viceroys for monarchs and rejected them on sight. A second set of birds, the controls, were offered only swallowtails and viceroys; these birds ate most of their viceroys. The experiment showed clearly that the scrub jays exposed to the sickening monarchs subsequently rejected look-alike viceroys on sight, whereas the control jays that had never tasted a monarch attacked or ate most of the viceroys. With this experiment, scientists had their first controlled study confirming the theory of Batesian mimicry.

Since this study, many other experiments have been done with other species of caged predators, such as birds, lizards, and monkeys. These experiments have supported both Bates's hypothesis—that good-tasting creatures mimic bad-tasting ones to avoid being eaten—and Müller's hypothesis—that bad-tasting creatures mimic each other to decrease the number of individuals eaten by predators. All of these experiments, however, were done in the laboratory under artificial conditions. How could mimicry be tested in a natural situation? If mimics survive at a higher rate than nonmimics, as theorized, then a field experiment should be able to test this prediction. But a suitable insect for such a test would have to be found.

The problem with using most insect species for experiments in nature is that once they are released in the wild, they tend to disperse quickly so that it is almost impossible to recover them. As a result, the insects that scientists wish to study tend to disappear, making it difficult, if not impossible, to obtain any experimental results.

A field experiment that I designed in the 1960's, along with entomologist Lawrence Cook of Manchester University in England, was intended to solve this problem. It involved using a large silk moth, *Callosamia promethia*, found in the Northeastern United States. This moth had one unique feature that ensured we could recover it in the wild. The male of *C. promethia* is attracted to the scent of the virgin female of this species. The female releases a *pheromone* (an irresistible chemical perfume) that attracts males from downwind for several kilometers. This pheromone has such a distinct scent that no other species of insect is attracted by it. We could release the male into the wild and use the female to entice him back, so that our experimental subjects would not disappear. And we could keep the female in a trap so that she could not disappear. Because the female's mating scent is so strong, we were confident that most of the males who did not return to the female had probably been eaten.

Another important feature of this species of silk moth is that the male's courtship flight to the female takes place in daylight, from afternoon to dusk. At this time, the male is exposed to a variety of bird predators. Most silk moths are nocturnal and fly only at night, when the majority of birds are not active. So the male silk moth of *C. promethia* gave us an ideal experimental subject.

The next step in our experiment was to paint some males the same color as unpalatable butterflies and to paint others—the controls—so that they would not resemble any known unpalatable butterflies. By painting individuals of only one species of silk moth, we could be sure that the only variable in the experiment was the moth's color.

It was a good idea, but, as sometimes happens in science, our experiment didn't work. We had conducted our experiment in Trinidad where there are great varieties of moths and bird predators. Therefore, the conditions of the natural setting may have been too complex for our experiment.

Nevertheless, it did work in the Great Lakes region of the United States, where entomologist Gilbert Waldbauer and his colleagues at the University of Illinois in Urbana-Champaign repeated the experiment in the 1970's, using the same species of silk moth. Waldbauer's group painted some of the silk moths to resemble the unpalatable monarch butterfly. When they counted the moths that returned, they found that moths painted to resemble monarchs survived better than moths painted to resemble the local palatable tiger swallowtail butterfly. Moreover, beak marks on the wings of the returning moths indicated that birds were attacking the moths painted to look like swallowtails much more often than those painted to look like monarchs. This study yielded strong experimental evidence that Batesian mimicry did indeed operate in the natural environment.

Batesian mimicry is one of the most successful forms of deception known, but what happens if it becomes too successful and eventually there are more good-tasting mimics than bad-tasting models? Will predators have more experience with good-tasting insects than bad-tasting ones?

Such a possibility could easily occur. For example, each year a new crop of young birds, lizards, and other predators are born and at some point they must begin feeding on their own. If a young fledgling bird sees a good-tasting mimic before encountering a bad-tasting model, it will attack and find the mimic palatable. Since the mimics are brightly colored, the young bird will have an easy time discovering more—and it will also find the model, which it will attack. The more mimics there are, the less chance that the young bird will first attack the model, find it disgusting, and learn to avoid both model and mimic. Thus we can reason that for Batesian mimicry to work efficiently, the mimic must be rare and the model common to increase the likelihood that the predator's first attack is on the model.

But now an interesting dilemma emerges: Batesian mimicry increases the mimic's reproductive success, so individuals in the mimicking species will likely survive, reproduce, and increase the population of the species. Eventually the mimic's success may be its downfall, because it may become so common the young predators will first taste the mimic and associate tastiness with its color pattern.

Nature has evolved at least one almost incredible solution to this predicament: Individuals of one butterfly species can resemble not one but several different models. This is called *polymorphism* and means that one species has individuals that come in many different forms. *Taxonomists* (scientists who specialize in the classification of animals) can determine from other characteristics which polymorphic individuals belong to the same species.

The most famous example of mimetic polymorphism is found in the African swallowtail butterfly, *Papilio dardanus*. An individual African swallowtail can have one of eight different forms that

Bamboozling a Bee

Mimicry has also evolved among some plants. A species of orchid, *above,* needs insects to carry its pollen to other flowers and thus ensure its reproduction. But it has no nectar to attract insects. Instead it looks, smells, and feels like a female bee and thus attracts male bees. When a male tries to mate with the orchid, *left,* it picks up pollen.

perfectly mimic eight very different-looking unpalatable models. Scientists have bred African swallowtails and carefully examined their offspring. They have discovered that the offspring of one female butterfly can take several mimetic forms. By imitating more than one model, this species can increase its numbers without running the risk of appearing too common.

Another problem scientists have studied is how the evolution of mimicry in its initial stages could have helped a species survive. How could the first small changes in color, for example, possibly dupe the predators? Mimicry could not have evolved quickly in a generation or two because a *mutation* (a change in a gene) that causes radical changes in color and pattern usually results in sterile or sickly individuals that die before they can reproduce. But if color pattern changes must be small and gradual, how then can the early stages of mimicry be advantageous?

Research on the heredity of wing color patterns in a group of North American butterflies, together with experiments on how birds learn to avoid unpalatable insects, have offered a solution. Studies on how birds learn to avoid unpalatable butterflies have shown that birds will tend to avoid even a small resemblance to a model rather than risk being sickened. So even an imperfect mimic—a mimic in its earliest stages—enjoys a slight advantage. The advantage is just great enough for individuals to survive and reproduce at a higher rate than individuals in the species that are not becoming mimics. As the early but imperfect mimic gains this survival and reproduction advantage, additional genetic variations producing a greater resemblance to the model can occur in the offspring. As these variations accumulate over thousands of generations, the butterfly species gradually evolves into a nearly perfect mimic.

One group of butterflies that were the object of the heredity studies belong to the genus *Limenitis*. Scientists once thought they were three species—a butterfly that is not a mimic called *Limenitis arthemis*; *L. astyanax*, a black-and-blue mimic of an extremely foul-tasting swallowtail butterfly; and *L. archippus*, commonly known as the viceroy butterfly, the famous mimic of the poisonous monarch butterfly. Entomologist Austin Platt of the University of Maryland discovered in the 1970's, however, that *arthemis* and *astyanax* are two forms of the same species. The viceroy evolved from *arthemis* and is now a separate species.

In the Northern United States and Canada, *arthemis* individuals have a white-banded pattern. The broad white bands across its otherwise dark wings produce what is called *disruptive coloration*, making the butterfly extremely hard for bird predators to see as it flies through the alternating light and dark color patterns in its forest habitat. In the South, all the way to Florida, *arthemis* individuals are very different in appearance. Rather than retaining the disruptive coloration, *arthemis* individuals in Southern habitats changed from a

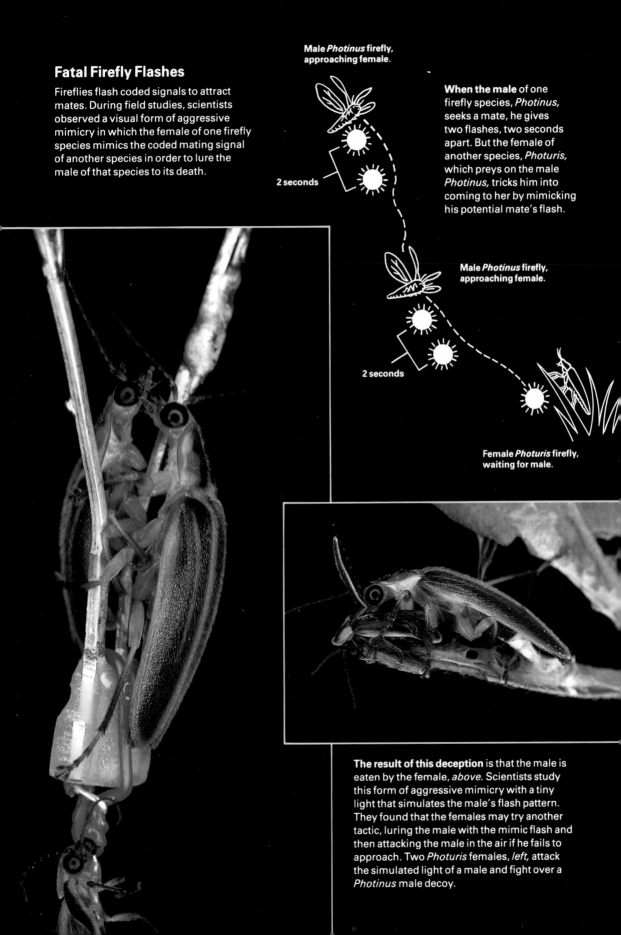

Fatal Firefly Flashes

Fireflies flash coded signals to attract mates. During field studies, scientists observed a visual form of aggressive mimicry in which the female of one firefly species mimics the coded mating signal of another species in order to lure the male of that species to its death.

Male *Photinus* firefly, approaching female.

2 seconds

When the male of one firefly species, *Photinus*, seeks a mate, he gives two flashes, two seconds apart. But the female of another species, *Photuris*, which preys on the male *Photinus*, tricks him into coming to her by mimicking his potential mate's flash.

Male *Photinus* firefly, approaching female.

2 seconds

Female *Photuris* firefly, waiting for male.

The result of this deception is that the male is eaten by the female, *above*. Scientists study this form of aggressive mimicry with a tiny light that simulates the male's flash pattern. They found that the females may try another tactic, luring the male with the mimic flash and then attacking the male in the air if he fails to approach. Two *Photuris* females, *left*, attack the simulated light of a male and fight over a *Photinus* male decoy.

Testing Mimicry Theory in the Laboratory

The theory of Batesian mimicry holds that a good-tasting species mimics a bad-tasting one to avoid being eaten by predators. Researchers tested this using the bad-tasting monarch butterfly and its mimic, the good-tasting viceroy. They offered a scrub jay a monarch, *below left.* The bird ate the monarch, *below center,* and became sick, *below right.* When offered a look-alike viceroy, the bird refused to eat it, even though viceroys taste good to birds.

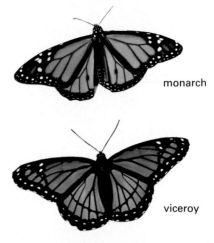

monarch

viceroy

black-and-white butterfly to a black-and-blue butterfly, a Batesian mimic of the foul-tasting black-and-blue southern pipevine swallowtail butterfly. And this is why scientists originally thought it belonged to a separate species, which they called *L. astyanax.*

In 1983, Platt proved that *astyanax* and *arthemis* freely interbreed in the region where they cohabit, proving they are of the same species. The region is a narrow geographic belt that stretches from New England westward to the Great Lakes region. There, where the two forms interbred in the wild, they produced variations in the color patterns ranging from one form to the other (blue and white to black and blue). By repeatedly crossbreeding *arthemis* and *astyanax* for nearly 20 years in the laboratory, Platt obtained the same variations in color patterns found in the natural interbreeding region. So Platt's studies also lent experimental support to the theory of how the evolution of a mimic in its earliest stages can benefit individuals. He showed that only a small number of genetic mutations were necessary to change color patterns and that a major mutation resulting in a single large color change was not necessary to explain the evolution of mimicry.

This finding was reinforced in a separate experiment in which Platt bred *arthemis* with the viceroy. His hybrid butterflies again clearly showed that a small number of genetic variations converted the white-banded *arthemis* into a nearly perfect mimic of the black-and-orange monarch. Thus, the field and laboratory findings together enabled Platt to reconstruct thousands of years of evolution.

Once the fact that mimicry does evolve as a result of small and gradual changes was established, my colleagues and I conducted a series of experiments to determine how strongly birds associate patterns of color with unpleasant experiences. Our experiments involved butterflies in the genus *Heliconius*, which are foul-tasting, and another species belonging to a distinct genus known as *Biblis* that is palatable. The foul-tasting species, *Heliconius erato*, is black with a big red patch on each wing, and the palatable *Biblis* is black with red borders only on its hind wings. The two species share the same basic colors, but the patterns are totally different. In our experiment, after birds had a bad experience tasting the unpalatable *erato*, they also rejected the palatable *Biblis*, despite the differences in color patterns. Then, in another experiment, we painted the red borders of the palatable *Biblis* black so that this butterfly appeared all black, rather than black and red like the foul-tasting model. Even then, the birds rejected several all-black butterflies. We concluded that just a single color in common—black—was sufficient warning.

From this, we deduced that a mimic does not have to have the same color pattern or even exactly the same colors. As long as it looks somewhat like a model, its initial genetic variation, though slight, may be enough for it to gain an advantage. The risk of eating the model and being sickened is apparently too great for the bird to chance. As individuals in later generations begin to look more like the model, predators will tend to eat fewer of these better mimics. The slightly better mimics will leave more offspring, and so eventually the highly detailed, nearly perfect mimic will evolve.

Studies of mimicry have driven home to scientists how complex and at the same time how marvelous protective adaptations are in nature. As long as the natural laboratories in the tropical regions of the world remain intact, many more amazing discoveries await those who seek to understand natural selection through the diverse cornucopia of mimicry.

For further reading:

Brower, Lincoln Pierson. "Ecological Chemistry." *Scientific American*, February 1969.
——— *Mimicry and the Evolutionary Process*. University of Chicago Press, 1988.
Owen, Denis. *Camouflage and Mimicry*. University of Chicago Press, 1982.

Astronomers are building a new generation
of giant telescopes that promise to see farther
into space than ever before.

New Eyes
on the Sky

BY STEPHEN P. MARAN

High atop mountains in Hawaii and Chile, astronomers are preparing for a new generation of giant telescopes that in the 1990's may provide answers to such perplexing questions as:

■ How do stars form?

■ Do other stars have planets orbiting around them, just as Earth and the other planets of our solar system orbit the sun?

■ How did *galaxies*—the vast systems that comprise hundreds of billions of stars—form and evolve?

■ How was the universe formed—and what will be its fate?

The new telescopes that may provide the answers will be *optical telescopes*, which—like our eyes—see visible light that is given off or reflected by other objects. These telescopes use mirrors to gather the light, and the ones now being built will dwarf the famous 5-meter (200-inch) mirror of the Hale telescope atop Palomar Mountain near San Diego. The Hale can collect a million times as much light as the human eye. Using the Hale, Dutch-born American astronomer Maarten Schmidt in 1963 identified the first quasar. (*Quasars* are the most distant and energetic objects in the universe.) Using the new giant telescopes—with mirrors and mirror combinations that will have light-gathering power equal to mirrors ranging from 6.5 to 16 meters (about 260 to 630 inches)—astronomers hope to unlock secrets of the universe that might otherwise remain hidden.

How a Reflecting Telescope Works In a reflecting telescope, mirrors gather and focus light from distant objects. The light enters the telescope tube and strikes a primary mirror, which reflects the light onto a smaller, secondary mirror. The secondary mirror reflects the light back through a hole in the primary mirror, to form an image at the focus. The image can be viewed with the eye, but astronomers usually record it on film or use electronic detectors that may be connected to computers. The larger the primary mirror, the more light it can collect, and thus, fainter and more distant objects can be seen.

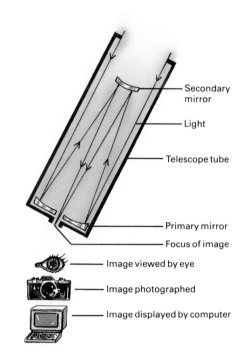

Secondary mirror

Light

Telescope tube

Primary mirror

Focus of image

Image viewed by eye

Image photographed

Image displayed by computer

The author:
Stephen P. Maran is a senior staff scientist at the National Aeronautics and Space Administration-Goddard Space Flight Center in Greenbelt, Md. The views expressed are his own.

Astronomers once believed it was impractical to try to build a telescope larger than the Hale, but this is no longer the case. The giant telescope projects have been started for two principal reasons. First, new technologies have made it possible economically to build giant mirrors. Second, astronomers have discovered that it is possible to obtain good images of celestial objects with larger mirrors by insulating and cooling observatory domes.

Throughout history, new scientific instruments have led to major discoveries. The first use of the telescope for astronomy by the Italian astronomer and physicist Galileo Galilei in 1609 was no exception. Galileo examined the broad band of light known as the Milky Way and found that it was not a river of "luminous fluid," as some had suggested, but a vast collection of individual stars.

The first telescopes operated on the principle of *refraction* (the bending of light by a lens or other device). In a refracting telescope, a lens at one end of the telescope tube known as the *objective lens* bends incoming light so that the light comes together at a point called the *focus*. An eyepiece at the other end of the tube magnifies the image formed at the focus.

The refracting telescope has certain disadvantages. To our eyes, the visible light of the sun and most stars appears white, but white light is actually a mix of the different colors of the rainbow. When white light passes through the objective lens of a refracting telescope, each color is focused at a slightly different point, rather than at a common point. This results in a fuzzy image.

Recognizing this problem, the English astronomer and mathematician Sir Isaac Newton constructed the first *reflecting* telescope in 1668. The reflector or reflecting telescope uses mirrors rather than lenses to collect and focus light from the stars. A large mirror at the bottom of the telescope known as the *primary mirror* gathers the light from the object under study. The mirror curves inward with a concave shape so that the light rays are reflected back at an angle and meet at a focal point known as the *prime focus* to form an image of the object. Because the different colors in white light are reflected at the same angle in a concave mirror, they are focused at the same point, eliminating the image blurring that occurred with refracting telescopes.

Following Newton's invention, other astronomers began to make and use larger reflectors, knowing that the larger the primary mirror, the more light was collected from a given star to form a brighter, sharper image of the star. A larger primary mirror was also able to detect images of faint stars. Larger refractors were also made. The largest refractor ever built had a lens with a diameter of 102 centimeters (40 inches). But among the most famous telescopes made were reflectors built by the German musician William Herschel, who moved to England in 1757 and became an astronomer, and Irish astronomer William Parsons, the third Earl of Rosse.

Herschel was a craftsman who built mirrors as large as 1 meter (48 inches) in diameter. He was skilled at shaping the mirrors to exactly the desired curvature so that their focus was sharp. Herschel's reflectors allowed him to discover that what appeared through less powerful telescopes to be *nebulae* (clouds of gas and dust) were actually groupings of many individual stars. In 1785, he wrote that these objects "may also be called milky ways." Thus, long before astronomers accepted the idea, Herschel guessed at the existence of other galaxies like our own Milky Way. He had the right idea—though from the wrong evidence— since many of the nebulae that he resolved into stars were actually star clusters in our own galaxy, not other galaxies beyond the Milky Way.

The major contribution of Lord Rosse was to build the first really large telescope in 1845, a 1.8-meter (72-inch) reflector. This powerful in-

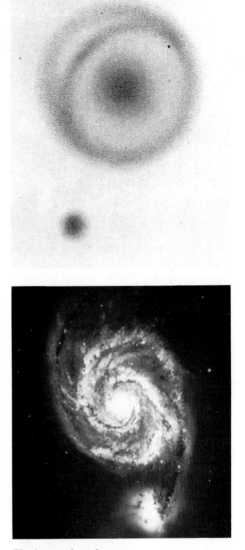

The larger the mirror, the more light collected

As astronomers built ever larger telescope mirrors, fainter and more distant objects were revealed in greater detail. Using a 47-centimeter (18.7-inch) telescope mirror, Sir John Herschel viewed what was thought to be a cloud of gas called M51, and in 1833, he published a sketch of it, *top.* Using the 5-meter (200-inch) Hale telescope, which was completed in 1948, contemporary astronomers were able to see that M51 is made of stars. Called the Whirlpool, it is a spiral galaxy, *above,* with a separate, smaller galaxy near it.

strument revealed peculiar pinwheel-shaped structures with spiral arms surrounding a bright central region in certain objects that were thought to be nebulae. These objects were neither gas clouds nor star clusters, and for generations afterward, astronomers debated whether these curious spiral systems were other separate galaxies or part of the Milky Way.

The final answer to the question came in 1924, when the American astronomer Edwin P. Hubble observed what was then called the Andromeda Nebula through the 2.5-meter (100-inch) Hooker reflector at Mount Wilson Observatory near Pasadena, Calif. With the great light-gathering power of this telescope, it was possible to photograph numerous stars in the Andromeda nebula. By using brightness measurements to determine their distance, Hubble proved that these stars were so far away they could not be part of the Milky Way galaxy but were part of a separate galaxy.

Following the completion of the Hale telescope in 1948, few astronomers gave any thought to the need for a larger telescope. They believed there were two basic problems with making telescopes larger than 5 meters: the expense, and the blurring of images due to turbulence in Earth's atmosphere, so that the images formed by a giant telescope might not be any sharper than those formed by the Hale telescope.

Only the Soviet Union attempted to build a telescope larger than the Hale. Its 6-meter (236-inch) telescope—the largest in the world—was installed at Zelenchukskaya in 1976. But it has failed to provide sharp images.

Since the time the Hale was built, large tele-

Improving Telescope "Vision"
Astronomers use various tools of modern technology to improve the images seen with large telescopes. An astronomer uses an infrared camera, *above,* to check for unwanted heat sources inside an observatory in Hawaii. Even a body can be a source of heat that produces warm air currents that blur telescope images.

Electronic detectors called *charge-coupled devices* (CCD's) produce better images than photographic film because they are a hundred times more sensitive to incoming light. An image of a star cluster taken with CCD's, *left,* reveals more stars and more detail than an image of the same cluster recorded on film, *far left.* Changes such as these led to plans for building bigger mirrors.

scopes had become extremely expensive. For example, doubling the diameter of a primary mirror could easily increase a telescope's cost eight times. This was because bigger mirrors were heavier, and the greater the mirror's diameter, the longer the telescope tube needed to be. So bigger telescopes were longer, had heavier structural elements and bigger machinery, and needed larger buildings to house them. Most astronomers believed therefore that the Hale telescope—with its 500 metric tons (550 short tons) of precision-moving machinery and glass and its cost of $6.5 million (a huge sum in 1948)—was about as large as was practical to build.

A more fundamental constraint on telescope size seemed to be the atmosphere itself. Pockets of warm and cool air are constantly in motion in the atmosphere, and the atmospheric turbulence this creates causes a blurring effect. For example, when we look at a star, it does not appear as a steady point of light. Instead, it appears to twinkle due to the atmosphere's blurring effect. With large telescopes, the blurring effect is greater because these telescopes look through a greater width of the turbulent atmosphere than do small telescopes. The belief that telescopes larger than the Hale were impractical was reinforced when the 6-meter telescope in the Soviet Union proved very costly and produced relatively poor images. The poor image quality, however, was more likely due to a combination of poor mirror quality, especially turbulent atmospheric conditions at the observatory site, and turbulent air currents around the telescope mirror caused by the mirror itself.

Beginning in the mid-1970's, some astronomers were encouraged to start thinking about larger telescopes as a result of an improved understanding of air currents in and around observatories. Astronomers found that much of the blurring effect that had been attributed to turbulence in the atmosphere above observatories was actually due to warm air currents rising from the observatories themselves. For example, telescope mirrors get warm during the day as they absorb heat from the air. When exposed to cool night air, the warm air currents rise from the mirror and create a shimmering effect, much like the shimmering you can see as hot air rises above a radiator. The problem became clear when the Multiple Mirror Telescope on Mount Hopkins in Arizona went into operation in 1979. This instrument combines light from six 1.8-meter mirrors to achieve a light-gathering power equal to a 4.5-meter (176-inch) mirror. When astronomers were testing the telescope, they concluded that differences in image blurring with different mirrors were a result of air turbulence near the mirrors.

As a result of these findings, astronomers now sometimes air-condition telescope domes during the day to keep the telescopes at nearly the same temperature as the night air. And large exhaust fans are used to remove heat from electrical and electronic equipment at night. In addition, astronomers use infrared cameras that detect heat

New Advances in Telescope Design

The new giant telescopes are made possible by technological breakthroughs in mirror design that keep their weight and cost low. The three advances in mirror design are the honeycomb spin-cast mirror, the segmented mirror, and the meniscus spin-cast mirror.

The Honeycomb Mirror

In the honeycomb design, *above*, the mirror has a solid reflecting surface supported by a honeycomb-shaped structure that is largely hollow to reduce weight. Both the surface and the honeycomb structure are made at the same time by a process called *spin-casting*, a technique that replaces the costly and laborious process of grinding a mirror's surface to the proper concave shape. As molten glass spins in a huge electric oven, at a carefully controlled rate, centrifugal force molds the reflecting surface into a concave shape.

to locate warm and cold spots on the telescope tube. They then use special tapes and paints to keep the telescope at a nearly uniform temperature and thereby minimize air turbulence.

In 1973, the new technology of light-sensitive electronic detectors known as *charge-coupled devices* (*CCD*'s) also allowed astronomers to use existing telescopes to the limits of their light-gathering capabilities. Once existing telescopes were pushed to those limits, astronomers wanted larger telescope mirrors that could collect even more light. CCD's consist of light-sensitive silicon chips—similar to computer chips—able to record between 70 and 100 per cent of the *photons* (particles of light) striking a telescope mirror, compared with photographic film, which can record only 1 of every 1,000 photons that strike a telescope mirror. With CCD's, the Hale telescope could record fainter objects than ever before, as became apparent in 1982 when it detected Halley's Comet at a greater distance than ever before. The comet was 20 million times fainter than the faintest star that the human eye can see.

In addition, larger mirrors make it possible to obtain sharper images in the infrared. Infrared radiation is not visible to the human

The Segmented Mirror

The segmented mirror, *below*, designed for the Keck telescope on Mauna Kea in Hawaii, combines 36 1.8-meter (72-inch) mirrors that fit together like bathroom tiles for a total diameter of 10 meters (400 inches). A technician, *right*, watches the cutting of a mirror segment into its hexagonal (six-sided) shape.

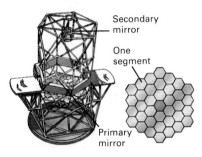

Secondary mirror

One segment

Primary mirror

The Meniscus Mirror

A meniscus mirror for the Very Large Telescope is so thin that it requires computer-controlled devices called *actuators, left,* to keep the mirror in the proper shape. The mirror rests on a bed of actuators, *below,* which can individually push or pull on the mirror when sensors indicate a section of glass is losing its shape.

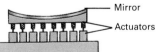

Mirror

Actuators

The Very Large Telescope (VLT), a project of the European Southern Observatory, will combine the light of four 8-meter (315-inch) mirrors to achieve the light-gathering power equal to a 16-meter (630-inch) mirror. Each mirror will also be used singly. A unique feature of the VLT, *above,* is the flexible dome, *inset, above,* which folds down around the telescopes during observations, eliminating the cost of a building made of concrete and a dome made of metal.

eye but is collected with optical mirrors that focus the light onto detectors that are sensitive to infrared rays. Atmospheric turbulence limits the quality of visible-light images, but mirror size is what limits the quality of infrared images. The reason is that infrared light is blurred less by the atmosphere than visible light.

Finally, some astronomers began to experiment with new designs and methods of making telescope mirrors that would greatly reduce their weight and cost. By designing mirrors in different ways and by devising different methods of constructing them, astronomers found the means to make larger telescopes affordable.

A key factor in keeping costs low is the shape of the primary mirrors, which are much more concave in the new telescopes. This causes light rays to be focused at a place much closer to the primary mirror. With a shorter focal length, the telescope tube can be shorter, and thus weigh less. For example, in the 5-meter Hale telescope, the prime focus is about 17 meters (55 feet) from the primary mirror, but a much larger 8-meter (315-inch) primary mirror of a future telescope will have a focal length of 10 to 15 meters (32 to 48 feet).

The giant telescopes under development now are so short in proportion to the diameter of their mirrors that they will resemble searchlights, compared with existing telescopes, which resemble cannons, according to astrophysicist Harland W. Epps of the

University of California at Los Angeles, who has worked on the optical design of many telescopes. A new 8-meter telescope, for example, will collect more than twice as much light as the 5-meter Hale telescope. But it will weigh less and fit inside a smaller dome than the Hale telescope.

Making lightweight, economical mirrors was another hurdle the new telescope makers had to conquer. A conventional telescope mirror is made by casting molten glass in a mold. The glass cools and hardens into a thick circular disk called a *mirror blank*. Opticians grind the top surface of the blank into a concave shape. Then, fine abrasive powders are used to polish the mirror surface. The entire process is extremely laborious, costly, and time-consuming. It took 10 years to complete the Hale telescope.

One of the new telescope makers has fashioned an entirely new process for molding mirrors. Under the stands of the football stadium at the University of Arizona in Tucson, astronomer Roger Angel has built a rotating electric oven. The huge oven resembles a giant turntable as it spins many times per minute. Angel's method— known as *spin-casting*—involves putting lumps of glass in a mold inside the oven. The glass is then spun just fast enough that *centrifugal force* molds the glass, as it melts, into a concave shape. (Centrifugal force causes the surface of a liquid to move outward as the liquid spins.) The shape the liquid glass flows into is almost exactly the correct shape for a telescope mirror.

Several different mirror designs have also been proposed for the new giant telescopes. No one knows as yet which new design concept is best. Each of these designs takes a unique approach to reducing the weight of the mirror, which is due to the volume of glass. The larger in diameter a single glass mirror is, the thicker it has to be to avoid sagging under its own weight.

The major designs fall into three categories. A *segmented mirror* combines many small mirrors to form one large mirror. A *meniscus mirror* is one large, extremely thin mirror that must have an underlying structure to support it. The *honeycomb mirror*—designed by Angel—is one large but almost hollow mirror with spaces that cause the mirror to resemble the honeycomb in a beehive.

The segmented mirror was designed by astrophysicist Jerry E. Nelson of the University of California at Berkeley for the future 10-meter (400-inch) Keck telescope, an $87-million joint project of the California Institute of Technology and the University of California. Each mirror segment for the Keck telescope is only 1.8 meters across and only 7.5 centimeters (3 inches) thick, compared with the Hale telescope's 60-centimeter (24-inch) thickness along its outer rim. Although the segments combine to form a 10-meter diameter, the total weight of glass in the Keck's segmented mirror amounts to 13 metric tons (14.4 short tons), compared with 37 metric tons (41 short tons) for the Soviet Union's single-piece 6-meter mirror. The weight

The Giant Telescope Projects

Telescope	Type and size of mirror	Location	Expected date of completion	Sponsoring organization
Multiple Mirror Telescope Conversion	6.5-meter (260-inch) honeycomb mirror	Mount Hopkins, Ariz.	1993	University of Arizona and Smithsonian Astrophysical Observatory
Magellan	8-meter (315-inch) honeycomb mirror	Chile	Undecided	Carnegie Institution of Washington, Johns Hopkins University, and University of Arizona
National 8-meter Telescopes	8-meter honeycomb mirror	One in Northern Hemisphere and one in Southern Hemisphere	Undecided	National Optical Astronomy Observatories
Spectroscopic Survey Telescope	8-meter segmented mirror	Fort Davis, Tex.	1990	Pennsylvania State University and University of Texas
Japan National Telescope	8-meter meniscus mirror	Mauna Kea, Hawaii	Undecided	Japanese government
Columbus	Twin 8-meter honeycomb mirrors (light-gathering equal to 11.3-meter [445-inch] mirror)	Mount Graham, Ariz.	Undecided	Italian institutions, Ohio State University, and University of Arizona
Keck	10-meter (400-inch) segmented mirror	Mauna Kea, Hawaii	1991	California Institute of Technology and University of California
Very Large Telescope	Four 8-meter meniscus mirrors (light-gathering equal to 16-meter [630-inch] mirror)	Chile	Mid-1990's	European Southern Observatory

of the structure needed to support the Keck mirror is also proportionately less.

The segmented mirror has a disadvantage, however. The segments must work in unison to create a common, perfectly shaped surface. To do this, the segments must be aligned to an accuracy of less than 0.000025 of a millimeter (0.000001 of an inch). This may prove difficult even with precision computerized controls. The Keck telescope will have a surface of 36 mirror segments, each with a *hexagon* (six-sided) shape, that will fit together like tiles in a mosaic.

Several things could cause the mirror segments to become misaligned. As the telescope moves to point to different parts of the sky, Earth's gravitational force acts on the mirror segments at different angles, causing them to sag or bend by tiny amounts that would give their surfaces the wrong shapes if not corrected by their support systems. Temperature changes around the telescope could also cause the mirror surface to deform slightly. And wind blowing against the telescope mirror and structure could also cause misalignments. Along each seam between mirror segments, the Keck telescope will have two sensors able to detect a misalignment as small as one *nanometer* (one-billionth of a meter) between the two adjoining segments. Computers will monitor the sensors twice each second and immediately adjust the mirror segments to keep them aligned.

Of all the new giant telescope projects, the Keck telescope is nearest completion. It is funded largely by a $70-million grant from the W. M. Keck Foundation (named after William M. Keck, the founder of Superior Oil). The dome for the observatory atop Mauna Kea, an inactive volcano in Hawaii, was completed in November 1988. The mirror segments are scheduled to be installed in early 1990, and by 1991, the Keck telescope will be ready for observations.

The single-piece meniscus mirror design was chosen by European astronomers building the Very Large Telescope (VLT)—a $235-million project of a group of West European nations. The VLT will be installed on an as-yet-undetermined mountain in Chile. Because the meniscus mirror is so thin, its weight is relatively low. And it is easier to make because of its single-piece design. But because the meniscus mirror is only 20 centimeters (8 inches) thick, strong winds and gravitational forces could cause it to bend out of shape if it were not for 350 computer-controlled devices called *actuators* on its back surface. The actuators push or pull constantly on the mirror to keep it in the correct concave shape.

The Europeans' VLT actually will consist of four separate telescopes placed in a row, each with an 8-meter meniscus mirror. The light from the four telescopes can be channeled to a common focus point and combined to equal the light-collecting area of a single 16-meter mirror.

Another unique aspect of the VLT is the complex of four collapsible domes that will surround the telescopes. Most observatories have rigid metal domes with relatively narrow slits that can be opened to view the sky. Because Earth rotates, telescopes must have the ability to move in order to track a star as it appears to change position in the sky. So the heavy telescope dome must rotate along with the telescope to keep the star in view. The dome itself and the machinery required to rotate it add considerably to the cost of a telescope project. The collapsible domes of the VLT will fold down around the telescopes during observations and are much cheaper than conventional metal domes.

Like the Keck telescope, the VLT Project has made considerable headway. The funds necessary to build the four telescopes were approved in December 1987 by the member nations of the European Southern Observatory (ESO), which is headquartered in Garching near Munich, West Germany. France, West Germany, and Italy will be the main financial supporters. In September 1988, the ESO issued a contract to a West German manufacturer to spin-cast the four primary mirrors out of a special glass-ceramic material called Zerodur that contracts or expands very little as a result of temperature changes. The ESO has already produced a prototype of these new mirrors—the 3.5-meter (140-inch) New Technology Telescope. This instrument was installed in 1988 at ESO's observatory on Cerro La Silla mountain in northern Chile and is making observations to test the new technology designed for the VLT. The VLT is expected to be ready for operation in the mid-1990's.

The third type of design—the honeycomb mirror—is incorporated in the plans for the Columbus Project, twin 8-meter telescopes which will be mounted in a way that resembles a giant binocular. The combined light of the two mirrors will yield the light-gathering power of a single 11.3-meter (445-inch) reflector. The Columbus Project, intended to celebrate the 500th anniversary of Christopher Columbus' voyage to America in 1492, is a joint undertaking of Ohio State University, the University of Arizona, and a group of astronomers at several institutions in Italy. In 1988, the United States Congress approved a site atop Mount Graham near Tucson for the observatory. The honeycomb mirrors for the Columbus Project will be made using Angel's spin-casting technique. In 1988, Angel successfully made a forerunner of the Columbus Project—a 3.5-meter honeycomb mirror to be installed on Sacramento Peak near Sunspot, N. Mex., for the Astrophysical Research Consortium, an organization formed by astronomers from several U.S. universities.

Another giant telescope project is the Spectroscopic Survey Telescope (SST), a $6-million project of the University of Texas and Pennsylvania State University. The SST will be placed at the McDonald Observatory near Fort Davis, Tex. Like the Keck telescope, the SST will have a segmented mirror, but there the resemblance ends. The hexagonal shapes of the Keck mirror segments fit together snugly, but the 85 SST mirror segments will be round, about 1 meter (40 inches) in diameter. The total diameter of the SST will be 9 meters (360 inches), but due to the empty spaces between the segments, its light-collecting power will equal that of an 8-meter mirror.

Unlike all of the other giant telescope projects, the SST will be a single-purpose telescope. It will be used exclusively for *spectroscopy*, the analysis of the light spectrum from stars and galaxies. Spectroscopy analyzes an object's light to determine its chemical makeup, and so tells astronomers much about the nature of the object and how it evolved. With its massive light-gathering ability, the SST will be able to analyze the faint light from distant galaxies and quasars.

Other giant telescope projects planned by U.S. astronomers await funding approval by sponsoring organizations. Some wait their turns for mirrors from the casting facilities.

When the Keck, VLT, Columbus Project, and other giant telescopes come into operation, they should be able to see as far as, if not farther than, the Hubble Space Telescope. With a scheduled launch into orbit by the space shuttle in 1990, the Hubble will be free of the blurring effect from Earth's atmosphere. But its mirror is relatively small at only 2.4 meters (95 inches) in diameter. Although the Hubble's mirror will not be able to collect as much light and therefore see as far as the giant ground-based telescopes, it will obtain sharper images than can be obtained with ground-based telescopes and be able to study ultraviolet light by using electronic detectors sensitive to ultraviolet radiation.

Together, the Hubble and the giant telescopes on Earth should help answer many questions in astronomy. Finding planets around other stars is one important goal. One study, as yet unconfirmed, suggests that perhaps half of the sunlike stars in our galaxy might be orbited by planets as large as Jupiter. Such planetary objects would give off infrared radiation. With their expected ability to resolve sharp images in the infrared, the giant telescopes should be able to detect these Jupiter-like objects around nearby stars—if these planets exist.

Astronomers also will look for *supernovae*—explosions of massive stars—in distant galaxies. Finding such supernovae may shed light on the theory that at the very beginning of the universe, many giant stars formed. Some astronomers believe that the explosions of these stars may have triggered the formation of galaxies. They hope that the new telescopes may detect these explosions and thus help answer the most fundamental questions of how objects in the early universe came into being. And if history is any guide, the most exciting discoveries will be those we cannot even imagine.

For further reading:

Henbest, Nigel. "The Greatest Telescope Race." *New Scientist*, Oct. 29, 1989.
King, Henry C. *The History of the Telescope*. Dover, 1979.
Waldrop, Mitchell M. "The Mirror Maker." *Discover*, December 1987.

BY JERRY F. FRANKLIN

A Mountain Bounces Back

The 1980 eruption of Mount St. Helens
turned lush forests into a moonscape,
but life returned with greater speed
and vigor than anyone expected.

The landscape below our helicopter should have been green with the new leaves of spring. Instead, it appeared totally barren, a moonscape in shades of gray and brown. The devastation had been caused by one of the few active volcanoes in the United States—Mount St. Helens in southwestern Washington state. On May 18, 1980, Mount St. Helens erupted with the force of a nuclear explosion. The blast killed 57 people, knocked down trees as if they were blades of grass, and wiped out wildlife for kilometers around.

Now, two weeks after the May 18 eruption, our team of 10 U.S. Forest Service researchers was flying to the blast zone. We would be the first scientific personnel on the ground—an exciting prospect. What an opportunity, I thought. At last, we would be able to study ecological succession—the changes in plant and animal populations that occur over time—starting from a totally barren area. Over the years, we could trace how long it took various organisms to reenter the area and in what order they would reappear.

Our first stop was Ryan Lake, nearly 32 kilometers (20 miles) from Mount St. Helens, on the edge of the blast zone. Our helicopter skimmed across a landscape studded with carcasses of dead trees, some standing and others scattered like toothpicks, and settled toward an ash- and debris-covered road. "Don't get out until the rotors have completely stopped," warned the helicopter pilot, sensing our eagerness to set foot in the blast zone. The door finally slid open, and we dropped to the ground. A strange mixture of scorched and rotting smells assaulted us. "Stay close," he ordered, "so we can get out of here quickly if the mountain acts up."

I stepped across a ditch into what had been an area cleared of trees by loggers prior to the eruption. A tiny patch of green caught my eye in the gray-brown scene. I dropped to my knees for a closer look. A green plant had pushed its way up through a crack in the blanket of ash—a fireweed sprout. This tall plant with pink flowers often appears on recently burned land. As I looked, I noted two, then six, then many more sprouts in the area around me.

Two strides brought me to a low bank, where I could see signs of recent excavations by tiny burrowing animals called pocket gophers, who had survived the blast in their underground homes. Movement caught my eye. Numerous ants—other underground survivors—were foraging about.

Later that day and in the following weeks, my colleagues and I saw many more survivors of this great eruption, including trees, dozens of other plants, beetles, deer mice, fish, frogs, and salamanders. Life had survived, and in many forms. The reinvasion of organisms from undamaged nearby areas would certainly be important, but, for the most part, the organisms were already there. Recovery had begun.

Nine years later, in the summer of 1989, the Ryan Lake area is lush with leafy plants and a scattering of young trees. Elk roam there, birds fly overhead, and insects abound. Only a few short stumps and fallen trees, still visible through the blanket of green, bear witness to the 1980 catastrophe.

The author:
Jerry F. Franklin is Bloedel Professor of Ecosystem Analysis at the University of Washington College of Forest Resources in Seattle.

Elsewhere in the Mount St. Helens area, the picture is much different, depending on the type of volcanic destruction that affected the area and on human efforts to speed recovery. Some landscapes remain barren, with only a few small plants providing sparse cover. At the other extreme are the woodlands replanted by foresters, now thick with young, rapidly growing trees. By studying the various types of recovery at Mount St. Helens, scientists have learned much about nature's ability to heal itself and how human beings can assist the healing process.

Before the eruption at Mount St. Helens, towering evergreen forests covered much of the mountain. Alaska cedar, Douglas-fir, noble fir, Pacific silver fir, western red cedar, and western and mountain hemlock dominated the forests. Some of these woodlands were magnificent old-growth forests with trees ranging from 350 to 750 years old. Other forests in the area were growing back after recently being cut down by loggers. Clear, cold lakes dotted the region, including Spirit Lake at the northern foot of Mount St. Helens. Earlier volcanic activity had created this lake by damming the upper reaches of the North Fork of the Toutle River.

Many kinds of destruction

The events that turned these lush forests and sparkling lakes into a giant ashpit began in the spring of 1980. The north side of Mount St. Helens began to bulge as liquid rock called *magma* rose from deep within Earth and collected inside the volcano under great pressure. On the morning of May 18, a series of earthquakes triggered an avalanche of rocks and debris on the north slope of the mountain. The landslide "uncorked" the superheated magma inside the mountain, producing a great explosion at 8:32 a.m. The force of the blast was directed sideways to the north, rather than all around a central opening at the top as is typical of most volcanic eruptions. The blast knocked down trees and wiped bare much of the landscape for nearly 520 square kilometers (200 square miles), an area called the *blast zone*. In a narrow surrounding belt called the *scorch zone*, trees remained standing but were scorched. The blast and scorch zones, along with the entire region where plant and animal life was destroyed or severely disrupted, make up an area that scientists decided to call the *devastated zone*.

The avalanche of rocks and debris filled the valley of the North Fork of the Toutle River to depths of more than 180 meters (590 feet) for 32 kilometers (20 miles). Apparently, no living things survived because they were so deeply buried. At the foot of the mountain, the landslide also dashed the waters of Spirit Lake out of their bed, leaving a "bathtub ring" of debris on mountain slopes more than 150 meters (490 feet) above lake level.

The blast and the avalanche of debris were only two of the results of the Mount St. Helens eruption, though they were among the most destructive. A column of hot gases, liquid magma, and solid rocks

Glossary

Debris flows: Thick, sticky floods of mud, rock, and other material.

Ecosystem: The group of plants and animals living in an environment, together with the nonliving features of the environment, such as soil and water.

Magma: Molten rock inside Earth.

Pyroclastic flows: Streams of extremely hot gases, gravel, and rock.

Succession: The changes in plant and animal populations in one area that occur over time.

Tephra: Airborne volcanic material, ranging in size from dust to rocks.

A Patchwork of Destruction

The 1980 eruption of Mount St. Helens created a patchwork of various kinds of destruction in the surrounding area. Streams of hot gases and rock called *pyroclastic flows* poured down the mountain, leveling everything in their path. Debris avalanches filled the beds of lakes and rivers. Other sites were blanketed by *tephra,* airborne volcanic dust and rocks.

Mount St. Helens

Spirit Lake

Toutle River

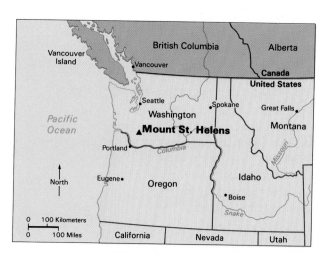

The eruption of Mount St. Helens on May 18, 1980, hurls clouds of hot gases and liquid and solid rock high into the air, *right.*

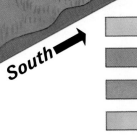

South

Pyroclastic flow

Rock and debris avalanche

Debris flow

Blast zone

Trees lie scattered like toothpicks about 6 kilometers (4 miles) from the volcano after the 1980 eruption, *below.*

from inside the mountain shot thousands of meters into the air and produced a rain of volcanic material called *tephra* (pronounced *TEHF ruh*). Tephra is a general term for all airborne volcanic deposits, regardless of particle size or origin, including ash, dust, sand, gravel, and rock. At Mount St. Helens, the tephra—commonly, but incorrectly, called ash—blanketed hundreds of square kilometers with up to 50 centimeters (20 inches) of material. On the south side of the mountain, the eruption deposited a layer of tephra but otherwise did little damage.

Mount St. Helens continued to erupt for several hours. From time to time, the eruption lost strength, and the column of volcanic material no longer shot into the air but instead fell back onto the mountain slopes, producing flows of extremely hot gases and rock called *pyroclastic flows*. The temperature of these flows exceeded 365°C (690°F.), killing everything in their path and creating some of the most desolate vistas on the volcano.

The heat of the eruption also melted ice and snow on the slopes of the mountain. The resulting water mixed with soil, rock, and other debris to produce thick, sticky floods of mud and debris called *debris flows*. These powerful flows—which had the consistency of wet cement—uprooted trees, lifted concrete bridges off their piers, and floated heavy objects for long distances. The debris flows filled valleys to the southeast and west of the mountain. One flow traveled down the valley of the North Fork of the Toutle River, eroding and mixing with the debris avalanche that had already filled the valley.

Although Mount St. Helens appeared initially to be a uniformly devastated landscape, the eruption had, in fact, varied in its effects from site to site, depending upon the type of volcanic disturbance— such as blast, debris avalanche, debris flow, or tephra fall. Survival of living organisms also varied depending on the amount of snow cover and other factors. The eruption created a vast and varied laboratory for study of ecosystem recovery and ecological succession.

Studying ecosystem recovery

Mount St. Helens gave scientists a unique opportunity to study how an ecosystem heals itself after a catastrophic disturbance. (An *ecosystem* consists of the plants and animals living in an environment and the nonliving features of the environment, such as soil and water.) Previous scientific concepts of ecosystem recovery had been dominated by the view that catastrophes destroy nearly all life and that new life must reinvade from outside the disturbed region. Therefore, scientists had concentrated on various processes of dispersal, such as how seeds are carried into a devastated region by winds and animals. Most catastrophes, however, do not wipe the "biological slate" clean. This is true of devastating windstorms, floods, forest fires, and other disturbances—even the eruption at Mount St. Helens. A catastrophe may decimate the organisms on a site, but it rarely kills everything. Over large areas, furthermore, destruction is usually irregular, leaving a patchwork with some patches devastated and other patches relatively intact.

A volcanic eruption or other disturbance may seem devastating but actually leaves a rich biological legacy—the remnants of earlier life that give new life a head start. This biological legacy includes not only living organisms but also organic remains, such as downed trees and the carcasses of animals. A fallen dead tree, for example, provides shelter for insects, other small animals, and plants that live in it and under it, and nutrients that nourish new life and replenish the soil. This biological legacy results in a much more rapid and diversified recovery than would otherwise take place. Let's look at how this principle was proved by events at Mount St. Helens, where life has returned with a rapidity and vigor that no one expected.

Research at Mount St. Helens began within days of the May 18, 1980, eruption with a reconnaissance of the mountain, the devastated zone, and the adjacent areas affected only by debris flows or tephra fall. The survey of the damage was done by interdisciplinary teams of scientists—including plant and animal ecologists, who study the relation of plants and animals to the environment; mycologists, who specialize in studies of fungi; entomologists, who study insects; soil scientists; aquatic biologists; and geomorphologists, who analyze changes in Earth's surface features. Gradually, the scientists formulated theories and began systematic research to study recovery at various distances from the mountain and in areas affected by different events, such as pyroclastic flows or debris avalanches. Researchers established large numbers of permanent sample plots for long-term observation of changes in plant and animal populations; such studies of ecological succession typically extend over many decades. In some areas, researchers tested how deliberate alterations, such as removal of tephra, affected the rate of recovery.

A herd of Roosevelt elk gallop across the devastated landscape near the North Fork of the Toutle River in 1981, a year after Mount St. Helens erupted. Elk moved back to the blast zone soon after the eruption.

Subsurface Survivors

Many living things survived the volcanic blast because they were underground or covered by snow. These buried survivors included, *clockwise from above,* pink-flowered fireweed, which sprouted from rootlike stems called *rhizomes;* frogs, which were hibernating in the mud at the bottom of lakes; trees and shrubs that were buried in snowbanks; and burrowing animals called pocket gophers, which survived in their underground homes.

In other areas, scientists conducted detailed studies of the relationships organisms have with one another and with their environment. One early study of such relationships concerned the links between pocket gophers, soil conditions, and plant growth. The gophers, who are industrious burrowers, assisted regrowth of vegetation by mixing rich old soil with the new, nutrient-poor tephra. The gophers also spread the spores of certain fungi that aid plant survival and growth. These fungi grow in or on the roots of green plants in mutually beneficial associations called *mycorrhizae* (pronounced *my kuh RY zee*). The fungus absorbs water and certain nutrients from the soil and passes them on to the green plant, which in turn supplies the fungus with carbohydrates. Evergreen trees, such as Douglas-fir and hemlock, need to form mycorrhizae to thrive.

The research at Mount St. Helens quickly revealed that life had survived in many forms and places using a wide variety of "strategies." Over most of the devastated zone, organisms and parts of organisms that were below the surface of the ground escaped destruction. These underground survivors included seeds, plant roots, insects, spiders, and small mammals such as deer mice and pocket gophers. Plants that sprout from roots, from rootlike stems called *rhizomes,* or from other underground structures had only to push their way up through a relatively thin layer of tephra—typically 20 to 30 centimeters (8 to 12 inches) deep. Numerous "weedy" green plants—pink-flowered fireweed, yellow-blooming groundsel, thistle, pearly everlasting, bracken fern, and even false dandelion—soon appeared. These aggressive species had become established in open areas that had been cleared by loggers prior to the eruption. After the eruption, these so-called weeds grew back quickly and provided plant cover.

Similar patterns of recovery have already appeared in Yellowstone National Park, where forest fires raged out of control in the summer of 1988. The Yellowstone fires roamed over nearly 650,000 hectares (1.6 million acres). But approximately 12 per cent of that area escaped the flames entirely, and nearly 35 per cent of the burned area suffered only a surface fire that left the tree canopies unburned. Even in the severely burned areas, the fires were erratic, enabling trees and other plants to survive in large numbers. The park's scattered meadow areas provided refuge for animals.

Natural recovery at Yellowstone began almost immediately. Grasses sprouted. Many tightly closed cones of lodgepole pines were not destroyed by the fire. Instead, the heat of the blaze caused the cones to open. After the fire passed, they shed their enclosed seed. Millions of tiny tree seedlings appeared at Yellowstone in the spring of 1989. In the Science File section, see ENVIRONMENT (Close-Up).

Erosion, usually so harmful, actually aided plant recovery at Mount St. Helens in the years following the eruption. The runoff from rain water and melted snow removed the cover of tephra and created gullies where new plants could grow.

Saved by snow

Snow also played a role in the recovery of some areas. Spring comes late to the slopes of Mount St. Helens, and at the time of the May 18 eruption, accumulations of snow, called *snowpack*, still remained in many areas. The snowpack varied from scattered drifts on warm exposures at elevations of 1,200 meters (3,900 feet) to a continuous, deep snow cover—3 meters (10 feet) or more thick—at higher elevations. The snow provided protection from heat and blast and also reduced the smothering effect of the blanket of tephra.

Snowpack areas contributed some unexpected survivors to the devastated landscape. Small trees—both seedlings and saplings—of hemlock and Pacific silver fir survived within the snowpack, as did many shrubs and leafy plants. The snowpack provided almost the only areas within the devastated zone where trees could—and did—survive. Nine years after the eruption, the seedlings that escaped the blast under the snow have grown into young trees and are beginning to produce seeds. The snowpack protected many mountain meadows so well that they came through the eruption almost unscathed.

Aquatic (water) environments also contributed many surviving organisms. Amphibians, such as frogs and salamanders, and crustaceans, such as crayfish, were still hibernating in the mud at the bottom of many lakes. These animals survived to repopulate the area following the eruption.

Conditions in lakes changed rapidly after the eruption. Within the devastated zone, all lakes and ponds received heavy doses of organic matter—shredded material from the forests that was blown into them by the blast. Some bodies of water, such as Spirit Lake, were also heated by the volcanic activity. The added organic material and sudden warming created a *eutrophic* (enriched) "soup," with an overabundance of phosphates, nitrates, and other nutrients. These nutrients promoted rapid growth of bacteria, algae, and microscopic animals called *zooplankton*, which depleted the water of oxygen. Aquatic insects survived the eruption to mature in this highly altered environment. Insect species that breathe through air tubes, such as mosquito larvae and rat-tailed maggots, became prominent in the poorly oxygenated waters during the first two years after the eruption.

Spirit Lake once sparkled in a setting of green trees. Its waters were cold and clear, with many fish. Today, the lake sits in barren shores, its waters gray and devoid of fish. Fish remained alive, however, in lakes that were less disturbed by the eruption.

Immigration and dispersal

Animal immigration—the movement of animals to new habitats—has also made important contributions to recovery at Mount St. Helens. The eruption totally wiped out animals that lived above-ground, such as birds, many mammals, and insects. Some of these species, such as the Roosevelt elk, moved back to the devastated zone almost immediately following the eruption. Others took longer to return. Some, such as the northern spotted owl, will probably not return until the forests mature. In general, however, the character-istic birds and mammals of the region are back.

Reestablishment of trees is a slower process. Although the snow-pack protected patches of small trees at high elevations, the eruption wiped out all the trees throughout most of the devastated zone. The evergreen trees of this region do not sprout from underground roots or other structures, nor do they store seed in the surface soil. As a result, the development of new seedlings depended upon dispersal of seed from forests around the edges of the devastated zone. In fact, noble fir, western hemlock, Douglas-fir, red alder, and other species are growing deep within the devastated zone—kilometers from existing seed sources. The seeds of those trees are all wind-disseminated.

In addition to seeds, other airborne arrivals—"subsidies" from outside the devastated zone—have been important. Many spiders have immigrated into the region carried on the wind by the silk threads they spin. Entomologist John S. Edwards of the University of Washington at Seattle has estimated the daily fall of organic material—both living and dead—at about 5 milligrams per square meter (0.5 ounce per square mile). Over time, even this small amount of airborne material contributes substantially to the build-up of organic carbon and nutrients in the barren habitats within the devastated zone.

Scientists often describe succession as a highly ordered process whereby certain organisms—usually simpler life forms—establish themselves first and function as pioneers, preparing the way for, or at least preceding, a series of other, more complex organisms. A theoretical example is the early establishment of lower plants, such as mosses and lichens, followed by herbs, shrubs, and, ultimately, trees.

Actually, succession is rarely so orderly. At Mount St. Helens, all types of plants became established together at most sites within the devastated zone, and there has been no evident progression of types. Where tree seed was available, tree seedlings are growing among shrubs, herbs, and mosses. On some sites, such as areas covered by the debris avalanche or pyroclastic flows, trees are not only the first but also the only green plants present. Their presence shows that trees can serve as "pioneer" plants in disturbed environments.

Human influences on recovery

Human activities can greatly influence the patterns and rates of ecosystem recovery following a catastrophic event. In fact, contrasts in recovery due to human intervention are already obvious in various parts of the devastated zone around Mount St. Helens. Important human activities have included salvage logging of fallen trees, grass seeding, reintroduction of fish, and tree planting.

Congress designated Mount St. Helens, a large portion of the devastated zone, and some adjacent land as the Mount St. Helens National Volcanic Monument on Aug. 26, 1982. Much of the 44,345-hectare (109,578-acre) monument was already federal property—part of the Gifford Pinchot National Forest. The federal government purchased additional acreage from the Weyerhaeuser Company—a forest products firm—from other private landowners, and from Washington state. The U.S. Forest Service manages the monument with the objectives of " . . . [protecting] the geologic, ecologic, and cultural resources . . . [and] allowing geologic forces and ecological succession to continue substantially unimpeded." This, then, is a *control* area where scientists can observe how ecosystem recovery occurs when nature is left alone.

Although some trees have reappeared naturally throughout most of Mount St. Helens National Volcanic Monument, the landscape will remain mostly grassy plain with few trees for many decades. Long-distance, wind-borne seed dispersal is a slow process.

Foresters have intensively rehabilitated most of the land outside the national monument to speed its return to productive forestland. This rehabilitated area includes part of Gifford Pinchot National Forest and lands owned by the Weyerhaeuser Company. Rehabilitation typically consisted of salvage logging of dead trees followed by planting of tree seedlings. Because the quality of the wood was not reduced by the blast, loggers recovered much valuable timber where

A Mosaic of Recovery

By mid-1989, nine years after the eruption, the landscape around Mount St. Helens reflects various stages of recovery, ranging from barren areas with sparse vegetation to lush, young replanted forests.

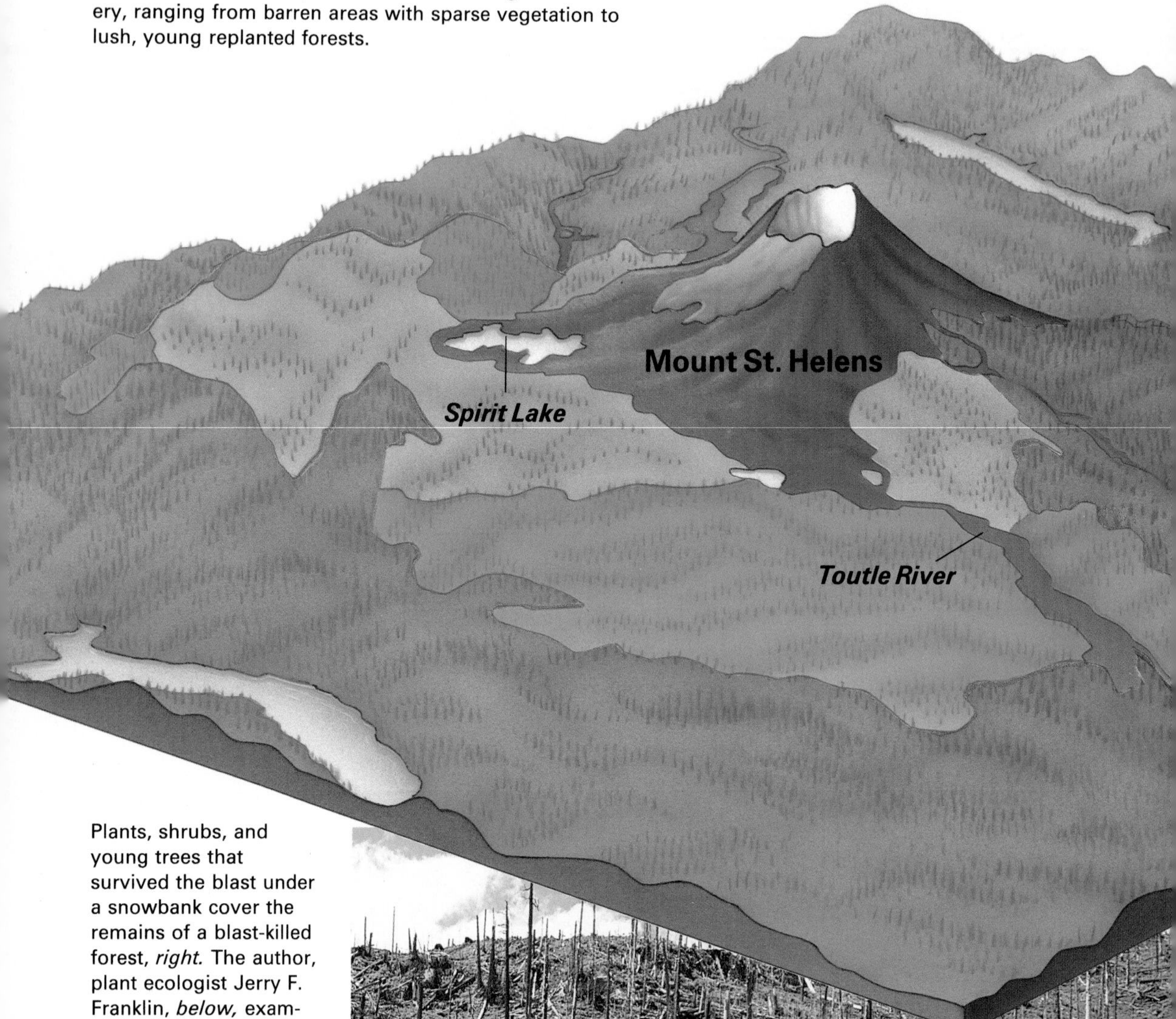

Mount St. Helens

Spirit Lake

Toutle River

Plants, shrubs, and young trees that survived the blast under a snowbank cover the remains of a blast-killed forest, *right.* The author, plant ecologist Jerry F. Franklin, *below,* examines grasses in a recovered meadow.

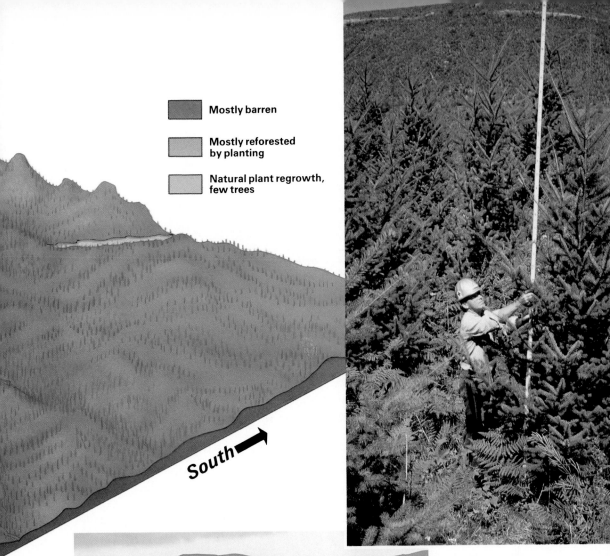

- Mostly barren
- Mostly reforested by planting
- Natural plant regrowth, few trees

South ➤

A Weyerhaeuser lumber company worker plants tree seedlings in 1981, *left,* by digging through volcanic deposits to set the tree roots in soil. A forester measures young Douglas-fir trees flourishing in Weyerhaeuser's replanted plot in 1988, *above.*

111

Mount St. Helens over the past 5,000 years has undergone several cycles of volcanic eruption and recovery. Spirit Lake sparkles at the foot of the mountain before the 1980 eruption, *top.* The lake is covered with floating debris after the blast, which blew off the top of the mountain, *above.* By the summer of 1989, *right,* the landscape around Spirit Lake was beginning to bloom again, and the cycle of recovery was once again underway.

virgin forests had existed prior to the eruption—more than 1.4 million cubic meters (590 million board feet) of timber from national-forest lands alone in the three years following the eruption. This was enough to build more than 50,000 homes.

Tree planting has greatly increased the speed with which dense forests will develop in devastated regions around Mount St. Helens. Reforestation efforts have consisted of planting more than 26 million one- to three-year-old seedlings on more than 10,000 hectares (25,000 acres) of devastated forestland.

The replanting program has been extremely successful, with high levels of seedling survival and growth. Some trees have grown more than 5 meters (16 feet) tall in eight years. This success is partially because there are few other plants to compete with the trees for sunlight, water, and nutrients in the soil. In addition, the surface blanket of tephra acts like a mulch, reducing the growth of competing weeds and shrubs and conserving soil moisture. Reforestation, however, has skewed the makeup of the forest toward tree species of greater commercial value. For example, Douglas-fir is the primary species in planted areas, but this species is much less important in naturally regenerated areas.

Mount St. Helens provided scientists with an incomparable opportunity to observe natural recovery processes. Knowledge gained from research there has improved our understanding of how ecosystems bounce back from catastrophic disturbances. It has renewed scientific interest in the importance of *biological legacies*—the remnants of earlier life, including surviving organisms, seeds, spores, and other organic materials.

Foresters are also beginning to incorporate the lessons of biological legacies in their management of forests for wood production. The controversial practice of *clearcutting*—the removal of all trees in a forest—can be made much less destructive with some simple modifications. For example, loggers can preserve habitats for many animals on clear-cut areas by leaving some standing dead trees and fallen logs, rather than totally clearing the site. Even better, loggers might leave a few living trees in the harvested area. Human beings and nature, working together, can do a better job of restoring an ecosystem than either could do alone.

For further reading:

Aylesworth, Thomas G., and Aylesworth, Virginia L. *The Mount St. Helens Disaster: What We've Learned.* Watts, 1983.

Bilderback, David E., ed. *Mount St. Helens 1980: Botanical Consequences of the Explosive Eruptions.* University of Calif. Press, 1987.

Franklin, Jerry F., and others. "Ecosystem Responses to the Eruption of Mount St. Helens." *National Geographic Research,* Spring 1985.

MacMahon, James A. "Mount St. Helens Revisited." *Natural History,* May 1982.

Most of the matter in the universe appears to be invisible, and the stuff it's made of may be unlike anything we know.

The Case of the Dark Matter

BY JOEL R. PRIMACK

"When you have eliminated the impossible, whatever remains, however improbable, must be the truth," said the great fictional detective Sherlock Holmes.

Mounting evidence has led astronomers to just such an improbable conclusion: At least 90 per cent and possibly 99 per cent of all the matter in the universe is completely invisible. Astronomers call this invisible stuff *dark matter*, and as a result of its discovery, they are faced with two of the biggest mysteries in modern science: What is dark matter, and how much of it exists?

It may be that dark matter is unlike anything we know of—or can even imagine—and will require a completely new understanding of what makes up our universe. And learning how much dark matter exists may answer the greatest question of all—the ultimate fate of the universe. To resolve these mysteries, astronomers and other scientists have adopted many of the methods detectives use to solve a crime. We are gathering evidence, examining it, and using our powers of deduction to come up with a solution.

An astronomer first reported the invisible matter after noting some unusual behavior in visible matter. In 1933, Swiss astrophysicist Fritz Zwicky observed that galaxies in a cluster of galaxies had higher speeds than expected. He concluded that something was causing strange gravitational effects on these galaxies.

Galaxies are like vast islands in deep space containing billions of stars that are held together by the force of gravity. Some galaxies are part of larger systems called *clusters*, which contain many galaxies. Most galaxies, however, belong to smaller systems called *groups*. Groups and clusters in turn form even larger structures known as *superclusters*. Just as the force of gravity keeps stars together in galaxies, so the force of gravity appears to keep galaxies together in clusters.

This same force of gravity keeps planets orbiting around the sun, rather than flying off into space. How great a force gravity exerts depends on the mass of the objects attracted and the distance between them, a principle discovered in the mid-1600's by English astronomer and mathematician Sir Isaac Newton. The amount of mass and the distance between objects also determine how fast the objects travel as they orbit each other. For example, in our solar system, the sun is the most massive object, making up about 99.8 per cent of the mass of the solar system, and the force of its gravity keeps Earth and the other planets in orbit around it. The orbital speeds of the planets decline with increasing distance from the sun. The planet nearest the sun, Mercury, travels at an orbital speed of 48 kilometers (30 miles) per second, while the distant planet Pluto orbits at a speed of 4.7 kilometers (2.9 miles) per second.

Using Newton's equations, astronomers can calculate the amount of mass or matter present in the solar system—or in a galaxy or cluster of galaxies—providing they know the orbital speeds and distances of the orbiting bodies. In the cluster Zwicky observed, the galaxies were traveling at tremendous speeds relative to each other.

Astronomers are able to determine the speeds of galaxies by measuring their *red shifts*—the shift in the wavelength of light given off by the galaxies toward the longer, or red, wavelengths of the *spectrum* (the pattern of colors that make up visible light). Lines of particular colors in the spectrum, which correspond to the radiation emitted or absorbed by the atoms of different elements, are shifted toward the red end of the spectrum when the source of the light is moving away from an observer. The amount of this red shift can be measured precisely, and this amount tells astronomers just how fast the galaxies that gave off the light are traveling away from us.

By measuring the speeds of the galaxies in the cluster, Zwicky could calculate how much mass there was in the cluster. He determined that there was a far greater amount of matter present in the cluster than was visible through telescopes. To Zwicky, the only logical conclusion was that the predominant form of matter in the cluster could not be seen. In fact, his measurements showed that there was more than 10 times as much *unseen matter* as visible matter in this cluster of galaxies. In 1933, Zwicky's suggestion was considered so improbable that few astronomers accepted it.

The case of the dark matter had been opened, however, and more

The author:
Joel R. Primack is professor of physics at the University of California at Santa Cruz.

Evidence for Dark Matter

Evidence that there is more matter in the universe than is visible rests on a theory of gravity, the force that keeps planets, stars, and other celestial objects in their orbits. The strength of this force depends on the mass of the orbiting objects and the distance between them. The amount of mass in the objects and their distance from each other determine the orbital speeds of the objects. Knowing orbital speeds and the distance between objects, astronomers can calculate the total mass in the orbital system.

LIKE CARS TRAVELING AT DIFFERENT SPEEDS.

25 35 55

THE PLANETS NEAREST THE SUN ORBIT FASTER THAN THOSE FARTHER AWAY. THIS IS BECAUSE THE SUN ACCOUNTS FOR ALMOST ALL OF THE MASS IN OUR SOLAR SYSTEM.

PLANETS

SUN

STARS IN GALAXIES ORBIT AT ABOUT THE SAME SPEEDS NO MATTER HOW FAR THEY ARE FROM THE MASSIVE GALACTIC CENTER. SO THERE MUST BE MUCH MORE MATTER IN THE OUTER REACHES OF THE GALAXY THAN IS VISIBLE.

LIKE CARS WITH THEIR CRUISE CONTROLS SET AT THE SAME SPEED.

55 55 55

CENTER OF GALAXY

STARS

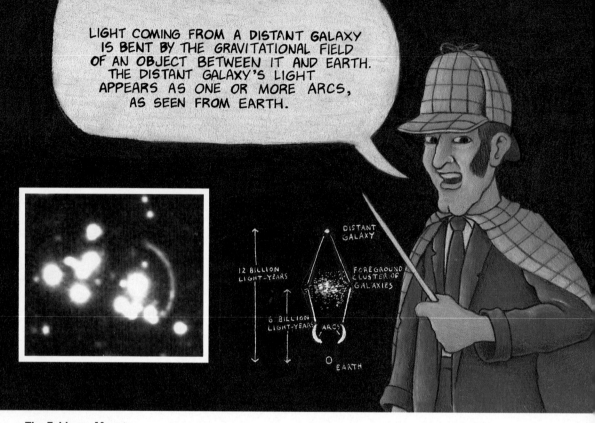

LIGHT COMING FROM A DISTANT GALAXY IS BENT BY THE GRAVITATIONAL FIELD OF AN OBJECT BETWEEN IT AND EARTH. THE DISTANT GALAXY'S LIGHT APPEARS AS ONE OR MORE ARCS, AS SEEN FROM EARTH.

DISTANT GALAXY

12 BILLION LIGHT-YEARS

FOREGROUND CLUSTER OF GALAXIES

6 BILLION LIGHT-YEARS

ARCS

EARTH

The Evidence Mounts

A strange arc of light appears around a cluster of galaxies, photo *above*. In 1987, astronomers determined that the arc was light from a distant galaxy and that the light was bent into an arc shape by the cluster's gravitational field. From the arc's size, they calculated how much matter there must be in the galaxy cluster to cause the bending. They found the total amount of matter was much greater than what was visible and concluded that most of the matter must be invisible dark matter.

clues pointing to the existence of dark matter were found in the 1970's. These clues were uncovered after years of painstaking research by astrophysicist Vera C. Rubin and her colleagues at the Carnegie Institution of Washington in Washington, D.C. These astronomers measured the orbital speeds of stars and clouds of gas in more than 60 *spiral galaxies*. Most large galaxies, like our own Milky Way galaxy, are called spiral galaxies because they have a pinwheel shape with a bright central region and several spiral arms. The bright central region is called the *central bulge* because it is the thickest part of the galaxy, where most of the stars are located. The region of the spiral arms is known as the *disk* because it is relatively thin and flat like a phonograph disk.

Rubin found that stars and gas clouds in the outlying regions of the disk rotated around the central bulge at roughly the same orbital speeds as stars in the inner regions of the disk close to the bulge. It was as if the stars and clouds were automobiles all traveling in circular tracks with their cruise controls set to the same speed. Their orbital speeds did not decline with distance from the central bulge the way the orbital speeds of the planets decline with distance from our sun. This finding indicated that there was more matter in the outlying regions of the disk than there was near the bulge. Optical telescopes, however, clearly revealed that visible matter was concentrated in the bulge. Rubin calculated that there was 3 to 5 times as much invisible or dark matter as there was visible matter in the form of stars, gas clouds, and dust.

118

Astronomers using radio telescopes found evidence of still more dark matter around spiral galaxies. Visible light is only part of the range of radiant energies known as the *electromagnetic spectrum*, which also includes the long wavelength energies of radio waves. Thin clouds of hydrogen gas extending from the outermost regions of a galaxy disk cannot be seen from Earth with optical telescopes but can be detected with radio telescopes. Radio astronomers measured the orbital speeds of these outer clouds and discovered that they, too, were orbiting at the same speed as stars in the disk, confirming that there was a great deal of mass in the outermost regions. This increase in mass obviously could not come from the clouds of hydrogen gas because they are so tenuous, contributing a negligible amount of mass. So the greater amount of mass must be in the form of dark matter.

The astronomer-detectives came to another logical—though im- probable—conclusion: All spiral galaxies are surrounded by huge, roughly spherical halos of dark matter that cover vast regions of space. Most astronomers now think that these halos of dark matter explain why gas clouds in the outermost regions of galaxies orbit at the same speed as stars in the inner disk. No one can be certain, but some astronomers estimate that the halo around the Milky Way, for example, may extend as far as 500,000 *light-years* from the central bulge. (One light-year is the distance that a beam of light travels in one year, about 9.5 trillion kilometers [5.9 trillion miles].) By contrast, the radius of the visible matter in the Milky Way is only about 50,000 light-years.

Like all good detectives, astronomers require more than circum- stantial evidence—even if the few clues are solid—to reach a firm conclusion. For more than 50 years after 1933, the evidence for dark matter around clusters of galaxies consisted solely of measurements of the speeds of the galaxies. Then another clue was discovered in January 1987, by astronomers Roger Lynds of the Kitt Peak National Observatory in Tucson, Ariz., and Vahé Petrosian of Stanford University in California.

Lynds and Petrosian discovered faint arcs of light around the centers of two galaxy clusters. The French astronomer Genevieve Soucail and her colleagues measured the red shift of the light from one of the arcs and found that the light came from a distant galaxy, about twice as far away from Earth as the cluster, which is known as Abell 370. Physicist Albert Einstein had predicted in 1936 that such arcs could occur due to gravitational bending of light. The arc is an optical illusion, like a mirage, caused when the light from the distant galaxy is bent as it passes near the gravitational field of the galaxy cluster. This bending of light from a distant object by the gravity of a foreground object is called a *gravitational lens*. In effect, a gravitational lens is the greatest telescope in the universe, collecting and focusing the light of distant galaxies that otherwise would be much too faint for us to see. From the size of the arc, astronomers can deduce the amount of mass in the cluster causing the gravitational bending of light. In the case of Abell 370, scientists calculated that the total mass in this cluster was about 60 times greater than the cluster's visible mass. This discovery independently confirmed the existence of dark matter around a galaxy cluster. Zwicky's conclusion—seemingly improbable in 1933—had become an accepted theory by the 1980's.

But what is dark matter made of? No one knows for certain. One possibility is that dark matter is made of atoms, the building blocks of the ordinary matter that we see and touch in everyday life. Many astronomers, however, suspect that the dark matter is not made of atoms at all, but rather is some exotic unknown form of matter.

Ordinary matter either gives off radiation in the form of light, as stars do; or reflects it, as planets do; or absorbs it, as dust does. If dark matter is made of ordinary matter that gives off radiation in some form, it should have been detected with telescopes and instruments that are sensitive to visible light, infrared rays, radio waves, X rays, or any other form of electromagnetic radiation. With such telescopes, astronomers have surveyed the universe at all wavelengths of the electromagnetic spectrum and have been unable to find any radiation in the dark matter halos. This has led some astronomers to conclude that dark matter is not ordinary matter.

Another argument that has led astronomers to conclude that dark matter is probably not ordinary matter is that the halo is so much

Suspect:
Jupiter-Sized Objects

Dark matter might be ordinary matter. Some scientists have thought, for example, that there might be objects such as balls of gas about the size and mass of the planet Jupiter and that they might be the dark matter. At very great distances, such as in the vast halo of dark matter that seems to surround spiral galaxies, these objects would be too small and too cool for our telescopes to detect.

more spread out than the visible matter in a galaxy. If the dark matter were made of ordinary matter, its distribution should be more like that of the visible parts of the galaxy.

As far as astronomers can tell, if dark matter is made of ordinary matter, it could take only two forms that would not conflict with observations already made by astronomers. One form could be balls of gas comparable in size to Jupiter and located mainly in the halos surrounding the galaxies. Although Jupiter is the largest planet in the solar system, it is small in comparison with stars. Jupiter has a diameter of 142,700 kilometers (88,700 miles), compared with the sun's diameter of 1,392,000 kilometers (865,000 miles). We can easily see Jupiter with the unaided eye because it is within our solar system and reflects light from the sun. But at the vast distances of the dark matter halo, objects the size of Jupiter would be too small and too cool to be detectable with current instruments.

The other form could be *black holes*—the collapsed cores of dead stars that have become so dense that not even light can escape their gravitational field. If enough black holes existed, they could account for the dark matter, yet could be detected only indirectly by their gravitational influence on visible objects. (Other dead stars with collapsed cores, such as white dwarfs and neutron stars, still give off enough radiation to be detected. There do not appear to be enough of these dead stars to account for the dark matter.)

Many astrophysical detectives doubt that ordinary matter suspects are responsible for the dark matter. Motive, always something a

Suspect: Black Holes
Dark matter might consist of black holes, which are very strange but could still be made from ordinary matter. A black hole can form from a star that has collapsed to become so dense that not even light can escape from its gravity. Black holes are powerful enough to suck in anything that comes too close to them.

detective looks for, seems to be missing in the case of both suspects. For example, if black holes accounted for the dark matter, there would have to be about 10 billion black holes in our galaxy alone. But black holes are the remnants of extremely massive stars, and such unusually massive stars are rare today. Most stars in our galaxy have about the same mass as the sun.

Moreover, only black holes that are remnants of supermassive stars could be dark matter candidates. Astronomers and physicists have calculated that only stars several hundred times more massive than the sun could evolve into black holes without ejecting most of their mass in gigantic explosions known as *supernovae*. Stars with less mass but still about 20 times more massive than the sun would become black holes after exploding as supernovae and ejecting matter rich in heavy elements, such as carbon and silicon. But the amount of heavy elements that would have been produced in our galaxy if a great number of such explosions had occurred has not been observed. So black holes from less massive stars can be· ruled out, leaving only black holes that evolved from supermassive stars as dark matter suspects. Astronomers can't think of a good reason why stars so much more massive than the sun would have formed and then collapsed to black holes in large enough numbers to account for the dark matter.

Motive is also a problem with the gas-ball suspects. Astronomers can't think of a good reason why objects much smaller than the sun, such as Jupiter-sized balls of gas, would have formed in large enough numbers to account for the dark matter. The sun, which is 1,047

Suspect: WIMP's

Dark matter may not be made of atoms, the building blocks of ordinary matter. The theory of supersymmetry says that in the early universe every elementary particle we know of had a counterpart, a "mirror image," called a *supersymmetric partner.* They would be *weakly interacting massive particles* (*WIMP*'s). The lightest supersymmetric partner of a force particle, such as the photon, the Z boson, or the hypothetical Higgs boson, might still be around today and could be the dark matter that makes up most of the universe.

times more massive than Jupiter, makes up 99.8 per cent of all the mass in our solar system. If dark matter were made up of Jupiter-sized, undetectable balls of gas, there would have to be 10,000 such objects for every star in the galaxy, which has about 100 billion stars. Yet it seems unlikely that there could be so many billions of Jupiter-sized objects in the galaxy halos without some of these objects becoming massive enough to burn nuclear fuel and become visible as stars. For example, an object just 80 times more massive than Jupiter would have temperatures hot enough to ignite nuclear reactions.

Motive, however, is the trickiest part of any detective work. Although no one can think of a reason why such gas balls should have formed, one day someone may find a reason. The motive may be there; we just haven't discovered it yet.

One important reason why many astronomers think the dark matter is not made of atoms is based on the observed amounts of elements in the universe and on a theory of *cosmology* (the study of the origin and history of the universe). This theory, known as the *inflationary theory*, predicts a certain value for the average density of matter in the universe called the *critical density*.

Using the spectral lines that are given off by the atoms of different elements, astronomers have surveyed the universe with their telescopes and have calculated the relative amounts of the elements that make up visible matter. These studies have shown that about 75 per cent of the visible matter in the universe consists of ordinary hydrogen atoms. Helium atoms form about 25 per cent of the visible matter, and all the elements heavier than helium make up less than 1 per cent of the visible matter in the universe. Deuterium, a heavy form of hydrogen, accounts for only about a thousandth of 1 per cent of the visible matter. Although only a tiny percentage of visible matter, the amount of observed deuterium is important because it indicates the density of matter in the early universe.

The observed amounts of elements agree with the *big bang nucleosynthesis* theory developed by nuclear physicists. This theory describes how the lightest atomic elements would have been *synthesized* (formed) soon after the *big bang*, the explosive event that scientists think created the universe. According to this theory, the temperature in the early universe was so high that the universe was a giant nuclear fusion reactor, creating deuterium, helium, and other nuclei from neutrons and protons. The relative amounts of the different kinds of nuclei were determined by the density of matter in the early universe. Deuterium is a sensitive indicator of the density of matter in the early universe. The more ordinary matter there is, the less deuterium is produced. Moreover, deuterium cannot be created in stars but can only be destroyed in stars. As a result, there could not have been any less deuterium in the early universe than the amount observed today. Knowing the amount of deuterium, scientists can calculate an upper limit on the density of ordinary matter in the early universe.

The calculations indicate that the total density of ordinary matter in the universe is not greater than about 14 per cent of the critical density predicted by the inflationary theory. So if ordinary matter cannot exceed 14 per cent of critical density, then the remaining matter—at least 86 per cent of the total matter in the universe—must be made of something other than atoms.

What could this other exotic matter be? Detectives working in the field of *particle physics* (the study of elementary particles) have theorized about the existence of particles they call *w*eakly *i*nteracting *m*assive *p*articles (WIMP's) that could be the dark matter. Physicists came to propose the existence of unknown new particles, including WIMP's, as they studied an entirely different problem—the search for a master force in the universe. Particle physicists divide the fundamental elementary particles into two types: *fermions* and *bosons*. Fermions include all the particles that make up matter, such as the protons and neutrons that make up the atom's nucleus and the electrons that whirl about the nucleus. Subatomic particles called *quarks*, which are the basic building blocks of protons and neutrons, are also considered fermions.

Bosons are particles that transmit forces between fermions. All the forces that hold together the fermions in an atom are due to the emission and absorption of bosons. For example, the electron is bound to the nucleus by the electromagnetic force, one of the four fundamental forces in nature. The boson that transmits this force is called a photon. The exchange of photons between the electron and the nucleus is what keeps the electron bound to the nucleus.

In addition to the electromagnetic force, physicists have identified three other fundamental forces that govern the universe: the *strong force*, the *weak force*, and gravity. The strong force holds quarks together to form protons and neutrons, and this force is transmitted by a boson called the *gluon*. The weak force, which is responsible for certain forms of radioactivity, is due to the exchange of bosons called *W* and *Z* particles. Gravity is due to the exchange of hypothetical bosons called *gravitons*. All of these bosons and fermions, except the graviton, are known to exist because they have been detected in experiments.

The problem that particle physicists were trying to solve when they speculated on the existence of new particles was whether in the earliest moments of the universe's creation, the four fundamental forces were part of a single, unified force. An idea that seems to be vital to any theory that unifies all the forces is called *supersymmetry*. Supersymmetry predicts that for every kind of boson there is a corresponding kind of fermion, and for every kind of fermion there is a corresponding kind of boson. For example, the photon would have a fermion partner called a *photino*. The electron would have a boson partner called a *selectron*, and each kind of quark would have a boson partner called a *squark*. In other words, every force or matter particle now known to exist would have a hypothetical partner, and physicists call these *supersymmetric partner* particles. Supersymmetry can be tested in laboratory experiments that attempt to create supersymmetric partner particles using particle accelerators. Physicists currently are working on such experiments at all the large particle accelerators in the world.

Most of these supersymmetric partners would have been unstable and would have gone out of existence long ago in the early universe. But, according to the theory, the lightest supersymmetric partner particle would be stable and would still be in existence today, an exotic relic of the big bang that could be the dark matter—as physicist Heinz R. Pagels and I pointed out in 1982. Supersymmetric theories indicate that this particle would have a mass several times greater than a proton and yet would interact weakly with other particles. It would be a weakly interacting massive particle, or WIMP.

WIMP's would be very hard to detect because of their weak interactions with ordinary matter. In fact, many of the WIMP's that form the dark matter in our galaxy could be going through your body as you read this without your being aware of it. Once in a great while, however, one of these WIMP's would strike the nucleus of an atom of ordinary matter. Physicists have shown that several kinds of very sensitive detectors could be built in underground laboratories to detect this kind of event. For example, if a crystal of a substance such as pure silicon were cooled to a very low temperature, just a thousandth of one degree above *absolute zero* ($-273.15°C$ [$-459.67°F$.]), the collision of just one dark matter WIMP with the nucleus of a silicon atom could raise the temperature of the crystal enough to be measured. In 1989, experimental physicists in the United States and several European countries began building WIMP detectors to test these theories.

Other physicists were building detectors to trap another dark matter suspect, the *axion*, a hypothetical particle. The existence of axions, like supersymmetric WIMP's, was predicted by theories of elementary particle physics that had nothing to do with astronomy. Only later did axions become dark matter suspects. Axions would be like WIMP's in that they, too, would interact very weakly with ordinary matter. Axions, however, would be much less massive than WIMP's. In a strong magnetic field, an axion would be transformed into a photon. The experiments now being designed to determine if axions exist would detect this transformation.

The line-up of suspect particles has also included the *neutrino*. Unlike WIMP's and axions, the neutrino is known to exist. There are three types of neutrinos produced when atomic nuclei or subatomic particles disintegrate. Since 1980, scientists have conducted experiments to determine if these neutrinos have mass, but the results have

Astronomers want to know for sure whether dark matter exists so they can calculate how much matter there is in the universe. The total amount of matter will determine the ultimate fate of the universe, which right now is expanding rapidly in all directions like an enormous balloon.

> IF THERE IS NOT ENOUGH MATTER, THE UNIVERSE WILL CONTINUE TO EXPAND FOREVER UNTIL ALL THE STARS BURN OUT. THIS ICY ENDING WOULD BE *THE BIG CHILL.*

BIG CHILL

> IF THERE IS TOO MUCH MATTER, THE UNIVERSE'S EXPANSION WILL EVENTUALLY HALT DUE TO THE FORCE OF GRAVITY, AND THE UNIVERSE WILL BEGIN TO SHRINK UNTIL IT COLLAPSES IN WHAT IS CALLED *THE BIG CRUNCH.*

BIG CRUNCH

been inconclusive. If any of these neutrinos has a mass about one-hundredth of 1 per cent of the mass of the electron, it could be the dark matter particle.

Many astronomers doubt, however, that any neutrino could be the dark matter. Neutrino dark matter, also called *hot* dark matter, would have led to what astronomers call *top-down galaxy formation*. According to the top-down theory, superclusters of gas and neutrinos would have formed first, then later broken down into galaxies. But much observational evidence appears to rule out this theory. For example, astronomers have determined that galaxies are old, but superclusters are young.

For this and other reasons, many astronomers think the dark matter must be what they call *cold* dark matter. WIMP's and axions are cold dark matter particles. Cold dark matter would lead to what astronomers call *bottom-up galaxy formation*. This theory maintains that galaxies formed first and later came together to form clusters and superclusters.

Many astrophysicists in the 1980's used computers to simulate galaxy formation with either cold or hot dark matter particles. The computer models that used cold dark matter produced a picture of how galaxies are distributed that is remarkably similar to what astronomers actually observe. The hot dark matter models, however, produced clumps of galaxies unlike anything observed.

There are deeper aspects to the dark matter case than just pinning down the right suspect. Finding out what the dark matter is will help answer one of the most important questions in astronomy: Will the universe continue to expand? We know that the universe is expanding because when astronomers observe all but the nearest galaxies, the light from those galaxies is red-shifted, indicating that they are moving away from us. In fact, galaxies are speeding away from each other in all directions due to the expansion of space itself. Whether the universe will continue to expand forever or whether the expansion will slow and ultimately reverse itself depends on how much matter there is in the universe.

If there is little matter, the expansion will go on forever long after all stars in the universe have burned out in an icy end. But if there is a lot of matter, the expansion will halt due to the force of gravity, and the universe will eventually contract to infinite density—the *big crunch*. A third possibility is that there may be just enough matter in the universe to achieve critical density. In this case, the expansion will continue but at an ever slowing rate.

Uncovering the composition of dark matter will help astronomers determine whether there is enough matter—both visible and invisible—to reach the critical density. But for now, the case is still open.

For further reading:

Disney, Michael. *The Hidden Universe.* Macmillan, 1984.
Tucker, Wallace and Karen. *The Dark Matter.* Morrow, 1988.

Human activities, from farming to burning
fossil fuels, are releasing gases that may
trap too much heat in the atmosphere.

Is Earth Overheating?

BY ARTHUR FISHER

The summer of 1988 brought record high temperatures throughout the United States. New York City suffered through more than 40
consecutive days of abnormally high heat and humidity. The
temperature in Los Angeles reached 43.3°C (110°F.) in September.
Record heat and widespread drought in the Midwest ruined or
stunted crops such as corn and soybeans. Water levels on the
Mississippi River fell sharply, stranding barges carrying cargo to and
from ports on the Gulf of Mexico. In other countries, too, the
summer was unusually hot. In the Soviet Union, for example,
Moscow recorded its hottest summer of this century.

In fact, throughout the 1980's summers have been unusually hot.
The six warmest years since 1901 have occurred in the 1980's, and
1988 saw the century's highest *global average temperature*, the average
of surface air temperatures recorded at locations all over the planet.
But the 1988 heat wave focused public attention on an issue that
scientists have been watching for some time—a potentially disastrous
rise in Earth's temperature.

The high temperatures of the 1980's are part of a definite upward
trend in the global average temperature. Since the 1880's, this
temperature has risen about 0.5 of a Celsius degree (0.9 Fahrenheit
degree). This may not sound like much of an increase, but scientists
consider that much of a rise in 100 years to be a rapid climb.

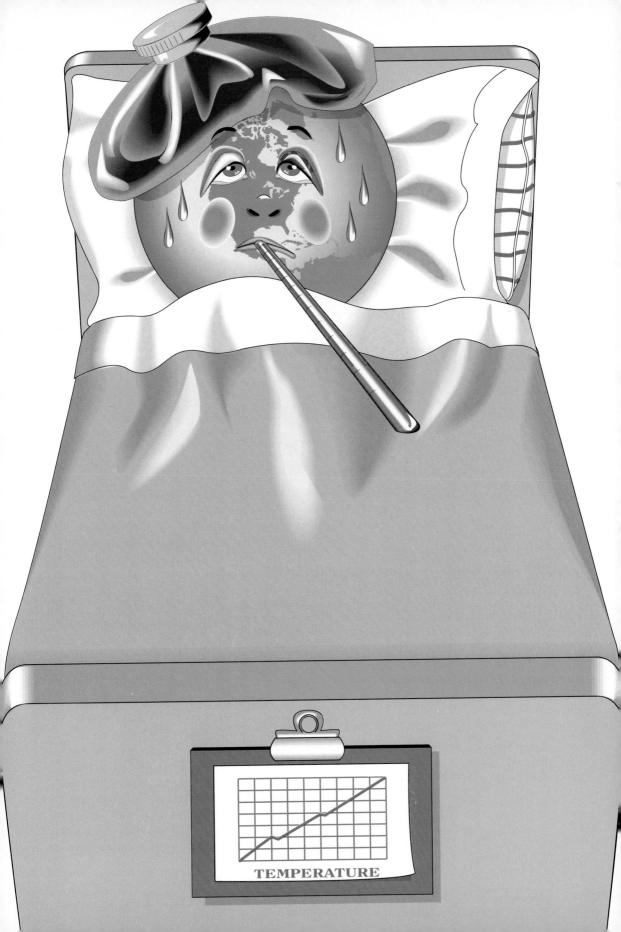

TEMPERATURE

Dust buffets farmland in Colorado during the unusually hot and dry summer of 1988. Although meteorologists believe short-term weather patterns were responsible for the hot summer, the unusual weather focused public attention on a long-term global warming trend.

The author:

Arthur Fisher is science and technology editor of *Popular Science* magazine and the author of the Special Report PLUGGING INTO SUPERCONDUCTORS in the 1989 edition of *Science Year*.

Although scientists cannot rule out the possibility that the current warm period is merely a natural variation in our planet's complex climate, many believe that a rapid shift is underway, triggered by human activity. They believe the upward trend is being caused mainly by the increased pumping of so-called *greenhouse gases*—especially carbon dioxide—into the atmosphere. Carbon dioxide and other greenhouse gases such as water vapor and methane are a natural part of the atmosphere. They make life on Earth possible by capturing some of the heat from the sun. They trap this heat in the atmosphere by a complicated process known as the *greenhouse effect*.

A number of human activities, especially the burning of *fossil fuels* such as coal, oil, and natural gas, release carbon dioxide into the atmosphere. Such activities have increased tremendously since the mid-1700's as the Industrial Revolution—powered chiefly by fossil fuels—has changed Western society by generating enormous growth in the production of many kinds of goods.

The increase in these activities is consistent with the belief that the greenhouse effect is causing the temperature to climb. James E. Hansen, an atmospheric physicist and director of the National Aeronautics and Space Administration's (NASA) Goddard Institute for Space Studies in New York City, says the acceleration in the rise in global average temperature over the last decade is almost certainly due to human activities that increase the greenhouse effect. If he is correct, the results may be dire. In 60 years, the amount of carbon dioxide in the atmosphere might be twice what it was in the mid-1700's. This might result in a rise of about 2 to 5 Celsius degrees (3.6 to 9 Fahrenheit degrees) in the global average temperature.

This increase in temperature would be much larger in some regions of the world, much smaller in others. In general, the closer to the poles, the more dramatic would be the ultimate change. Some of Greenland's cover of glacial ice would melt, raising sea levels by as much as 30 centimeters (12 inches). This would threaten low-lying coastal areas of such cities as Boston; Miami, Fla.; New York City; and Vancouver, Canada; with more frequent flooding. Shifting patterns of rainfall and heat could cause water levels in the American West to drop, making hydroelectric dams a much less reliable source of electricity for millions of residents in the Northwest. The same shifting patterns might devastate some grain-growing regions of the United States and Canada while opening up other parts of those countries to farming. Northern areas of the Soviet Union would have much longer growing seasons, but perhaps also more dry spells. Bangladesh would be hit by even more destructive typhoons and floods. And summers would be hotter. New York City, for example, might swelter in 35°C (95°F.) heat and 95 per cent humidity for most of the summer.

It may be difficult to believe that a rise of only 4 Celsius degrees or so in the global average temperature could cause such effects. After all, the temperature in areas where most of us live fluctuates at least that much from day to day without drastic results. The key to understanding how these effects could occur lies in knowing the difference between *weather* and *climate*.

We tend to use these terms interchangeably to refer to atmospheric conditions, but scientists make a distinction that involves both area and time. The term *weather* refers to local changes in the atmosphere lasting a relatively short time. A thunderstorm, for example, might

Glossary

Climate: Long-term pattern of temperature and precipitation in a particular region.

Global average temperature: The average of air temperatures from locations all over Earth.

Greenhouse effect: The trapping of *infrared* (heat) radiation by certain gases in Earth's atmosphere, just as glass in a greenhouse traps heat from the sun.

Greenhouse gases: Gases in the atmosphere that cause the greenhouse effect. These include carbon dioxide, methane, and water vapor.

Weather: Brief events involving temperature and precipitation, such as a winter snowstorm or a summer heat wave.

Climate Versus Weather

The difference between climate and weather involves both time and area. Climate involves weather conditions lasting thousands of years over a large region, such as the Arctic climate that created the Greenland ice cap, *below.* Weather is short-term temperature and precipitation, such as winter snow in the Midwest, *below right.*

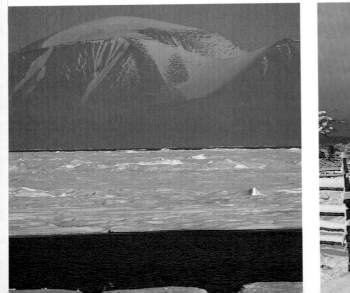

Reading Nature's "Diary"

A scientist, *below,* examines a cylinder of ice drilled from the ice cap in Greenland. Such ice cores are a frozen "diary" of past concentrations of atmospheric gases. Researchers analyze bubbles of air trapped as the ice formed over tens of thousands of years to determine how the concentrations of gases changed and to correlate the gas changes to past climate changes. To bring the "diary" up to date, scientists use such tools as a gigantic weather balloon, *right,* to measure the gases that make up the atmosphere today.

The jet stream usually flows across North America in a track during spring and summer that directs rainstorms to the Midwest. By pushing the jet stream far north of its normal track in the spring of 1988, the La Niña could have diminished rainfall in the Midwest.

Climatologists (scientists who study the climate) base their knowledge of Earth's past and present climate—and their ideas about the future climate—on information gathered by researchers working in a variety of scientific fields. From meteorologists, they gather information on temperature, humidity, wind speed and direction, and other weather phenomena at various parts of the globe. Meteorologists have recorded accurate weather data for more than 100 years. Today's meteorologists also analyze samples of air to determine percentages of certain gases in the atmosphere.

From oceanographers come results of research on samples of seawater collected at great depths. Chemical analysis of such water helps determine amounts of carbon dioxide absorbed by the ocean from the atmosphere.

Geologists examine evidence of glacial movements such as grooves scratched into bedrock by boulders or rock fragments dragged along by glaciers. Biologists analyze tree rings to determine plant growth in various years. This growth depends in part on the amount of carbon dioxide in the atmosphere. Insect specialists measure gas emissions from holes dug in the ground or mounds built by termites—a natural source of methane, another greenhouse gas. Astronomers measure changes in the brightness of the sun.

Paleoclimatologists (scientists who study the climate of prehistoric times) analyze *cores* (long, thin cylinders) drilled out of sediments deposited on ocean floors over millions of years. They also examine cores taken from deep within the ice sheets that cover Greenland and Antarctica, where ice has been steadily laid down for hundreds of thousands of years. These cores are "diaries" of Earth's atmosphere from eons ago until the present. Analyses of plants and animals in sediment cores reveal how much the temperature of the ocean has changed. Ice cores enable scientists to tell how much carbon dioxide has been in the atmosphere because the ice contains trapped bubbles of atmospheric gases.

Evidence from ice cores shows that over the past 160,000 years there has been a close correlation between global average temperature and the amount of carbon dioxide in the atmosphere. The major periods of glaciation match those times when carbon dioxide made up a relatively small amount of the gas in the atmosphere—about 200 parts per million (ppm). (One ppm equals $\frac{1}{10,000}$ of 1 per cent.) And the warmer, interglacial periods match those times when the carbon dioxide level was relatively high—about 280 ppm.

Ice cores show also that this level has been climbing sharply. In 1800, before the Industrial Revolution began to take full effect, the carbon dioxide level was about 280 ppm. By the 1890's, the carbon

Natural Causes of Climate Change

Scientists believe that at least some long-term climate changes, such as major ice ages, are caused by Earth's position in relation to the sun.

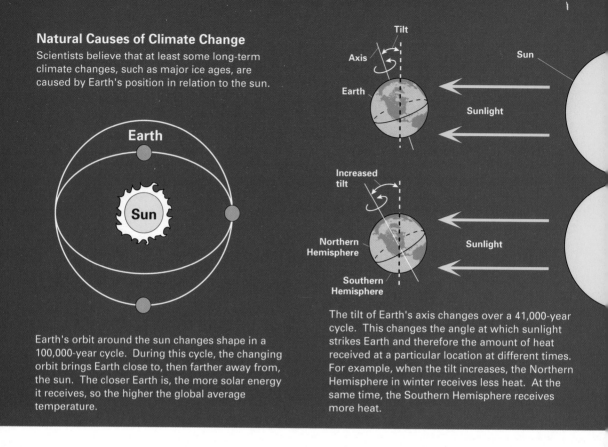

Earth's orbit around the sun changes shape in a 100,000-year cycle. During this cycle, the changing orbit brings Earth close to, then farther away from, the sun. The closer Earth is, the more solar energy it receives, so the higher the global average temperature.

The tilt of Earth's axis changes over a 41,000-year cycle. This changes the angle at which sunlight strikes Earth and therefore the amount of heat received at a particular location at different times. For example, when the tilt increases, the Northern Hemisphere in winter receives less heat. At the same time, the Southern Hemisphere receives more heat.

dioxide level had risen to perhaps 290 ppm. Today, according to analyses of air samples, the level is more than 350 ppm, 25 per cent higher than the 1800 level. To many experts, the past linkage between increasing levels of carbon dioxide and rising temperatures and the current sharp climb in the amounts of greenhouse gases are evidence that we are due for a drastic shift in the climate due to the greenhouse effect—this time, with human causes.

Further evidence comes from global climate *models* (mathematical descriptions) constructed by climatologists to evaluate the scientific information available to them. Researchers manipulate global climate models in some of the world's most powerful computers to analyze the past and predict Earth's future climate. The climate is so complex that no one has come close to building a model that includes all the important physical, chemical, and biological processes from the top of the atmosphere to the bottom of the ocean. Furthermore, the models vary considerably in their details, resulting in a wide range of temperature predictions. Nevertheless, all of them predict that the greenhouse effect will raise the global average temperature sharply in the decades ahead.

How does the greenhouse effect work? Why do the amounts of carbon dioxide and certain other gases in the atmosphere make any difference to Earth's temperature?

The greenhouse effect gets its name from what happens inside a glass greenhouse—the structure used to grow "hothouse" vegetables, fruits, and other plants out of season. The inside of the greenhouse stays warm in the winter even without artificial heating because sunlight coming through the glass heats the interior and the glass retards the escape of heat.

In Earth's greenhouse effect, the atmosphere plays the role of the glass in an ordinary greenhouse, and the heat-trapping phenomenon depends upon differences in radiant energy. The sun and objects heated by the sun—including Earth—emit various forms of electromagnetic radiation, which differ from one another in their *wavelength*, the distance between successive wave crests.

The wavelengths of energy radiated by an object depend generally on the temperature of the object—the hotter the object, the shorter the wavelengths. The surface of the sun has a very wide band of temperatures—ranging up to thousands of degrees—so the sun's radiation covers a wide range of wavelengths. In order of decreasing wavelength, forms of electromagnetic radiation emitted by the sun include radio waves, microwaves, infrared (heat) rays, visible light, ultraviolet rays, and X rays. Most of the sun's total emitted energy is either visible light or infrared radiation.

Of the solar energy reaching Earth's atmosphere, about 30 per cent is reflected back to space, scattered by clouds, by dust particles and certain kinds of molecules in the atmosphere, and by objects on the surface itself. The polar icecaps, for example, reflect part of the sunshine that strikes them. The remaining 70 per cent of this solar radiation is absorbed by the atmosphere, bodies of water, the ground, vegetation, and other surface objects.

Whatever absorbs this radiation becomes hotter and, in turn, reradiates energy. Because Earth is so much cooler than the sun, however, the reradiated energy has a much longer wavelength than does solar radiation. Most of Earth's radiation is in the *far infrared*, whose wavelength is some 10 times longer than that of visible light.

Greenhouse gases in Earth's atmosphere allow about 50 per cent of the shorter waves of incoming solar radiation to pass through to Earth's surface. But the gases absorb 80 to 90 per cent of the longer infrared rays reradiated from Earth's surface, preventing these rays from journeying outward into space and also heating the atmosphere. The gases then reradiate some of the energy into space, but most of it is reradiated back to warm Earth.

Another natural process, the carbon cycle, has a profound influence on the amount of carbon dioxide—a major greenhouse gas—in the atmosphere and thus on Earth's temperature. This process involves the ocean waters and all plants (including algae), animals, and bacteria. In fact, it is fundamental to life on Earth.

The ocean waters readily dissolve the gaseous carbon dioxide from the atmosphere—though warm water can take up less of the gas than

Human Causes of Climate Change

Scientists believe that human activities, from increased burning of fossil fuels to increased land clearing and farming, are adding gases to the atmosphere that cause the average global temperature to increase.

The Natural Greenhouse Effect

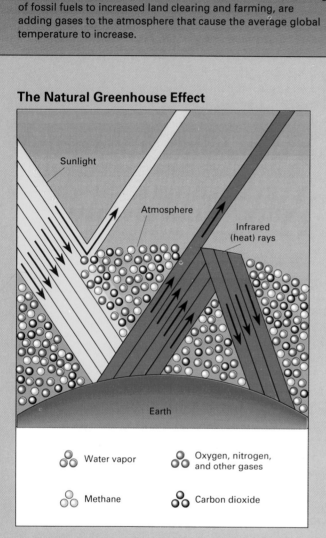

The Natural Greenhouse Effect

Concentration of Carbon Dioxide

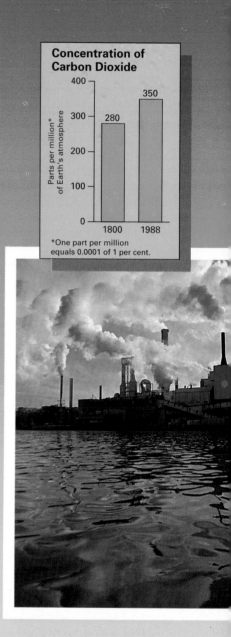

*One part per million equals 0.0001 of 1 per cent.

The Natural Greenhouse Effect

Gases such as water vapor, carbon dioxide, and methane are naturally present in Earth's atmosphere. These so-called greenhouse gases trap heat from the sun, making Earth warm enough for life. Like greenhouse windows, these gases allow most rays of sunlight to pass through the atmosphere and heat Earth's surface. The surface, in turn, emits *infrared* (heat) rays into the atmosphere. The greenhouse gases absorb most of this heat and radiate it back down to the surface — beginning another cycle of absorption, heating, and radiation.

Burning coal, oil, and other fossil fuels has increased the amount of carbon dioxide (CO_2) in the atmosphere since 1800, when all the atmospheric CO_2 occurred as the result of natural processes. Factories account for 29 per cent of the CO_2 added by the burning of fossil fuels; electric power plants, 28 per cent; motor vehicles, 27 per cent; and furnaces for homes and businesses, 16 per cent.

The level of atmospheric methane has more than doubled since 1800, due largely to increased agricultural production. Microbes in the guts of cattle and in rice paddies break down plant material and release this gas, which traps heat 25 times as well as carbon dioxide does.

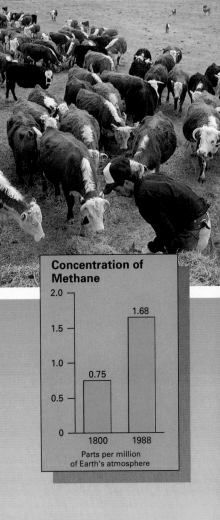

Concentration of Methane

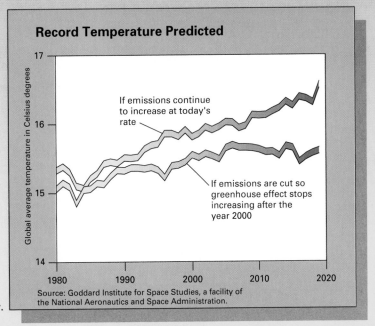

(graph values: 0.75 at 1800; 1.68 at 1988)

Parts per million
of Earth's atmosphere

Concentration of Chlorofluorocarbons

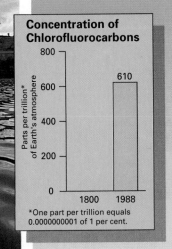

Parts per trillion*
of Earth's atmosphere

(graph value: 610 at 1988)

*One part per trillion equals
0.0000000001 of 1 per cent.

Only tiny amounts of chlorofluorocarbons, artificial gases used mainly as refrigerants and propellants in spray cans, have entered the atmosphere, but their levels are increasing by 5 per cent each year. And they trap heat 25,000 times more efficiently than does carbon dioxide.

Climate specialists predict that the greenhouse effect will push the global average temperature up steadily — unless the release of greenhouse gases due to human activity is cut back sharply.

Record Temperature Predicted

Global average temperature in Celsius degrees

If emissions continue to increase at today's rate

If emissions are cut so greenhouse effect stops increasing after the year 2000

(x-axis: 1980, 1990, 2000, 2010, 2020; y-axis: 14, 15, 16, 17)

Source: Goddard Institute for Space Studies, a facility of the National Aeronautics and Space Administration.

Possible Greenhouse Effects

If the global average temperature rises between 2 and 5 Celsius degrees (3.6 to 9 Fahrenheit degrees), climate changes might occur. Some areas of the world could become hotter; others, wetter. Crop-growing areas might shift to the north.

Cities in the United States might suffer extended summer heat waves. Dallas in the Southwest, for example, could have 160 days of temperatures above 32° C (90° F.), while Chicagoans might swelter through two months at this temperature.

Rainfall might increase sharply in the tropics, causing extensive flooding.

Hotter summers and shifting patterns of rainfall might jeopardize farming in areas such as the Midwestern United States, while making lands to the north in Canada and Siberia prime crop-growing regions.

can cool water. Plants in the ocean and on land also take up carbon dioxide and use it to make their food. In this process, called *photosynthesis*, they release oxygen.

Plants also release some carbon dioxide. But they produce much less carbon dioxide than they consume. Animals take in oxygen and release carbon dioxide in the process of *respiration*—known as *breathing* in animals with lungs.

In addition, the burning of plants combines carbon and oxygen to produce carbon dioxide, as does the decay of plants and animals. Decay does not affect all the carbon in the dead bodies of plants and animals, however. In fact, soil and ocean sediments are vast storehouses of carbon from dead plants and animals, and from animal wastes. Fossil fuels formed deep within Earth from plants and animals that died millions of years ago represent another major reserve of carbon.

For eons, the carbon cycle has maintained a rough equilibrium between the carbon dioxide in the atmosphere and the carbon dioxide dissolved in the oceans. And this equilibrium—via the greenhouse effect—has kept the temperature of the lower atmosphere (the global average temperature) approximately the same year after year. If there were no greenhouse effect at all, this temperature would be nowhere near its present 15°C (59°F.). Instead, it would be closer to −18°C (0°F.), much too low to support life.

This equilibrium is now threatened. The amount of carbon released into the atmosphere in the form of carbon dioxide has begun to outstrip the amount of carbon dioxide absorbed by the oceans and by plants for photosynthesis.

According to scientists, by far the greatest cause of this increase in atmospheric carbon dioxide is the worldwide burning of fossil fuels. Global oil consumption, for example, skyrocketed from 149 million barrels in 1890 to more than 20 billion barrels by 1988. Other major causes include the burning of wood for cooking and heating and the burning of vast tropical rain forests to clear land in Central and South America.

Indeed, the clearing of rain forests is throwing nature a "quintuple whammy," reinforcing the greenhouse effect in five ways:
■ The burning of trees adds substantially to the amount of carbon dioxide in the atmosphere.
■ The decay of unburned vegetation produces carbon dioxide and methane.
■ The killing of the trees and other vegetation decreases the rate of removal of carbon dioxide from the air by photosynthesis.
■ The unburned vegetation stimulates a massive invasion of termites, which produce large amounts of methane.
■ The use of cleared land as pasture adds to the generation of methane, because bacteria in the digestive systems of cattle produce large amounts of this gas.

Decomposing organic matter in rice paddies also produces methane. Both the raising of cattle and the cultivation of rice have been increasing at a steady rate, and so has another human activity that adds methane to the atmosphere—the mining of coal. Methane seeps out of underground coal mines. With all this activity, the amount of methane in the atmosphere is increasing even faster than the percentage of carbon dioxide.

Among the greenhouse gases affected by human activities, carbon dioxide has caused about 66 per cent of the rise in global average temperature since 1880. Methane has been responsible for 15 per cent of the rise. Next in line—at 8 per cent—are chlorofluorocarbons, artificial chemicals extensively used in aerosol sprays in Europe and used in refrigerators and air conditioners throughout the world.

Evidence gathered in the last decade has provided ample warning that human activity may cause a drastic shift in Earth's climate. But scientists have been warning us about the greenhouse effect for almost 100 years. In the late 1890's, Swedish chemist and physicist Svante A. Arrhenius said that because of the greenhouse effect, a doubling of atmospheric carbon dioxide would cause the global average temperature to rise by about 5 Celsius degrees (9 Fahrenheit degrees). Skeptics ignored Arrhenius' warnings, however.

Stephen H. Schneider, a climatologist at the National Center for Atmospheric Research (NCAR) in Boulder, Colo., has been sounding the alarm about the possible consequences of the greenhouse effect for more than 15 years. "I felt very lonely out there talking about the greenhouse effect in 1973," he says. "I believed that the upper limit to world growth was the level of carbon dioxide, not because there was any clear sign in the climate that greenhouse warming was coming, but just from the physics of the problem. . . .There's no bell that rings and says 'Greenhouse detected.'"

Now that we understand the threat of a rapid global warming, what can we do to prevent an environmental catastrophe? "There is no way to turn the clock back," says Michael McElroy, chairman of the Department of Earth and Planetary Sciences at Harvard University in Cambridge, Mass. "It would be unrealistic to expect society to accept voluntarily a reduced standard of living, . . . [but] ultimately, we should drastically curtail our use of fossil fuel."

Many scientists believe we should turn to other forms of energy. Nuclear energy from splitting atoms produces no carbon dioxide, for example, and nuclear power plants are used to generate electricity in many parts of the world. Three major industrial nations—France, Japan, and the Soviet Union—are building more such plants. But nuclear energy is plagued by so many other problems—including the disposal of radioactive waste and a fear of serious nuclear accidents—that many governments are reluctant to increase its use.

Instead, they may turn to alternative energy sources that have been under study for decades—photovoltaic cells, for example, which convert sunlight directly into electricity, and so-called wind farms dotted with giant wind turbines that generate and store electricity. Other prospective sources include devices that tap the energy of the seas. These include wave power machines, turbogenerators driven by the rising and falling tides; and ocean thermal energy conversion power plants, which use the temperature difference between warm surface waters in the tropics and colder bottom waters to provide energy to run turbogenerators. In the distant future, scientists and engineers may develop *fusion* power plants that operate on energy released when two or more atomic nuclei fuse together—the type of nuclear reaction that gives the sun its energy (in the Science File section, see PHYSICS, SUBATOMIC [Close-Up]).

Another long-sought goal is the use of solar energy to split molecules of water into oxygen gas and hydrogen gas. These gases might be an almost ideal fuel. When hydrogen burns in pure oxygen, its only waste product is water.

One of the easiest approaches to solving the greenhouse problem, however, is to make our use of energy more efficient. An outstanding example of success in this area is the increase in gasoline mileage achieved by automobile manufacturers since the late 1970's. Most engineers say that much more fuel economy can be built into cars.

Still another approach involves attacking the other side of the carbon dioxide dilemma—increasing the absorption of the gas from the atmosphere. In September 1988, Daniel J. Dudek, a senior economist for the Environmental Defense Fund, an independent organization, proposed such an approach to the Senate Committee on Energy and Natural Resources. Dudek said that 4 million hectares (10 million acres) of new forest could absorb all the carbon dioxide emitted by all the U.S. power plants likely to be built in the next decade. Replanting that many hectares of farmland as forest would cost between $1 billion and $2 billion, according to Dudek, but would be a cost-effective alternative in battling global warming.

Was the very hot summer of 1988 caused by the greenhouse effect, or was it just a random variation in Earth's fickle weather? It really does not matter, say many atmospheric scientists. Global warming is on the way, and it is time, according to them, to take action to avoid a worse outcome than nature itself decrees.

As Schneider puts it, "It is often said that we do not so much inherit the world from our forebears, but rather we borrow it from our children. It is increasingly urgent that we act to prevent our debt from growing out of control."

For further reading:

Gay, Kathlyn. *The Greenhouse Effect*. Watts, Franklin, Inc., 1988.
"CO$_2$ on the Rocks." *Discover*, April 1988.
Marshall, Eliot. "Using Forests to Counter the Greenhouse Effect." *Scientific American*, December 1987.

Researchers are developing sophisticated radar
systems and other devices to help pilots avoid
wind shear, which has caused more aircraft
fatalities than any other weather hazard.

Science Versus
Wind Shear

BY DIANA SOMERVILLE

Disaster struck in New York City when an Eastern Airlines Boeing 727 crashed on approach to John F. Kennedy International Airport on June 24, 1975, killing 113 people. On July 9, 1982, a Pan American World Airways Boeing 727 crashed shortly after take-off from New Orleans International Airport, claiming 153 lives. And on Aug. 2, 1985, a Delta Air Lines Lockheed L-1011 Tristar coming in for a landing at Dallas-Fort Worth International Airport hit the ground short of the runway, killing 137 people.

All three disasters had the same cause—*wind shear*, a swift change in wind speed and direction. Wind shear causes aircraft to lose altitude rapidly. Plunges of more than 200 meters (650 feet) in just a few seconds have been reported. For an aircraft flying at a normal cruising speed and altitude, such a loss of elevation is only a minor problem. But a jetliner taking off or approaching an airport for a landing is flying both slowly and low, so even a small drop is a matter of life and death.

Wind shear has caused more aircraft fatalities than any other weather hazard, according to a study released in 1983 by the National Research Council, an independent group that advises the United States government on scientific and technical matters. This study cited wind shear as the cause of 27 aircraft accidents accounting for nearly 500 deaths in the United States between 1964 and 1982. Since 1982, the National Transportation Safety Board (NTSB), an agency of the U.S. government, has investigated at least three more wind-shear incidents, including the Dallas-Fort Worth crash.

Because of its potential to cause such crashes, the problem of wind shear has become a major area of scientific research. Meteorologists have been using sophisticated radar systems and other research equipment to examine the weather conditions that can lead to wind shear. What they have learned is being applied at airports in the United States to help pilots avoid these deadly winds.

Scientists now know that the most dangerous form of low-level wind shear occurs when an aircraft flies inside a *microburst*—a narrow, brief, but extremely violent downward flow of air. When a microburst strikes the ground, air flows out rapidly along the surface in all directions from the center of impact.

A microburst is a type of *downburst*, which is any intense downward flow of air. Meteorologists classify downbursts according to size. A microburst is 4 kilometers (2.5 miles) or less across, while a *macroburst* is larger. Air also flows downward beneath thunderstorms, but not violently enough to qualify as downbursts. When it strikes the ground, this air creates an outward-flowing pattern, the leading edge of which is called a *gust front*. Macrobursts and air flowing beneath thunderstorms can cause relatively mild forms of wind shear.

It may seem strange to use so many terms to describe what is essentially a single phenomenon—a column of air striking the ground and spreading in all directions along the surface. But differences in the size and intensity of such columns are the keys to understanding the dangers of low-level wind shear, as University of

The author:
Diana Somerville is a free-lance writer.

Chicago meteorologist T. Theodore Fujita determined in the mid-1970's. In fact, Fujita coined the term *microburst* in 1974 to describe a phenomenon he identified when studying damage patterns caused by a series of tornadoes, and he first used the term *downburst* in 1975 while investigating the Eastern Airlines crash. Since then, researchers working with the Federal Aviation Administration (FAA) and other government agencies have been developing instruments and techniques to detect low-level wind shear and enable pilots to avoid it during the crucial periods of take-off and landing.

Microbursts do not behave like most other winds. Scientists have long known that winds are caused by differences between the pressures of neighboring masses of air. These pressure differences are often brought on by temperature variations. For example, warm air has a tendency to rise. When a mass of warm air rises, the pressure decreases in the area vacated by this air. Colder air then rushes into this area, increasing the pressure and causing wind.

We can think of Earth as being surrounded by an "ocean" of air, with restless, moving waves; deep flowing currents; and violent whirlpools. Energy from the sun powers this motion of the air by heating the atmosphere unevenly. There is always a temperature difference, for example, between Earth's equator and the North and South poles. Because warm air is lighter than cool air, air at the equator rises as it gets warmer. The cold—and therefore heavy—air at the poles sinks down and moves toward the equator.

Earth's rotation influences the general circulation of air in both the Northern and Southern hemispheres, generating the *prevailing winds* that encircle the globe. The *prevailing westerlies* blow from west to east in two belts between the latitudes of about 30° and 60° north and south of the equator; and *trade winds* blow from east to west at latitudes from the equator up to 30° in both hemispheres.

Earth's irregular surface also affects wind. Flat, dry deserts, for example, heat up quickly and reflect heat from the sun. The resulting rapid rise of warm air acts as a powerful wind generator. Mountain ranges act as irregular heat sources, churning up turbulence in the air passing over them.

Areas next to oceans, seas, and large lakes experience a regular, twice-daily shift in the wind, around sunrise and sunset. This shift occurs because energy from the sun raises the temperature of land surfaces much more rapidly than the temperature of large bodies of water and because, when the sun sets, land cools more rapidly than water. The warmer surface heats the air above it. As the heated air rises, cooler air rushes in to replace it, so breezes flow from water to land in the morning and from land to water in the evening.

Meteorologists distinguish between these large-, medium-, and small-scale weather patterns with special terms. Huge weather patterns or systems that are roughly the size of several states are called *macroscale* (large-scale) systems; *mesoscale* (middle-scale) systems

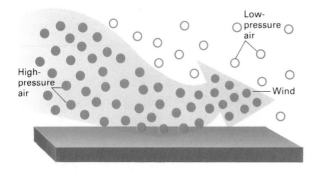

Pressure Differences Cause Wind
Wind is caused by differences in air pressure. Cool
and dense high-pressure air rushes into areas of
low-pressure air, *above,* creating wind that blows
horizontally, bending trees and sending waves crash-
ing onto shore, *right*.

encompass an area about 15 to 30 kilometers (9.3 to 19 miles) in
diameter; *microscale* (small-scale) systems indicate a weather pattern
about the size of a city, or smaller. Microbursts belong to the last and
smallest group.

Fujita discovered the power of microbursts while making an aerial
survey of damage created by a series of 148 murderous tornadoes
that had churned across the central and southern United States on
April 3 and 4, 1974. They created a swath of damage that stretched
for about 4,200 kilometers (2,600 miles), killing 315 people and
injuring more than 5,000 others. No stranger to the violent power of
winds, Fujita had earned the nickname of "Mister Tornado" for his
studies of the dynamic, dramatic births and deaths of these winds.

From his airplane, Fujita saw a number of unusual patterns of
damage on the ground. The wind had blown objects such as building
materials, crops in fields, and even large trees outward, in a starlike
pattern—as if an explosion had occurred. The starbursts were
markedly different from the swirling patterns tornadoes usually
leave. "One could easily simulate a starburst by pointing the nozzle of
a garden hose downward so that a jet of water hits the surface to
generate a starburst outflow," Fujita explained.

Fujita concluded that microbursts had caused the starburst patterns. Fujita's proposal was controversial. Downward flows of cold air
were associated with turbulent thunderstorms, but few people
accepted the idea of a flow strong enough to fell large trees.

Little more than a year later, Fujita was presented with the
opportunity to both prove his theory and demonstrate that violent
downward flows of air were a hazard to aviation. The pivotal incident
was the Eastern Airlines crash near New York's Kennedy Airport on
June 24, 1975. While coming in for a landing, the Boeing 727 had
encountered heavy rain at an altitude of 150 meters (500 feet). At

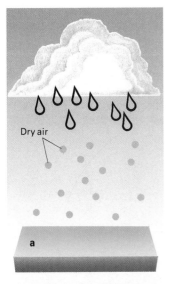 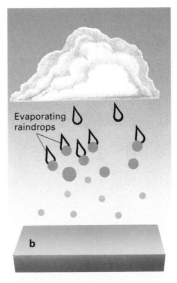 

Dry air

Evaporating raindrops

a

b

c

The Making of a Downburst

A downburst is a wind that blows straight down toward the ground. A downburst can develop when rain falls into a region of dry air, *above, a.* Raindrops evaporate quickly in this air, *b,* thereby cooling the air and making it denser. Eventually, the air becomes so dense that it plunges to Earth as a downburst, *c.* As the downburst strikes the ground, winds blow out in all directions. A downburst develops over Denver's Stapleton International Airport, *left,* creating hazardous take-off and landing conditions.

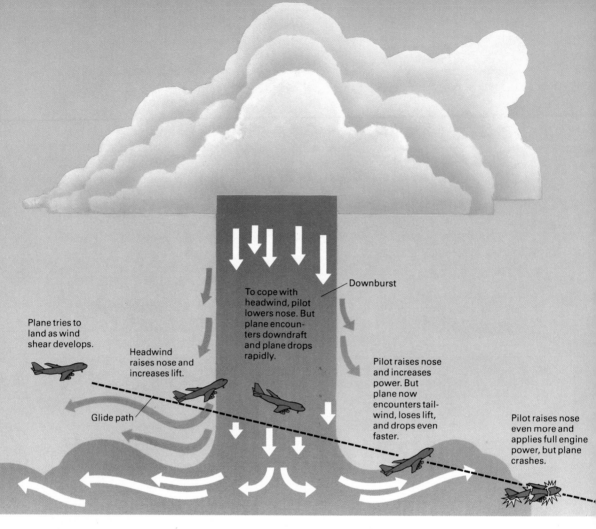

Downburst

Plane tries to land as wind shear develops.

Headwind raises nose and increases lift.

To cope with headwind, pilot lowers nose. But plane encounters downdraft and plane drops rapidly.

Pilot raises nose and increases power. But plane now encounters tailwind, loses lift, and drops even faster.

Glide path

Pilot raises nose even more and applies full engine power, but plane crashes.

How Wind Shear Causes Planes to Crash

A plane approaches for a landing as a downburst develops over the runway. The downburst creates wind shear, an abrupt shift in wind speed and direction. Wind shear can rob a plane of altitude so swiftly that the pilot cannot avert a disaster.

120 meters (400 feet), the plane experienced an abrupt loss of *air speed* (the speed of an aircraft relative to the surrounding air). This decrease reduced *lift* (the supporting force of the air that keeps a plane aloft). As a result, the aircraft crashed short of the runway.

Several airlines asked Fujita to investigate the strange wind conditions of that fateful afternoon. Fujita learned that another Eastern aircraft had attempted to land on the same runway less than 10 minutes before the crash. That aircraft also had encountered extremely heavy rain and experienced a drop in air speed, but the pilot had been able to pull the plane out of the approach, regain altitude, and fly to another airport. Fujita pieced together weather reports from the airport and reports from 14 pilots who had attempted landings on the same runway during a 26-minute period to develop a concept of a special type of low-level wind shear, caused by what he called a downburst.

Confirmation of Fujita's concept came about six weeks later, on August 7, when an airliner crashed at Denver's Stapleton International Airport. A Continental Airlines Boeing 727 began its take-off, ran into light rain on its path down the runway, and lifted off normally. As the aircraft climbed to 45 meters (150 feet), it lost 77 kilometers per hour (48 miles per hour) of air speed in less than 10 seconds and hit the ground. Fifteen people were injured, but no one was killed. The plane apparently encountered a downburst on take-off, according to an analysis of the wind measurements, radar observations, and flight recorder data examined by Fujita and Fernando Caracena, a physicist with the National Oceanic and Atmospheric Administration (NOAA) in Boulder, Colo.

Before Fujita investigated the crashes, many meteorologists had believed that such dangerous encounters between airliners and winds were due to gust fronts caused by thunderstorms. But Fujita amassed an overwhelming amount of data to support his concept of downbursts. His proof includes detailed reports of dozens of aircraft encountering downbursts throughout the world, as well as photographs of starburst patterns of damage in forests and cornfields.

A downburst begins to form when falling raindrops, hailstones, or other precipitation evaporates rapidly in midair. This evaporation cools the surrounding air. The rapid cooling suddenly increases the density of this air. The denser air, heavier than the air surrounding it, plummets to the ground.

The most dangerous type of downburst, the microburst, sometimes packs the wallop of a tornado but lasts only a matter of minutes. Precipitation may or may not reach the ground in a microburst depending on how rapidly it evaporates in the air.

Since Fujita first discovered microbursts, scientists have learned what happens when a microburst hits the ground. Cold air is forced out along the ground and waves of turbulence tumble out from the center of the impact. The rapid changes in wind speed and direction a pilot encounters in a microburst depend not only on whether the plane is landing or taking off, but also on whether the plane is encountering the turbulent air head-on or along its edges.

Aircraft routinely land into a *head wind*, a wind blowing along the length of the plane from front to back. When a plane approaching an airport for a landing enters a microburst head-on, however, it first encounters an extremely strong head wind. This wind decreases the speed of the plane relative to the ground but increases its air speed, lifting its nose and causing the plane to rise above its intended path of descent. As the plane encounters the downdraft, the head wind changes abruptly to a violent downward thrust. The resulting loss of air speed forces the nose down. Finally—as the plane continues on through the downburst—comes a *tail wind*, which blows from the back of the plane to the front, decreasing air speed even more. This wind can cause a sharp drop in lift. So in a matter of only a few seconds, the pilot struggles against the forces of wind shear, first attempting to correct for a head wind that lifts the plane, only to be buffeted by a tail wind that robs it of lift.

Doppler Radar—A Major Aid to Wind-Shear Detection

Scientists are experimenting with radar systems that apply the *Doppler effect,* a compression and expansion of waves, to detect wind shear at airports. Pictures produced by Doppler radar systems can show the differences in air speed and direction that indicate hazardous wind-shear conditions.

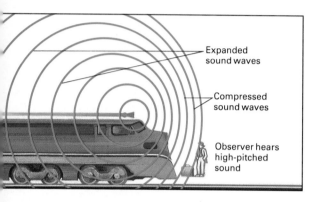

Expanded sound waves

Compressed sound waves

Observer hears high-pitched sound

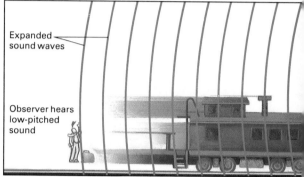

Expanded sound waves

Observer hears low-pitched sound

The Doppler effect refers to the compression of waves traveling in the same direction as the source of the waves and the expansion of waves moving in the opposite direction. A familiar example of the Doppler effect involves sound waves. Sound waves from the whistle are closer together in front of the moving train, *above left,* than behind the train, *above right.* And the farther apart the waves, the lower the sound's pitch. So as the train passes, a listener standing still hears the pitch of the whistle sound drop.

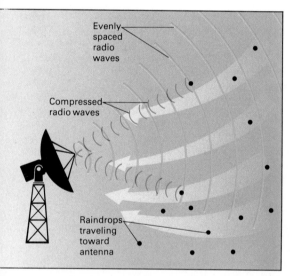

Evenly spaced radio waves

Compressed radio waves

Raindrops traveling toward antenna

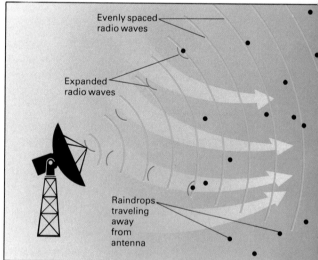

Evenly spaced radio waves

Expanded radio waves

Raindrops traveling away from antenna

Doppler radar uses this principle and sends out radio waves to detect the unusual wind patterns of a downburst. Evenly spaced radio waves bounce back like echoes from raindrops and insects carried along by winds. The radio waves returned to the radar antenna by particles moving toward it are compressed, *above left,* and waves bounced back from particles moving away are expanded, *above right.* Electronic detectors measure the round-trip travel time of returning waves and the spacing between them, then display the data on a televisionlike screen as a color-coded image indicating wind speeds and directions.

The appropriate response to a microburst during a landing goes against most of a pilot's traditional flight training. Rather than lower the nose and decrease power and air speed when encountering head wind, the correct response in a microburst is to raise the nose of the plane, increase speed, and climb as rapidly as possible. The pilot of an aircraft that encounters wind shear during take-off should respond in the same way. In both cases, the plane's chance of survival depends upon its speed and altitude.

Regardless of how a pilot responds, however, many microbursts are not survivable. The best way to deal with microbursts is to avoid them. The challenge is to develop wind-monitoring systems that will detect the conditions that make take-offs and landings extremely dangerous and to warn pilots of these conditions.

Until World War II (1939-1945), the only practical wind detector was the *anemometer*, a device that spins in the wind and measures wind speed. Then during the war, scientists developed *radar* (*radio detection and ranging*) devices to detect enemy aircraft and ships. During World War II, pilots learned to use radar to avoid dangerous weather.

A radar antenna emits a beam of radio waves that bounce off distant targets—planes, raindrops, or snowflakes, for example—and return to the antenna. Electronic devices determine how much time the reflected waves, or echoes, take to return to the antenna. The

A Doppler radar image of winds blowing along the ground near Denver's Stapleton International Airport is made up of small rectangles whose colors indicate wind speed and direction relative to the radar antenna, which is out of the picture to the right. This picture shows the characteristic Doppler pattern of a downburst—a center at which there is virtually no horizontal movement of air, and winds blowing outward from this center in all directions and at various speeds.

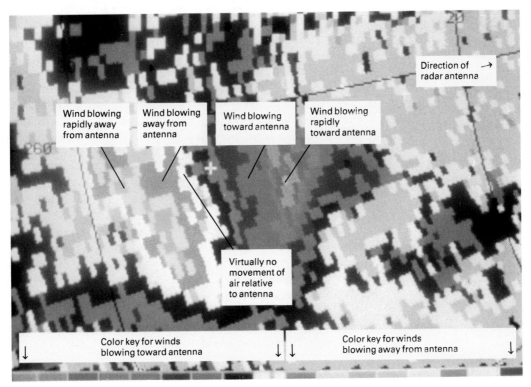

Direction of →
radar antenna

Wind blowing rapidly away from antenna

Wind blowing away from antenna

Wind blowing toward antenna

Wind blowing rapidly toward antenna

Virtually no movement of air relative to antenna

Color key for winds blowing toward antenna

Color key for winds blowing away from antenna

time lapse indicates the distance to the target plane or storm. Then the returning echoes are translated into a picture displayed on a televisionlike screen. Researchers use radar to track and probe thunderstorms, hurricanes, tornadoes, and other weather systems.

Doppler radar, first developed in the late 1940's, has added the dimensions of speed and direction to the measurement of weather systems. Doppler radar not only reveals the size of a storm system but also indicates the speed and direction—relative to the antenna—of the system's internal winds. Doppler radar uses the *Doppler effect*, the change in *wavelength* (distance between successive wave crests) caused by relative motion between a source of waves and their observer. If the source and the observer are moving closer together, the wavelength shortens. But if the source and the observer are moving farther apart, the wavelength becomes longer.

The Doppler effect is familiar to us in the realm of sound. As a sound moves toward us, the sound waves are *compressed* (decreased in wavelength). This raises the pitch of the sound. So if, for example, an ambulance is coming toward you as you stand on a street corner, the pitch of the siren will be higher than it would be if the ambulance were not moving. As the ambulance speeds away from you, the pitch will drop as the sound waves *expand* (increase in wavelength).

Doppler radar bounces radio waves off moving objects, and the movement of these objects causes the waves to compress or expand. In the case of a weather system, these might be raindrops, snow-flakes, or even flying insects swept along by clear air.

As in conventional radar, the echoes of Doppler radar are displayed on a TV-like screen. In a Doppler display, however, the picture is color-coded to indicate the change in wavelength, which shows how rapidly the various objects are moving toward or away from the radar antenna.

The development of Doppler radar as a meteorological tool has occurred hand in hand with an improved understanding of wind shear and with improvements in aviation weather warning systems. In the late 1970's, the FAA, working with NOAA, developed the Low-Level Wind Shear Alert System (LLWAS), a network of six anemometers that detect gust fronts by sensing the speed and direction of ground-level wind at an airport. The devices are connected to a computer that calculates an overall wind speed and direction for various sectors of the airport. Control-tower personnel then radio this information to pilots, who use it to determine the risk of taking off or landing. By the early 1980's, such networks had been installed at about 100 airports in the United States.

But the LLWAS observations of ground conditions were not sufficient to detect microbursts. The LLWAS missed about 75 per cent of the microbursts occurring within the sensor network.

In 1982, researchers from the National Center for Atmospheric Research (NCAR) in Boulder, Colo., began an FAA-funded project

A flight simulator containing a mock-up of an aircraft cockpit helps pilots learn how to react to wind shear by mimicking the violent changes in orientation that a plane undergoes when it encounters these dangerous and rapidly shifting winds.

to improve the network. They set out to expand the network from 6 anemometers to 12, develop mathematical formulas that would enable the computers to determine when a microburst is present, prepare wind shear information for each runway, and develop ways to communicate this information instantaneously so that pilots can use it during the crucial seconds of take-off and landing.

The enhanced LLWAS was field-tested in Denver in 1987. Pilots reported that the system was significantly more valuable than the earlier one, especially because the new system did not require pilots to do mental mathematics to calculate the risk of wind shear on their runways while trying to get their planes up or down. The FAA has indicated it plans to enhance all of the LLWAS networks in the United States. Nevertheless, even the improved, enhanced LLWAS still misses microbursts and developing microburst conditions outside the network of anemometers.

In 1982, the University of Chicago and NCAR conducted a program called Joint Airport Weather Studies (JAWS) in the Denver area to develop a physical description of microbursts, examine detection and warning systems, and determine how aircraft perform in microbursts. One of the most important contributions of the JAWS project was a demonstration that Doppler radar could detect wind shear conditions effectively.

JAWS and other projects demonstrated that Doppler radar is less limited than LLWAS in detecting wind shear because the radar scans the skies, spotting dangerous winds as they develop. Consequently, in the mid-1980's, the FAA began a program to add Doppler radar to major airports throughout the United States.

Detecting Potentially Deadly Winds

Doppler radar systems, which can detect downbursts that produce wind shear, are being installed at major airports. A Doppler radar antenna, *right,* scans the skies around Denver's Stapleton International Airport, the first to have such a system. Data from the radar is used to construct computer images of wind patterns, *below,* which a meteorologist analyzes for signs of downbursts. A large red dot on the computer screen to her right identifies an area of downward flowing air and possible wind shear.

The wind shear warning is sent to the airport's control tower, *right,* where air traffic controllers can reschedule takeoffs or landings until the downburst is over.

The Doppler system to be installed was developed in part from results of the JAWS project and work at the Massachusetts Institute of Technology in Cambridge. The system, called Terminal Doppler Weather Radar, is designed to detect microbursts and gust fronts, predict wind shifts near the terminal, and provide graphic displays of precipitation. The FAA plans to have such systems operating in 47 airports by the mid-1990's.

Some airliners have wind shear avoidance and guidance systems on board. At least five U.S. manufacturers have developed airborne devices that can sense dangerous wind conditions and alert a flight crew to these conditions before wind shear begins to buffet the aircraft severely. A guidance system connected to the device helps a flight crew respond to wind shear, but all this equipment gives the crew only a slight time advantage in coping with wind shear.

To overcome this disadvantage, researchers at the National Aeronautics and Space Administration's Langley Research Center in Virginia are working on airborne Doppler radar and *lidar* (*light radar*) systems to detect wind shear conditions ahead of an aircraft. Lidar is like radar but uses laser light beams, rather than radio waves.

Freeing aircraft from dependence on ground-based detection would be another significant advantage of such airborne detection systems. Many airports, especially small ones and those in developing countries, may not be able to afford expensive ground-based systems such as the terminal Doppler system.

Education offers a less expensive approach to airline safety. Pilots seldom receive refresher courses in aviation meteorology, yet the final decision about whether to take off or land in questionable weather rests with the pilot. A significant step has already been taken with the development of the Wind Shear Training Aid. This program, developed by Boeing Company under an FAA contract, provides a strategy for avoiding hazardous weather and a series of recommendations on what to do when encountering it.

Continued research on wind shear and downbursts may allow computers to calculate the actual risks of wind shear hazard rather than merely produce advisory information. And perhaps the FAA will develop national standards defining when the weather is too dangerous for take-offs and landings.

Given the whims of the winds and the dangers of downbursts, adopting stringent guidelines will inevitably mean that air travelers will face more weather-related delays. Such delays, however, seem a small price to pay for arriving safely at one's destination.

For further reading:

Low-Altitude Wind Shear & Its Hazard to Aviation. National Academy Press, 1983.
Monastersky, Richard. "Mastering the Microburst." *Science News*, March 21, 1987.
"Wind Shear Technology Advances" (special section). *Aviation Week & Space Technology*, Sept. 22, 1986.

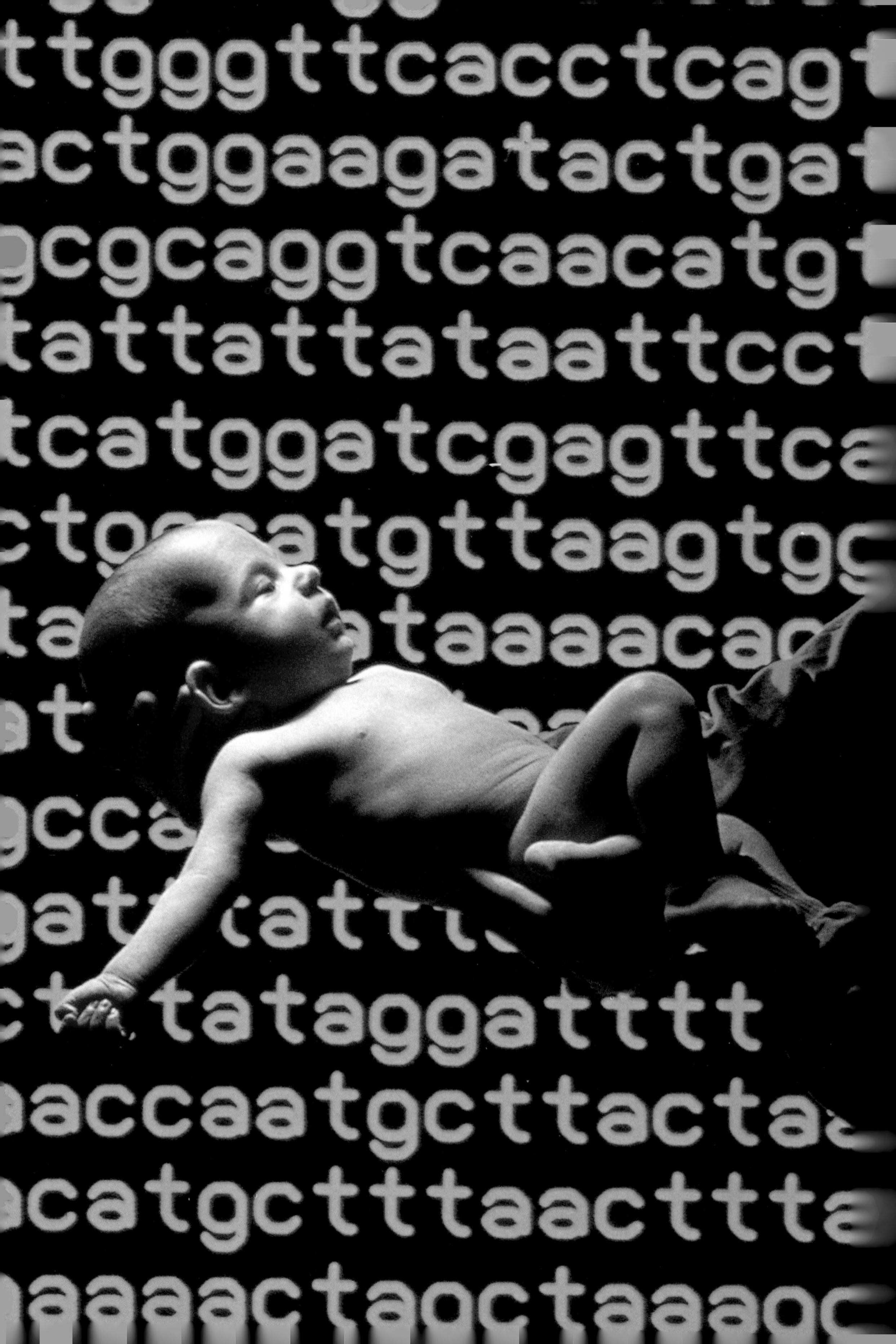
ttgggttcacctcag
actggaagatactga
gcgcaggtcaacatg
tattattataattcc
tcatggatcgagttca
aaccaatgcttacta
acatgctttaacttta

A massive and controversial effort to identify all human genes promises to revolutionize the medical and biological sciences.

Creating the Ultimate Map of Our Genes

BY BOYCE RENSBERGER

Imagine a ladder with 3 billion rungs rising more than 800,000 kilometers (500,000 miles) above Earth—more than twice as high as the moon. Imagine also that each rung is divided by a line and that on either side of the line is stenciled one of four letters of the alphabet. Finally, envision yourself climbing the ladder and writing down the pairs of letters that make up each rung. If you could climb one rung per second, recording the letters in notebooks as you go, it would take you approximately 100 years to reach the top of the ladder. Your notebooks would contain enough information to fill 5,000 books the size of a typical novel.

This imaginary task gives some idea of the challenge facing biologists in the United States and elsewhere as they embark on a monumental project: deciphering all the coded information in the human *genome*, all the genes in a human cell. Genes, the basic units of heredity, guide the development and functioning of our bodies. All plant and animal life on Earth is governed by genes, and every species has its own individual genome. We human beings have a genetic makeup that is uniquely our own.

The project to achieve a complete understanding of the genome is by far the largest coordinated effort ever undertaken in the biological sciences. It involves hundreds of scientists working full-time and may take 15 years and $3 billion to complete. But supporters of the idea

Left: The human genetic code contains complete instructions for making a human being.

The author:
Boyce Rensberger is science editor at *The Washington Post.*

say the results should more than justify the labor and expense. They predict that a complete understanding of the human genetic code would provide untold benefits for humanity. For example, those advocates claim that medical science would gain powerful new abilities to diagnose, cure, and eventually prevent many diseases caused by faulty genes. And biologists, they say, would acquire a far deeper understanding of life itself—how life began, how it evolved, how embryos develop, how the brain works, and why people age and die. So great is the challenge of deciphering the genome, and so far-reaching the possible benefits, that many scientists have called that goal the Holy Grail of biology.

Nevertheless, the project is controversial. Many biologists say it will not lead to practical applications any faster than studying individual genes, one at a time. For one thing, they note that merely reading the code of a gene tells you little about that gene's role in life. Up to now, the usual approach in learning about human genes has been to start with a known disease, track down the gene (or genes) involved, and decode it. That method is comparable to reading only books that you know something about. The tack being taken in the genome project is more like the opposite—reading every book in the library to find those with information of value to you.

Gene mapping as "Big Science"

Despite the controversy, the idea of a major national effort to read all the "books" in the human "genetic library" began gaining support among biological scientists in the mid-1980's. Early advocates of a genome project urged the U.S. government to adopt a so-called Big Science approach comparable to the Apollo moon-landing program of the 1960's and 1970's. To the initial alarm of many scientists, such proposals came not from the biomedical research community but from the Department of Energy (DOE), which oversees the nation's production of nuclear weapons. The DOE's interest stemmed from its study of genetic damage caused by nuclear radiation.

The DOE's efforts to become the leader in genome research were countered by another federal agency, the National Institutes of Health (NIH), which has long been the center of American biomedical research. The NIH has never favored the Big Science approach to research, preferring instead to fund many independent, small-scale projects. A classic Washington, D.C., power struggle ensued as the two agencies vied for control of the genome project. The dispute was finally settled in 1988 when NIH and DOE officials reached an agreement: Genome research would be carried out at a number of laboratories under the agencies' separate but coordinated leadership. In mid-1988, however, the NIH leaped into an apparently commanding position by appointing Nobel laureate James D. Watson as associate director of its segment of the genome project. Watson, director of the prestigious Cold Spring Harbor Laboratory on New York's Long Island, is one of the scientists who in the 1950's discovered the structure of the molecule of which genes are made (in the People in Science section, see JAMES D. WATSON).

The United States efforts are only part of a worldwide movement to decipher the genome. A Center for the Study of Human Polymorphisms (genetic variations) has been established in Paris, and molecular biologists in Great Britain, Denmark, Finland, West Germany, Italy, and Japan are also involved in the research.

Thus, there is no single human genome project; instead, there are many such projects, each concentrating on just part of the problem. To coordinate this global undertaking, geneticists meeting at the Cold Spring Harbor Laboratory in April 1988 launched the Human Genome Organization (HUGO). HUGO will award fellowships to researchers, conduct workshops, and issue annual reports on the progress of the international effort to decipher the genome.

What genes are and what they do

Just what *are* genes, and how do they function? Genes provide a complete blueprint for the creation and maintenance of any living thing. In human beings, they determine eye color, skin color, height, and other obviously inherited characteristics. They also ensure that we are born with two arms and two legs, that our head is atop our neck, and that our heart is connected to the circulatory system. In addition, genes govern all the day-to-day events that enable life to continue: the absorption by cells of oxygen from the bloodstream, the extraction of energy from food, and countless other functions.

Human beings have between 50,000 and 100,000 genes—the exact number has yet to be determined. The genes are located in the nucleus of every cell (except red blood cells, which have no nucleus)

What Genes Are

Genes are located within the cell nucleus on tiny structures called *chromosomes*. There are 23 pairs of chromosomes in human cells. The genes are sections of *deoxyribonucleic acid* (DNA), a molecule shaped like a twisted ladder. The rungs of the ladder are made of four *bases*: adenine (A), guanine (G), thymine (T), and cytosine (C). A always joins with T, and C with G. The sequence of these base pairs carries the genetic code for all living things.

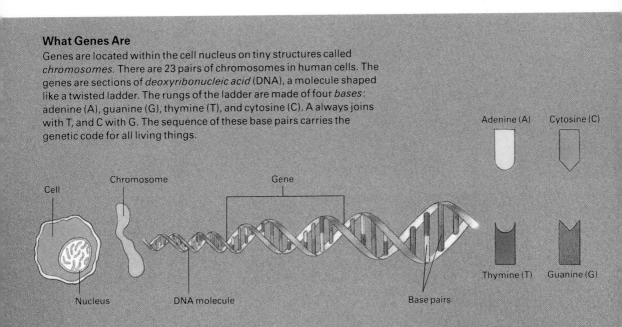

What Genes Do

Genes are responsible for passing on physical traits from parents to children, *below*, and they direct thousands of day-to-day life functions in the body, such as telling cells when to divide. Genes that are defective can cause diseases, such as sickle cell anemia, a disorder of blood cells mainly affecting black people. Normal red blood cells, *bottom left*, are round and flexible and flow freely through blood vessels. Sickle cells, *bottom right*, are rigid and deformed and tend to jam up in small blood vessels, preventing oxygen and nutrients from reaching tissues and organs.

on tiny, threadlike structures called *chromosomes*. There are 23 pairs of chromosomes in a human cell. The chromosomes have recognizable shapes under the microscope, and scientists have numbered the pairs—1 through 22, plus the two sex chromosomes that determine a person's gender. One set of 23 chromosomes is inherited from one's mother, the other set from one's father. Chromosomes vary in size, but on average they contain more than 1,000 genes apiece.

Genes are made of *deoxyribonucleic acid* (DNA), a complex molecule constructed like a long, twisted ladder. The DNA ladder is made up of units called *nucleotides*. Each nucleotide consists of a sugar molecule, a phosphate molecule, and a compound called a *base*. The sides of the ladder are made of alternating sugar and phosphate molecules, and two bases joined together form each rung.

There are four kinds of nucleotides, and each has its own unique base. The four bases are called *adenine*, *thymine*, *guanine*, and *cytosine*; they are usually referred to by their initials—A, T, G, and C. To make up the rungs of the DNA ladder, A always joins with T, and G always joins with C. These joined bases are called *base pairs*. The human genome contains approximately 6 billion base pairs, 3 billion in each set of 23 chromosomes.

The particular sequence of base pairs in our DNA is what carries the coded genetic information, and it is the sum total of that encoded information that determines who we are. Two unrelated individuals differ by roughly 6 million base pairs, or about 1 base pair out of 1,000. People from the same family have fewer genetic differences, and identical twins have exactly the same sequence of base pairs.

The genetic code of a human being or any other organism is a "recipe" for the production of protein molecules. Proteins are the workhorses of the cell. Some proteins give shape to the cell in much the same way that steel girders provide the framework for a building. Other proteins, like legions of tireless workers, carry out the cell's many biochemical reactions. When a protein is to be manufactured by a cell, the code for that protein is copied into *ribonucleic acid,* a molecule that is a sort of mirror image of DNA. Other molecules then assemble the protein from materials in the cell.

Only about 5 per cent of our DNA codes for the proteins used in our bodies. The other 95 per cent includes sequences that regulate the activity of genes, but the vast majority of our DNA seems to have no function. These sequences, often called "junk DNA," may be remnants of genes that were important in our evolutionary past but that have long since ceased to have any purpose.

Many of the 6 million base pairs by which one human being differs from another occur within these junk sequences. Other base-pair differences, however, occur in coding regions and account for the variations—hair and eye color, for example—that make us unique individuals. Some base-pair differences can be harmful, resulting in malfunctioning proteins that cause or contribute to disease. More than 3,000 diseases—including sickle cell anemia, muscular dystrophy, heart disease, cancer, and even some forms of *schizophrenia* (a severe mental disorder)—have been linked to defects in genes. Some of those diseases, including sickle cell anemia, are caused by a single incorrect base pair.

The first gene maps

Scientists have identified about 1,200 genes in the human genome since the early 1970's. They did this by tracing genes to particular chromosomes, and then to progressively smaller segments of chromosomes. Determining the location of genes on chromosomes is called *mapping*.

The first maps, called *chromosomal banding maps*, were produced in the early 1970's. Scientists were able to create these maps because chromosomes, when extracted from cells that are in the process of dividing, can easily be seen under the microscope. They look like fuzzy sausages. When the scientists treated the chromosomes with

The First Gene Maps

Finding where genes are located on chromosomes is called *gene mapping.* The first gene mapping efforts focused on finding the location of a particular gene and trying to pinpoint it as closely as possible on a particular chromosome.

The first step was to determine on which of the 46 human chromosomes the gene was located. Scientists did this by fusing human and mouse cells to produce hybrid cells with just a single human chromosome. If the hybrid cells manufactured a particular human protein, then the gene coding for the protein had to be located in that chromosome. We can liken this to searching for a particular United States city, such as Houston. Finding the correct chromosome was roughly like determining that Houston is located in the state of Texas.

Chromosomes

Chromosome containing sought-for gene

The next advance in gene mapping involved finding the general area of the chromosome where the gene was likely to be. Scientists found that a chemical stain applied to chromosomes creates a pattern of bands. The pattern is almost the same for everyone's chromosomes. Once scientists determined the normal banding patterns, they could compare them with the banding patterns on chromosomes from people with an inherited disease. If a band was missing or arranged differently on a chromosome, the defective or missing gene causing the abnormality or disease was probably in or missing from that area of the chromosome. This would be like determining that Houston is located somewhere in eastern Texas.

Band missing

Normal banding

Staining chromosome

An abnormal gene can be pinpointed even more closely using genetic engineering techniques to examine genes from families in which an inherited disease occurs. Scientists cut up DNA from members of these families with "biochemical scissors" called *restriction enzymes,* which cut the molecules only at certain places. They then compare the cut-up pieces of DNA with those from people without the abnormal gene. If they find that the DNA from those family members affected by the disease always cuts in an unusual place, they call this cut a *marker.* If the marker is close to the abnormal gene that causes the disease, the marker and the abnormal gene are usually inherited together. Finding a genetic marker can be likened to discovering that Houston lies somewhere near the geographical "marker" Galveston Bay. Finding Galveston Bay would mean that Houston cannot be far away.

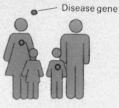

Disease gene

Biochemical scissors (Restriction enzymes)

DNA

Family with history of a genetic disease

or

Probable location of abnormal gene

Normal cutting site

Abnormal cutting site

special chemical stains, light and dark bands formed on them, making each chromosome resemble a raccoon's tail with rings of varying width. Scientists do not know why the bands show up, but the banding pattern is the same in almost everyone's chromosomes.

By studying chromosomes from families with inherited diseases, geneticists found that some diseases are associated with unusual chromosomal banding patterns. As a result of such studies, the scientists concluded that the gene or genes responsible for a given disease must be located in a certain abnormally formed or missing band. By the end of the 1970's, researchers had mapped more than 200 genes to the bands of various chromosomes.

Exploring for other particular genes

In the 1980's, the introduction of genetic engineering techniques provided a way to determine the location of many more genes. Genetic engineering—cutting DNA apart and reassembling it in different ways—was made possible by the discovery of "biochemical scissors" called *restriction enzymes*. Each type of restriction enzyme cuts DNA at a specific short sequence of base pairs wherever that sequence occurs. A particular enzyme thus cuts a DNA strand into hundreds or even thousands of pieces of varying size.

If people were genetically identical to one another, a given restriction enzyme would cut everyone's DNA into the same number of pieces, and the pieces from one person's genome would match up exactly with the pieces from another person's genome. But since people differ genetically, the cutting sites for specific restriction enzymes occur at different places in one person's DNA than in another person's. So everyone's genome produces a unique batch of DNA segments.

Because restriction-enzyme cutting sites are so numerous and are scattered throughout a chromosome's DNA, geneticists theorized that some sites might lie near certain genes that cause hereditary diseases. They also speculated that people who inherit a disease gene from their parents would usually also inherit a particular cutting site that is seen in their parents' DNA. In such cases, that cutting site—and the DNA segment of unusual length that would result from it—would serve as a *marker*, or identifying "flag" signaling the presence of the gene.

That theory was correct. Researchers studying the inheritance of diseases in several generations of large families found that individuals with an unusual cutting site almost always developed the disease. By the late 1980's, scientists had located markers for many hereditary disorders, including Huntington's disease and cystic fibrosis.

When scientists discover a marker for a gene, they do not know exactly where that gene is in relation to the marker. They determine the likely distance between a marker and a gene by studying how often they are inherited together in families. If a marker and a gene are always inherited together, they must lie very near to each other

Texas

Approximate location of Houston

Houston

Galveston Bay

Mapping the Entire Genome

Rather than exploring chromosomes in search of a particular gene, scientists working on the human genome project are surveying all the DNA in the genome to determine the location and function of every gene. This is somewhat like trying to create a map that would ultimately show every building on every street in every city and town in the United States.

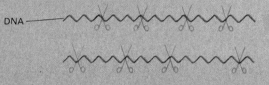

DNA

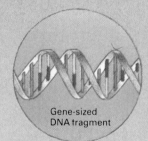

Human DNA fragment

DNA

Bacterium

1. Scientists begin this enormous project by cutting the DNA molecule into smaller parts. But they must keep track of the order in which the parts were organized in the original chromosomes. They do this by using two types of restriction enzymes, with which they cut up two identical chromosomes taken from different cells. Because each enzyme cuts at a different place, the result is pieces of DNA with overlapping sequences of base pairs. These overlapping sequences will enable researchers to determine the original order of the DNA pieces.

2. Next, the scientists make *clones* (identical copies) of each DNA piece. They do this by splicing a DNA piece into the DNA of a rapidly reproducing bacterium (or other microorganism, such as yeast). The bacterium acts as a biochemical factory, reproducing exact copies of the human DNA each time the bacterium reproduces. Thus, enough DNA fragments are produced to be studied by many researchers.

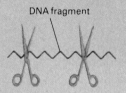

DNA fragment

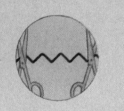

Gene-sized DNA fragment

4. The gene mapping will grow progressively more detailed as scientists cut the DNA fragments into smaller and smaller pieces with other types of chemical scissors. As they do this, they must always establish and keep track of the order in which the DNA fragments belong.

6. The gene-sized pieces of DNA will then be placed in a machine called a *sequencer*, which "reads" the sequences of base pairs that make up the gene.

Sequencer

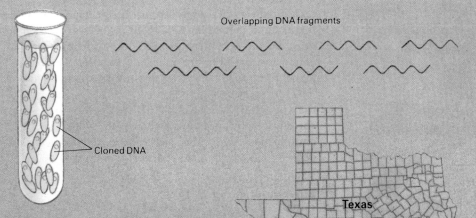

Overlapping DNA fragments

Cloned DNA

Texas

3. Cutting the DNA of one chromosome into about 1,000 of these relatively large fragments and then determining how those fragments were originally ordered in the chromosome is somewhat like surveying the entire state of Texas and determining where the boundaries of all its counties lie.

5. Eventually, scientists will be able to cut the DNA into pieces that are about the size of a single small gene. They will also know the position of each of these fragments within the DNA molecule that makes up the chromosome. The map that this will produce can be likened to one that shows the locations of every city and town in every county of Texas.

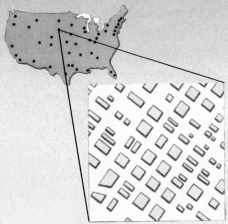

7. The long string of A's, T's, C's, and G's that come out of the sequencer will be the final achievement of the human gene mapping project; scientists will then know the exact order of some 3 billion base pairs making up the human genome. This will produce a gene map equivalent in detail to a map of the United States showing the location of every building or other structure on every street in every city and town.

At this institution in Costa Rica, for 25 years
a leading center for tropical biology, scientists
are seeking ways to save the world's rain forests.

The Organization for Tropical Studies

BY ROBIN L. CHAZDON AND ROBERT K. COLWELL

Six times a month, Costa Rican biologist Maria Marta Chavarría takes a midnight walk in a tropical rain forest. Leaving behind the lights of an isolated research facility in a heavily forested preserve in the lowlands of northern Costa Rica, Chavarría hikes along a dark, well-used trail. She is headed for a large area of virgin rain forest set aside for research in tropical biology.

At this hour, the daytime players—the parrots, howler monkeys, brilliantly colored butterflies, day-blooming plants, and a host of others—have left the forest stage, and the night creatures have emerged to play their parts. The light from Chavarría's headlamp picks out a three-toed sloth, moving in slow motion up a nearby tree to reach the tasty young leaves in the upper branches. A little nine-banded armadillo, nosing about in fallen leaves, scuttles quickly into the forest as the biologist approaches. The fragrant scent of a night-blooming tree floats on the warm air, while an out-of-tune symphony of animal sounds issues from the surrounding blackness.

A few minutes into the forest, Chavarría sees ahead of her an eerie purple glow that marks the site of her work. At the side of the trail, a battery-powered ultraviolet light, which she switched on at dusk, illuminates a white bedsheet hanging as if from a clothesline. But you

Opposite page: In a rain-forest preserve at the Organization for Tropical Studies' (OTS) La Selva Biological Station in northern Costa Rica, a scientist ascends into the *canopy*—the leafy upper levels of the trees—to study the forest's ecology and look for new species.

wouldn't want to put this sheet on your bed; it is peppered with moths of every size, shape, and color that have been attracted by the light, some of them new to science.

Working with tropical biologist Daniel Janzen of the University of Pennsylvania in Philadelphia, Chavarría has for several years been collecting and cataloging moths in Costa Rica. But there are so many kinds of moths in this tiny Central American country, and so little is known about them, that Janzen estimates 30 years of hard work will be required to find and classify them all. In the research preserve alone, there may be 3,000 or more species of moths.

Unfortunately, the two biologists may not have 30 years—or even 10—to complete their work. The rain forests of Costa Rica, like those elsewhere in the tropics, are being cut down at an alarming rate that accelerates each year. As the destruction continues, thousands of species of plants and animals are becoming extinct. Meanwhile, scientists are trying to learn all they can about the remaining forests and the incredible variety of life they contain.

Scientists such as Chavarría and Janzen are aided in their work by a unique institution—the Organization for Tropical Studies (OTS). The OTS is a research and education consortium of 46 universities and research institutions—4 in Costa Rica and the rest in the United States and Puerto Rico. The OTS owns and maintains three research and teaching centers in Costa Rica. Foremost among them is La Selva (The Forest) Biological Station, regarded as one of the world's leading centers of tropical biology, where Chavarría collects her moths. The organization has two headquarters—one in the capital city, San José, and the other at Duke University in Durham, N.C.

The OTS marked its 25th year in 1988. To celebrate its silver anniversary, the organization held a weeklong international symposium in June in Miami, Fla., and at several locations in Costa Rica. Reviewing the state of tropical biology, participants at the meetings agreed that scientific knowledge of tropical organisms had increased dramatically in the previous quarter century and that the OTS could claim much of the credit for that development.

During its lifetime, the OTS has provided training in tropical biology for more than 2,000 graduate students from more than 20 countries. It has also come to play a leading role in the preservation of key areas of Costa Rica's rain forests and has launched research projects that may lead to more ecologically sound uses of forestlands in the tropics.

The authors:
Robin L. Chazdon and Robert K. Colwell teach biology and ecology at the University of Connecticut at Storrs.

Tropical rain forests ring the globe between the Tropic of Cancer and Tropic of Capricorn, a region of perpetual warmth. Aptly named, rain forests receive about 200 to 400 centimeters (80 to 160 inches) of rainfall annually and thus are moist and green throughout the year. These lush forests, the richest *ecosystem* (plants and animals interacting with their environment) in the world, present biologists with a vast field of study. Although they cover only 7 per cent of

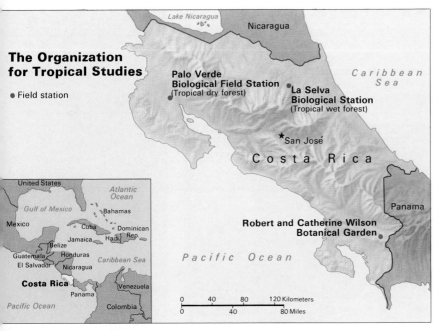

The Organization for Tropical Studies

● Field station

Lake Nicaragua

Nicaragua

Palo Verde
Biological Field Station
(Tropical dry forest)

La Selva
Biological Station
(Tropical wet forest)

Caribbean
Sea

★San José

Costa Rica

Panama

Robert and Catherine Wilson
Botanical Garden

Pacific Ocean

United States

Atlantic
Ocean

Gulf of Mexico

Bahamas

Mexico

Cuba

Dominican
Rep.

Jamaica

Haiti

Belize

Guatemala

Honduras

Caribbean Sea

El Salvador

Nicaragua

Costa Rica

Venezuela

Panama

Pacific Ocean

Colombia

0   40   80   120 Kilometers
0   40   80 Miles

The OTS operates three facilities in Costa Rica, *above left:* La Selva, the Palo Verde Biological Field Station, and the Robert and Catherine Wilson Botanical Garden. At the botanical garden, *above,* the field house is surrounded by the wide variety of tropical plants that researchers come here to study.

Earth's land surface, tropical rain forests are home to more than half of the plants and animals on the planet. For example, tropical forests may have 200 or more species of trees per hectare (2.5 acres), compared with only 10 or so tree species in the same area of a forest in a cooler climate. Animal life is even more diverse. Biologist Terry Erwin of the Smithsonian Institution in Washington, D.C., estimates that as many as 30 million insect species alone may be found in tropical rain forests.

The great majority of tropical birds and mammals are now known to scientists. But thousands upon thousands of tropical plants, insects, and other organisms—millions, if Erwin is correct—remain to be discovered and classified. Far more is known about the plants and animals of La Selva than about those of any other comparable rain forest area in Latin America, yet even at La Selva researchers discover hundreds of new species every year—especially *arthropods* (insects, spiders, mites, and their relatives). In most tropical areas, only a tiny fraction of the plant and animal species have been cataloged, and the great majority of species still await discovery. Unfortunately, many of those species will be lost for all time—driven to extinction by the devastation of their forest homes.

Human destruction of tropical forests accelerated greatly following World War II (1939-1945), as the demand for tropical land and lumber increased. In the 1980's, tropical forests are being destroyed faster than any other natural ecosystem in the world. In Latin America, cattle ranching is the chief force behind deforestation, but elsewhere in the tropics—notably in Africa and Southeast Asia—

The Tropical Rain Forests' Endangered Treasures

The warm, moist forests of the tropics are home to more than half the world's species of plants and animals. The forests also absorb vast amounts of carbon dioxide from the atmosphere. Rain-forest destruction, spurred by growing demands for lumber and land, has accelerated greatly since the 1940's. Scientists warn that unless this plunder is brought under control, mass extinctions and changes to Earth's climate will result.

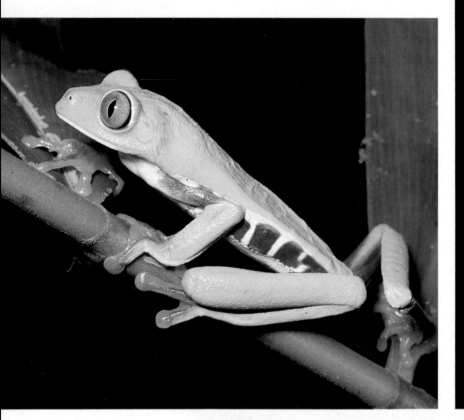

Among the species in the Costa Rican rain forests are a number of amphibians, such as the red-eyed tree frog, *above*. The forests also have thousands of insects and plants, such as the giant saturniid moth, *right*—with a wingspread of 20 centimeters (8 inches)—and colorful passionflowers, *opposite page.*

Vast areas of rain forest
are cut and burned
each year throughout
the tropics. Some of the
worst devastation is oc-
curring in the Amazon
region of South Amer-
ica. In western Brazil,
smoke from a burning
expanse of rain forest
turns day into night,
above.

farming, logging, mining, and other activities also play an important role in forest destruction. Already, the tropics' original forest cover has been reduced by at least 50 per cent, and conservationists predict that, at present rates of destruction, almost 20 per cent of the world's remaining tropical rain forests will be completely gone or seriously damaged by the end of the 1900's. Costa Rica, with the highest rate of deforestation in Latin America, stands to lose 80 per cent of its surviving forests.

Aside from causing the extinction of countless species, the large-scale clearing of tropical forests could have a drastic effect on global climate by altering the balance of carbon dioxide (CO_2) in the atmosphere. Plants remove carbon dioxide from the air during *photosynthesis*, the process by which they build their tissues from CO_2 and sunlight. Because tropical rain forests are so vast, they absorb huge amounts of the gas. As the forests are cleared, less and less CO_2 is absorbed, and so it builds up in the atmosphere. Moreover, the burning and decay of cleared forests release even more CO_2 into the air. Large-scale burning is an especially critical problem in the Amazon region of South America.

The level of carbon dioxide in Earth's atmosphere has been increasing throughout this century. Although most of the excess CO_2 has been caused by the burning of fuels in the industrialized countries, forest destruction has also played a major part in the build-up. Many scientists think the rising concentration of atmospheric CO_2 is trapping heat from the sun and slowly raising global temperatures. This *greenhouse effect*, if it is indeed occurring, could by sometime in the next century partially melt the polar icecaps—flooding seacoasts around the world—and change the distribution of rainfall on every continent. In the Special Reports section, see Is Earth Overheating?

Potential climatic disaster and the loss of huge numbers of species because of destruction of rain forests are alarming prospects, and the OTS is taking them very seriously. The organization has long been committed to the wise use of tropical lands, through both the preservation of untouched forests and the replanting and sustained use of forests that have already been cut. This twofold approach to conservation, OTS scientists believe, offers the best chance for preventing total destruction of the rain forests.

The OTS was founded as a nonprofit corporation in 1963 by a small group of visionaries from six U.S. universities and the University of Costa Rica. The main purpose of the organization, which was funded chiefly by the United States National Science Foundation (NSF), was to promote research and education in tropical biology. Conservation was at that time a less prominent goal.

The organization's facilities and programs took shape slowly at first. It was not until 1968 that the OTS purchased La Selva, a 468-hectare (1,170-acre) tract of rain forest about 70 kilometers (44 miles) north of San José. The organization purchased the property from a forester who had set it aside as a preserve. The first OTS building erected at La Selva was a modest, two-story wood-and-screen structure—shared with rats in the walls and giant spiders and bats under the eaves. The building served as dormitory, kitchen, dining hall, laboratory, and library. The only source of electricity was an unreliable diesel-powered generator, and the only access to the outside world was by dugout canoe along the Puerto Viejo River to the small town of Puerto Viejo de Sarapiquí.

At about the same time that it acquired La Selva, the OTS built the Palo Verde Biological Field Station in Costa Rica's northwestern Guanacaste Province. The station lies within the Palo Verde National Park and adjoins the Lomas Barbudal Biological Reserve to form a protected area covering more than 19,000 hectares (47,000 acres). The land there supports seasonal dry forest—with a definite wet and dry season every year—rather than rain forest, enabling scientists to conduct comparative ecological studies on the vegetation and soils in these two different kinds of tropical forest.

Most of the trees in the Palo Verde area lose their leaves during the six-month dry season, from November through April. For the duration of the dry season, birds and mammals crowd into narrow bands of year-round greenery in *gallery forests*—wooded areas along streams and rivers. In the rainy season, extensive wetlands form in the national park. There, crocodiles bask in the sun, and thousands of water birds nest and raise their young.

The third OTS holding, the Robert and Catherine Wilson Botanical Garden (formerly Las Cruces Botanical Garden), was donated to the organization in 1972. Located high in the rolling hills of southern Costa Rica near the Panamanian border, this 158-hectare (391-acre) field station includes a magnificent collection of tropical plants in addition to areas of natural forest.

Shortly after its founding, the OTS began offering courses to graduate students from universities in Costa Rica, other Central American countries, and the United States. Then, as now, the curriculum included a number of specialized classes focusing on such topics as tropical parasites and rain-forest plants. But the mainstay of the educational program soon became a twice-annual overview course titled "Fundamentals of Tropical Biology: An Ecological Approach." In 1974, the OTS introduced a parallel Spanish-language course, called "Ecología de Poblaciones" (Population Ecology), that it presented once a year. The 20 graduate students participating in each offering of "Fundamentals," as it came to be called, were drawn primarily from OTS member institutions; students in the "Poblaciones" course came from countries throughout Latin America and from Spain.

Having no permanent faculty, the OTS relied on visiting U.S. and Costa Rican professors to teach the eight-week classes. With rare

Exploring the Forests
OTS scientists and students spend much of their time outdoors studying the plants and animals of the forests. On many expeditions, tents become their "home away from home," *right.*

exceptions, these professors worked without pay, dividing their time between teaching and their own research projects. That arrangement worked well and has been continued up to the present, though in recent years some of the professors have been offered a fee for their teaching services.

Students taking either of the basic courses spend nearly all their time in the field, visiting the three OTS field stations and several other sites in Costa Rica. They sweat in rain forests, wade through coastal waters, and shiver in the cloud-swept *páramo*, a high, cold plateau covered with brush and grasses.

For both students and teachers, these field courses are an intensive and exhausting—but exhilarating—experience. Everyone is on the go for 15 to 18 hours a day, 7 days a week, with only a couple of rest days midway through the term. At each site, the first day or two is devoted to "orientation," a dignified term for a scramble to absorb as much information as quickly as possible about the bewildering variety of plants and animals in that locale. Students spend the remainder of their time at each site doing field research. Many of these research projects are designed on the spot by the students themselves—with faculty guidance—one of the best ways to learn about the art of scientific research.

As the OTS course offerings have expanded, so too have its facilities. At La Selva—to the distress of romantics but to the relief of anyone serious about research—only the forest is the same as it was

Much of the work done by OTS researchers consists of finding and cataloging new species. In a section of rain forest lush with undergrowth, a botanist collects specimens of plants, *above.* The great majority of newly discovered species are insects. Working in a makeshift field laboratory, an entomologist classifies insects he has found in a nearby forest area, *left.*

in 1963. The station, which is now easily accessible by road, accommodates 72 people comfortably in modern surroundings. Three air-conditioned, computer-equipped laboratories house up-to-date equipment, electricity is now reliable, and a microwave telephone link connects La Selva with the outside world. Plans for the future include improved, all-weather hiking trails, illustrated guides to the forest's plants and animals, and special family housing for long-term researchers with small children. Officials of the OTS are currently seeking funding for those projects.

The financing of OTS operations has never been easy, and during one touch-and-go period in the mid-1970's the organization went through a financial crisis. Fortunately, the organization was rescued by the able leadership of its executive director, botanist Donald E. Stone of Duke University, who obtained grants from private foundations and from new NSF programs. Largely because of Stone's efforts, the OTS reached age 25 in strong fiscal condition. To ensure future financial stability, an effort is underway to establish a permanent endowment fund for the organization.

Beginning in the late 1970's, conservation became one of the OTS's top priorities. That change of emphasis occurred because researchers at La Selva could no longer ignore the destruction going on around them. Vast stretches of Costa Rican rain forest were being cut down to make way for cattle ranches, and it appeared that La Selva would soon be an island of forest in a sea of stump-dotted pasturelands.

In 1981, deforestation came knocking at the very door of La Selva as the owner of property just outside the field station's western

Gravely concerned about the destruction of tropical rain forests, the OTS has made conservation a top priority. At La Selva, tree seedlings used in reforestation studies grow in an outdoor nursery, *below*. OTS scientists are experimenting with a variety of seedlings in an effort to determine which tree varieties would be best suited for planting on eroded pasturelands.

boundary suddenly began chain-sawing his trees. The man said he would stop clearing his land if the OTS would agree to purchase it. The organization thus launched an emergency fund-raising effort that succeeded in collecting $300,000 to acquire the 600-hectare (1,500-acre) tract. That area, now known as the Western Annex, was incorporated into La Selva in 1983.

At about the same time, the OTS undertook another major fund drive. The goal of that campaign was to establish a protected corridor of forest connecting La Selva with Braulio Carrillo National Park in a mountainous region 35 kilometers (22 miles) to the south. The corridor would preserve a continuous range of ecosystems, from La Selva's lowland rain forest to the cloud-enveloped mountain rain forest of the national park, some 3,000 meters (10,000 feet) above sea level. To purchase a 7,600-hectare (19,000-acre) strip of forest, the OTS needed to come up with $2 million.

The organization's fund-raising efforts got a boost in 1984 when the John D. and Catherine T. MacArthur Foundation—a philanthropic organization in Chicago—awarded a grant of $1 million to the OTS toward purchase of the protection zone. The OTS helped raise another $1 million in contributions from individuals and several conservation groups, enabling the Costa Rican National Park Foundation to buy the ribbon of forest. In April 1986, the corridor was officially incorporated into Braulio Carrillo National Park.

Realizing that the protection of Costa Rica's forests depends in large part on the support and cooperation of the citizenry, the OTS devotes much of its energies to the task of public education. In 1984, the organization began offering basic courses in forest ecology to Costa Rican teachers. And since 1986, hundreds of schoolchildren have visited La Selva to learn firsthand about the rain forest and its wildlife. Many of the children had never before walked in an undisturbed rain forest. The OTS has also offered a series of environmental education programs at the Wilson Botanical Garden. The organization hopes to extend its programs throughout Costa Rica and to other parts of Latin America.

Another important educational project, supported by the OTS, was the publication in 1983 of *Costa Rican Natural History*. This monumental work, written by 174 experts in tropical biology, describes hundreds of Costa Rica's plants and animals. A Spanish translation of the book was nearing completion in 1989.

But land purchases and public education programs can accomplish just so much. Ultimately, saving the rain forests—in Costa Rica and throughout the tropics—will depend to a large extent on the wise management of forests as permanent public resources rather than as private possessions to be cut down for short-term gain. Here too, OTS scientists are vitally involved as investigators and advisers.

The OTS is engaged in several major research projects aimed at improving methods of forest management and finding ways to

BY BEN PATRUSKY

"Magic Bullets" Against Disease

Disease-fighting molecules that track down and destroy viruses and cancer cells may one day cure many deadly diseases, and even the common cold.

Magic bullets. That term sounds like the invention of a fantasy writer, but in fact, it represents a long-standing dream of medical scientists. The dream: to find ways of homing in on and destroying diseased cells, such as cancer cells, while leaving healthy cells unharmed. It is a tantalizing idea but a highly elusive one, and for years researchers could not quite make it work.

By 1989, however, the development of magic bullets was making great headway, and it appeared that the dream of hunting down specific cells in the body might be on the verge of coming true in a very big way. Scientists were experimenting with several new kinds of laboratory-created molecules designed to carry out these "search and destroy" missions. Some researchers were developing altered versions of the body's own disease-fighting molecules to battle cancer cells. Others were constructing a different type of magic bullet by joining various kinds of protein molecules. These *fused proteins* were being tested as a possible treatment for several diseases, including AIDS.

The search for magic bullets began early in this century with the work of a brilliant German bacteriologist, Paul Ehrlich. Ehrlich, who

187

coined the term magic bullets, noticed that certain dyes were taken up by a variety of infectious microorganisms. That observation led him to the idea of chemically hitching a *toxin* (poison) such as arsenic to a dye to kill the *microbes* (germs) that cause syphilis and other diseases. Although his efforts had only limited success, they led to the concept of *chemotherapy*, the use of chemicals to treat disease.

In later years, other investigators began looking for chemicals to kill cancer cells that have *metastasized*, or spread to other parts of the body. Metastasis is what makes cancer so deadly. A cancerous tumor can be removed surgically. But if even one or two cancer cells have broken away from a tumor, they can travel through the circulatory system and start new tumors elsewhere in the body. By the 1980's, researchers had developed some 40 drugs for killing cancer cells. These chemicals generally act by entering and destroying cells that are in the process of dividing rapidly. The problem is that many normal cells, such as hair cells and the cells of the intestines, also reproduce rapidly, and so they too absorb a large dose of the chemical. That is why cancer patients receiving chemotherapy often experience hair loss, nausea, and other unpleasant side effects. That is also why chemotherapy usually does not cure a patient with metastasized cancer. If enough of the drug is given to kill all the cancer cells, the drug may well kill the patient, too.

Medical scientists have long been unhappy with chemotherapy's scattershot approach to gunning down cancer cells; they wanted very much to become sharpshooters. The answer, they felt, lay in the immune system, which produces its own kinds of magic bullets.

One of the immune system's major lines of defense against viruses, bacteria, and other invading microorganisms is a type of white blood cell called a *B lymphocyte*, or B cell. B cells create molecules called *antibodies*, which "recognize" and fasten onto identifying molecules, called *antigens*, that dot the surface of those foreign invaders. Each B cell makes antibodies that fit just one shape of antigen, just as a key will fit only one lock.

When a B cell encounters an antigen it recognizes, it reproduces rapidly. The multiplying B cells release millions of copies of the antibody into the bloodstream to track down all the microbes by fastening onto their antigens. Other elements of the immune system then converge on the immobilized invaders to make the final kill.

The lock-and-key arrangement that enables specific antibodies to grab hold of specific antigens is not unique to the immune system; in fact, it is seen everywhere at the cellular level. Cells have molecular "doors" called receptors on their surface through which many other kinds of molecules, such as hormones and nutrients, enter the cell. Each receptor lets just one kind of helpful molecule through. Harmful viruses, however, often have the right "keys" to unlock certain of these doors, and that is how they gain entrance to cells.

The various locks and keys by which cells and molecules interact

The author:
Ben Patrusky is a free-lance science writer and a media consultant to several scientific institutions.

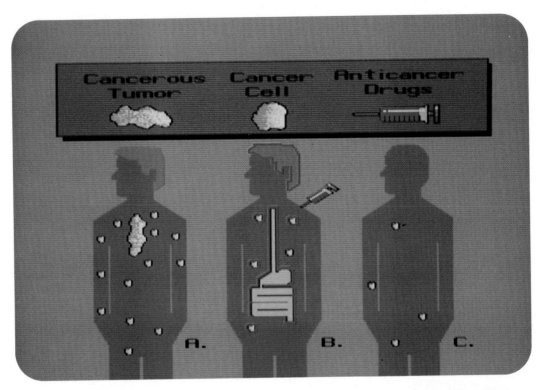

Cancerous Tumor   Cancer Cell   Anticancer Drugs

A.   B.   C.

suggested to scientists a number of ways to zero in on diseased cells and viruses and destroy them. But it was antibodies, and their possible use in combating cancer, to which medical scientists first turned their attention.

One of the first major advances was made in the early 1970's by a Swiss scientist, Jean-Pierre Mach. Mach was studying an antigen that had been isolated from the surface of human colon-cancer cells. He injected the antigen into rabbits, thereby stimulating the animals' immune systems to produce antibodies. Mach then extracted anti-body-rich fluid from the rabbits' blood and injected it into mice in which human colon tumors had been implanted. Soon, the antibodies were swarming over the tumors. Although the mice were not cured, Mach's experiment demonstrated that, in the bodies of living animals, antibodies could distinguish between normal cells and cancer cells and bind to only the cancer cells.

Scientists were confident that antibody therapy could be developed into a powerful weapon against cancer. But before they could proceed toward that goal, they needed a reliable way to produce unlimited numbers of any desired kind of antibody. That need was answered in 1975 when two immunologists in England—Cesar Milstein and Georges Köhler of the Medical Research Council laboratories in Cambridge—devised a method for churning out an endless supply of exact-replica antibodies, called *monoclonal antibodies*.

The Medical Arsenal Needs Magic Bullets

A tumor can be removed surgically, but often cancer cells break loose and travel to other parts of the body, where they start new tumors (A). Anticancer drugs are injected to seek out these fast-growing cancer cells (B). But the drugs also kill fast-growing healthy cells, such as hair and intestinal cells, causing serious side effects. Thus, the drug dose must be limited, and sometimes it is not sufficient to kill all the cancer cells (C). So doctors want something that will kill only cancer cells.

189

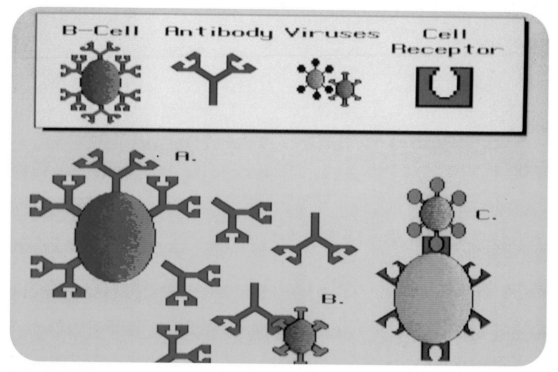

B-Cell   Antibody   Viruses   Cell Receptor

A.

B.

C.

Designing Bullets from Locks and Keys

A biological system of locks and keys allows body cells to interact with foreign invaders such as bacteria and viruses. The body's immune system uses this principle to make its own magic bullets called *antibodies.* These are tailor-made by immune system cells called *B cells* (A) to fit an identifying molecule, called an *antigen,* on a germ or cancer cell (B). Body cells have "doors" called *receptors* that allow hormones and nutrients to enter. But viruses have keys that unlock some of these doors (C), allowing the viruses to slip in.

The production of monoclonal antibodies works like this: An antigen from cancer cells is injected into a mouse, whose B cells then produce antibodies against the foreign molecule. The B cells are removed from the mouse's body and, with the aid of a chemical that causes cells to melt together, are fused with cancerous mouse B cells. Like other cancer cells, those B cells can live and reproduce indefinitely. The fused cells, called *hybridomas,* live and divide endlessly and make the desired antibody. Hybridomas thus are like little factories, spewing out limitless quantities of antibody molecules. They are called *monoclonal* antibodies because they are manufactured by *clones* (multiple exact copies) of a single hybridoma. (Mono comes from the Greek word for *one.*)

As it turned out, making monoclonal antibodies against cancer cells was not quite the straightforward proposition that scientists had expected it to be. Although researchers had assumed that some antigens on cancer cells would be found nowhere else, they soon learned that all cancer-cell antigens also occur on normal cells. Subsequent studies revealed, however, that some antigens are present in greater numbers on cancer cells than on normal cells. Scientists hoped these so-called *tumor-associated antigens* would give them the edge they needed for developing monoclonal antibodies effective against cancer.

In the late 1970's, researchers tested monoclonal antibodies on patients with a variety of advanced cancers, including breast, lung, and colon cancer and leukemia. The monoclonals proved safe but only moderately effective. In most cases, patients experienced only a temporary *remission* of their disease (the complete or partial disappearance of detectable symptoms). Almost invariably, the patients' cancers recurred.

There were several reasons for these disappointing results, as scientists were quick to determine. One reason related to the mechanism by which antibodies help rid the body of invaders. Think of an antibody as a Y-shaped molecule. The "arms" of the Y contain small variations that form the specific key to the antigen lock. The "tail" of the Y is essentially identical in many antibody molecules. Once the arm region of an antibody engages an antigen, it is the tail region that sets up the kill by calling in other elements of the immune system. These "terminators" include various kinds of white blood cells and cell-destroying chemicals. Researchers discovered that while there was no limit to the amount of monoclonal antibodies they could give to people with highly advanced cancers, the patients' immune systems were so weakened that they were incapable of producing a sufficient quantity of cell-killing agents. Thus, the supply of those terminators was rapidly exhausted, and the cancers reappeared.

A second reason for the unsatisfactory results was something called HAMA—short for *h*uman *a*nti-*m*ouse *a*ntibody—which is produced by the patient's body. Monoclonal antibodies, derived as they are from mouse cells, are foreign substances to the human body. As such, they are attacked by the immune system, just as germs are, and cleared from the bloodstream within a week or two. From then on, the immune system is on guard against that monoclonal. The individual is for all intents and purposes permanently "vaccinated" against it, so further doses do no good.

There was yet another problem with monoclonals. The antibodies are designed to track down a specific antigen, but researchers learned that not every cancer cell in a patient's body has the target antigen on its surface. Consequently, cells without the antigen are likely to escape monoclonal antibodies and develop into new tumors that threaten the patient's life.

To overcome these limitations, scientists in the early 1980's began developing a new monoclonal-antibody strategy. Instead of using monoclonals alone, they coupled toxins and *radioisotopes* (radioactive forms of elements) to the antibodies. In this approach, a monoclonal antibody is not so much a bullet as a guided missile carrying a deadly warhead.

Research on toxins has centered on three poisonous proteins. Of those three, the most intensively studied is a substance secreted by the bacterium that causes diphtheria. The other two are ricin, a protein derived from the seed of the castor bean; and a toxin produced by a bacterium called *Pseudomonas aruginosa*. Although these toxins are dissimilar in most respects, they have several important characteristics in common. In the first place, each is astonishingly lethal; just one molecule is often enough to kill a cell. Moreover, they all kill in the same way: by interfering with the manufacture of proteins vital to a cell's survival. The three poisonous proteins also have a similar chainlike structure. One part of the chain contains the "binding site" that allows the toxin to link up with a cell and penetrate its outer membrane. Once inside the cell, another part of the molecule does the killing.

Researchers use these toxins in either of two ways. In some cases, they attach the entire toxin to the monoclonal antibody. Other times, they chemically cut the toxin into its two main parts and hook only the killing fragment onto the antibody. The latter technique is preferred because, with its binding site removed, the toxin is far less likely to enter and destroy normal cells. Which method is used depends on the monoclonal antibody. If the antibody itself can enter the cell, only the killing part of the toxin is needed. If not, researchers must rely on the cell-penetrating power of the complete toxin molecule. Both forms of the toxins are now being tested in cancer patients at several major medical centers in the United States. For example, molecular biologist Ira Pastan and his colleagues at the National Cancer Institute in Bethesda, Md., are treating women suffering from advanced ovarian cancer with a monoclonal antibody carrying the full-bodied pseudomonas toxin. Other experimental human trials are underway elsewhere to test antibody-ricin combinations against colon cancer; melanoma, a frequently fatal skin cancer; and glioma, a deadly tumor of the brain.

But toxin "warheads" have one basic drawback: They are effective only if the monoclonal "missiles" deposit them right on target. With those cancer cells that lack the targeted antigen, that cannot occur. It is for this reason that scientists are looking into using radioactive warheads.

A major advantage of using a radioisotope on a monoclonal is that the antibody does not have to get into a cell to kill it. The radiation itself will penetrate and destroy the cell. More to the point, however, a sufficiently powerful radioisotope will kill not only the cell that the monoclonal has landed on but nearby cells as well. Thus, as long as some of the cells in a small tumor have the targeted antigen on their surface, monoclonals carrying a radioisotope should be able to destroy the entire cell cluster. One drawback to this approach is the possibility that normal cells near the tumor will also be killed. Animal studies with radioactive monoclonals, however, have indicated that the amount of damage caused to normal cells is insignificant.

Human trials with radioisotope-bearing monoclonals are underway at the National Cancer Institute under the direction of immunologist Jeffrey Schlom. Schlom and his associates are also trying to stimulate cancer cells to produce more antigens on their surface to

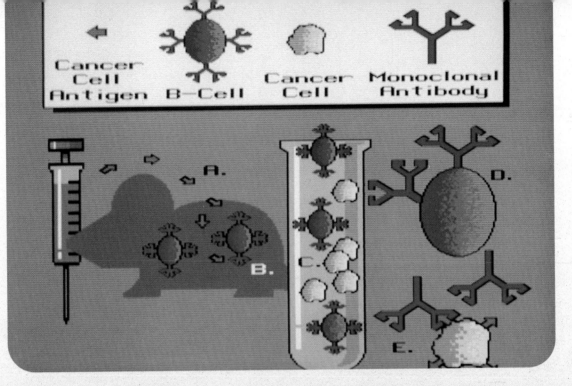

The First Artificial Magic Bullets

Scientists made the first magic bullets by injecting a mouse with antigens from human cancer cells (A). The mouse's B cells made antibodies (B) to fight the antigens. B cells were then fused with rapidly dividing cancer cells (C) to create an antibody "factory." The fused cells (D) produced antibodies called *monoclonal antibodies* (E), to track down the human cancer cell antigens.

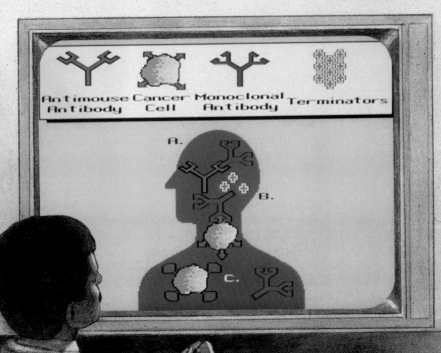

Monoclonal antibodies did not work perfectly. First, the antibodies were from mice, and the body's immune system fought them as it would any invader (A). Second, antibodies call in other elements of the immune system, including so-called killer cells, but in patients weakened by cancer there were not sufficient numbers of these "terminators" (B). And third, some cancer cells did not have the targeted antigen (C), and so they escaped destruction completely.

193

Building Better Bullets

To overcome the shortcomings of monoclonal antibodies, scientists add "warheads" that can destroy cancer cells or viruses.

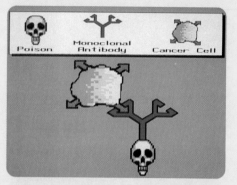

With a poison attached to it, a monoclonal antibody can kill a cancer cell with no help from the immune system's terminators. The poison enters the cell and destroys it.

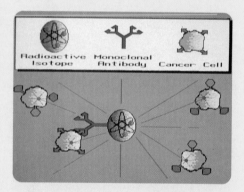

A monoclonal antibody that is linked with a radioactive particle kills not only the cancer cell it attaches to but also nearby cancer cells that lack the targeted antigen.

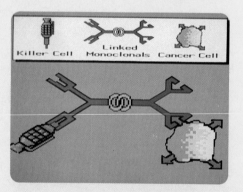

Joining a monoclonal that seeks a cancer antigen with one that attracts a natural killer cell may avoid the problem of putting poisons or radiation in the body.

create a better "bulls-eye" for the monoclonal antibody. The researchers' initial laboratory findings suggest that a natural body substance called interferon will do just that when given to patients in amounts over and above what the body itself produces.

Among magic-bullet researchers, there are some who continue to see merit in using monoclonals without warheads. One such researcher is Ronald Levy, a cancer specialist at the Stanford University Medical Center in California. Levy thinks the key to boosting the tumor-fighting potential of monoclonal antibodies is to direct them not at antigens that merely serve to distinguish cancer cells from normal cells but rather at the surface receptor molecules that may be essential to cancer-cell growth. Levy scored what may be the first long-term cure with monoclonal antibodies in the treatment of a patient suffering from a type of cancer called lymphoma. That patient, treated in 1983 with monoclonals alone after all other therapy had failed, remained alive and cancer-free in 1989.

Levy later had far less success with other patients afflicted with the same form of cancer. In every case, the cancer eventually recurred. Rather than concentrating on the failures, Levy asked himself why his treatment of the first patient was such a success. The answer, he thinks, is that he and his colleagues inadvertently produced a monoclonal antibody that targeted a receptor molecule vital to cancer cell development.

David Segal, a researcher at the National Cancer Institute, is experimenting with an ingenious monoclonal strategy that brings so-called *killer cells* into play. These cells, a type of white blood cell, are one of the terminators of the immune system. Segal and his associates use chemicals that link two different monoclonal antibodies end-to-end by their tails. One antibody seeks out and binds to a receptor on a killer cell; the other, to an antigen on a tumor cell. In this way, the linked antibodies bring cancer cells and killer cells together. The killer cells then release substances that penetrate and destroy the cancer cells. In test-tube studies in 1985, these antibody "bridges" proved highly effective in killing cancer cells.

In animal tests of linked monoclonals, Segal has succeeded in blocking the growth of colon and ovarian tumors. By mid-1989, three human trials had been launched—in the United States, the Netherlands, and Japan.

For all the wonderful inventiveness surrounding monoclonal technology, one major problem remains: HAMA. Because of the immune reaction to the foreign antibodies, researchers essentially have just one shot at a patient's cancer, and one shot is unlikely to be enough. But HAMA may soon be a worry of the past. Scientists think that a new class of monoclonals called *chimeric* antibodies, which are part mouse and part human, may offer a solution.

To create these "humanized" antibodies, scientists make use of gene-splicing techniques developed in the 1970's and 1980's. Using special chemicals that function as "biochemical scissors," the researchers cut apart mouse hybridoma genes. They then separate out the portion of the gene that codes for the part of the antibody that fastens onto the antigen (the arms of the Y). Next, they link that gene fragment to the human gene fragment coding for the tail region shared by many human antibody molecules. Copies of the hybrid mouse-human gene are then inserted into laboratory-grown animal cells, where they take up residence in the cells' own genes. In response to the instructions of the transplanted genes, the cells produce great numbers of the chimeric antibody.

Although the testing of chimeric antibodies was still in its initial stages in 1989, preliminary results have been encouraging. Scientists at Cambridge University in England, for instance, obtained good results with two patients suffering from lymphoma. The patients, both of whose cancers went into remission, were given repeated doses of chimeric monoclonals, with no hint of an immune reaction. Such trials suggest that the chimerics are more effective than regular monoclonals at calling in the immune system's cell-killing agents.

Scientists are now experimenting with new forms of antibodies. Among the latest developments is a molecule containing little more than the antigen-binding region of the arms. This bare-bones monoclonal, connected to a toxin or radioisotope, kills target cells more quickly.

Gene-splicing technology has also sparked a growing interest in molecules other than antibodies as possible magic bullets. In one promising avenue of investigation, researchers isolate the gene coding for the cell receptor (a protein) that a particular virus uses to enter the cell. They then join the cell receptor gene to a gene coding for a toxic protein. Inserted into animal cells, the linked genes manufacture a fused protein consisting of a cell receptor linked to a poison molecule. This fused protein is essentially a molecular booby trap. In some cases, the targeted virus "mistakes" the free-floating receptor as the door to a cell, hooks up with it, and is destroyed by the poison.

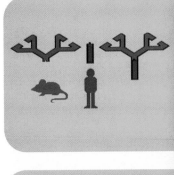

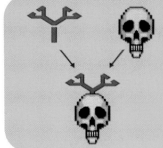

New "Missiles"
To avoid being thwarted by the body's immune system, better delivery systems are being developed. One, *top,* is a monoclonal antibody with mouse "arms" but a human "tail" that is less likely to set off an immune response in the patient's body. Another, *above,* consists of just the part of the antibody that fastens to the antigen, linked with a poisonous molecule. This streamlined antibody is designed to kill target cells faster than a regular monoclonal antibody.

Most fused proteins, however, work by destroying cells that the virus has infected. Those cells produce viral antigens on their surface. The receptor part of the fused protein hooks onto the antigen, and the toxin then enters the cell and kills it. The virus, which can reproduce itself only with the "machinery" of a living cell, is thus prevented from spreading its infection.

In 1989, the fused-protein strategy was being tested against the AIDS virus by scientists at the National Cancer Institute and the National Institute of Allergy and Infectious Diseases in Bethesda. The AIDS virus infects white blood cells called *helper T cells*, which stimulate B cells to produce antibodies. Helper T cells have a receptor molecule known as CD4 on their surface; it is by way of CD4 that the AIDS virus enters the cell. The researchers fused a CD4 receptor to the pseudomonas toxin and produced a fused protein that in test-tube studies has been effective in killing cells that the virus has invaded.

In 1989, researchers at the National Cancer Institute and Genentech, Incorporated, a biotechnology company in California, reported an even newer wrinkle in the making of an anti-AIDS CD4 molecule. Their innovation was a genetically engineered fusion protein called an *immunoadhesion*. It consists of a portion of the CD4 cell receptor

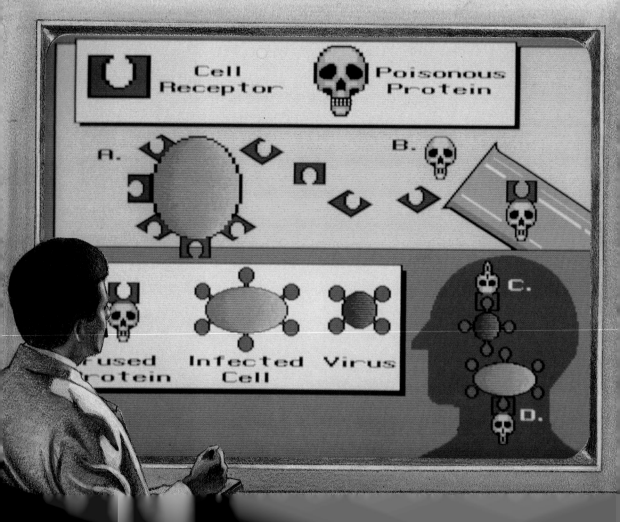

coupled to the tail of a human antibody. The receptor portion of the molecule attracts the virus, while the antibody part calls in the killing agents of the immune system.

Whether either of these fusion proteins will block the AIDS virus in patients remains to be seen; human trials will not begin for some time. But even if the strategy of using engineered cell receptors does not work against the AIDS virus, it may be effective against some other viruses. Scientists at Columbia University in New York City reported in March 1989 that they had identified a cell receptor that the polio virus uses to invade cells. At the same time, researchers in the United States and West Germany announced the discovery of a cell receptor used by rhinoviruses, the cause of many colds. So scientists are now looking into the possibility of developing engineered receptors that might one day provide cures for many illnesses—even the common cold.

There seems to be no end to these new search-and-destroy strategies against human disease. One of the more imaginative ideas, now in the earliest stage of development, involves a so-called Trojan-horse gene (named for the legendary wooden horse filled with soldiers that the ancient Greeks used to infiltrate and bring down the city of Troy). The Trojan-horse gene would code for a cell-destroying toxin. It would be administered to cancer patients— probably as part of a harmless virus—and would infiltrate cells throughout the body. The gene would be rigged with a "detonator," a genetic switch activated by specific proteins that are found only in cancer cells. Inside a cancer cell—but not a normal cell—the gene's toxin would be produced and the cell would be destroyed.

For now, Trojan-horse genes represent the cutting edge of magic-bullet research. And in fact, all forms of cell-targeted therapy are still entirely experimental. Further study is required to establish whether such therapy, in whatever guise, is effective and safe. But most medical researchers are optimistic. They say that as a result of anything but magic—by virtue of scientific ingenuity, hard-won knowledge about the immune system, laborious laboratory testing, and painstaking clinical evaluation—magic bullets will before too long become a prominent part of the modern medical arsenal.

For further reading:

American Cancer Society. *The American Cancer Society Cancer Book*. Doubleday, 1986.

Mizel, Steven B., and Jaret, Peter. *The Human Immune System: The New Frontier in Medicine*. Simon & Schuster, 1986.

Potts, Eva, and Morra, Marion. *Understanding Your Immune System*. Avon, 1986.

During the 50 years since television broadcasts began, researchers have been striving to produce better-quality TV pictures, and their newest effort is high-definition TV.

The Endless Quest for a Better TV Picture

BY WILLIAM J. HAWKINS

You enter your living room, sit back on the couch, click on the television set, and relax. In a moment, the screen on the wall in front of you comes alive with vivid, dazzling pictures, comparable in color and detail to films shown in movie theaters.

You are not watching a film, however. Rather, you are watching *high-definition television* (HDTV), the television of the future. Researchers believe that HDTV sets will be available to United States consumers by the mid-1990's.

HDTV represents the latest in a series of remarkable improvements in television images that have been made since the first successful TV system was built more than 60 years ago in an attic laboratory in London, England. There, on Oct. 25, 1925, humming electric motors spun large cardboard disks in front of the face of a ventriloquist's dummy named Bill. In the next room, 37-year-old John Logie Baird stared at a piece of glass a few centimeters high, looking for any image resembling the dummy's wooden face.

The disks were part of a crude TV camera that took Baird two years to build out of an old tea chest, a cake tin, scrap electrical equipment, knitting needles, a bicycle headlight, wires, string, and sealing wax. The disks contained a set of holes in a spiral pattern. Light reflected from Bill's face passed through the holes, emerging as what looked like a succession of lines, each made up of points of light

Opposite page: High-definition television (HDTV) promises to deliver supersharp images in the 1990's, as previewed in a telecast of a ceremony at the 1988 Olympic Games. HDTV would replace a system that has kept picture quality largely unchanged for four decades of a TV boom that has generated such hits as, *top to bottom,* "The Honeymooners" (1950's), "Bonanza" (1960's), "M*A*S*H" (1970's), and "The Cosby Show" (1980's).

like a row of tiny spotlights. The points of light struck a device that produced an electric current whose intensity varied with the brightness of each point. The current traveled over wire to the receiver that Baird was watching.

On the receiving end, the changing current varied the brightness of a light mounted behind a similar set of spinning disks, which were synchronized with the disks in Baird's "camera." As a result, a beam of light came through the holes in the receiving disks as a series of individual points, with the brightness of each point matching that of the corresponding point of light reflected from Bill's face.

The points of light illuminated the screen to form a succession of lines that produced a recognizable picture of Bill's face. And this is still the way all TV images are produced—as a series of horizontal lines.

Baird's picture, however, flickered because the disks could scan a scene only 10 times per second. And the image was fuzzy because the disks could separate the picture into only 30 lines.

Flicker and *low definition* (fuzziness) have remained serious problems for TV designers. Baird knew that flicker could be reduced by increasing the number of times a scene was scanned each second. Definition could be improved by increasing the number of lines used to "paint" the picture. Baird learned after many more years of work, however, that his mechanical system would never have the potential to produce a steady, detailed picture.

The first electronic TV

Meanwhile, in the United States, Russian-born physicist and electronics engineer Vladimir K. Zworykin was developing a nonmechanical TV system. Zworykin built a TV camera and a receiver based on a device called an *oscilloscope* that was used to display "pictures" of voltages. The main part of his oscilloscope was a large *vacuum tube*, a glass vessel from which most of the air had been pumped out. Inside one end of this tube was an *electron gun*, which fired a steady beam of electrons at a flat, circular surface at the other end. Covering the inside of that surface were thousands of tiny dots, each composed of a *phosphor*, a substance that glowed when struck by the electron beam.

Around the neck of the tube were two coils of wire that produced magnetic fields when electric currents flowed through them. One field guided the beam repeatedly from left to right. The other field, whose current was caused by the voltage being "pictured," moved the beam up and down. So, for example, if this voltage changed steadily to produce alternating current, the screen would show wavy lines.

Zworykin adapted the oscilloscope for use as a TV camera by replacing the phosphors with a metal plate and changing the operation of the coil that moved the beam up and down. The plate held a mica sheet coated with hundreds of thousands of drops of silver. In front of this silver sheet, he mounted a lens to capture light

The author:
William J. Hawkins is senior electronics editor of *Popular Science* magazine.

More Lines, Better Pictures

TV screen

Scan lines

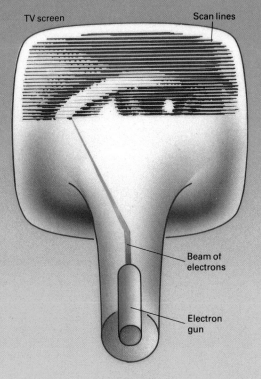

Beam of electrons

Electron gun

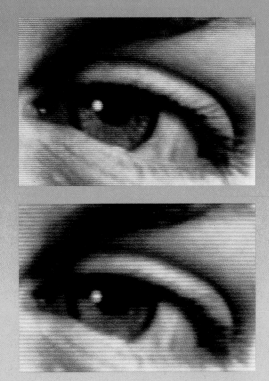

from a scene. Light reflected from the scene struck the silver drops. In each drop, the light created an electric charge whose voltage depended on how bright the light was. This broke up the light entering the lens into separate *pixels* (picture elements), equivalent to Baird's points of light.

The electron gun at the back of Zworykin's camera emitted a narrow beam of electrons that struck the silver layer. As in an oscilloscope, one coil produced a magnetic field that guided the electron beam from left to right; the other coil's field steered the beam down to the bottom of the screen, then shifted it back to the top. Zworykin's camera broke the picture up into 120 horizontal lines, compared with 30 lines for Baird's—and therefore improved definition considerably.

As the electron beam struck each silver drop, the silver discharged its voltage to the metal plate. The sequence of voltages represented the image. To broadcast the image, Zworykin borrowed techniques from the radio industry. Electronic devices translated the voltages so that a transmitter could broadcast a representation of the image into the air as radio waves.

An antenna picked up the waves and a receiver translated them back into voltages. These voltages went to another Zworykin adaptation of the oscilloscope, a TV picture tube.

This tube also had an electron gun, two wire coils, and a flat surface coated with phosphors. Zworykin set the scanning rate of the electron

The sharpness of a television image depends upon the number of lines that an electron beam in the picture tube, *above left,* uses to "paint" the image. The beam scans across the back of the TV screen, lighting up individual dots to create a picture line by line. The more lines used to make the image, the sharper the picture. A picture produced by a high-definition TV set that uses 1,125 scan lines, *top right,* is much sharper than a picture produced by a standard set, *above,* which uses only 525 scan lines.

The Quest for a Better Picture

The quality of a TV picture depends on three basic elements: the number of lines used to create the image; the number of times all the lines are displayed on the screen per second; and the range, or *bandwidth,* of radio waves available to transmit this information on a particular TV channel. The wider the bandwidth, the more information the channel can carry.

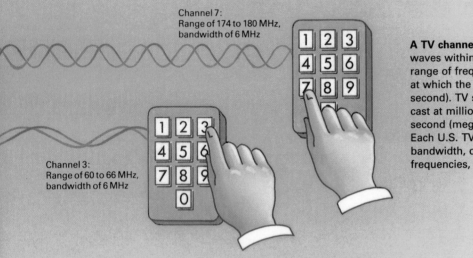

Channel 7:
Range of 174 to 180 MHz,
bandwidth of 6 MHz

Channel 3:
Range of 60 to 66 MHz,
bandwidth of 6 MHz

A TV channel consists of radio waves within a particular range of frequencies (the rates at which the waves vibrate per second). TV signals are broadcast at millions of cycles per second (megahertz [MHz]). Each U.S. TV channel has a bandwidth, or range of frequencies, that covers 6 MHz.

gun in the picture tube to match that of the electron gun in the camera. The incoming voltages varied the intensity of the electron beam as it scanned the face of the tube, thereby reconstructing the picture line by line. In 1929, Zworykin demonstrated the first all-electronic TV system, which still serves as the basis of TV.

Preparing for the TV industry

Television designers in the late 1920's and early 1930's were eager to improve picture definition by increasing the number of scan lines. But how many lines should be used? To promote the establishment of a television industry, potential TV broadcasters and manufacturers of TV equipment sought government approval of scanning standards that all segments of this new industry would have to follow.

The government agency responsible for the approval of such standards was the Federal Communications Commission (FCC), which was established in 1934. The FCC believed that it might limit TV's technical growth by deciding on a scanning standard too early. So, instead, it set a standard for the radio waves that carried the picture information and the accompanying sound. The FCC stated this standard in terms of wave *frequency*, the number of times a wave vibrates each second. The unit of measure for TV waves is the *megahertz*, and 1 megahertz equals 1 million vibrations per second. The FCC selected a range of frequencies for TV and divided these frequencies into *channels*. Each channel had a *bandwidth*, or frequency range, of 6 megahertz.

Standard television programs are each carried by a single channel. The channel selector sorts one channel from all those broadcast to the TV set. The image is constructed of 525 lines scanned in two stages. In 1/60 of a second, the electron beam scans all the odd-numbered lines, such as 1, 3, and 5. In the next 1/60 of a second, it scans all the even-numbered lines.

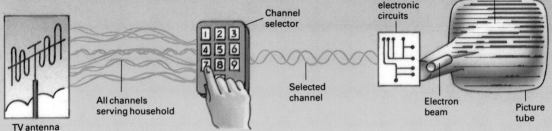

Scanning 525 lines in two stages of 1/60 second each

Standard electronic circuits

Channel selector

All channels serving household

Selected channel

TV antenna

Electron beam

Picture tube

Improved-definition television (IDTV) also receives programs from a single channel, but creates the entire 525-line image in 1/60 of a second. Computer chips instantaneously store and combine the information about odd- and even-numbered lines. IDTV, as a result, produces a sharper image with less flicker.

Scanning 525 lines in 1/60 of a second

Computer chips

High-definition TV (HDTV) might require programs to be broadcast over two channels. A standard channel would carry information for creating a 525-line picture, *below left.* Computer chips in an HDTV set would combine this with data broadcast over another channel, *below center,* to produce a very sharp image, *below right,* of 1,050 lines scanned in 1/60 of a second.

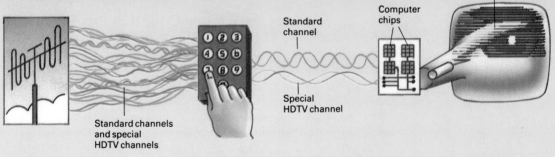

Scanning 1,050 lines in 1/60 of a second

Computer chips

Standard channel

Standard channels and special HDTV channels

Special HDTV channel

The National Broadcasting Company (NBC) began regular TV broadcasts on April 30, 1939, the day on which the owner of NBC, the Radio Corporation of America (RCA), opened its pavilion at the New York World's Fair. These broadcasts transmitted a 441-line picture. The broadcasts continued until July 1940, when the FCC selected a new range of frequencies to make way for sending the audio portion of the show via frequency modulation (FM), rather than amplitude modulation (AM). This change caused havoc in the budding TV industry.

U.S. standard of 525 lines set

On May 1, 1941, the FCC finally adopted a scanning standard that called for 525 lines. The 525-line system, which is still in use in the United States, is called an *interlaced* scanning system. A complete picture—a *frame*—is displayed in two separate scanning cycles called *fields*. The first field, shown in $\frac{1}{60}$ of a second, contains the odd-numbered lines such as 1, 3, and 5 that "paint" the picture on the screen. In the next $\frac{1}{60}$ of a second, the electron gun shifts back to the top and scans the even-numbered lines. Normally, not all 525 lines appear on the screen. For example, about 30 lines are invisible because the beam shifts from the bottom to the top during the time they would be scanned.

Scanning a frame in two fields minimizes flickering of the picture on the screen. And because both $\frac{1}{60}$-second fields are displayed within $\frac{1}{30}$ of a second, the brain puts the two together as one scene.

Commercial broadcasting begins

On July 1, 1941, the FCC granted broadcasters permission to use commercials to help pay costs. NBC and the Columbia Broadcasting System (CBS) soon began regular commercial broadcasts in New York City.

The United States entry into World War II in December 1941 delayed the commercial growth of TV, but broadcasting continued. In fact, CBS aired one of the most notable of the early shows that same month—a documentary on Japan's attack on Pearl Harbor. And the year 1943 saw the first musical comedy written for television, *The Boys from Boise.*

The manufacture of commercial TV equipment, however, ended almost entirely in 1942. But technical improvements in the laboratory continued at a more rapid pace because government officials thought television might have military uses. During the war, engineers developed new types of phosphors for TV picture tubes that greatly improved brightness and contrast. Clearer glass tubes helped to increase picture clarity.

After World War II ended in 1945, television stations sprang up throughout the United States. The year 1951 saw the first coast-to-coast telecast. A TV boom was underway.

But the TV image still differed from the scene being telecast in one significant aspect: The image lacked color. Since the late 1930's, researchers had experimented extensively with color-TV systems. In December 1953, the FCC paved the way for color broadcasting by establishing a standard, and in 1954 color sets went on sale in the United States.

In the color system, the light coming from the scene being photographed is broken into three colors—red, blue, and green—and the three colors are directed to three tubes inside the camera. The three signals are transmitted in such a way that they can be received on standard black-and-white as well as color sets.

The picture tube of a color TV set has three electron guns—one for each color. For every phosphor dot that would be on a black-and-white screen, the color screen has a set of three dots—one red, one blue, and one green. The three electron beams scan the screen in unison, each one striking the appropriate color dot.

Transistors enter the picture

The next improvement in both color and black-and-white TV pictures came in the 1960's, when small devices called *transistors* replaced the vacuum tubes in television sets. The most obvious immediate impact of transistors was a reduction in the size of TV sets. Vacuum tubes were almost as big as a light bulb. A typical cylindrical transistor measured only about 3 millimeters (⅛ inch) in both diameter and height. Furthermore, the transistors consumed so little electricity that a TV set could be battery powered. By the 1970's, TV's appeared in the backyard, on boats, and on the beach.

But an even greater influence on TV technology was on the way. Beginning in the late 1950's, researchers built transistors and other electronic components into a sliver of germanium—later, silicon—so that the sliver served as both a mounting for the components and all the electrical connections between them. The original devices contained fewer than 10 components—but these electronic chips evolved with breathtaking speed. By the early 1970's, a silicon chip no larger than a fingernail held 100 to 10,000 components.

A few chips soon replaced hundreds of separate TV components. The size of the TV shrank even further. Along with another development, the liquid-crystal display (LCD), the chip gave rise in the mid-1980's to handheld TV's with screens as small as 5 centimeters (2 inches).

A tiny LCD TV screen is made up of liquid crystals sandwiched between two layers of polarized glass, each layer acting as a filter by allowing light waves vibrating in only one direction to pass through. Light passing through the first layer must be twisted 90 degrees by the crystals to pass through the second layer. Whether the crystals twist the light depends on the presence or absence of voltages. The individual voltages regulate the passage of light through more than 50,000 points in an LCD.

The Evolving Television Image

Television pictures have improved tremendously in the 60 years since the invention of the all-electronic TV set. Small, flickering images rendered in black and white gave way to colorful, lifelike displays on ever-larger screens. And the future promises even more wonders—from supersharp high-definition TV to 3-D images.

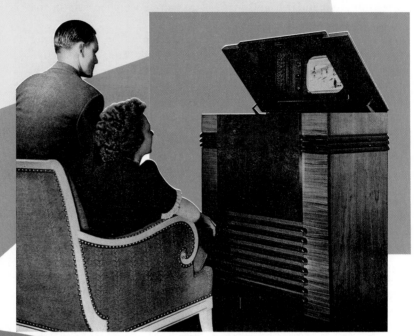

1939
Regular television broadcasts begin in the United States, received on black-and-white sets, some with a reflecting mirror.

1929
The first all-electronic television system is demonstrated, with picture scanned on a tiny round screen in 120 lines.

1954
The first commercial color TV sets go on sale in the United States.

1988
Computer chips provide such features as a picture-in-picture and very clear improved-definition images.

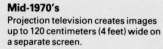

1984
Pocket-sized TV's replace the picture tube with liquid crystal displays.

Mid-1990's?
High-definition TV displaying supersharp images.

Late 1990's? Early 2000's?
Three-dimensional TV images.

Mid-1970's
Projection television creates images up to 120 centimeters (4 feet) wide on a separate screen.

At the same time that teams of designers worked to make the picture smaller, other researchers labored to make it bigger—much bigger. They created new picture tubes with superbright phosphors, lenses, and an assortment of reflective screens, and in the mid-1970's came up with a projection-TV system that displayed a picture that was at least 1.2 meters (4 feet) wide. But projection TV produced relatively fuzzy images.

Computer chips make a better picture

Meanwhile, researchers were experimenting with silicon chips to improve picture quality. Two types of chips had already begun to revolutionize computers. *Memory chips* stored information, while *microprocessors* performed arithmetical and logical operations.

The key to the computerization of TV is the chip's digital circuitry, which converts each pixel into a series of *binary digits*, or *bits*—0's and 1's. For example, a blue dot on the screen might be represented by the number 10011001. By converting the picture into bits—the "alphabet" of computers—digital circuitry enables memory chips and microprocessors to store and vary the picture.

Some new TV sets can store an entire picture field—2.5 million pieces of data—in a single memory chip. A microprocessor can then instruct the electron guns to display the captured color picture as a still image as long as the viewer wishes. Some sets can even display two shows at once, with one moving image shrunk and displayed in the corner of another.

Computer chips can also process the fields to clean up the image. For example, they can remove electrical interference created by a passing car.

Using microprocessors to store a field in memory has given rise to a new breed of TV called *improved definition television* (IDTV). An IDTV set first stores a field, then displays it along with the next one at twice the normal speed. In this way, it displays a complete 525-line frame every $\frac{1}{60}$ of a second, increasing detail and reducing flicker.

High-definition television

IDTV sets went on sale in the United States in 1988. But many experts consider IDTV to be merely a way station on the road to HDTV. Several organizations, such as the David Sarnoff Research Center of Princeton, N.J. (working for RCA and NBC), and Zenith Electronics Corporation of Glenview, Ill., have already developed proposed HDTV standards. Proposals for scan lines range from a low of about 650 lines (usually referred to as *enhanced definition*) to a high of 1,250 lines.

Some of these proposals would require the FCC to reassign broadcast frequencies. Researchers have succeeded in squeezing 650-line broadcasts into 6-megahertz bandwidths. Proposed 1,250-line systems, however, would require more than 6 megahertz, and so each TV station would use at least part of a second channel. Each channel would carry part of the image, and the parts would be put together electronically inside the HDTV set.

Once again, all eyes are on the FCC, whose decision about broadcast standards will affect the future of television viewing in the United States—and perhaps the future of the U.S. television industry. Foreign corporations, particularly Japanese firms, are further along in the development of HDTV than are U.S. companies. Many industry and government officials in the United States fear that unless the FCC decides on a system developed by one or more American-owned companies, all future HDTV development, manufacturing, and sales in the United States—with an annual potential of about $10 billion by the year 2010—will be lost to foreign firms.

So far, the FCC has ruled that a future HDTV system must not make present TV sets obsolete. The commission is scheduled to select a complete standard for HDTV by 1991. By 1995, high-definition television sets may be available in the United States.

By that time, other video marvels may be on the scene as well. One might be an outgrowth of liquid-crystal displays. The small flat LCD screens of today may give rise to large flat screens that hang on the wall like a picture.

Liquid crystals might also be used to help produce the illusion of a three-dimensional (3-D) TV image on a conventional television screen. Two cameras, separated by the same distance as human eyes, would shoot the same scene. On the TV screen, the left- and right-eye pictures would appear alternately as the two fields.

The viewer would wear glasses whose "lenses" would actually be liquid crystal panels that alternate between being clear and opaque. A remote-control device containing a computer chip would synchronize the glasses with the display so that the panels would allow each field to pass to the correct eye. The switching would be so rapid that the viewer's brain would combine the two fields as if the eyes were seeing both images at once, producing a 3-D effect. For the far future, researchers are experimenting with holographic displays, which require no screen at all. A hologram has three dimensions—you can actually walk around and view it from the front and the sides.

Perhaps one day a racing car will appear to scream through your living room. A Broadway star may seem to dance across your floor. Or your couch may appear to hold rival presidential candidates engaged in a lively discussion of the issues.

Impossible? Get the popcorn ready.

For further reading:

Douglas, Susan J. *Inventing American Broadcasting*. 1899-1922. Johns Hopkins University Press, 1987.

Friedman, Jeffrey B., ed. *Television Technology: A Look Toward the 21st Century*. Society of Motion Picture & Television Engineers, 1987.

———*Television Technology in Transition*. Society of Motion Picture & Television Engineers, 1988.

Science File

Science Year contributors report on the year's major developments in their respective fields. The articles in this section are arranged alphabetically.

Agriculture
Effects of drought
Crop and livestock research

Anthropology
Prehuman development
Ancient human beings
   and their behavior

Archaeology, New World
Excavations in North and
   South America
Close-Up:
   Ancient Peruvian tomb

Archaeology, Old World
Excavations in Africa, Asia,
   and Europe
Close-Up:
   Shroud of Turin dated

Astronomy, Extragalactic
Other galaxies
The universe

Astronomy, Galactic
Center of the Milky Way
Unusual stars
Other solar systems

Astronomy, Solar System
The planets and their moons

Books of Science

Botany
Plant research
Close-Up:
   Endangered plants

Chemistry
Biochemicals
Synthetic molecules

Computer Hardware
Computer chips
New computers, printers,
   and scanners

Computer Software
Hypermedia
New computer programs

Deaths of Scientists

Dentistry
Tooth repair
Oral hygiene
Gum disease

Drugs
Drug reactions
New medicines
Chemotherapy

Ecology
Greenhouse effect
Wildlife communities

Electronics
New cameras
Video technology

Energy
Alternative energy systems
Nuclear energy

Environment
Oil spills
Ozone hole
Toxic chemical pollutants
Close-Up:
   Yellowstone fires

Genetics
Human-gene mapping
Genetic engineering
Disease-causing genes

Geology
Ice ages
Earth-forming forces
Close-Up:
   Earthquake in Armenia

Immunolgy
Immune system research

Materials Science
New alloys
Computer chip materials
Close-Up:
   Microscopic motors

Medical research
New surgical techniques
Disease research
Preventive medicine

Meteorology
Drought and storms
Weather prediction

Neuroscience
Brain research
Nervous system disorders
Chemical messengers

Nobel Prizes

Nutrition
Vitamins and minerals
Surgeon general's report
   on nutrition

Oceanography
Ocean currents and
   temperatures
Deep-sea drilling
Ancient seas

Paleontology
Dinosaurs
Fossils

Physics, Fluids and Solids
Superconductors
Close-Up:
   Roller-coaster physics

Physics, Subatomic
Elementary particles
Close-Up:
   Cold fusion

Psychology
Emotions and disease
Animal and human
   intelligence
Behavior

Public Health
Trends in AIDS cases
Disease surveillance

Science Education
Educational statistics
Educational reform efforts

Science Student Awards

Space Technology
Space shuttles
Interplanetary spacecraft
Space stations

Zoology
Studies of animals

Agriculture

Drought conditions that seriously affected crops in much of the United States in 1988 persisted through the winter and spring of 1989. Agricultural officials said the driest conditions were in the nation's major wheat-growing regions in the upper Midwest. As a result, the 1989 harvest of winter wheat, which accounts for about 75 per cent of the U.S. wheat crop, was expected to be down 8 per cent from the previous year.

Drought was also severe in early 1989 in south Texas and parts of California. The Eastern United States, for the most part, got adequate rain during the first part of the year. See METEOROLOGY.

The 1988 drought greatly reduced harvests of several crops, including spring wheat, down 54 per cent from 1987; soybeans, down 21 per cent; oats, down 44 per cent; and corn, which fell by 34 per cent.

Drought resistance. The harsh 1988 drought focused attention on research aimed at increasing crop production to feed Earth's ever-growing population.

Some research was aimed at helping regions, such as Africa, where drought is a constant threat.

In a breakthrough that could help reduce crop failure and famine in developing nations, Purdue University researchers reported in March 1989 that they had grown a mature Indica rice plant from a single cell. Indica rice is grown in the tropics, where floods, droughts, and insect plagues frequently imperil crops. The ability to grow a rice plant from a single cell may enable scientists to introduce useful new genes into the nucleus of the cell. These genes may give the rice plant resistance to drought and insect pests.

Aflatoxin. The drought also focused attention on a potentially serious food problem: contaminated corn. U.S. agricultural scientists reported in early 1989 that amounts of *aflatoxin*, a cancer-causing substance produced by a fungus that infects corn and several other grain crops, had risen to possibly hazardous levels in portions of the 1988 corn crop. The increase was due to the drought, which caused acceler-

A solar-powered microchip may help scientists track the movements of so-called killer bees. The aggressive bees have been heading northward for years and may invade the United States from Mexico by late 1989. Shown here glued to the midsection of a regular honey bee, the chip transmits an infrared signal that can be received up to 1.6 kilometers (1 mile) away. The chip was developed by researchers at the Oak Ridge National Laboratory in Tennessee.

ated growth of the fungus on corn.

One-third of the corn samples tested by state and federal inspectors in Illinois and Iowa in early 1989 were found to contain dangerous levels of aflatoxin; lesser amounts of contamination were found in corn in five other Midwestern states. The U.S. Food and Drug Administration (FDA) tried to prevent aflatoxin-tainted corn from being shipped between states, but its efforts were spotty because of a shortage of inspectors.

In many cases, aflatoxin was detected by private food companies and prevented from reaching consumers. For example, dairies in several states dumped milk from corn-fed cows that was found to contain aflatoxin. A number of food-processing companies rejected shipments of tainted corn.

The FDA tried to calm public fears about aflatoxin. FDA officials repeatedly asserted that whatever contaminated grain escaped detection by inspectors was likely to be greatly diluted as it made its way through the food system and was mixed with grain free of aflatoxin. They assured consumers that it posed no serious health risk. Many food safety experts disputed that view, however.

Alar in apples. The public also became concerned in 1989 about residues of pesticides and other agricultural chemicals in food. One of the biggest controversies erupted in February, when the U.S. Environmental Protection Agency (EPA) reported that apples treated with Alar—the trade name for a chemical called daminozide—were unsafe for human consumption.

Alar is used on at least 5 per cent of the U.S. apple crop, primarily to increase the reddening of varieties such as Jonathan, McIntosh, and Delicious. The EPA estimated, based on studies with laboratory animals, that Alar residues on apples could produce 9 cancers per 1 million consumers over a 70-year period.

Later in the month, a study more favorable to Alar was reported by a national food-processing trade group. In that study, tests of 4,623 samples of apples and apple products found only traces of the chemical ranging from 1.0 to 1.3 parts per million (ppm). Those levels were far less than the 20 ppm allowed by the EPA. The U.S. Department of Agriculture (USDA) said the findings indicated that eating apples and apple products presented no danger to consumers' health.

Nonetheless, apple sales throughout the spring were down by about 20 per cent. In May, officials of the U.S. apple industry said growers would cease using Alar by fall. And in June, the maker of Alar, Uniroyal Chemical Company, Incorporated, said it would stop selling Alar in the United States until further notice.

Pesticide-free apples. Agricultural scientists in mid-1988 made progress toward developing pesticide-free apples with the introduction of three disease-resistant apple varieties. The varieties—William's Pride, Dayton, and McShay—were produced with traditional plant-breeding techniques in a cooperative program between Purdue University in Indiana, the University of Illinois, and Rutgers University in New Jersey. The apples are resistant to a common disease called apple scab, which is caused by a fungus.

Clue to poultry disease. A shortage of oxygen is apparently the cause of *ascites*, a disease afflicting chickens, a Texas researcher reported in summer 1988. Ascites (pronounced *uh SIGH teez*) is a disorder of the heart and lungs in chickens that causes a build-up of fluids in the abdomen. The disease is becoming increasingly common in the United States, killing thousands of chickens in commercial poultry operations every year.

Ascites has long been a problem for poultry producers in mountainous regions, such as parts of Mexico and South America. Because the air is thinner in such areas, agricultural officials wondered if ascites might result from too little oxygen.

To test that hypothesis, Don Witzel, a veterinary physiologist with the U.S. Agricultural Research Service in College Station, Tex., raised groups of chicks in chambers in which the oxygen content of the air could be controlled. The chambers simulated altitudes of up to 2,900 meters (9,500 feet) above sea level.

The results of the experiment were striking. Some chicks in each group developed ascites, but the incidence of

A U.S. Agricultural Research Service microbiologist gives a chick a dose of a natural sugar that blocks the growth of salmonella bacteria in the bird's intestines. The bacteria are a common cause of food poisoning in people, and many cases result from tainted poultry. The sugar treatment may offer a way to reduce the incidence of salmonella poisoning.

the disease was highest in the group that had breathed the thinnest air.

Witzel said he planned next to look for reasons why commercially raised poultry might be getting too little oxygen. He said the improper heating and ventilation of cages were likely factors.

Weed seeds that get mixed in with some grain shipments may not be a health hazard, but their effects on human health need more study. That conclusion was reported in March 1989 by scientists at the USDA's Food Safety Research Unit in Albany, Calif.

Seeds from a number of weeds can be harmful if eaten in quantity. When weeds are allowed to infest a field of grain, they get harvested along with the crop, and their seeds get mixed in with the grain kernels.

The higher the proportion of seeds, the lower the quality rating of the grain, and, if there are a great many seeds, the grain shipment is usually rejected by most U.S. grain purchasers. Such grain is normally exported, but the purchasers, particularly in Europe and Japan, have complained about the seeds and questioned the safety of eating the grain.

In response to such concerns, the USDA scientists tested the effects of several kinds of weed seeds on rats. They mixed varying amounts of seeds with the rats' food for 90 days. At the end of that time, the researchers examined the rats' body organs for evidence of tissue damage.

The results of the study were still being assessed in mid-1989, though according to a preliminary report on one seed—jimsonweed seed—no organ damage was found in the rats. The final report was expected in late 1989. The USDA will use the report's conclusions to set acceptable levels of seeds in grain for both domestic consumption and export.

New source of vegetable oil. Canola, a member of the turnip family, was attracting considerable attention in the United States in 1989 as a source of cooking oil. Canola is low in saturated fats, the kind of fats linked to heart disease. As a result, the food industry was expressing considerable interest in using canola oil.　　　[Steve Cain and Victor L. Lechtenberg]

In WORLD BOOK, see AGRICULTURE.

Anthropology

A question that has puzzled anthropologists for years—whether the uniquely human habit of *bipedalism* (walking upright on two limbs) developed suddenly among our ancient ancestors or occurred gradually over time—received new attention in September 1988. Anthropologist William L. Jungers of State University of New York (SUNY) at Stony Brook reported evidence that *australopithecines*, humanlike creatures who lived between 1 million and 4 million years ago, probably moved in a manner similar to both human beings and apes, suggesting that bipedalism was a gradual development in early human beings.

Jungers compared the hip and leg joints of modern people with the hip and leg joints of apes. He noted that in human beings these joints are exceptionally large relative to body size. This is because they bear all of the body's weight when a person is standing. In apes, however, the leg and hip joints are smaller because apes also use their forelimbs for support.

Jungers then examined the hip and leg joints of an australopithecine skeleton nicknamed Lucy and found that its joints display both humanlike and apelike characteristics. Jungers concluded that Lucy's physical development—as well as that of other australopithecines—falls somewhere between human beings and apes. While australopithecines may have walked in an upright manner, their gait was probably far different from the upright movement exhibited by modern human beings.

Ancient forearm. The belief that robust australopithecines were anatomically capable of making and using tools was supported at the April 1989 meeting of the American Association of Physical Anthroplogists in San Diego. Anthropologists at SUNY at Stony Brook, reported that the complete right *radius* (a bone of the forearm) from a smaller type of australopithecine that did not develop into modern human beings had ape and human characteristics. The scientists reconstructed the radius from bone fragments found at the Swartkrans site, near Johannesburg, South Africa.

The elbow end of the reconstructed radius from this australopithecine has a mushroom shape and a shallow rim similar to the radius found in apes. The shaft and wrist end of the bone, however, are clearly more humanlike, the scientists noted. Hand bones recovered at Swartkrans suggest that this australopithecine also had humanlike fingers capable of making and using tools like modern human beings.

Peking man site protected. The Chinese capital of Beijing (Peking) in early 1989 issued regulations that put the archaeological site of Zhoukoudian, located outside the city, under its protection. It was at Zhoukoudian that archaeologists in 1927 found the fossil remains of the famous *Homo erectus* called "Peking man." Between 1927 and 1937, the remains of more than 40 individuals dating from 250,000 to 500,000 years ago were found at the site. These disappeared during World War II (1939-1945), but the site is still a valuable resource for understanding human origins. The new regulations prohibit activities that could destroy the features and ecology of the land.

Israeli site grows older. Human fossils found at the cave site of Skhul, near Haifa, Israel, are actually 81,000 to 100,000 years old, thousands of years older than scientists had previously believed. Using a dating technique known as *electron spin resonance* (ESR), anthropologist Christopher B. Stringer and his co-workers at the British Museum in London came to this conclusion and reported it in April 1989. This discovery makes Skhul nearly the same age as Qafzeh, an Israeli cave site near Nazareth. It gives support to the theory that modern human beings inhabited the Arabian Peninsula about 50,000 years before they appeared in western Europe.

Stringer and his colleagues obtained the new date by performing ESR on two teeth from an ancient cow or ox that were found in sediment containing the remains of at least 10 early modern human beings. ESR is a technique that measures the amount of naturally occurring radiation absorbed by buried objects, such as bone, that contain the mineral calcite. The older the object is, the higher the level of radiation.

Prehistoric disease. The bones of prehistoric people from North America have revealed new information

Anthropology

Continued

HUNTER-GATHERERS, NORTH AMERICA, LATE 20TH CENTURY

about the origin of rheumatoid arthritis, according to a September 1988 report. Rheumatoid arthritis is a crippling inflammation of the tissue that surrounds the joints. Although it was first described in the 1780's, when and where the disease originated is still unknown.

Pathologist Bruce M. Rothschild of the New Arthritis Center of Northeastern Ohio in Youngstown and anthropologists Kenneth R. Turner and Michael A. DeLuca of the University of Alabama in Tuscaloosa reported that they found evidence of rheumatoid arthritis in the skeletons of six adults who lived in northwestern Alabama 3,000 to 5,000 years ago. According to the scientists, the arm, hip, and leg joints—and especially the wrists and ankles—had damage that was nearly identical to that seen in modern rheumatoid arthritis patients. This finding, combined with a lack of evidence of the disease in prehistoric human fossils in Europe, Africa, and Asia, suggest that rheumatoid arthritis originated in the Americas.

Compulsive tooth picking. The results of a study into the cause of grooves found in the teeth of ancient human beings who lived during the late Paleolithic Period (approximately 12,000 years ago) was reported in August 1988 by Vincenzo Formicola of the Anthropology and Human Pathology Institute of Pisa, Italy. Some anthropologists had suspected that the grooves were caused by either a chemical or by something abrasive that was inserted between the teeth.

Using a microscope, Formicola analyzed the upper and lower molars found at a site in Grimaldi, Italy. The molars had deep grooves that were highly polished. Formicola reported that the grooves were probably caused by some kind of wooden toothpicks that were originally used for removing trapped food or for some other hygienic activity. The depth of the grooves, however, suggests that the activity may have developed into a compulsive habit. [Charles F. Merbs]

In WORLD BOOK, see PREHISTORIC PEOPLE.

Archaeology, New World

Scientists from Peru dazzled the archaeological world in October 1988 when they reported the spectacular treasure found in an ancient burial site in Sipán. The tomb, constructed by a pre-Columbian civilization, is the richest ever uncovered by archaeologists. See Close-Up.

Clovis cache uncovered. Archaeologists in 1988 gained insight into the lives of a prehistoric people believed to be among the earliest groups of human beings in North America. In October, archaeologist Peter J. Mehringer at Washington State University in Pullman reported on the artifacts found in an apple orchard in Wenatchee, Wash.

The artifacts, dating back about 11,000 years, were identified as belonging to a prehistoric people called Clovis. The Clovis lived during the late *Pleistocene Epoch*, an ice age that ended about 10,000 years ago. Their culture is recognized by distinctive fluted *spearpoints* (or spearheads), found at various sites in North America.

This Clovis site was discovered in 1987 by workers installing an irrigation system. Archaeologists named the site "Richey-Roberts" after the Richey family, who own the orchard, and Richard Roberts, its manager.

A cluster of artifacts. The excavated area, only 2 square meters ($21\frac{1}{2}$ square feet) large, yielded an amazing array of spearpoints and other artifacts. Some of the Clovis spearpoints measured up to 23 centimeters (9 inches) in length, much larger than specimens found at other sites. This kind of discovery, where artifacts are clustered together in a small area, is called a *cache*.

What made the Richey-Roberts cache particularly interesting to the archaeologists was the appearance of the spearpoints. Many of them were unfinished. Mehringer speculated that the Richey-Roberts cache was the carefully stored kit of a Clovis toolmaker that for some reason was never retrieved. Or perhaps the cache had been used as a ceremonial or burial offering.

Although an important discovery on its own, the Richey-Roberts find fits into the pattern of Clovis caches previ-

An archaeologist in San Francisco's Chinatown, *above,* searches for artifacts at the site of what was a general store and residence during Gold Rush days in the early 1850's. At the site, unearthed during the construction of a bank, archaeologists found more than 100,000 ceramic items, including a vase, *right,* made in China.

Tomb of a Moche Priest

The discovery of the richest tomb ever excavated by scientists in the Western Hemisphere was reported in September 1988. The tomb was uncovered by Peruvian archaeologist Walter Alva at an ancient ceremonial site near the village of Sipán, which is located in the Reque Valley on the coast of Peru about 680 kilometers (420 miles) northwest of Lima. The tomb belonged to a pre-Columbian civilization we now call *Moche*, which flourished in this area between approximately A.D. 100 and 700.

Alva, director of the Brüning Archaeological Museum in Lambayeque, Peru, and his assistants began excavating at Sipán in April 1987, after a fabulously rich tomb had been looted there by grave robbers in February 1987. In June 1987, the archaeologists found an unlooted burial chamber. On the floor of the burial chamber was a plank coffin containing the skeleton of a man in a fully extended position, lying on his back with his arms along his sides. He was in his 30's when he died and was buried with an opulent array of elaborate garments, ornaments, and ceremonial implements, including a ceremonial rattle, crescent-shaped knives, scepters, spears, shields, and numerous exotic sea shells.

The buried man was lavishly adorned with gold nose and ear ornaments, necklaces, head-dresses, bells, and crescent-shaped knives. His feet were clad in copper sandals and around his wrist were bracelets consisting of hundreds of tiny gold and turquoise beads. Two gold eyes, a gold nose, and gold teeth were placed on his face at the time of burial. Some of his ornaments are among the most complex and sophisticated metal objects ever found in the Western Hemisphere, documenting a mastery of craftsmanship that was previously unknown.

Around the man's plank coffin were many other objects, including hundreds of ceramic vessels, the skeleton of a dog, and the skeletons of two llamas that had been sacrificed. There were also the bones of three young women, each approximately 18 years old: Two were at the head of the coffin and one was at the foot. On each side of the coffin was the skeleton of an adult male, approximately 35 years old—the same age as the man in the coffin. From careful analysis of the skeletal remains, the age and sex of each individual in the tomb was determined

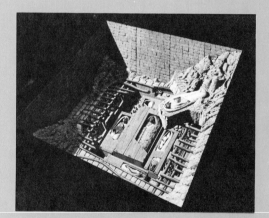

At the excavation site, *right,* of a tomb dating from the pre-Columbian Moche civilization in Peru, archaeologist Walter Alva (right) and an assistant examine a clay jar left behind as a burial offering. Among the objects in the tomb were gilded copper faces resembling jaguars, *far right.* The principal figure in the tomb, shown in a reconstruction, *above,* was probably a powerful warrior-priest, surrounded by the bodies of two men, three young women, and a dog.

by physical anthropologist John Verano of the Smithsonian Institution in Washington, D.C.

By comparing the objects from this tomb with those worn by individuals depicted in Moche art, I was able to identify the man in the coffin as a warrior-priest. In Moche society, the warrior-priest was an extremely important and powerful individual. Although the Moche people had no writing system, they left a vivid artistic record of themselves in beautifully modeled and painted ceramic vessels. These illustrate Moche architecture, implements, supernatural beings, elaborate ceremonies, and activities such as hunting, weaving, and combat. Among the ceremonies depicted in Moche art was one in which the warrior-priest appeared to be the primary figure, presiding over the sacrifice of prisoners of war.

The archaeologists working at Sipán have also discovered the location of several other royal tombs. One of these was being excavated in 1989, and appears to be similar to the first tomb. The excavations at Sipán, which are supported by the National Geographic Society, will continue for several years, and we expect that more royal tombs will be uncovered.

The Sipán project is proving to be a landmark in New World archaeology. Never before has it been possible to excavate such a wealth of artifacts and scientific information regarding the elite ruling class within a major pre-Columbian civilization—information that is helping us understand the ancient civilization of the Moche. [Christopher B. Donnan]

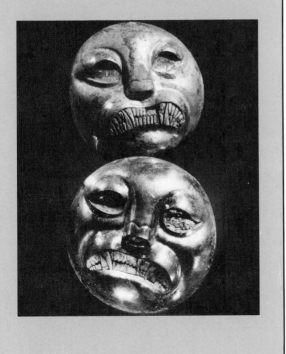

ously unearthed in Idaho, Montana, Colorado, and other Western states. These caches give archaeologists an important glimpse into the Clovis culture. They reveal the technology of Clovis stone toolmaking and sometimes indicate how tools were used. For example, preliminary studies show that three of the Richey-Roberts spearpoints still bear residues of animal blood, indicating that they may have been used for hunting.

Farming in ancient Peru. Research confirming that farmers of Chimu, an ancient Peruvian empire, turned swampland into agricultural land by constructing raised fields was reported in October 1988 by Jerry D. Moore, an archaeologist at the University of California in Santa Barbara. The Chimu empire, which preceded the Inca empire, existed from 900 to 1470.

Although the Incas are well known for their agricultural achievements, the Chimu empire also appears to have made its own contributions to agriculture, especially the construction of irrigation canal systems. But archaeologists had never found proof that farmers in ancient Peru built raised fields in swampland, a practice that was common among other ancient South and Central American people. Some archaeologists had suggested that such fields may have been built in the Casma Valley, an area along Peru's northern coast, but until Moore's study there was no proof that these fields existed.

In his study, Moore carefully scrutinized aerial photographs of the Casma Valley and noticed irregular ditches that suggested the presence of raised fields. Follow-up excavations in the valley revealed that there were raised fields, formed by digging narrow canals in *bogs* (swampland) near the Casma River. According to Moore, the Chimu apparently took the muck from the canals and mounded it up to create raised fields.

Moore's aerial studies and field work revealed 439 hectares (1,084 acres) of raised fields in the southern part of the valley and another 81 hectares (200 acres) in the northern part. He calculated that the Chimu could have built such extensive fields in about one year using 600 workers. Examination of pottery fragments found at the site revealed that the fields must have been constructed during the last phase of the Chimu empire, sometime between 1300 and 1470.

Ancient farm village. Near the raised fields, Moore found the ruins of a Chimu community, believed to have been a settlement of agricultural workers. The site, called *Quebrada Santa Cristina*, consisted of 284 rooms. Notably absent from this site were any remains of maize, beans, or other Chimu crops. Instead, Moore found many doughnut-shaped granite artifacts with heavily bashed edges, which he believes were implements used to break up clods of dirt. Since pottery from the site was the same as that found in the fields, Moore theorized that the village was occupied by workers responsible for building and maintaining the raised fields.

New discoveries at Teotihuacán. After years of being studied by archaeologists and visited by millions of tourists, the ancient city of Teotihuacán near Mexico City was thought to have few secrets left. But in January and April 1989, archaeologists at Brandeis University in Waltham, Mass., reported the details of mass burial pits they discovered on the perimeter of the city's Temple of Quetzalcóatl. (Quetzalcóatl was a god represented as a plumed or feathered serpent.) The graves contained the remains of 18 males ranging in age from 18 to 55, apparently victims of a ritual sacrifice.

The city of Teotihuacán predates the Aztec and Mayan civilizations and little is known about its inhabitants. During its peak around A.D. 400, Teotihuacán covered more than 21 square kilometers (8 square miles) and had a population of about 120,000. The temple is actually the site of two temples. The first temple built, called the *old temple*, was decorated with elaborate representations of Quetzalcóatl and Tlaloc, a rain and fertility god. Later, another temple was built over the foundation of the old temple.

The Brandeis archaeologists discovered the burial pits along the outside foundation of the old temple. Ten of the men found in the graves had their arms crossed behind their backs, indicating that they were bound at the time of death. Buried with the men were 169 obsidian spearpoints and some 4,000 pieces of carved shell. The archaeologists also found 14 human *maxillas* (upper jaws) that were worn as ornaments by some individuals.

According to the Brandeis scientists, the ages of the men in the graves and the type of weapons and other artifacts buried with them suggest that the men were soldiers from the city's army who were probably sacrificed as part of a ritual associated with the completion of the old temple.

Looting controversy. A report in the March 1989 *National Geographic* on the extent of the 1987 looting of a prehistoric American Indian burial site in Kentucky renewed concern over the destruction of archaeological remains in North America. It also highlighted the ongoing dispute among archaeologists, *physical anthropologists* (scientists who study human physical characteristics), and some American Indian groups about the excavation of burial sites and how skeletal remains and grave artifacts should be handled.

The scene of the 1987 vandalism was the Slack Farm near Uniontown, the site of an Indian cemetery dating from approximately 1450 to 1650. The looters paid the farm's owner $10,000 for the right to excavate the site. According to the report, they uncovered about 650 prehistoric Indian graves in a 16-hectare (40-acre) area. In digging up pottery and other artifacts to sell, the looters destroyed the graves and many historically valuable remains. Although some of the looters were later arrested on misdemeanor charges, the incident spurred the Kentucky legislature in 1988 to enact a law making it a felony to desecrate unmarked graves of American Indians and other ethnic groups.

Besides creating a furor among archaeologists and legislators, the Slack Farm incident also set off protests by some American Indian groups. Although scientific studies of the skeletons found at Slack Farm could not establish tribal affiliation, some Indian groups insisted that the looted remains be reburied.　　　[Thomas R. Hester]

In the Special Reports section, see WHO (OR WHAT) KILLED THE GIANT MAMMALS? In WORLD BOOK, see ARCHAEOLOGY; PERU (History).

Archaeology, Old World

The discovery in Iraq of the lost city of Mashkan-shapir, inhabited between 2050 and 1720 B.C., was announced in March 1989. The existence of the city was known from documents that tell how the Babylonian Emperor Hammurabi sent ambassadors there in about 1780 B.C. to negotiate a peace between two warring factions.

Archaeologist Elizabeth Stone of the State University of New York at Stony Brook identified the city through well-preserved cuneiform tablets found at the site. Because Mashkan was a capital city, many tablets were made in the "royal" manner using baked clay, which remains intact far longer than the unbaked clay used for ordinary tablets. The war between Iran and Iraq that began in 1980 prevented the archaeologists from examining the site from airplanes. But they were able to use a camera suspended from a kite flown over the city to identify the walls outlining the settlement, which was 1.3 kilometers (0.5 mile) square.

The find is especially remarkable because the city has remained undisturbed since its destruction by fire in 1720 B.C. Excavations might take decades, but archaeologists already have found a rare intact bridge that spanned a canal running through the city. Fragments of copper and bronze and other artifacts found so far suggest that Mashkan, about 140 kilometers (90 miles) southeast of Baghdad, was a major manufacturing center.

Greek ship proves seaworthy. The results of experiments made with a full-scale reconstruction of an important type of ancient Greek warship were reported in April 1989 by British Royal Navy architect John Coates. The type of ship, called a *trireme*, was a large wooden vessel equipped with a bronze battering ram for sinking enemy ships. Ancient Greek histories describe long sea voyages in which triremes averaged the impressive speed of 7.5 knots. But no remains of triremes have ever been found, and descriptions in art and literature are fragmentary.

Some clues to the construction of triremes do exist, however. Wrecks of other ancient Mediterranean sailing

A 3,000-year-old statue of the ancient Egyptian goddess Iunet, unearthed in Luxor, Egypt, in January 1989, is carefully brushed by an archaeologist. The statue was one of five perfectly preserved sculptures, dating from the height of ancient Egyptian culture, discovered buried in Luxor Temple.

ships provide some idea of general shipbuilding principles of the time. Archaeologists have excavated the remains of sheds in which triremes were berthed, which indicate that the ships were no more than 5.6 meters (18 feet 5 inches) wide and about 37 meters (121 feet) long. Ancient documents record that a trireme carried 170 oarsmen, a captain, about a dozen deck hands and officers, and 14 soldiers and archers. Coates' team used all this information to reconstruct a trireme.

In the past two years, the reconstructed trireme, named *Olympias*, has undergone tests on the Aegean Sea off Greece. The experimenters found that the *Olympias*, rowed by 170 volunteers, could go even faster than ancient records suggest—up to 9.5 knots. They believe that speed was the chief advantage of the trireme over other easily maneuverable warships of its time. The scientists concluded that the trireme was the optimum design for a warship that could be built within the limits of the ancient Greeks' resources and technology.

Polynesian beginnings. People have lived in Australia and New Guinea for more than 40,000 years. But when—and from where—did they reach other South Pacific islands thousands of kilometers east of Australia? In autumn 1988, archaeologist Patrick V. Kirch of the University of California at Berkeley shed light on the origins of the Polynesians, based on excavations in the Mussau Islands, about 700 kilometers (430 miles) off east New Guinea.

Kirch found the largest known site of Lapita culture, an early Polynesian culture that thrived from about 1600 B.C. to 500 B.C. Lapita artifacts, especially pottery decorated with distinctive stamped designs and lime paint, have been found on South Pacific islands thousands of kilometers farther east.

In addition to the artifacts, the Mussau site includes the remains of wooden posts and stakes that may have supported stilt-houses on the edge of the lagoons of the islands. This house style is now widely used throughout the islands off Southeast Asia and much of the South Pacific.

Because the oldest deposits at the site contain the most elaborate artifacts and no traces of a developing culture, Kirch suggests that the Lapita did not originate at Mussau, but came there from the west—probably from the Southeast Asian islands. The Lapita apparently spread swiftly across the South Pacific, covering some 4,500 kilometers (2,800 miles) of ocean in less than 500 years.

Roman letters. Some 700 personal letters written by Roman soldiers and their family members around A.D. 100 were among about 1,100 documents unearthed from beneath a Roman fortress in northern England. Archaeologist Robin Birley found most of the letters late in 1988 while excavating at Vindolanda, a frontier post just south of the Scottish border. Five rebuildings of a fort on that site had buried the discarded letters under clay and turf, preserving them. The early fort was replaced by a stone fortress in A.D. 128, when the Roman Emperor Hadrian built a wall across England.

The documents—the oldest examples of Roman writing ever found in Europe—were written in carbon ink on sheets of birch or alder wood, which were then hinged, folded, and tied through small holes in the edges. The letters provide an intriguing glimpse into the lives of ordinary people on the distant frontier of the Roman Empire. Their topics range from financial matters to soldiers' requests for leave. Other documents include rosters of troops, lists of provisions, and writing practice by schoolchildren. Only a small portion of the site has been excavated, and Birley expects to find many more documents.

One series of letters, from the wife of an official at a nearby fort to the wife of a commander at Vindolanda, contains what may be the earliest known handwriting by a woman of any culture. At the bottom of one letter written by a scribe, in which Claudia Severa invites Sulpicia Lapidina to attend her birthday party, Claudia Severa herself added, "Farewell, sister, my dear heart."

Oil of kings. Israeli archaeologists in February 1989 announced the discovery of a 2,000-year-old jug of oil of the type thought to have been used for anointing ancient Jewish kings. The jug was unearthed in the summer of 1988 in a cave near the Dead Sea.

The Old Testament of the Bible

Science Dates the Shroud

Scientific tests reported in February 1989 proved that the Shroud of Turin could not have been the burial cloth of Jesus Christ. After centuries of debate about the shroud's authenticity, researchers at long last subjected samples of the cloth to a technique called *radiocarbon dating*, which reliably dates any natural material. The results showed that the shroud is only about 660 years old and could not have dated from the time of Christ.

This remarkable and beautiful piece of cloth has stirred wonder and awe in many people since it was first displayed in about A.D. 1350 by a French knight, Geoffrey de Charny, in Lirey, France. Since 1578, the Roman Catholic Church has kept the shroud in a chapel in Turin, Italy. Stains on the linen cloth of the shroud form a life-sized image, both front and back, of a crucified man. It is a detailed image showing all the wounds associated with Christ's crucifixion as described in the Bible.

Shortly after the shroud's existence was first announced, Bishop Henry of Poitiers, France, declared it a fraud—"a work of human skill, and not miraculously wrought or bestowed." Bishop Henry claimed to know who the artist was but did not reveal the name. Nevertheless, many people over the centuries believed that the cloth could have been produced only by a miraculous burst of radiation that occurred as Christ rose from the dead. The church had long refused to submit the shroud to scientific testing that would reveal its age, because the only tests available would have destroyed a handkerchief-sized sample of the cloth.

The Vatican in 1988 agreed to allow the measurement of the shroud's age by a dating technique called *accelerator mass spectrometry*, developed in 1977 at the University of Rochester in New York. The method enables scientists to date valuable relics using a specimen of material no bigger than a postage stamp. Three laboratories—at the University of Arizona in Tucson, Oxford University in England, and the Federal Institute of Technology in Zurich, Switzerland—worked independently on the shroud dating, which was coordinated by the British Museum in London. The results were published in the Feb. 16, 1989, issue of the British scientific journal *Nature*.

The dating technique used was a type of radiocarbon dating, which is based on the fact that all living things—such as the flax used to make linen—constantly absorb carbon dioxide containing one atom of carbon 14 for every trillion atoms of ordinary carbon, called carbon 12. Carbon 14, also known as *radiocarbon*, is unstable and changes into nitrogen at a known rate. While an organism lives, it takes in as much carbon 14 as it loses. After the organism dies, the ratio of carbon 14 to carbon 12 begins to decrease at a known rate. Half of the carbon 14 disappears in 5,730 years, a period called the *half-life* of radiocarbon. By measuring the amounts of carbon 14 and carbon 12 present in a dead object, scientists can tell how long ago the object died. As a result, they could establish the year the flax was harvested to weave the linen of the Shroud of Turin.

Each of the three laboratories received a strip of the shroud measuring about 2.3 square centimeters (0.357 square inch) and three other similarly sized pieces of cloth whose ages were known to the British Museum but not to the laboratories. The ages of the other samples ranged from 2,000 to 700 years. The laboratory estimates for the ages for all four samples were within 100 years of each other. They found that the shroud was woven sometime between 1260 and 1390.   [Harry E. Gove]

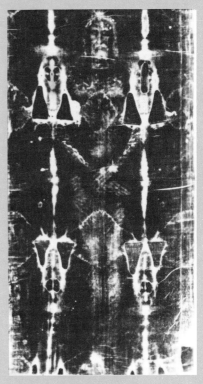

Section of the Shroud of Turin

An Egyptian researcher examines what may be the oldest known copy of the Biblical Book of Psalms, which has been dated to about A.D. 400. The book, handsomely bound in wood and leather, was discovered in a child's grave in an ancient cemetery for the poor south of Cairo, Egypt.

Archaeology, Old World

Continued

describes the use of fragrant oil for religious rites; in coronation ceremonies, it was poured over the heads of kings. Although the oil in the jug had lost its fragrance, it was chemically intact, and scientists concluded that it was extracted from a now-extinct ancient persimmon plant that was a valued source of natural perfume.

The jug was wrapped in palm leaves and buried in a pit in the cave, indicating that it may have been hidden by its owners, perhaps because it was valuable. Its age is uncertain, but a scroll found in the same cave in the 1950's discussed the hiding of sacred Jewish items from the Roman army in the years A.D. 66 through 68.

First fires. The earliest known evidence of the controlled use of fire—one of the most important milestones in human history—was reported in December 1988 by two South African anthropologists, C. K. Brain of the Transvaal Museum in Pretoria and Andrew Sillen of the University of Cape Town. Anthropologists believe that the fires, found at Swartkrans

Cave in South Africa, were made by *Homo erectus*, an early human species that lived between about 1.6 million and 300,000 years ago.

At Swartkrans, Brain and Sillen found 270 pieces of burned bone in a level dated to between 1 million and 1.5 million years ago. The researchers compared the chemical and microscopic characteristics of the burnt fossil bones to modern antelope bones that they had burned in an experimental campfire made from white stinkwood. Stinkwood trees grow near the cave, and bits of ancient stinkwood had been found in the fossil deposits. The scientists concluded that the fossil bones had been burned at temperatures between 200°C and 800°C (about 400°F. and 1500°F.), a range similar to that produced in their experimental campfire. This suggests that the bones were burned in a controlled, rather than an accidental, fire.   [Robert J. Wenke]

In the Special Reports section, see EXCAVATING HEROD'S DREAM. In WORLD BOOK, see BABYLONIA; GREECE, ANCIENT; JEWS; ROME, ANCIENT.

Astronomy, Extragalactic

Astronomers making observations of a *supernova* (exploded star) in a neighbor galaxy of our Milky Way found evidence in January 1989 of a *pulsar* (a rapidly rotating neutron star) at the site of the supernova explosion. The supernova was first observed in 1987 in the Large Magellanic Cloud and was named Supernova 1987A.

The standard theory of how stars evolve predicts that a star of a certain mass will end its life in a supernova and that the core of the star remaining after the explosion will collapse to form a pulsar. So the discovery of a pulsar at the site of Supernova 1987A had been long anticipated.

Pulsar unveiling. The evidence for the existence of a pulsar, however, as of mid-1989 consisted of a single optical observation by astronomers John Middleditch of Los Alamos National Laboratory in New Mexico and Tim P. Sasseen of Lawrence Berkeley Laboratory in California. Using the 4-meter (158-inch) telescope at Cerro Tololo Inter-American Observatory in Chile, the two astronomers observed rapid flickering in the light from the supernova. Their analysis of the flickering indicated the presence of a pulsar rotating almost 2,000 times per second, more than twice as fast as any previously observed pulsar.

As of June 1989, this phenomenon had not been seen again, and as a result, many astronomers were skeptical of the report. One explanation for why it was observed only once is that the pulsar is embedded in the center of clumps of material spewed out by the explosion. This debris obscures the pulsar's light so that it usually cannot be viewed from Earth. The single observation made in January might have been due to a chance hole in this cloud of debris.

Einstein rings. The discovery of what may be an *Einstein ring* was reported in June 1988 by a team of astronomers led by Jacqueline N. Hewitt of the Haystack Observatory in Westford, Mass. In 1936, physicist Albert Einstein predicted that any form of electromagnetic radiation, such as light or radio waves from a distant object, could appear distorted to an observer on Earth after passing through the gravitational field of a massive foreground object.

The light from the distant object would be bent or distorted by the foreground object's gravitational field. This phenomenon is known as a *gravitational lens*. If the distant object and the massive foreground lens are perfectly aligned as seen from Earth, the optical illusion created will be a ring, and this is called an Einstein ring.

Using the National Radio Astronomy Observatory's Very Large Array (VLA) telescope near Socorro, N. Mex., the astronomers obtained a radio image with a ringlike shape. Using the National Optical Astronomy Observatory's 4-meter telescope at Kitt Peak National Observatory near Tucson, Ariz., Hewitt and her colleagues found a visible light counterpart for the radio source that appears to be an elliptical galaxy. Data from the combined radio and optical observations suggested that the radio ring is from a large, distant galaxy that gives off most of its energy in the form of radio waves. Such a galaxy is called a *radio galaxy*.

This radio galaxy is apparently located directly behind an extremely massive but unseen object whose gravitational field has bent the optical and radio waves from the galaxy into the shape of an elliptical ring.

Previously, scientists had thought the probability of such a perfect alignment of a distant radio source and an intervening gravitational lens was small. Hewitt and her colleagues, however, pointed out that because radio galaxies are large and because there are a large number of them, the probability of the precise alignments occurring is more likely than previously thought.

Quasar images in galaxy. In September 1988, astronomers Michael M. DeRobertis of York University in Ontario, Canada, and Howard K. C. Yee of the Universite de Montreal in Quebec confirmed the authenticity of a previously suspected gravitational lens involving a distant quasar and a nearby galaxy. In 1985, astronomer John Huchra of the Harvard-Smithsonian Center for Astrophysics in Cambridge, Mass., had discovered a quasar with a red shift indicating that it was extremely distant. But the quasar was situated in the center of a galaxy with a red shift indicating that it was relatively close by.

Astronomy, Extragalactic

Continued

Astronomers use red shifts to determine how fast distant objects appear to be moving. Light given off from sources moving away from Earth, for example, is shifted toward the longer (red) wavelength of the object's *spectrum* (the range of colors that make up visible light). The greater this red shift, the faster an object is moving away, and the greater its distance from Earth.

Huchra concluded that he was observing a gravitational lens in which the galaxy's gravitational field bent the light from the quasar so that the quasar appeared to be at the galaxy's center.

The probability, however, that such an alignment would occur to create an image of a distant quasar at the center of a nearby galaxy is small. Also, only one image of a quasar was found, but a gravitational lens usually produces multiple images. So in 1985, astronomers concluded that more observational evidence was needed to confirm the lens hypothesis.

Further evidence came in May and June 1988 when Yee and astronomer Donald P. Schneider of the Institute for Advanced Study in Princeton, N.J.—using three different telescopes—reported the discovery of four objects near the center of the galaxy. Then, in September, DeRobertis and Yee reported that the four images have similar spectrums, and these spectrums are characteristic of quasars. This confirmed that the system is a gravitational lens. The alignment of this quasar and a nearby galaxy nucleus is highly unlikely, and this is why so much effort was needed to prove the lens hypothesis. It may well be that this lens system is unique, but if astronomers find other examples to show that it is relatively common, then there must be many more objects in the distant universe than previously thought. This is because a greater number of objects at vast distances increases the likelihood of finding more galaxy-quasar lens systems. Finding more objects in the distant universe may cause astronomers to revise their estimates of the total amount of matter in the universe.

Dark matter in galaxies. The discovery of a second example of an Einstein

Rings called *light echoes* surround Supernova 1987A, an exploding star in a nearby galaxy, in this July 1988 photograph taken at the Anglo-Australian Observatory in Australia. The light echoes are so-named because they represent light from the explosion that is being seen a second time. The original light from the explosion was observed in February 1987, but light reflected from clouds of gas and dust took longer to reach Earth. Studies of the light echoes could provide data about the early stages of the supernova and the nature of the gas clouds.

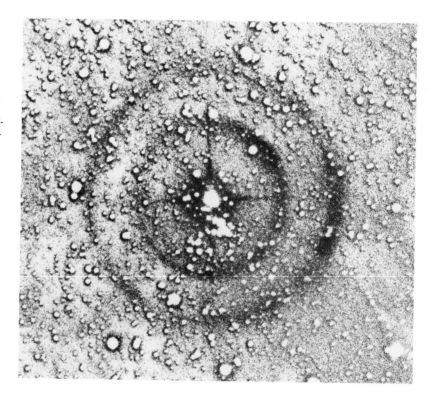

ring was announced in January 1989 by astronomer Glen Langston of the Max Planck Institute for Radio Astronomy in West Germany. His discovery provides new evidence to support the existence of substantial amounts of *dark matter* in the universe. Dark matter does not appear to give off or reflect electromagnetic radiation and so cannot be seen. Its existence only can be inferred from the way its gravity affects visible matter. In the Special Reports section, see THE CASE OF THE DARK MATTER.

The new ring was detected with the VLA. Like the previous Einstein ring, the ringlike shape of this object shows up only in radio observations. In visible light, this object appears as a pointlike *quasar* (an extremely energetic and distant object).

Unlike the situation with the first Einstein ring found, the details of this gravitational lens system are well known. The object that causes the lensing effect is a foreground galaxy. Using optical telescopes, Langston and his colleagues determined the distances to the galaxy and the quasar, based on their red shifts.

Knowing the distances of the quasar and the foreground galaxy, and the size of the Einstein ring, Langston and colleagues were able to calculate the total amount of mass in the galaxy that caused the gravitational bending of light from the quasar. They found that the total mass is equal to the mass of about 300 billion suns. This is far greater than the amount of visible mass in the galaxy, so the galaxy must contain a large amount of dark matter.

Distribution of dark matter. Findings about a gravitational lens that may shed light on how dark matter is distributed in a cluster of galaxies were reported in 1989 by a group of French astronomers. In this case, the lens is a cluster of galaxies whose gravitational field has bent light from a distant spiral galaxy into the shape of an arc. The arc was discovered near the cluster using the 3.6-meter (142-inch) Canada-France-Hawaii telescope in Hawaii.

Theoretical models of how this gravitational lens formed predicted that more than one arc image should be seen. The French astronomers found at least two other images that appeared

to be connected with the arc. The astronomers were then able to make a more detailed model of the lens system and calculate the total amount of matter in the galaxy cluster, both visible and dark matter.

These astronomers predicted that their model could reveal how dark matter is distributed in the cluster. If the dark matter is concentrated at the center of the cluster, it would have different properties than if it is found spread out around the cluster in a vast halo.

Dark matter not black holes. Dark matter probably does not take the form of *black holes* (objects so dense that not even light can escape their gravitational field) in numbers large enough to halt the universe's expansion. This conclusion was published in July 1988 by astronomer J. Anthony Tyson of AT&T Bell Laboratories in Murray Hill, N.J. Tyson noted that of the 4,000 quasars astronomers have discovered, only a few form multiple images as part of gravitational lens systems. If black holes were the dark matter, there should be many lensed quasars.

Since 1929, when American astronomer Edwin P. Hubble determined that the universe is expanding, astronomers have debated whether there is enough matter in the universe to halt this expansion through gravitational attraction. If not, the universe will go on expanding forever.

Tyson pointed out that if the expansion of the universe could be halted by the existence of a large amount of dark matter in the form of black holes, then there should be more instances of multiple images of quasars caused by black holes acting as gravitational lenses. This is because the gravitational field around a black hole is so strong that it would create many images of quasars. These images should have been easily detected by now. Instead, astronomers find that the objects that have caused most of the gravitational lensing of quasars are galaxies that appear to be surrounded by massive halos containing dark matter. Dark matter in the halos, however, appears to be spread out and so could not exist in the form of extremely compact objects such as black holes.   [Stephen S. Murray]

In WORLD BOOK, see ASTRONOMY.

Astronomy, Galactic

Our Milky Way galaxy may not have a massive *black hole* at its center—as some astronomers have suggested—according to findings reported in July 1988. A black hole is an object so dense that not even light can escape its gravitational field.

Astronomers have been debating about the nature of the center of our Galaxy, known as the *galactic core*. This core gives off tremendous emissions in the form of X rays, infrared light, and radio waves, suggesting that there may be a source of intense energy at the heart of the Galaxy. Astronomers have proposed that this source could be either a massive black hole or a compact cluster of massive stars.

Evidence against a black hole. The most compelling evidence for a black hole has been the existence of interstellar gas clouds moving at high speeds near the galactic core. The faster that things orbit near the center of the Galaxy, the greater the mass that must be concentrated there. Astronomers measure the speeds of the interstellar clouds by observing tiny changes called *Doppler shifts* in the wavelengths of light that they give off. When an object is moving toward Earth, its light is shifted toward shorter wavelengths; when it is moving away, it is shifted toward longer wavelengths. The faster the object is moving, the larger the wavelength shift.

In order to measure speeds of objects near the center of the Galaxy, astronomers must use infrared telescopes that detect infrared wavelengths or heat radiation. Infrared radiation can be detected through the thick clouds of gas and dust that lie between Earth and the galactic core.

Astronomers George and Marcia Rieke of the University of Arizona in Tucson reported in July that they had measured Doppler shifts at infrared wavelengths from stars near the galactic core. They found that these stars, unlike the interstellar clouds observed previously, are not orbiting faster than stars farther out from the center. This suggests that the gas clouds are moving rapidly for some other reason than the gravitational effect of a central object.

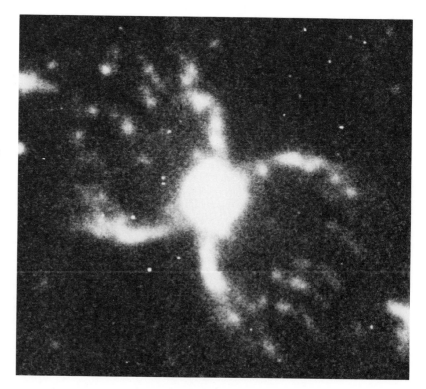

An object that has been dubbed the "Southern Crab" nebula was photographed in the southern sky in January 1989 by astronomers at the European Southern Observatory in La Silla, Chile. Astronomers speculate that the central "body" may consist of two stars, with an expanding layer of gas from one of the stars distorted to resemble the legs of a crab.

The new results also indicate that matter in the vicinity of the galactic core is spread out over a radius of at least 2 *light-years*. (A light-year is the distance light travels in one year, about 9.5 trillion kilometers [5.9 trillion miles].) This is a much larger region than would be the case if the galactic core had a massive black hole or a compact, massive star cluster.

More millisecond pulsars. Between June 1988 and June 1989, astronomers discovered four millisecond pulsars in *globular clusters* (spherical clusters of stars found in the outer portions of our Galaxy). A *pulsar* is a rapidly spinning, compact star composed almost entirely of *neutrons*, a type of particle found in the nucleus of atoms. As a pulsar spins, it gives off beams of radio waves that sweep across the sky like light beams from a lighthouse. Pulsars spin so rapidly that they complete a rotation once every few seconds. A *millisecond pulsar* spins even more rapidly, at hundreds of rotations a second.

The discovery of four millisecond pulsars in a single year has caused astronomers to revise their thinking about how these pulsars form. They apparently are much more common than was previously thought. Astronomers had speculated that millisecond pulsars formed in *binary* (double) star systems, involving a massive star. When this massive star exploded as a *supernova*, they theorized, its remaining core collapsed to become a pulsar. Then the pulsar captured matter from its companion star, and the added matter caused the pulsar to spin even more rapidly as a millisecond pulsar, according to this theory. Massive stars in binary systems, however, are too rare for this theory to explain the large numbers of millisecond pulsars being found.

In November 1988, Jonathan E. Grindlay and C. D. Bailyn of the Harvard-Smithsonian Center for Astrophysics in Cambridge, Mass., published their suggestion that millisecond pulsars could form in binary star systems in which one star is a *white dwarf* (a dying star that is no longer undergoing nuclear reactions). Such systems are more common and so could account for the relatively large numbers of millisecond pulsars.

Grindlay and Bailyn suggested that if the two stars are orbiting closely enough, the gravitational field of the white dwarf could capture matter from the companion star. As this transfer of matter continued, the white dwarf could become so massive that it would collapse and become a neutron star. In the process of collapsing, the white dwarf would increase its rotational speed so much that the resulting neutron star would be a millisecond pulsar.

Black widow pulsar. Further observations on a recently discovered millisecond pulsar, which became known as the *black widow pulsar*, were reported in 1988 and 1989. Astrophysicists at Princeton University in New Jersey first reported their discovery of this millisecond pulsar in a binary system in May 1988, using the giant radio telescope at Arecibo Observatory in Puerto Rico.

The astronomers deduced the existence of a companion star because the frequency of the pulsar's radio beams shifted slightly as it rotated, indicating the presence of an unseen companion. By measuring the pulsar's orbital speed, it was possible to deduce the mass of the unseen companion star. The mass turned out to be only about 2 per cent of the mass of the sun, far too small for any normal star. The unseen companion also blocks the pulsar's radio beam for a portion of each orbit, indicating that despite its small mass, it is larger in diameter than the sun.

The astronomers suggested that these puzzling observations could be explained if the companion is losing matter, which forms a surrounding dense cloud. That way the companion could have a small mass, but the dense cloud of matter it lost could be large enough to block the pulsar's radio beam periodically. The astronomers concluded that gas leaving the pulsar at nearly the speed of light is blowing matter off the companion and is evaporating it. Like the black widow spider, which eats its mate, the pulsar is vaporizing its companion star.

Other planetary systems? Findings indicating that there may be other planetary systems in our Galaxy were reported in August 1988 by two separate groups of astronomers. David W. Latham of the Harvard-Smithsonian Center for Astrophysics and Bruce

Astronomy suffered a major setback in November 1988 when the 90-meter (300-foot) radio telescope at Green Bank, W. Va., *above*, suddenly and mysteriously collapsed, *right*. An investigative panel reported in April 1989 that a fracture in a metal plate caused the collapse.

Astronomy, Galactic

Continued

Campbell of the University of British Columbia in Victoria, Canada, each headed a group seeking to detect periodic variations in the orbital speeds of nearby stars. Such variations would indicate the presence of a massive planet whose gravitational field is affecting the orbit of the star. For example, the mass of the planet Jupiter is sufficient to cause the orbital speed of the sun to vary by about 13 meters (43 feet) per second as the sun and Jupiter orbit a common center of mass. If there were no planet with the mass of Jupiter in our solar system, the sun's orbital speed would be constant and would never vary.

The slight variations in orbital speed are very difficult to measure. The new findings are based on different techniques developed by the two groups.

Each group used Doppler shifts but in different ways. Over a period of seven years, Latham's group accumulated enormous numbers of observations of Doppler shifts in the light of a given star, so that data on the orbital speed of the star could be averaged to determine if there were any regular variations. Campbell and his colleagues developed a new technique for making accurate measurements of Doppler shifts.

Both groups reported finding variations in orbital speeds. Latham reported periodic variations in the orbital speed of a sunlike star called HD 114762, indicating the presence of a massive companion. It is uncertain whether the companion to this star is a planet or a *brown dwarf* (an object too massive to be a planet but not massive enough to be a star). Campbell found periodic variations in the orbital speed of 9 stars out of a sample of 19 that his group had been studying. In the case of a star called HR 4112, the data implied the presence of a planet with about 50 per cent more mass than Jupiter. If all 9 of Campbell's suspected planetary systems are real, his results suggest that perhaps half of all sunlike stars have planets.   [Theodore P. Snow]

In the Special Reports section, see NEW EYES ON THE SKY. In WORLD BOOK, see ASTRONOMY; MILKY WAY; PULSAR.

Astronomy, Solar System

United States astronomers traveled to Australia and New Zealand in June 1988 to view for the first time the passage of a star behind the planet Pluto. This event, in which light from the distant star is eclipsed by the planet, is called an *occultation*. By watching the light from the star become weaker and distorted as the edge of Pluto began to eclipse the star, astronomers determined that Pluto, the planet farthest from the sun, has an atmosphere.

Observing the occultation with ground-based telescopes in Australia and New Zealand were astronomers from Lowell Observatory in Flagstaff, Ariz., the University of Tasmania, and the University of Arizona in Tucson. Flying high above them in the Kuiper Airborne Observatory, an aircraft equipped with telescopes and operated by the National Aeronautics and Space Administration (NASA), were scientists from the Massachusetts Institute of Technology (M.I.T.) in Cambridge.

Finding Pluto's atmosphere. For some time, astronomers have suspected that Pluto might have an atmosphere, based on analysis of the *spectrum* (range of colors in visible light) of sunlight reflected from Pluto. To obtain this spectrum, researchers passed the reflected sunlight from the planet through a grating, where it spread out into its component colors. Dark absorption lines that appear in the spectrum at certain wavelengths (or colors) are created by radiation given off by particular atoms or molecules. Analysis of the spectrum of Pluto had indicated the presence of methane on the planet, either as a solid ice, or as a gas in the atmosphere, or both. (On Earth, methane is produced by bacteria and other organisms; scientists believe that methane on Pluto was produced during the formation of the planets, not by any biological process.)

The astronomers analyzing the stellar occultation data from the June observations showed conclusively that Pluto has an atmosphere. They found that as the edge of Pluto passed in front of the star, the star's light became weak and distorted. They concluded that the light must have been *refracted* (bent) by gas molecules in the atmosphere, which extended out beyond the planet's edge. If Pluto did not have an atmosphere, then the star's light would have remained unchanged as the edge of Pluto passed in front of the star. Calculations showed that Pluto's atmosphere is thin, with a surface pressure roughly one-millionth the pressure at Earth's surface. The greater the density of gases in an atmosphere, the higher the surface pressure.

Pluto's gases. The scientists could not directly identify what gases make up the atmosphere. Because of their spectrum analysis, they considered methane to be a likely candidate, though there may be more than one gas. This possibility was suggested by a curious sudden dimming of the star's light before it passed behind the edge of Pluto. The M.I.T. astronomers observed this sudden drop and suggested that it might have been caused by a layer of haze in Pluto's lower atmosphere near the surface. If the haze exists, it is most likely a smog layer created when sunlight causes a chemical reaction that transforms molecules of methane into heavier substances.

Another explanation was proposed by Roger Yelle and me, both of the University of Arizona. Using calculations based on a theory about planetary atmospheres, we determined the temperature in Pluto's atmosphere at various altitudes. This is called a *temperature profile*. Knowing the temperature and the air pressure at various altitudes, we could calculate the average weight of gas molecules in the atmosphere. This average weight of Pluto's atmosphere is heavier than the weight of methane molecules alone, suggesting the presence of a second gas heavier than methane.

The temperature profile we calculated shows that temperatures become lower toward the surface. This could also explain the curious sharp decrease in starlight, since a colder gas is denser and refracts light more strongly than a warm gas. The identity of the second gas is not known, but it may be nitrogen or carbon monoxide.

Phobos missions end. The Soviet Union's planetary exploration program suffered a setback when contact was lost with two spacecraft—*Phobos 1* and *Phobos 2*—before they achieved their main goal of landing on the Martian moon Phobos in early 1989.

The two spacecraft were launched in July 1988. Soviet engineers lost control of *Phobos 1* in August 1988 due to an error by a flight controller. The spacecraft began tumbling and could not be recovered. The sister ship, *Phobos 2*, made measurements of interplanetary space and then entered Mars orbit in March 1989. Remote sensing devices on the spacecraft measured the composition of the Martian surface as it orbited the planet for several weeks. While the spacecraft was being prepared for its approach to the moon Phobos on March 27, an unexplained failure occurred that ended radio communications between Earth and the spacecraft's instruments.

Phobos and Deimos (the Greek words for *fear* and *terror*) are the two moons of Mars. They are much smaller than Earth's moon. Phobos is only about 23 kilometers (14 miles) across, compared with the moon's diameter of about 3,476 kilometers (2,160 miles). Many scientists believe that the moons of Mars may resemble *asteroids* (small bodies that generally orbit the sun in a region between Mars and the planet Jupiter). Scientists have been intrigued by the Martian moons since their discovery by American astronomer Asaph Hall in 1877.

The Soviet spacecraft contained a variety of scientific instruments to study Mars and its moons. Included in the mission were smaller craft on *Phobos 2*, which were called the *lander* and *hopper*. These were to be ejected from *Phobos 2* and were to land on Phobos to sample the surfaces directly with scientific instruments. The hopper was to jump across the surface of Phobos, taking advantage of the moon's weak gravitational field, and study several sites. Although the international team of scientists for the mission—including a number of U.S. scientists—was disappointed that the main mission goal was not achieved, important data, including detailed photographs of the surfaces of Mars and Phobos, were obtained by *Phobos 2*.

Ice volcanoes on Uranus' moons. Scientists at Cornell University in Ithaca, N.Y., in September 1988 announced evidence for ice volcanism on one, and possibly two, of the moons of Uranus. Researchers Steven W. Squyres and David G. Jankowski reported that they found this evidence by analyzing images returned by NASA's *Voyager 2* spacecraft when it flew by Uranus and its moons in January 1986. Several pictures of the Uranian moon Ariel showed evidence for volcanic flows. The thickness and appearance of the flows on Ariel, however, suggested that they were not liquid. Photographs of another Uranian moon, Miranda, contain hints of the existence of similar flows. The Cornell scientists proposed that water ice caused the flows.

Uranus is about 19 times farther from the sun than is Earth, and therefore temperatures are much colder there. A moon orbiting Uranus would have a temperature of roughly $-200°C$ ($-330°F$.). As a result, the moons of Uranus are made up of a mixture of rock and ice. (If these moons were as close to the sun as Earth is, they would melt, leaving behind a loose collection of rocks.)

Ice volcanism simply means that water ice is being pushed out onto the surfaces of the moons. The flows on the surfaces of the moons indicated that the ice was being either softened or melted due to heating from the moons' interiors. The source of this interior heat is unclear, however. Such heat may be generated either by *tidal forces* (changes in the gravitational pull of Uranus as the moon moves around it in a noncircular orbit) or by natural radioactivity in rocks deep in the interiors of the moons.

Jankowski and Squyres believe that the flows are too thick and have the wrong shape to be ice melted into liquid water. So in order for the ice to be sufficiently soft to move over the surface, the scientists suggested that it might contain small quantities of other materials such as methane or ammonia. Other astronomers have suggested instead that the flows are liquid mixtures of ammonia and water, which may move like molasses at very low temperatures. Whatever the flows are made of, their very existence tells scientists that the moons of Uranus were geologically active at some point in the past.   [Jonathan I. Lunine]

See also SPACE TECHNOLOGY. In WORLD BOOK, see ASTRONOMY; MARS; PLUTO; URANUS.

Books of Science

Here are 24 outstanding new science books suitable for the general reader. They have been selected from books published in 1988 and 1989.

Agriculture. *The Food of China* by E. N. Anderson describes the development of agriculture in China before 1800 and tells how small areas of cultivable land, through careful management, produced enough food for large numbers of people. (Yale Univ. Press, 1988. 263 pp. $30)

Astronomy. *Planets Beyond: Discovering the Outer Solar System* by Mark Littmann explores the origins of Uranus, Neptune, and Pluto and probes some of the unanswered questions that still surround those distant planets. Littmann includes photographs taken with telescopes and by the *Voyager 2* spacecraft. (Wiley, 1988. 286 pp. illus. $22.95)

The Starry Room: Naked Eye Astronomy in the Intimate Universe by Fred Schaaf is a collection of essays about sky phenomena visible to the unaided eye, including rainbows, meteors, *supernovae* (exploding stars), and *planetary conjunctions*, which occur when two planets appear near each other in the heavens. (Wiley, 1988. 264 pp. illus. $19.95)

Biology. *Axis and Circumference: The Cylindrical Shape of Plants and Animals* by Stephen A. Wainwright shows how the study of *functional morphology*—the branch of biology that deals with the form, structure, and function of plants and animals—can be used to explain why the cylinder is an ideal shape for living things. (Harvard Univ. Press, 1988. 132 pp. illus. $22.95)

In Praise of Imperfection: My Life and Work by Rita Levi-Montalcini, translated by Luigi Attardi, tells of the author's work in *embryology* (the branch of biology that studies development before birth), for which she was awarded the Nobel Prize for physiology or medicine in 1986. Levi-Montalcini, who worked first in Italy and later in the United States, writes that she tackled certain research problems mainly because of her tendency to underestimate the difficulties involved. (Basic Bks., 1988. 220 pp. illus. $18.95)

Toward a New Philosophy of Biology: Observations of an Evolutionist by Ernst Mayr strengthens the bridge between philosophy and biology, focusing on the growth of concepts instead of the search for laws in current scientific thought and on the properties that distinguish living systems from inanimate nature. (Belknap Press, 1988. 564 pp. $35)

Plantwatching: How Plants Remember, Tell Time, Form Partnerships, and More by Malcolm Wilkins is a beautifully illustrated guide to how plants live, work, and react to their environment. (Facts on File, 1988. 207 pp. illus. $29.95)

General science. *Flanagan's Version: A Spectator's Guide to Science on the Eve of the 21st Century* by Dennis Flanagan, a former editor of *Scientific American* magazine, discusses four fields that have been revolutionized in the author's lifetime: physics, astronomy, geology, and biology. (Knopf, 1988. 272 pp. $18.95)

Is Science Necessary? Essays on Science and Scientists by Max F. Perutz surveys the author's ideas about the usefulness of science, its relationship to health and to food and energy production, and the role of scientists during peacetime and war. Perutz, an Austrian-born British molecular biologist who won the Nobel Prize in chemistry in 1962 for determining the structure of the blood protein hemoglobin, also has suggestions on how to become a scientist. (Dutton, 1989. 255 pp. $19.95)

A Passion for Science by Lewis Wolpert and Alison Richards consists of interviews with 13 scientists, primarily British, in such fields as biology and chemistry. The discussions touch on how scientists do their work and on the pleasure they obtain from it. (Oxford Univ. Press, 1988. 206 pp. illus. $21.95)

The Symbiotic Universe: Life and Mind in the Cosmos by George Greenstein explains how life in the universe is made possible only because of several coincidences. Greenstein suggests that the theory of *quantum mechanics*, which explains that matter and energy have characteristics of both particles and waves, offers a key to understanding the unity of life and the universe. (Morrow, 1988. 271 pp. illus. $18.95)

Time in History by G. J. Whitrow discusses how ideas about time have developed. Whitrow explains conceptions of time in antiquity and in the modern world, how time has been measured through the ages, and how

these ideas of time are linked to the notion of progress. (Oxford Univ. Press, 1988. 256 pp. illus. $29.95)

The World Within the World by John D. Barrow explores the concept of laws of nature, discussing whether there are really laws waiting to be discovered, if they are the same everywhere, and why the laws of nature are mathematical. (Clarendon Press, 1988. 398 pp. illus. $24.95)

Geology. *Sand* by Raymond Siever shows how sand preserves a record of Earth's history and explains what we can learn from sand's mineral content, chemistry, surface shape, and distribution. (Scientific Amer. Lib., 1988. 237 pp. illus. $32.95)

History of science. *Let Newton Be!* edited by John Fauvel and others is a series of essays illustrating English scientist Sir Isaac Newton's contributions in physics, optics, and mathematics in the late 1600's and early 1700's. The essays also describe Newton's experiments with magic, his ideas about God, and the relevance of Newton's work today. (Oxford Univ. Press, 1988. 272 pp. illus. $29.95)

The Pasteurization of France by Bruno Latour, translated by Alan Sheridan and John Law, studies the revolution in medicine, biology, and hygiene begun in the late 1800's by the brilliant French chemist Louis Pasteur. The book also describes the tremendous impact Pasteur's discoveries had on public attitudes toward the sciences. (Harvard Univ. Press, 1988. 273 pp. $30)

Mathematics. *The Mathematical Tourist: Snapshots of Modern Mathematics* by Ivars Peterson is a guide to new discoveries on the leading edge of mathematics in such areas as the search for the highest *prime number* (a whole number such as 2, 3, 5, and 7 that cannot be divided evenly by any number except itself and 1), new solutions to problems in mapmaking, and the investigation of minimal surfaces, which explains why soap bubbles are round. (W. H. Freeman, 1988. 240 pp. illus. $17.95)

Mathematics and the Unexpected by Ivar Ekeland explores French mathematician René Thom's catastrophe theory, which proposes that numerous minor changes in a system can lead to a major catastrophic change. Ekeland also explains how mathematical laws governing the physics of the universe give rise to the complex and chaotic behavior of the actual world. (University of Chicago Press, 1988. 146 pp. illus. $24)

The Scientific Companion: Exploring the Physical World with Facts, Figures, and Formulas by Cesare Emiliani uses physical measurement and mathematical formulas to describe the universe, space and time, matter and energy, the solar system, the early development of life, and the history of Earth during the last 500 million years. (Wiley, 1988. 287 pp. illus. $24.95)

Natural history. *The Arctic Wolf: Living with the Pack* by L. David Mech records the day-to-day life of the wolf in the Arctic and includes the author's discovery of a den of wolf pups. This personal account by a naturalist who has devoted his life to the study of wolves is accompanied by superb photographs. (Voyageur Press, 1988. 128 pp. illus. $27.95)

The Honey Bee by James L. Gould and Carol Grant Gould is the story of the complex society of bees, their foraging behavior, how they navigate, and how they communicate with other members of their colony. (Scientific Amer. Lib., 1988. 239 pp. illus. $32.95)

People of the Tropical Rain Forest edited by Julie Sloan Denslow and Christine Padoch contains photographs and essays on the ecology of the rain forest; the ways in which peoples and forest interact; and the impact of logging, forestry, and cattle raising on tropical woodlands. (University of Calif. Press, 1988. 231 pp. illus. $39.50)

Paleontology. *Before the Indians* by Björn Kurtén describes North America and its wildlife from the beginning of the Pleistocene Epoch about 2 million years ago to its end about 10,000 years ago, including the arrival of human beings. Kurtén considers some of the unanswered questions surrounding the extinction of many species. (Columbia Univ. Press, 1988. 158 pp. illus. $29.95)

Technology. *American Genesis: A Century of Industrial and Technological Enthusiasm, 1870-1970* by Thomas P. Hughes argues that the work of such inventors as Thomas A. Edison and Henry Ford laid the groundwork for the technological society the United States has become. (Viking, 1989. 530 pp. illus. $24.95)   [William G. Jones]

Botany

The world's first plant biotechnology laboratory that is open to the public was unveiled in October 1988 at Walt Disney World's EPCOT Center in Orlando, Fla. The laboratory has more than 1 million *plantlets* (tiny immature plants) growing in sterile containers. Research focuses on using genetic engineering to develop improved varieties of peanuts, strawberries, and several other crops. Visitors can observe the scientists at work and even see closeups of what they are doing on video screens. The laboratory is a joint project of Walt Disney World; Kraft, Incorporated; and the U.S. Agricultural Research Service.

A new kind of movement operating in flowering plants was described in March 1989 by Luraynne C. Sanders and Elizabeth M. Lord, botanists at the University of California at Riverside. The scientists reported that such plants apparently secrete a substance that carries sperm cells to the ovary.

The female part of a flower, the *carpel*, is often a cylindrical structure, swollen at its base. The top of the carpel, a sticky surface known as the *stigma*, is connected to the base by a tube called the *style*. When a pollen grain lands on the stigma, it sprouts a pollen tube that grows inside the style down to the base of the carpel, where the *ovary*, or reproductive organ, is located.

Botanists had always assumed that the movement of the pollen tube down the style was caused by its own growth. They thought that the tube followed some kind of chemical signal produced, perhaps, in the ovary.

Sanders and Lord discovered that this is not the case. They placed red microscopic latex beads on the stigmas of several kinds of flowering plants and observed them with a microscope. They found that the beads moved down the styles of each of the flowers just as pollen tubes do—and at about the same speed. To make sure that gravity was not a factor, the scientists also placed beads in flowers that were laid horizontally rather than standing vertically. That change had no effect on the movement of the beads.

Since the beads could not move by themselves, the researchers concluded that their movement must have been caused by a material secreted by the flower. Further research will be needed to identify that substance.

Hardy hybrids. An explanation for the phenomenon of *hybrid vigor*—the tendency of hybrid plants to be larger, stronger, and more fertile than their inbred parents—was offered in September 1988 by a group of Canadian and Australian plant physiologists. The scientists said that hybrid vigor seems to result because hybrid plants produce greater amounts of some important hormones.

America's Endangered Plants

A total of 253 plant species in the United States and its territories are in danger of becoming extinct within the next five years. Another 427 species of American plants may disappear in the five years after that. Moreover, nearly 8 per cent of those 680 species may already be extinct in the wild and are surviving only in the protected environment of botanical gardens.

Those estimates were released in December 1988 by the Center for Plant Conservation in Boston, a consortium of 19 botanical gardens and *arboreta* (tree gardens). The center's report, the first comprehensive survey ever made of the estimated survival time of endangered U.S. plant species, was based on a list of 800 imperiled species that was reviewed by 89 American botanists. The botanists, all experts in the conservation of rare native plants, predicted how soon each species might become extinct. They also added a number of other endangered plants to the list.

The experts agreed that the pace of plant extinction has been accelerating rapidly. They pointed out that perhaps 200 U.S. plant species have become extinct during the past 200 years. Before that, the entire world lost only about one plant species each 1,000 years, so a loss of 680 species in just one decade and in just one part of the globe would be truly catastrophic.

Looking beyond the 10-year period, the botanists estimated that some 3,000 native plant species may become extinct in the foreseeable future—more than 10 per cent of the approximately 25,000 species of plants in the United States.

The situation is the same or worse in most other parts of the world. It is estimated that about 20 per cent of Earth's approximately 300,000 plant species are in danger. Most of these plants are in the tropical rain forests that are being cut down, and many have not even been identified yet.

Why is extinction imminent for so many U.S. species? The main reason is the destruction of habitats. This destruction is caused, especially in the Eastern United States, by land development, such as the construction of shopping malls and housing tracts. In the Western states, the poor management of public lands has been a critical factor. There, many habitats have been destroyed by the spread of *exotic* (foreign) plant species. For example, June grass, which was introduced from Europe in the late 1800's, has invaded hundreds of square kilometers of Western lands, pushing out some native species of grass that are less able to compete for the usually scarce moisture.

Public apathy has also contributed to the problem. Americans have rallied to the cause of endangered animals such as whooping cranes and African elephants, but they seem unconcerned about endangered plants. Perhaps they consider wild animals to be public property, but plants are the property of the owner of the land on which they grow.

The consequences of habitat destruction are often most serious in the tropics and subtropics. Those regions have a much greater number of

Among the U.S. plants facing extinction are the *Amsinckia grandiflora, above,* a plant with large yellow-orange flowers that grows at only one site in California; *Chionanthus pygmaeus, right,* a flowering shrub found at various locations in Florida; and *Lesquerella pallida, far right,* a very rare Texas plant with delicate white flowers.

plant species than are found in cooler climates. And many species grow in only a small area, increasing the probability of their being wiped out. It is not surprising, therefore, that nearly 75 per cent of the 680 species on the most-endangered list are located in just four states and Puerto Rico. Hawaii has 21 per cent of the 680 species; California, 19 per cent; Texas, 12.2 per cent; Florida, 10.6 per cent; and Puerto Rico, 10.1 per cent. But nearly all of the 50 states have at least a few native plants that are among those facing extinction.

Saving endangered plants is important for several reasons. Among those plants, there may be some that produce substances that would be of value in making medicines. Others might possess genetic traits that could be used to improve crop plants. We might also find that some plants are worth growing for their own sake—as food or perhaps for the oils in their seeds. But beyond such practical applications, there is a sense of loss when any species—a plant as much as an animal—disappears from the face of the Earth forever.

What can we do to save our native plants? The best course of action is to preserve the habitats of endangered species so they can continue to exist as part of a natural plant community. One way to accomplish that is by establishing preserves in which plant life is protected. Another approach is to improve the management of public lands to minimize damage from grazing animals and crowding out by exotic plant species.

Unfortunately, such steps are not always possible. In many cases, either habitats are too far gone to be saved or exotic plants are so widespread that they cannot be eliminated. In those situations, the only alternative is to preserve plants and seeds in botanical gardens and seed banks until the day when the species can be reestablished in the wild. Of the 680 native plants in danger of becoming extinct during the next 10 years, only 91 are presently being preserved this way.

Such preservation is no easy task. A species reproduced by seed year after year in a botanical garden may become "domesticated." That is, the characteristics that best suit the species to the mild, artificial environment tend to persist, while characteristics that the plant needed to survive in its natural habitat—and the genes that produced those traits—may disappear.

For this reason, preserving plants in enclosed surroundings is not a satisfactory solution to the extinction problem, but for many endangered species it is the only solution available. Where our options for effective action are so limited, we have no choice in the matter but simply to do the best we can.   [Frank B. Salisbury]

To investigate hybrid vigor, the researchers crossed four strains of corn to produce a number of hybrids. As expected, all the hybrids were taller and more productive than the parent plants. The scientists theorized that the parents were less vigorous than the offspring because they had lower levels of important plant hormones called gibberellins (GA's).

To test their theory, the scientists applied a gibberellin called GA_3 to all the parent and hybrid plants. They found that the parent plants responded to the GA_3 much more than the offspring did, suggesting that the parents had less of the hormone. And an analysis of the plants' tissues revealed that nearly all of the parent plants did contain smaller amounts of GA's.

GA's are produced in corn plants with the aid of proteins called *enzymes*. The researchers speculated that hybrid corn plants have more of the needed enzymes than inbred plants and thus can produce larger quantities of hormones. If so, the same situation may hold true for other kinds of plants, though the specific enzymes and hormones involved might vary from species to species.

Auxin and stem growth. Botanists have long theorized that *auxin*, an important plant hormone, is involved when plant stems bend upward in response to gravity. In January 1989, researchers at the University of Missouri at Columbia announced findings supporting the idea that auxin causes cells on the bottom side of horizontal stems to grow more quickly than cells on the opposite side.

The investigators found that certain molecules of *ribonucleic acid* (RNA) increased in the lower half of soybean stems that had been laid on their side and decreased in the upper half. RNA is a molecule that "reads" genes to carry out the production of proteins in both animal and plant cells. The type of RNA they studied appears only when plants are treated with auxin. Auxin stimulates plant cells to manufacture the RNA molecules, which produce enzymes essential for cell growth.

When cell growth is more rapid on one side of a stem than on the other, the stem bends toward the side of lesser

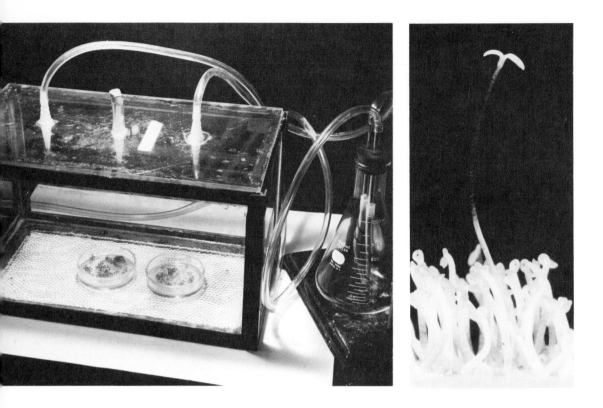

Botany

Continued

Mouse-ear cress plants, *above,* grow in a chamber filled with the gaseous compound ethylene in an experiment at Michigan State University in East Lansing. Small amounts of ethylene are normally produced by plants to regulate growth and other processes. A *mutant* (genetically altered) mouse-ear cress plant that is resistant to ethylene, *above right,* towers above the normal plants. Little is known about how ethylene controls growth, but studies with such mutant plants may lead to a better understanding of this compound.

growth. Stems bend upward because of such variations in cell growth. Scientists theorized that auxin—responding in some unknown way to gravity—causes the more rapid cell growth on the lower side of the stems.

To test that theory, the Missouri scientists made careful measurements of the RNA content of the stem tissues after the stems had been laid horizontally. They found that the RNA molecules began to increase in the bottom side of the stem, and decrease in the top side, after the position change but before any noticeable stem bending had occurred. This result strongly supported the notion that the differences were caused by differences in response to auxin.

Auxin sensitivity. Botanists recently questioned whether the increase in RNA in the bottom part of a horizontal stem meant that the amount of auxin had also increased. In December 1988, scientists at Utah State University in Logan reported evidence indicating that, instead, it is plant tissues' response to auxin that is elevated.

The researchers, under the direction of plant physiologist Frank B. Salisbury, placed stem segments from sunflower seedlings in a horizontal position in solutions of auxin of varying strength. They found that as the strength of the solution increased, the stems responded less to gravity. In the most concentrated solutions, in fact, the stem pieces bent downward.

Measurements of growth showed that an increase in auxin actually inhibited cell growth in the lower side of the stems. In that half, auxin already present in the tissues was enough to make cells grow at close to their maximum rate. More auxin was too much for the cells, slowing rather than stimulating growth.

In the upper half of the horizontal stems, however, increased auxin had stimulated growth. Because much more auxin was required by upper tissues than lower tissues to cause maximum growth, the upper tissues were much less sensitive to auxin than the lower tissues.   [Frank B. Salisbury]

In WORLD BOOK, see BOTANY; PLANT.

Chemistry

Two chemists shocked the scientific community in March 1989 when they announced that they had created a fusion reaction in a tabletop device at room temperature. B. Stanley Pons of the University of Utah and Martin Fleischmann of the University of Southampton, England, said that they operated the device successfully for 100 hours and that it gave off four times as much energy as they had put into it.

A fusion reaction joins atomic nuclei and releases a tremendous amount of energy. Fusion provides the energy of the sun and the other stars. In an effort to harness this powerful process to produce useful energy, physicists have spent billions of dollars on massive machines that reproduce the extreme temperatures and pressures that bring about fusion in the sun.

The chemists claimed that they had success with a device you could hold in your hand. If their claims prove true, this breakthrough holds tremendous promise for an inexpensive, nonpolluting, and almost limitless source of energy. But there are many doubters. See PHYSICS, SUBATOMIC (Close-Up).

Growth aid tested. A development that may help up to 80 per cent of the 12,500 United States children who suffer from dwarfism and other growth disorders was reported at the national meeting of the American Chemical Society in April 1989. Chemist Arthur Felix of Hoffmann-La Roche, Incorporated, in Nutley, N.J., told colleagues that an artificially produced version of a substance called *growth hormone releasing factor* (GHRF) could cause the human body to release normal amounts of *human growth hormones* (HGH), substances that promote growth. When children's bodies produce too little HGH, their growth is stunted.

Only a few years ago, dead bodies were the only source of extra HGH, and the substance was in short supply. Today, the main type of HGH is produced in laboratories by genetically engineered bacteria and supplies are plentiful.

Unfortunately, patients require large amounts of the genetically engineered

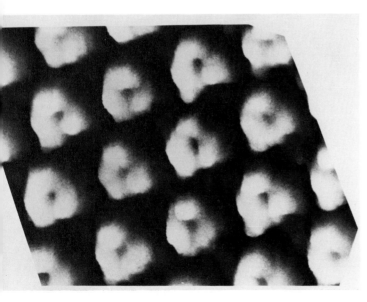

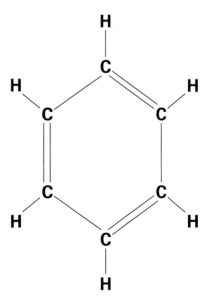

Chemists since the 1860's have envisioned the benzene molecule to be a hexagonal ring, *above right,* made up of carbon atoms (C) bonded to hydrogen atoms (H). The first picture of benzene molecules, *above,* taken by IBM scientists in San Jose, Calif., with a scanning tunneling microscope, revealed that they are indeed shaped like six-sided rings.

Chemistry

Continued

hormone, and it must be injected up to three times a week. Furthermore, because this substance is only one type of HGH, it does not help patients as much as would the full spectrum of natural growth hormones.

The search for a better treatment for growth disorders began in 1982 when scientists at the Salk Institute in La Jolla, Calif., discovered natural GHRF. Researchers learned to manufacture the substance by genetic engineering and in November 1988 began clinical tests of the engineered product in children.

The GHRF is 50 to 150 times more powerful than an equal weight of genetically engineered HGH, so doses of GHRF can be smaller than HGH doses. Furthermore, the GHRF molecule is smaller, consisting of 44 *amino acids*, the building blocks of proteins, compared with HGH's 191 amino acids. Because GHRF is both smaller and more potent, it may be possible to deliver the drug through a patch worn on the skin or by inhalation of a GHRF mist instead of by injection.

Harvesting sunlight. Green plants turn solar energy into chemical energy—stored primarily in sugars—by a process called *photosynthesis*. Chemists James E. Guillet and his colleagues at the University of Toronto in Canada reported in December 1988 on the invention of a *photozyme*, a synthetic chemical that also uses sunlight to perform a chemical reaction yet is not consumed by the reaction.

Guillet's invention, a *polymer* (chain of molecules) called PSSS-VN, is a virus-sized molecule, part of which is spherical. In water, PSSS-VN attracts *organic* (carbon-containing) molecules that are repelled by water molecules. The PSSS-VN molecules concentrate the organic molecules in their spherical regions, isolating them from the water molecules.

To test the effectiveness of the polymer as a photozyme, the Toronto scientists put a perfume ingredient into a water solution containing PSSS-VN. The perfume molecules traveled to the photozyme's spherical regions. When exposed to light, the perfume mole-

A bottle made of an experimental heat-resistant soft plastic called Cleartuf HP holds its shape better than does a bottle made of a conventional polyester when used to boil water. Cleartuf HP was developed by Goodyear Tire and Rubber Company, which says the material also retards spoilage in bottled foods during storage.

Ecolyte, a new plastic, disintegrates in sunlight and so may help solve the problem of littering. A food tray made of Ecolyte, *top left,* has fallen to pieces, *top right,* after 30 days' exposure to sunlight. After 40 days, *right,* little of the tray remains. And after 55 days, *far right,* it has vanished.

Chemistry

Continued

cules broke apart nine times more rapidly than they did when exposed to light in a solvent not containing the photozyme. The Toronto chemists cited two reasons for the speed-up: The perfume molecules in the PSSS-VN solution were more highly concentrated, and certain groups of atoms on the polymer captured sunlight and transferred some solar energy to the "guest" molecules.

Photozymes open up the prospect of using solar energy to produce fuels. In addition, they might enable the chemical industry to perform certain *organic reactions* (reactions involving carbon compounds) in water, rather than in the organic solvents presently used. Water is not only less expensive than these solvents but also cleaner.

Growing new body tissues. Chemical engineer Robert S. Langer of Massachusetts Institute of Technology in Cambridge reported in April 1989 that he is developing polymers that may help adults and children who suffer from liver diseases. Each year, about 30,000 people die of liver diseases in

the United States. Physicians have limited the death toll somewhat in children by transplanting into their bodies healthy livers removed from individuals who have recently died. Of the children listed as candidates for liver transplants, however, 25 per cent die before a liver becomes available for transplant, and many other children wait for weeks and months before receiving new livers.

Langer's polymers provide a framework for growing new body tissues in the laboratory. Atoms in the polymers form, in effect, microscopic scaffolds to which growing tissue clings. Doctors may one day use such polymers to grow liver tissues. For example, a parent would donate cells from his or her liver for a child. The doctors would place the cells in the scaffold and supply the cells with nutrients. The cells would eventually grow into a substantial amount of tissue, which surgeons would implant in the child.

In experiments with rats, Langer and physician Joseph Vacanti of Boston's Children's Hospital have already

241

Chemistry
Continued

"seeded" polymer systems with liver, cartilage, and intestine cells removed from rats. The cells grew to form tissues, which were transplanted successfully into rats.

The researchers monitored the structure and function of the transplanted tissues for up to three months. In one study, the scientists confirmed that transplanted liver cells produced the protein albumin while in the animals. This protein is a major constituent of blood. After implantation, substances in the body gradually break down the scaffold polymers chemically so they can be removed from the body by natural processes.

Scientists must do much more work before newly grown tissues can become a viable alternative to human transplants. They must test them in small animals for much longer than three months, test them in large animals such as monkeys, and finally test them in people.

Bye-bye, blue jeans. A new chemical process may provide relief for people who are bored by the blueness of blue jeans. Chemist Robert J. Harper, Jr., of the U.S. Department of Agriculture's Southern Research Center in New Orleans reported in April 1989 that a new fabric treatment method makes "just-in-time" dyeing of apparel possible. As a result, red, yellow, and even green jeans may become as common as blue jeans.

Today, fabrics must be dyed before they are treated for wrinkle resistance, so dyeing is generally done in large lots. No merchandiser wants to get stuck with a warehouse full of pink dungarees, so color choices tend to be conservative.

But the new USDA wrinkle-resistance treatment can be applied to just one side of the fabric, leaving the other side available for dyeing. A wholesale merchant therefore could keep generic white garments on hand and dye them in small lots as orders for various colors of jeans come in.   [Peter J. Andrews]

In the Special Reports section, see Is EARTH OVERHEATING? In WORLD BOOK, see CHEMISTRY; GROWTH; HORMONE; POLYMER.

Computer Hardware

Faster microprocessor chips for computers appeared in early 1989, when both Intel Corporation of Santa Clara, Calif., and Motorola Corporation of Schaumburg, Ill., announced advanced chips containing more than 1 million transistors. These are suitable for technical work stations that require tremendous computing power.

Faster chips. Until early 1989, the leading microprocessors in the personal computer world were models 80286 and 80386, manufactured by Intel. The 80286 chip handles 16 *bits* of data at a time. (A bit is a 0 or a 1, the smallest piece of information a computer can handle. All computer data is composed of arrangements of 0's or 1's.) Model 80386 can move 32 bits of data at a time. This chip has a major advantage over 80286 in addition to its bit rate: A computer using the 80386 chip can handle more than a single program at a time.

In April 1989, however, Intel introduced a faster 32-bit microprocessor, model i486. This chip can carry out 12 million to 24 million instructions per second, compared with 4 million to 8 million instructions per second for an 80386 chip.

International Business Machines Corporation (IBM) claimed in June 1989 that it had developed the world's fastest memory chip. This dynamic random access memory (DRAM) chip can store 1 million bits and can retrieve a bit in 22 billionths of a second. The new chip is two to three times faster than previous DRAM chips. DRAM is the computer's "live" or temporary memory, which holds programs and data that are manipulated by microprocessor chips.

Laptop computers continued to gain popularity during the year as they grew smaller and more powerful. NEC of Wood Dale, Ill., in October 1988 introduced an extremely small laptop, the UltraLite, which weighs less than 2 kilograms (4.4 pounds) and is about the size of a notebook. Instead of traditional disc drives, the UltraLite uses battery-powered chips to store both software and data in memory. Software for the UltraLite is stored on cards that

Computer Hardware

Continued

are inserted into the machine much as video game cartridges are put into game machines. The UltraLite sells for about $3,000.

Jobs's NeXT machine. In October 1988, Steven P. Jobs, president of NeXT, Incorporated, of Palo Alto, Calif., introduced a machine called the NeXT Computer System. Jobs was a founder of Apple Computer, Incorporated, of Cupertino, Calif. His new computer attracted a great deal of attention because of Jobs's reputation as an entrepreneur and because the machine has several innovative features. Among these are an erasable optical storage disc that holds 256 million characters of information (equivalent to 128,000 double-spaced typewritten pages), high-fidelity sound, 8 million characters of RAM, and a wide array of software that includes not only word-processing, database, and other programs but also a dictionary, thesaurus, and even the works of William Shakespeare. NeXT is aimed at the higher-education market and is priced at $6,500.

Laser printers, already well established in the office, gained popularity among consumers in 1988 and 1989 as manufacturers responded to competition by cutting prices. A crucial component in desktop publishing, laser printers operate in a manner similar to photocopiers, delivering sharp images and text. By the summer of 1989, a host of laser printers were available for less than $2,500.

In August 1988, Qume Corporation of Milpitas, Calif., introduced the CrystalPrint Publisher, which uses liquid crystal technology to achieve laser printing results. Conventional laser printers focus images with a rotating cylindrical mirror. The CrystalPrint Publisher, by contrast, uses a liquid crystal shutter, which provides a less distorted image and increases printing speed. The $4,499 CrystalPrint Publisher was developed for use with Apple Macintosh computers.

New scanners. A number of optical scanners went on the market during the year. For example, Hewlett-Packard Company of Palo Alto, Calif.,

The Wizard electronic organizer, available from Sharp Electronics Corporation, can function as seven different devices, including an appointment diary, personal computer, calendar, telephone directory, and clock that tracks time zones all over the world. Add-on software cards can convert the Wizard into a language translator, a dictionary and thesaurus, or a time manager.

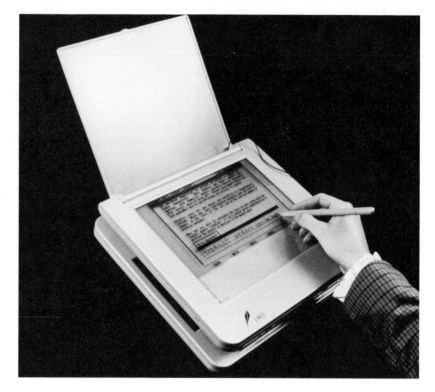

The Write-Top computer made by Linus Technologies of Reston, Va., needs no keyboard for typing in letters and numbers. Instead it has a transparent pad that "reads" hand-printed letters and other symbols and displays them on a liquid crystal screen. Training the machine to read an individual's printing takes about half an hour.

Computer
Hardware
Continued

in January 1989 introduced the Scan-Jet Plus optical scanner that produces images in 256 shades of gray. It works with either an IBM PS/2 or a Macintosh computer and costs $2,190.

An optical scanner converts both text and images on a paper page into digital data that can be stored on computer discs and incorporated into desktop publishing documents. Scanners use light sensors and special chips called charge-coupled devices (CCD's). A CCD records patterns of light and darkness on a scanned page, and the information is then converted into digital data.

Bus revolt. Computers made by IBM and computers that are compatible with IBM machines continued to dominate the market for desktop computers in 1988 and 1989. Recent developments in hardware, however, almost certainly will split this group of products into two segments.

The developments centered around the computer *bus*, the pathway of circuits through which the computer distributes information among its various

parts. In 1987, IBM introduced a bus called Micro Channel Architecture (MCA) for its Personal System/2 (PS/2) computers. IBM intended this bus to help differentiate its new machines from the competition. While the bus meets many needs of the next generation of computers, it will not accommodate computer boards and internal devices designed for PC's.

A group of IBM's competitors in October 1988 responded to the MCA challenge. Led by Compaq Computer Corporation of Houston, IBM's leading competitor, and Tandy Radio Shack of Fort Worth, Tex., the largest computer retailer, the group announced a personal computer design standard called Extended Industry Standard Architecture (EISA). Computers built to this standard will use the IBM PC bus, so boards and internal devices purchased for IBM PC's will work on EISA machines. More than 100 companies announced support for the EISA standard. [Keith Ferrell]

In WORLD BOOK, see COMPUTER; COMPUTER, PERSONAL.

Computer Software

Computer viruses continued to spread in 1988 and 1989, with more than 30,000 virus infections reported in November and December 1988 alone. A *computer virus* is a small piece of software designed to spread from machine to machine and to do mischief. Some viruses even damage the computers they infect or damage or destroy data.

Concerns about data security heightened in November 1988, when a virus spread through Arpanet, a United States government computer network that allows scientists at various universities and other research institutions to share information. Robert T. Morris, Jr., a graduate student in computer science at Cornell University in Ithaca, N.Y., allegedly created the virus and released it on November 2 from his terminal at Cornell. The virus caused no damage, but the cost of removing it and the computer time lost was estimated at close to $100 million.

As a result of the infection, legislators sought to strengthen laws such as the 1986 Computer Fraud and Abuse Act, aimed at protecting businesses and individuals from damage caused by computer viruses. Proposed changes would provide stiff penalties for deliberately distributing a virus. Software designed to detect viruses also found a ready market in 1988 and 1989.

HyperCard programs. Software producers continued to issue HyperCard programs for business, education, and entertainment in 1988 and 1989. HyperCard, produced by Apple Computer Incorporated of Cupertino, Calif., for its Macintosh computers, functions as both a database and a programming language. Users store information as linked "stacks" of "cards," the fundamental units of the HyperCard database. Using a mouse to point a cursor at a symbol or word representing a card or stack, the HyperCard user can browse through related information quickly.

Activision of Menlo Park, Calif., in August 1988 introduced the Manhole, a HyperCard entertainment package that enables players to explore a fairy-tale world filled with animation. In January 1989, Silicon Beach Software

Optical scanners improved during 1988 and 1989. In the Apple Scanner, *above,* a photograph is laid flat while the scanner translates the light and dark areas into the 0's and 1's of computer language. Scanned photos can be processed by computer programs that reproduce the image as up to 256 shades of gray. Final picture quality depends on the printing device's resolution. A 2,540-dot-per-square-inch (dpi) print from a Linotronic typesetting machine, *bottom right,* is sharper than a 300-dpi laser print, *top right.*

Heard and Seen on the Grapevine

Grapevine, a hypermedia program, enables a student to search a database for information about the historical setting of John Steinbeck's novel *The Grapes of Wrath* (1939), *right.* The information can then be presented in audio and video forms through speakers, a videodisc player, and TV set connected to the computer. For example, the computer monitor, *below,* shows a list of 1930's radio programs that a student could listen to while viewing old photographs of families listening to the radio. To study politics of the Great Depression, the student can watch, among other things, a filmed speech on the New Deal by President Franklin D. Roosevelt, *bottom.* Other kinds of information available on Grapevine include magazine articles, posters and other artwork, and even songs.

STEINBECK

THE GRAPES OF WRATH

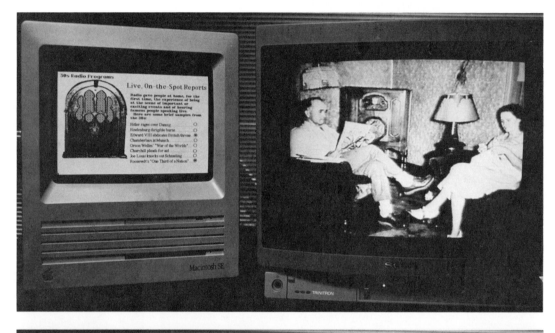

Computer Software

Continued

of San Diego released Supercard, a program that is compatible with HyperCard but, unlike the Apple product, also works with color monitors. A Bible study program, HyperBible, was also released during the year in both King James and New International versions.

Hypermedia growth. HyperCard gave rise to a rapidly growing field of software called *hypermedia*, which makes use of a number of media to present data. HyperCard and similar programs present only text and graphics on the computer screen. Hypermedia programs also steer users to related pieces of information in the computer database. But the information can then be heard through speakers and viewed through video equipment. The searches through the database are conducted by HyperCard.

Several hypermedia programs appeared in 1988 and 1989. Apple Computer worked with teacher Patricia Hanlon and librarian Robert Campbell of Lowell High School in San Francisco to develop Grapevine, a hypermedia program to help students studying *The Grapes of Wrath*, John Steinbeck's novel of the Great Depression of the 1930's. Students use a videodisc player and a computer to call up depression-era films, still photographs, magazine articles, and radio programs.

Filmmaker George Lucas' Lucasfilm studio developed a hypermedia program featuring Paul Parkranger, a cartoon character who asks the computer user to help determine why ducks are abandoning their marshy homeland. To gather background material, the user can open up "notebooks" and "file cabinets" containing such sources of information as filmed interviews with game wardens and hunters, animated maps, and articles about ducks.

Outlining software. Lotus Development Corporation of Cambridge, Mass., in July 1988 released *Agenda*, its version of a type of program called Personal Information Manager (PIM) and intended for business managers and executives. These programs have a built-in outline format that lets the user link ideas, names, financial data, dates, and sales projections to provide status reports on various companies. The main feature of a PIM is that a busy executive can "throw" into it tremendous amounts of unrelated, unorganized information of virtually any length and format, then return to the program later to organize the information under headlines and subheads.

Advanced graphics packages. Adobe Systems of Mountain View, Calif., in mid-1988 introduced *Illustrator 88*, a professional graphic arts tool for Macintosh users. At about the same time, the Aldus Corporation released a similar program called Freehand. The software takes advantage of PostScript—a computer language that translates graphic information into data for a laser printer or typesetter. PostScript enables the printer to reproduce, for example, curved edges without the jagged lines often associated with computer graphics, as well as shading that gives images a realistic look.

Educational programs. Wolfram Research Incorporated of Champaign, Ill., in June 1988 introduced Mathematica, a Macintosh program that covers algebra, calculus, and other complex mathematics. This software can be used both to solve problems and to teach math. The user types in everything up to the equal sign, and Mathematica and the Macintosh do the rest.

Tandy Radio Shack of Fort Worth, Tex., in July 1988 released School-Mate, an educational version of its DeskMate business program. School-Mate automates grade averaging, record keeping, and other numerical work for teachers and serves as the central control for classroom computer networks.

Entertainment software continued to grow in popularity in 1988 and 1989. The program that attracted the most attention was a Soviet game called Tetris, a simple but challenging game of skill involving the manipulation of pictures of falling objects. Versions of Tetris for all popular computers were released in the United States during the second half of 1988.

Nobunaga's Ambition, imported from Japan in July 1988 by Koei of Torrance, Calif., enables players to "re-create" ancient Japan and react to challenges faced by leaders hoping to unify the country. [Keith Ferrell]

In WORLD BOOK, see COMPUTER; COMPUTER, PERSONAL.

Deaths of Scientists

Notable scientists and engineers who died between June 1, 1988, and June 1, 1989, are listed below. Those listed were Americans unless otherwise indicated. An asterisk (*) indicates that a biography appears in THE WORLD BOOK ENCYCLOPEDIA.

*Alvarez, Luis W. (1911-Sept. 1, 1988), physicist who won the Nobel Prize in 1968 for his use of *bubble chambers*—containers filled with superheated liquid—to detect new subatomic particles. He and his son Walter, a geologist, proposed the theory that the impact of a comet or asteroid led to the extinction of nearly 70 per cent of Earth's species, including the dinosaurs, about 65 million years ago.

Anderson, Herbert L. (1914-July 16, 1988), physicist who helped build the first nuclear reactor in 1942 and the first atomic bomb in 1945 as part of the U.S. government's top-secret Manhattan Project.

Andrewes, Sir Christopher (1896-Dec. 31, 1988), British virologist who helped discover the influenza virus and studied the causes of the common cold.

Austin, Oliver L., Jr. (1903-Dec. 31, 1988), ornithologist who wrote the definitive study *Birds of the World* (1961).

Bond, James (1900-Feb. 14, 1989), ornithologist and expert on the birds of the West Indies whose name was borrowed by British author Ian Fleming for his fictional secret agent.

Bourne, Geoffrey H. (1909-July 19, 1988), Australian-born nutritionist, anatomist, and expert on primates. He directed the Yerkes Primate Research Center in Atlanta, Ga., from 1962 to 1978.

Brickwedde, Ferdinand G. (1903-March 29, 1989), physicist who helped discover *deuterium*, a hydrogen isotope also called *heavy hydrogen*. Chemist Harold C. Urey headed the deuterium research team and received the Nobel Prize in chemistry for the discovery in 1934.

Burk, Dean (1904-Oct. 6, 1988), biochemist at the National Cancer Institute in Bethesda, Md., from 1939 to 1974. He helped develop the *nuclear magnetic resonance scanner*, a device that uses magnetic fields and radio waves to produce clear images of the internal organs. Burk also was a codiscoverer of *biotin*, one of the B family of vitamins.

Dart, Raymond A. (1893-Nov. 22, 1988), Australian anthropologist who in 1924 in South Africa discovered the Taung skull, the fossil remains of an apelike creature called *Australopithecus*.

Festinger, Leon (1919-Feb. 11, 1989), psychologist who developed the theory of *cognitive dissonance*, a state of mental agitation that occurs when two simultaneously held thoughts, opinions, or beliefs are inconsistent.

Fox, Daniel W. (1923-Feb. 15, 1989), chemist who invented a tough plastic called Lexan for the General Electric Company.

Glushko, Valentin P. (1908-death reported Feb. 2, 1989), Soviet rocket scientist who helped design the engine for the world's first intercontinental ballistic missile, launched in 1957.

Gollan, Frank (1909-Oct. 5, 1988), Czechoslovak-born pediatrician who isolated the polio virus in 1948 and invented the heart-lung machine.

*Hirohito (1901-Jan. 7, 1989), marine biologist who reigned as emperor of Japan from 1926 until his death.

Holmes, Thomas H., III (1918-Dec. 24, 1988), psychiatrist who along with Richard H. Rahe created the Holmes-Rahe stress scale, which measures on a scale of 11 to 100 the effects of such life changes as the death of a spouse, marriage, and retirement.

Hurley, Lucille S. (1922-July 28, 1988), Latvian-born nutritionist who linked dietary deficiencies with birth defects.

Klots, Alexander B. (1903-April 18, 1989), an authority on butterflies and other insects who wrote the best seller *A Field Guide to the Butterflies of North America* (1951). From 1933 to 1967, he taught biology at what is now City University of New York.

Ledoux, Paul (1914-Oct. 6, 1988), Belgian astrophysicist known for his studies of stellar structure, stellar stability, and *variable stars* (stars that change in brightness).

*Lorenz, Konrad Z. (1903-Feb. 27, 1989), Austrian naturalist who shared the Nobel Prize in physiology or medicine in 1973 with Nikolaas Tinbergen of Great Britain and Karl von Frisch of Austria for their pioneering work in *ethology*, the study of animal behavior in natural environments. Lorenz developed the theory of *imprinting*, the

Luis W. Alvarez

James Bond

Raymond A. Dart

Deaths
of Scientists
Continued

Konrad Z. Lorenz

Emilio G. Segrè

Felix Wankel

bonding between young animals and a mother figure, and did many experiments trying to prove that most animals are instinctively aggressive.

Ma Haide (George Hatem) (1908?-Oct. 3, 1988), Chinese physician, born in the United States, who led the effort to wipe out leprosy and venereal disease in China.

Pagels, Heinz R. (1939-July 24, 1988), physicist and author of popular books about science, including *The Cosmic Code* (1982) and *Perfect Symmetry* (1985).

Richter, Curt Paul (1894-Dec. 21, 1988), psychobiologist credited with the discovery of *biorhythms*, an internal clock that governs eating, sleeping, and sexual behavior.

Ruben, Samuel (1900-July 16, 1988), electrochemist who patented more than 300 inventions, including the alkaline battery.

Sears, Robert R. (1908-May 22, 1989), developmental psychologist known for his studies of how childhood discipline affects personality and behavior. He headed the psychology department at Stanford University in California from 1953 to 1961.

Segrè, Emilio G. (1905-April 22, 1989), Italian-born nuclear physicist who shared the 1959 Nobel Prize in physics with Owen Chamberlain for demonstrating the existence of the *antiproton*, a negatively charged antimatter counterpart of the positively charged proton. Segrè also contributed to the discovery of the elements plutonium, technetium, and astatine.

Shimkin, Michael B. (1912-Jan. 16, 1989), Russian-born medical researcher who helped establish the link between smoking and lung cancer while working at the U.S. National Cancer Institute from 1939 to 1963.

Spieth, Herman T. (1905-Oct. 20, 1988), zoologist who studied the behavior and evolution of various fly species.

Steyermark, Julian A. (1909-Oct. 15, 1988), botanist who discovered and described more plant species than any other botanist of recent times.

Stone, Marshall H. (1903-Jan. 9, 1989), mathematician known for his work in *Hilbert space*, an imaginary space with an infinite number of dimensions named for German mathematician David Hilbert. Stone received the National Medal of Science in 1983.

Tinbergen, Nikolaas (1907-Dec. 21, 1988), Dutch-born British biologist who shared with Konrad Lorenz and Karl von Frisch the 1973 Nobel Prize for physiology or medicine for his studies of animal behavior.

Tishler, Max (1906-March 18, 1989), chemist who developed the processes for mass production of cortisone, penicillin, and several vitamins. He was awarded the National Medal of Science in 1987.

Uhlenbeck, George E. (1900-Oct. 31, 1988), Dutch-born physicist who codiscovered, with Samuel A. Goudsmit, that electrons spin. Their discovery proved to be a cornerstone in understanding the nature of atoms. Uhlenbeck received the National Medal of Science in 1977 and shared the Wolf Prize in 1979.

Wankel, Felix (1902-Oct. 9, 1988), West German engineer who developed the Wankel rotary engine. Once used in Mazda automobiles, the Wankel generates more power in less space than conventional piston engines do.

Warner, John Christian (1897-April 12, 1989), chemist who supervised plutonium research on the Manhattan Project that developed the first nuclear bomb in 1945. He served as president of Carnegie Institute of Technology (now Carnegie-Mellon University) in Pittsburgh, Pa., from 1949 to 1965.

White, Jack E. (1921-July 2, 1988), surgeon and medical researcher who studied cancer among blacks. He taught surgery at Howard University in Washington, D.C., from 1951 to 1986.

Whitney, Hassler (1907-May 10, 1989), mathematician whose specialty was the study of geometric figures. He received the National Medal of Science in 1976 and the Wolf Prize in 1981.

Wolman, Abel (1892-Feb. 22, 1989), sanitary engineer who pioneered the use of chlorine to purify drinking water, ending such water-borne diseases as cholera and typhoid in many nations. He received the National Medal of Science in 1975.

ZoBell, Claude E. (1904-March 13, 1989), deep-sea scientist known as the father of marine microbiology. He was the first researcher to recover and cultivate living organisms from ocean depths greater than 6,000 meters (20,000 feet). [Sara Dreyfuss]

Dentistry

A research team from Marseille, France, in November 1988 reported on the use of computer-aided design and computer-aided manufacturing (CAD-CAM) in the construction of crowns, toothlike caps that are cemented onto damaged or decayed teeth.

The conventional method of making a crown involves a complex series of steps. The dentist must remove the damage or decay and grind the remaining tooth so that a crown will fit over it. The dentist then takes an *impression* (mold) of the prepared tooth with a puttylike material that hardens.

Next, dental technicians make a wax model in the size and shape of the desired crown. They then cover the wax model with plaster, heat it to melt out the wax, and fill the space with molten gold, creating the crown.

The CAD-CAM system of making crowns does away with impression materials, wax models, and gold casting. Instead, after the dentist has prepared the tooth, an optical probe system records the exact dimensions of the tooth. The information is put into a computer, which creates an electronic model of the tooth. Using this information, the dentist designs the crown on a video screen and transmits the final dimensions electronically to a computer-aided manufacturing system. The CAM system automatically shapes the crown.

The CAD-CAM technique also can be used to make *inlays* (shaped pieces of gold or porcelain that are cemented into a tooth as a filling) and *bridges* (sets of artificial teeth fastened to real teeth on both sides).

Dental psychology. Most cases of tooth decay and gum disease could be prevented if people used proper oral hygiene—that is, brushed after every meal and used dental floss every day to remove *plaque* (a film of food particles and bacteria). Most dentists find, however, that their attempts to motivate patients to reform poor oral hygiene are time-consuming and generally ineffective. French dental surgeon François Alcouffe in November 1988 reported a study using a psychological approach to the problem.

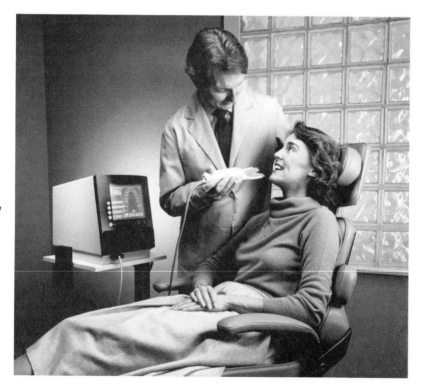

A computerized device may replace the wax molds or coated papers used by dentists to determine how well the upper and lower teeth meet when a person bites. The patient bites down on a sensor covered with a metal grid that conducts electricity. A computer screen displays the force of the bite and shows how the teeth meet.

Dentistry
Continued

The study group involved 26 volunteers with *periodontal disease*, infection of the gums and jawbone that may destroy the tissue supporting teeth, causing them to fall out. None of the volunteers maintained adequate oral hygiene as measured by a standardized plaque index score.

The patients were divided into two equal groups. The participants in one group took part in individual interviews with a psychologist, while the patients in the second group—a control group—did not. The interviews took about one hour for each person and focused on the patient's perception of periodontal disease, the relationship with the dentist, and the role of oral hygiene in the prevention and treatment of gum disease.

The interviewed group showed a significant improvement in plaque index scores after six months and maintained the improvement throughout a two-year study period. The control group showed no improvement. Involving a psychologist in periodontal treatment of unmotivated patients may prove more effective than repeated instructions by dentists.

Gum-disease drug. A new drug that fights periodontal disease was reported in November 1988 by researchers at the Harvard School of Dental Medicine in Boston. They found that a drug called *flurbiprofen* reduces the rate of jawbone destruction in people with periodontal disease. Flurbiprofen belongs to a group of medications called *nonsteroidal anti-inflammatory drugs*, including aspirin and ibuprofen, that are usually used to treat arthritis.

The drug trial involved 15 adult patients with active periodontal disease. Eight of them received flurbiprofen for two months, while the remaining seven were given *placebos* (look-alike substances with no active ingredients). Neither the patients nor the researchers knew which patients were getting the drug.

After two months, the flurbiprofen-treated patients showed less bone loss and more bone gain than the control group had.   [Paul Goldhaber]

In WORLD BOOK, see DENTISTRY.

Drugs

People from different racial backgrounds may respond differently to medication, according to a March 1989 report by a research group at Vanderbilt University in Nashville. The researchers gave 10 male Chinese-Americans and 10 male white Americans a series of increasingly powerful doses of propranolol, a medication commonly used to slow the heartbeat or lower blood pressure.

The scientists discovered that the Chinese-Americans were able to eliminate the drug from their bloodstreams faster than the white volunteers. The volunteers of Chinese descent also showed a much greater slowing of their heart rate, and a two to three times greater decrease in blood pressure.

Physicians have long been aware that two patients with the same medical problem may require different doses of medication. Some patients are said to be "sensitive" to a medicine, needing only a small amount, while others are resistant to its effects. But the idea that patients with different racial or ethnic backgrounds—which reflect genetic differences—may need different doses of medications is a new and important one. The significance of this ethnic or racial factor for medicines other than propranolol clearly indicates a need for further study.

Electric skin patch. A new, more effective skin patch for administering medication was described in December 1988. Researchers at North Shore University Hospital-Cornell University Medical College in Manhasset, N.Y., reported on a test of a patch, developed by Drug Delivery Systems, that uses an electric current to help medication pass through the skin.

Skin patches impregnated with medicine have been used for years to give steady doses of medicine for periods as long as one week. The patches have been used to administer only a handful of drugs, however, because human skin is an effective barrier that does not absorb many compounds.

The newly designed skin patch is unique in that it contains a battery and electrical circuitry, which passes an extremely low level of electric current

Drugs

Continued

across the skin. The current, too mild to be felt, lessens the skin's resistance to the absorption of drugs.

The Cornell investigators used the new patch to administer a medication to 13 healthy male volunteers. The drug was absorbed and increased the level of the medication in the volunteers' bloodstream without injuring the skin. The volunteers reported that they felt no sensation while wearing the patches. When the same volunteers were given a skin patch without electric current, the drug was not absorbed.

The new patch may allow a wider variety of drugs to be comfortably administered by means of skin patches rather than by injections.

Breast cancer chemotherapy. Four studies reported in the Feb. 23, 1989, issue of *The New England Journal of Medicine* found that giving drug treatment to all breast cancer patients decreased the likelihood that they would develop a recurrence of cancer within four to five years after the cancer was surgically removed. The reports involved the work of many scientists from hospitals around the world, who had agreed to work together to determine whether or not such treatment improved the cancer-free survival rate for women whose tumors did not appear to have spread at the time of surgery.

The traditional treatment of breast cancer usually begins with the surgical removal of the tumor in the breast. If the surgeon finds cancer cells in the lymph nodes near the tumor, it is likely that cancer cells have spread to other organs and may grow into tumors in their new sites. To prevent a recurrence of cancer in these patients, doctors treat them after the surgery with *chemotherapy* (the use of drugs to treat disease and infection).

Unfortunately, about 20 per cent of the patients who do not have cancer cells in their lymph nodes nonetheless develop a recurrence of cancer within a few years. For this reason, some scientists have argued that all breast cancer patients should be treated with chemotherapy. Other researchers have disagreed, contending that such a policy

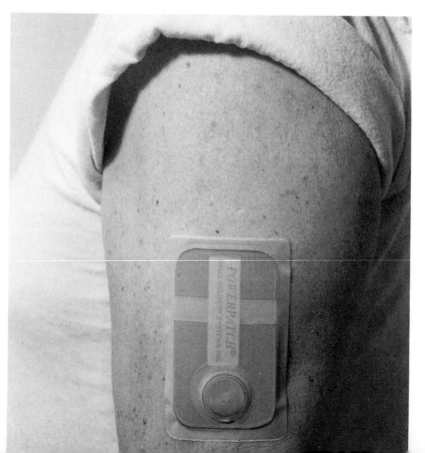

A battery-powered skin patch uses a mild electric current to help medication cross the barrier of the skin and pass into the bloodstream. The patch, developed at North Shore University Hospital-Cornell University Medical College in Manhasset, N.Y., may allow a wider variety of drugs to be administered through the skin.

A drug that in the laboratory seems to kill only cells infected with the AIDS virus is displayed by a researcher who helped develop it at the University of California, San Francisco. The new drug, which is derived from the root of a Chinese cucumber plant, is the only drug that can kill macrophages, immune-system cells that harbor large quantities of the AIDS virus.

Drugs
Continued

would subject many women to unnecessary and potentially dangerous treatment, because chemotherapy can cause serious side effects such as nausea, hair loss, and sterility.

The publication of the reports documenting the effectiveness of giving chemotherapy to all breast cancer patients did not put an end to the controversy, however. Some cancer experts, such as William L. McGuire of the University of Texas Health Science Center at San Antonio, argue that further research is needed to better determine which patients will truly benefit from chemotherapy.

Hepatitis B drug. An experimental drug therapy for a previously untreatable viral inflammation of the liver called chronic hepatitis B infection was reported in July 1988 by scientists from Washington University in St. Louis, Mo.

Hepatitis B is the most severe type of hepatitis and is usually spread via contaminated blood. Despite the fact that testing of donated blood has decreased the amount of hepatitis B transmitted

by blood products, this infection remains a major health problem for people who need frequent transfusions and for health-care workers.

Approximately 300,000 new hepatitis B cases are diagnosed in the United States each year. Between 5 and 10 per cent of the cases develop into chronic infections, which can lead to liver failure or liver cancer. In this way, chronic hepatitis B infection leads to 5,000 deaths each year in the United States—and many more throughout the world.

The Washington University researchers used a combination of two drugs—prednisone, a steroid hormone; and alpha 2b interferon, an artificially produced, but natural, protein that helps cells resist viral infection. Nine months after treatment began, 22 per cent of the patients treated with these drugs had no evidence of hepatitis. Although only 18 patients were treated with the new drug, the results were seen as encouraging. Another study involving more patients began in mid-1989. [B. Robert Meyer]

In WORLD BOOK, see DRUG.

Ecology

The predicted warming of the planet by the so-called greenhouse effect is likely to produce great changes among Earth's plants and animals. That prediction emerged from a meeting of ecologists, conservationists, and government officials in Washington, D.C., in October 1988.

The greenhouse effect is the retention in the atmosphere of energy from the sun. Carbon dioxide and certain other gases prevent heat produced by absorbed sunlight from being radiated away from the planet. As these gases build up in the atmosphere—the result of the burning of fossil fuels, such as coal and oil, and the destruction of forests—the greenhouse effect increases. In the Special Reports section, see IS EARTH OVERHEATING?

Life and global warming. The effects of atmospheric warming on life cannot be predicted with certainty, participants at the Washington meeting agreed, but they are likely to be significant. The experts said that many plants and animals in the warmest regions on Earth and in coastal areas that would be flooded by rising ocean levels would probably become extinct.

Plants and animals living in natural habitats that have become surrounded by cities, farms, and roads will probably also have a high rate of extinction. In such areas, most species will be prevented from migrating to a cooler or wetter climate.

The experts also predicted, however, that some organisms are apt to thrive in the warmer conditions—including weeds, parasites, and crop-eating insects. If so, agricultural output—which in many parts of the world would already be in decline as a result of heat and drought—will be reduced by insect damage, and the incidence of many tropical diseases will rise.

Sunspots and wildlife. Ecologists have long suspected that sunspot activity, by altering Earth's weather patterns, can affect some populations of wild animals. In 1989, ecologists were investigating the possibility that a link between sunspots and at least one group of animals had been found.

That link relates to a discovery made in 1987 by meteorologists at the Free University in West Berlin, West Germany. The German researchers reported evidence that sunspots are responsible for certain periods of warming in the Northern Hemisphere. Those periods correspond to increases in the number of snowshoe hares, an animal found in northern and mountainous parts of North America. The snowshoe hare's predators also increase in number.

The snowshoe hare and the animals that prey on it—notably the lynx, a type of wildcat—go through population cycles that last 10 to 11 years. After reaching a peak, the animals' numbers decline until the cycle begins anew.

Although there has been no general agreement about what causes the ups and downs in numbers of hares, some ecologists have suggested that the population cycles are somehow related to sunspots, magnetic "storms" that also occur in cycles of about 11 years. During peaks of sunspot activity, the sun sends out large amounts of charged particles, interrupting radio communications on Earth.

Scientists theorized for many years that sunspots also affect Earth's weather, but the German researchers were the first to find a convincing connection between sunspot activity and climate. The correlation they discovered is a relationship between sunspot activity and the effects of stratospheric winds over the equator.

The investigators discovered that when sunspot activity is at a minimum and these winds are blowing from the west, the Northern Hemisphere tends to be warmer than average. At that same time, the populations of snowshoe hares and lynxes begin to increase. That may occur because the warmer temperatures produce more edible greenery, enabling a habitat to support more hares. And with more hares to eat, lynxes also increase in number.

Although some meteorologists think that the correlation announced by the German researchers may be disproved, ecologists are intrigued by the possibility that sunspots can affect Earth's animals.

Genetically engineered organisms. The Ecological Society of America published a report in April 1989 spelling out its policy on the release into the environment of organisms that have

Of Owls and Voles

A barn owl, *left,* a bird common in most of North America, holds its favorite prey, a ratlike rodent called a vole. The owls have been vanishing from the Midwestern United States because the voles' habitat— meadows and pastures—is being destroyed by urban growth and by farming practices that favor row crops over grassy fields. Barn owls also catch mice and rats, so the birds are welcome tenants on farms, and efforts are being made to bring them back to the Midwest. Conservationists in New Jersey— where the owls are numerous and can be more easily studied—observe owl behavior with night-vision goggles, *below,* and check on a nesting box, *below left,* where parent owls can raise their young, *bottom.* Owls will take up residence in a box only if there are voles nearby, however, so preserving vole habitats is a key factor in keeping barn owls on the farm.

Ecology
Continued

been genetically engineered. Such organisms include bacteria and other microbes that have been given genes taken from other organisms. In some cases, these genetically altered microorganisms are designed to be released outdoors. For example, scientists have engineered bacteria that can be sprayed on crop plants to protect them from frost.

There has been a great deal of controversy over the release of these and other genetically altered organisms. Opponents contend that such organisms could harm communities of plants and animals or cause unforeseen problems in the environment.

The seven authors of the report, headed by ecologist James M. Tiedje of Michigan State University in East Lansing, said that while most engineered organisms would probably pose no danger to wildlife or the environment, one might occasionally be potentially hazardous. Thus, they concluded, all proposed releases of engineered organisms should be scrutinized until there is no doubt as to their safety.

Sources and sinks. Animal habitats vary in quality. Some habitats are better places to live, and, because they suit the needs of animals better than other habitats, they tend to be more densely populated. In November 1988, ecologist H. Ronald Pulliam of the University of Georgia in Athens cautioned that these variations in local habitat must be taken into consideration in any study of animal populations.

Ecologists refer to better habitats as *sources* and poorer habitats as *sinks*. Being the more desirable habitats, sources get filled up first; animals move into sinks when there is no room left in the sources.

Pulliam said ecologists must study sources and sinks together to get a true picture of a species' numbers in a general area. He noted, for example, that if a scientist studied only a species' sink population, the researcher might conclude that the overall population of the species in that area was stable.

If a nearby source population were also included in the study, however, it would be clear that the sink population was maintained by the dispersal of animals from the source. In such a situation, the overall population of the species, rather than being stable, might actually be increasing.

Death of North Sea seals. A previously unknown virus has been killing seals in the North Sea, British scientists reported in November 1988. The virus, which they named the *phocine* (seal) distemper virus, has killed at least 10,000 harbor seals in the North Sea, an arm of the Atlantic Ocean between Great Britain and the European mainland. The total population of harbor seals in the North Sea had been estimated at 15,000 to 16,000.

The virus was designated a distemper virus because it is very similar to the virus that causes canine distemper, an illness that afflicts dogs and their genetic cousins, such as wolves and foxes. In fact, researchers at first thought that the seals had somehow contracted canine distemper, perhaps from Arctic foxes.

A Netherlands scientist reported in September 1988 that the canine distemper virus had been isolated from the bodies of seals that had died of the mysterious disease. The virus later proved to be a new strain within the same class of viruses.

The epidemic first came to public attention in April 1988, when dying seal pups were discovered on an island off the Swedish coast. Investigators soon suspected that the canine distemper virus, or a related virus, was involved, because sick seals suffered from the same lung and nervous-system infections seen in dogs with distemper. In addition, organs taken from dead seals showed damage typical of distemper.

Some researchers speculated that pollution also played a part in the seals' illness. The North Sea is heavily polluted with industrial wastes, and the filthy water could have weakened the animals' immune systems. That theory was still considered a possibility in mid-1989 but had not been confirmed.

Meanwhile, scientists feared that the disease might spread to other seal populations. Some biologists suggested that the virus might also infect porpoises, which range far across the ocean. If so, the porpoises could conceivably carry the disease to every coastal area in the world.   [Robert H. Tamarin]

In WORLD BOOK, see ECOLOGY.

Electronics

The U-Force home video game controller made by Nintendo sends out beams of infrared light to form an invisible three-dimensional light grid that senses and measures the positions of the player's hands. This eliminates the need for a joystick or any other control device that must be touched. Instead, the player uses only hand movements to manipulate images on the television screen.

The video revolution continued in 1988 and 1989, providing consumers with more ways to record, transmit, and play back pictures. These included a filmless camera for still images and a battery-powered portable videocassette recorder (VCR) for moving pictures. And manufacturers slashed the price of the *videophone*, a telephone combined with a television camera and screen so people talking on the phone can see each other.

Filmless cameras for still color pictures reached the United States consumer market in September 1988 when Canon USA, Incorporated, of Lake Success, N.Y., introduced its Xapshot and Sony Corporation of America in New York City brought out the Mavica. These products, called *still-video cameras* (SVC's), took several years to develop for the consumer market. Sony had unveiled an experimental version of the Mavica in 1981.

The SVC's were expensive. In mid-1989, Xapshot cost $1,000 and the new Mavica sold for $900.

Like a video camera or camcorder, an SVC focuses light reflected from the image being shot on a device that translates the light into electric signals. These signals are then recorded as magnetic patterns on a rapidly spinning disk measuring 5 centimeters (2 inches) in diameter. The disk can store up to 50 shots.

The photographer can display the "snapshots" immediately by connecting the camera to an ordinary television set. Each picture fills the entire TV screen. The photographer can erase any of the images and reuse the empty area on the disk.

Prints made from SVC's are not as sharp as conventional film snapshots. For this reason, neither Canon nor Sony offers a printer for its consumer-version SVC.

Portable VCR. In August 1988, Sony introduced the Video Walkman Model G8, a combined color TV set and VCR that is about the size of a paperback almanac. It weighs about 1 kilogram (2.2 pounds) and runs on batteries or ordinary household current. The device uses 8-millimeter videocassettes,

Electronics

Continued

which are slightly smaller than conventional audio tapes, and has an 8-centimeter liquid crystal display screen.

The Video Walkman can record and play back up to four hours of programs, and can play ordinary TV broadcasts as well as prerecorded 8-millimeter tapes. When introduced, the Video Walkman sold for $1,300.

Inexpensive picturephones entered the U.S. consumer market in mid-1988. Mitsubishi Electric Sales America, Incorporated, of Cypress, Calif., introduced the Visitel LU-500, with a price tag of $400, and Sony announced a $500 videophone called PCT-15. Before these products were introduced, videophones designed for the consumer cost about $1,500.

Both new products transmit and receive black-and-white still images over ordinary telephone lines. These pictures are no match for the moving images transmitted in color by videophones that corporations use for teleconferences. But business videophones cost tens of thousands of dollars and require special telephone lines.

All consumer videophones can communicate with one another. And telephone companies do not charge extra when a customer uses a videophone.

The front of a consumer videophone contains a video camera and a 10-centimeter (4-inch) televisionlike screen. To send a picture, a caller first poses for the camera while viewing the pose on the screen. When satisfied, the caller presses a button to freeze the image on the screen and store the image on a computer memory chip.

To transmit the stored image, the caller presses another button. During transmission, the image on the screen slowly disappears, line by line, from bottom to top. At the same time, the picture appears line by line on the videophone screen at the other end and is stored on a memory chip there. It takes 5 to 10 seconds to transmit a picture.   [Stephen A. Booth]

In the Special Reports section, see THE ENDLESS QUEST FOR A BETTER TV PICTURE. In WORLD BOOK, see ELECTRONICS; VIDEO CAMERA; VIDEOTAPE RECORDER.

Energy

The discovery of an astonishingly simple—and inexpensive—way to harness the energy of the atomic nucleus was claimed in March 1989 by chemists working at the University of Utah in Salt Lake City. B. Stanley Pons of Utah and Martin Fleischmann of the University of Southampton in England said that they had caused atomic nuclei to *fuse* (join) in a jar-sized container at room temperature.

A fusion reaction gives off a tremendous amount of energy. In fact, fusion powers the sun and other stars. In an effort to tap fusion's potential as an energy source on Earth, governments throughout the world have spent billions of dollars on huge, highly complex machines that heat nuclei to temperatures higher than in the center of the sun.

The size of the two chemists' device, and the fact that their experiment cost only $100,000, suggested to some observers that the development of practical fusion machines might be much less expensive than had been expected. Many scientists, however, contended

that fusion had not even occurred in the chemists' device. See PHYSICS, SUBATOMIC (Close-Up).

Batteries for power plants. An assembly of 8,256 lead-acid battery cells began operating in August 1988 in Chino, Calif., to demonstrate that it is practical to use battery storage to meet varying electric power demand.

The demand for electricity in the United States varies widely during a typical week. The amount used at 4 a.m. on a Sunday, for example, is less than half that used at 4 p.m. on a Monday. Utility companies meet this variable demand by operating two types of plants. They run the first type—coal, hydroelectric, and nuclear plants—24 hours a day. These plants produce an excess of power during off-peak periods but a shortage when demand is high. Such plants, however, are much cheaper to operate for long time periods than are plants burning natural gas or oil.

During the week, as demand exceeds the power provided by these units, the company starts to use additional plants

Energy

Continued

A vertical axis wind turbine (VAWT), towering 50 meters (164 feet), generates electricity during tests conducted in 1988 and 1989 by its developer, Sandia National Laboratories. The turbine's rotor speed can be changed to obtain maximum electric power output as wind speed varies. The machine was built near Bushland, Tex. It can generate 500 kilowatts of electricity when rotating 37.5 revolutions per minute in a wind blowing at 45 kilometers (28 miles) per hour.

that burn oil or gas, because plants burning these fuels can start and stop quickly. But because oil and gas are expensive, the use of the additional plants drives up the average cost of power.

Southern California Edison Company designed the Chino Battery Energy Storage Facility to store excess energy generated during off-peak periods and to discharge this energy when demand is high. This minimizes the need for expensive power generated by oil- or gas-fired plants.

The battery cells contain more than 1.8 million kilograms (4 million pounds) of lead. The cells are similar to those in an ordinary automobile battery. Unlike car battery cells, however, the Chino units can discharge all their energy without wearing out.

During times of peak demand, the batteries supply 10 million watts of power for four hours. This is enough power for 5,000 homes. The battery system can return 75 per cent of the energy it receives from the power lines.

Battery storage offers three major advantages to power companies that need to increase their peak generating capacity. First, systems of various sizes could use the same basic design. The main difference would be in the number of batteries used, so companies could save a great deal of engineering time. In addition, a battery system would take much less time to build than does an oil- or gas-fired plant. And finally, a battery system has a negligible impact on the environment.

Air to store power. Construction began on the first commercial compressed-air energy storage facility in the United States in October 1988. The Alabama Electric Cooperative in McIntosh expects to begin operating the plant in early 1991.

In this kind of plant, an electric motor uses electricity generated during low-power demand periods to drive an air compressor. The resulting compressed air is stored in underground caverns. During peak periods, this high-pressure air is released, heated by burning gas, and expanded in a turbine to spin the turbine blades. The

Nuclear reactors, *left*, at a plant on the Savannah River, *above*, were shut down completely in August 1988 after cracks were discovered in the reactor vessels. The plant is the only U.S. source of tritium (radioactive hydrogen) for nuclear weapons.

An engineer at the Savannah River plant, *above right*, tests ultrasound sensors attached to a computer-controlled robot arm, *above left*, designed to inspect and locate cracks in welds or in the stainless steel surface of the reactor vessels.

motor that drives the compressor during the charging cycle is connected to the turbine during the discharge process and therefore acts as a generator. To save energy, the hot exhaust leaving the turbine preheats the compressed air before this air is heated by the burning gas.

The use of the stored compressed air gives the turbine and generator three times the electrical output of a conventional gas turbogenerator that consumes the same amount of gas. As a result, Alabama Electric expects the use of the facility to decrease the total cost of generating electricity.

Plans call for the McIntosh facility to compress air for 8 hours per day Monday through Friday and for 40 hours over the weekend. The compressed air will be used about 10 hours per day Monday through Friday to generate 110 million watts.

Alabama Electric plans to create the cavern for the compressed air by mining a salt dome. First, a drill will bore a hole into the salt dome. Next, pumps will force fresh water into the hole to dissolve a large amount of salt. Finally, the resulting salt water will be pumped out. The cavern will be 425 meters (1,400 feet) belowground, about 50 meters (160 feet) in diameter, and 180 meters (600 feet) long.

Nuclear waste processing. New equipment at a nuclear fuel reprocessing plant reduced the volume of about 280,000 liters (75,000 gallons) of radioactive liquid waste by 90 per cent in 1988. This work was part of the West Valley (New York) Demonstration Project, which began in May 1988 and could run until the mid-1990's. Lessons learned from this project may be applied at other reprocessing plants and at nuclear reactors.

The West Valley plant, located about 55 kilometers (35 miles) south of Buffalo, had reprocessed more than 600 metric tons (660 short tons) of commercial nuclear fuel rods from 1966 to 1972, enabling much of the fuel to be reused. The reprocessing operation generated more than 2.1 million liters (550,000 gallons) of highly radioactive liquid waste.

The waste was stored in an underground tank 23 meters (75 feet) in diameter that was built in 1967 and designed to last for 40 years. Since then, the waste has separated into a sludge on the bottom of the tank and a liquid on the top.

The plant's new liquid-waste treatment process begins by passing the fluid through filters filled with *zeolite* (a sandlike clay), removing 99.996 per cent of the radioactive wastes. The liquid that has passed through the filter—now containing low levels of radioactive waste—is then concentrated by heating it to evaporate most of the water. Finally, the remaining liquid with highly concentrated radioactive waste is mixed with cement and solidified in 273-liter (72-gallon) steel drums. The drums are stored aboveground in a special building.

Plans call for all the low-level waste to be solidified by early 1990. Work is then to begin on the high-level waste in the sludge.

Solar cell breaks record. Scientists at Sandia National Laboratories in Albuquerque, N. Mex., reported in August 1988 that a stacked photovoltaic cell had set a record by converting 31 per cent of the sunlight striking it to electricity. By comparison, commercially available cells of this type are 18 to 20 per cent efficient.

The stacked cell, with a top surface area of 0.317 square centimeter (0.049 square inch) is made up of two photovoltaic cells, each converting a different color of the spectrum of sunlight to electricity. (The spectrum is all the rainbowlike colors of visible light.) To increase the output of the cell, a lens focuses sunlight on it.

After passing through the lens, sunlight strikes the upper cell. This cell, produced by Varian Associates of Palo Alto, Calif., is made up mainly of gallium arsenide and converts sunlight from the blue end of the spectrum to electricity. The remaining colors are either reflected or pass through this cell to the lower cell, which is made of crystalline silicon. The lower cell converts sunlight mostly from the red end of the spectrum. Researchers at Stanford University in Stanford, Calif., produced this cell.   [Marian Visich, Jr.]

In the Special Reports section, see Is EARTH OVERHEATING? In WORLD BOOK, see BATTERY; ENERGY SUPPLY; FUSION; NUCLEAR ENERGY; SOLAR ENERGY.

Environment

The supertanker *Exxon Valdez* ran aground on a reef in Alaska's Prince William Sound on March 24, 1989, setting off the worst oil spill in United States history. Within a month, more than 240,000 barrels of crude oil spread out into the sound, fouling more than 2,600 square kilometers (1,000 square miles) of sea and pristine coastline.

Alaska's top environmental official, Dennis Kelso, commissioner of the Alaska Department of Environmental Conservation, criticized the cleanup efforts of the Exxon Shipping Company. Only 8 per cent of the petroleum had been recovered by the end of the first three weeks. With each succeeding week, the oil became more tarry, less buoyant, and more difficult to retrieve. Exxon said it planned to clean 491 kilometers (305 miles) of shoreline by mid-September.

Environmentalists predicted that the spill would have devastating effects on wildlife, particularly sea otters, migrating birds, herring, and the already endangered bald eagles. They noted that the spill occurred when herring were beginning to spawn and migrating birds were arriving in the sound.

Antarctic spill. Diesel fuel from an Argentine supply ship that ran aground off Antarctica on January 28 washed ashore near Palmer Station, a U.S. research installation on the Antarctic Peninsula. It was the first major oil spill in Antarctica.

The ship, named the *Bahía Paraíso*, reportedly carried about 950,000 liters (250,000 gallons) of diesel fuel. Thousands of shrimplike fish called *krill*, which are key to the food chain in Antarctica, were killed by the spill, and more than 30,000 birds, including many *rookeries* (colonies) of penguins, were endangered.

Thinning ozone layer. A layer of ozone high in Earth's *stratosphere* (upper atmosphere) shields plants and animals from harmful ultraviolet radiation emitted by the sun. A potentially dangerous seasonal thinning in this layer over the South Pole—commonly known as the Antarctic *ozone hole*—appeared again in late August 1988. But ozone concentrations in the worrisome hole fell only 10 to 15 per cent below normal for that time of year,

which is late winter in Antarctica. This decline was half what scientists with the National Aeronautics and Space Administration (NASA) had expected. The scientists speculated that this smaller ozone loss might have been due to unusual weather patterns that altered chemical reactions in the stratosphere. These reactions are responsible for destroying ozone each spring.

On Dec. 1, 1988, physicists at the State University of New York in Stony Brook reported evidence that reactions involving chlorine monoxide molecules—ordinarily rare in the stratosphere over Antarctica—were causing the ozone losses. Their studies also for the first time confirmed what had long been suspected—that industrial chemicals called *chlorofluorocarbons* (CFC's) contribute most of the chlorine involved in these reactions.

In April 1989, University of Chicago scientists announced they had found the first evidence that the hole was indeed allowing excessive ultraviolet radiation to reach the surface at the South Pole. Although the ozone hole in 1988 was smaller, they detected a doubling of ultraviolet radiation reaching the surface during spring.

Scientists returning from flights over the Arctic in February 1989 reported finding chlorine monoxide levels in the stratosphere comparable to those over the Antarctic. While an Arctic ozone hole has not yet been seen, scientists who observed the Arctic stratosphere in January and early February 1989 now suspect one may develop there. See METEOROLOGY.

Poisoned paper. Researchers from around the world began publishing data in 1988 showing that extremely toxic chemicals known as *dioxins* and *furans* contaminate a range of paper products—from coffee filters and disposable diapers to paper towels, newspaper, and facial tissues. In August, at a conference in Sweden, Canadian chemist John J. Ryan presented evidence indicating that these paper contaminants—formed by the paper-bleaching process—were entering the food supply. Ryan found trace quantities of identical dioxins and furans in milk and in its cardboard cartons, suggesting that the chemicals entered the milk from the containers.

The map shows:

Fairbanks

Alaska
(U.S.)

Canada

Anchorage • Valdez •
● **Oil spill**

*Prince William
Sound*

Juneau •

Pacific Ocean

0   200 Kilometers
0   200 Miles

Oil trails from the *Exxon Valdez, top,* which ran
aground in March 1989 in Alaska's Prince
William Sound, *above,* creating the worst oil
spill in United States history. Oil washed up on
beaches leaving a tarry black coating on rocks,
and killed many animals, including sea otters,
right.

Yellowstone Fires: Let Them Burn?

A massive conflagration swept through Yellowstone National Park during the hot, dry summer of 1988. Fires consumed more than 240,000 hectares (600,000 acres), about one-third of the park's total area, which is located largely in northwest Wyoming. The amount of wood that fueled the blaze was equal to about 400 billion liters (100 billion gallons) of gasoline.

"People who had been fighting fires professionally for 30 years were in awe at this one," observed John Varley, head of research at Yellowstone. "This one was so completely beyond our control it was terrifying at times."

The blaze also ignited a heated debate in the United States over the correct policy for fighting forest fires.

Since 1972, park managers in Yellowstone had followed what came to be known as the "let-it-burn" policy, one that many biologists believe is best for the long-term ecological health of the park. But dramatic images of forests burning out of control, seen daily in television and print news media during the summer of 1988, quickly fueled condemnation of that policy.

"It is clear that this let-it-burn policy has been a disaster," said Secretary of the Interior Donald P. Hodel. "From now on, the policy will be putting the fires out when they see the flames," declared Senator John Melcher (D., Mont.).

Many Americans' perceptions about fires in the wild have been shaped by the U.S. Forest Service's appealing and powerful image of Smokey the Bear. "Remember: Only YOU can prevent forest fires," admonished Smokey, who first appeared on the forest scene in 1945. The underlying message was clear: Forest fires are bad things. This attitude accurately reflected official Forest Service policy of the time, that all fires—no matter the cause—must be suppressed. The policy had been in place ever since Yellowstone was established as the world's first national park in 1872, and it embodied the notion that in order to protect nature, human beings must try to control nature.

"Anything that seemed to perturb the natural state of the park's habitat was regarded as a threat," according to ecologist and forestry expert Norman Christiensen of Duke University in Durham, N.C. "And there is nothing more potentially perturbing to a forest than fire."

Attitudes began to change in the mid-1960's, prompted by the publication in 1963 of a report by wildlife biologist Starker Leopold of the University of California at Berkeley. The Leopold report stated that, rather than protecting the forests from destruction by fire, the policy of constant fire suppression actually increases that danger in the long term. Constant fire suppression allows the steady accumulation of highly inflammable debris on the forest floor. Given enough time and the right conditions, this debris will eventually fuel a massive conflagration, according to the report.

Commissioned by the secretary of the interior, the Leopold report made two recommendations. First, controlled burning should be undertaken where necessary to remove the accumulated debris. And second, fires that begin naturally—as the result of lightning, for example—should be allowed to burn themselves out, unless human life or property is threatened. This is the basis of the somewhat misnamed let-it-burn policy currently applied in all national forests.

Ecologists were enthusiastic about the policy, because by the 1960's, scientific theory had come to recognize the importance of fire in the dynamics of the ecosystem. Changes caused by fire came to be recognized as an aid in maintaining a large diversity of species in an ecological community. "By periodically destroying parts of a habitat, fire helps maintain a diversity of species in that habitat," explains ecologist Linda Wallace of the University of Oklahoma in Norman. "In the absence of fire, one or just a few species can quickly dominate and crowd out the rest."

Between 1972—the beginning of the let-it-burn policy in Yellowstone National Park—

Fire fighters are dwarfed by the towering flames of 1 of 13 fires that engulfed Yellowstone National Park during the hot, dry summer of 1988.

and the summer of 1988, forest fires were a constant element in the ecological picture. Several thousand separate fires occurred during that 16-year period, burning about 14,000 hectares (34,000 acres). Then, beginning in July 1988, 13 separate massive blazes roared over half of the park's land area. Why were there so many fires, destroying so much forest, in so brief a time?

"One reason was that there had been a hundred years of accumulation of debris," says biologist William Romme of Fort Lewis College in Durango, Colo. Romme also points out that 1988 saw the hottest, driest summer the area had experienced in a long time. More significant, however, was the history of fire in the park, which Romme studied along with his colleague Don Despain of the National Park Service.

They studied the pattern of fires in one area of the park and concluded that the pattern was determined in part by the nature of the lodgepole pine, the major tree species in much of the Yellowstone forests. "Lodgepole pines don't burn very readily until they are about 200 years old," Romme explains, "and from then on they become more and more combustible."

In other words, major conflagrations among stands of lodgepole pines won't happen very often, not until a sufficient proportion of the trees are older than 200 years. When this time comes, a fire may sweep through large areas, destroying the stands completely and thereby clearing large areas for a new generation of lodgepole pines. The cycle can then begin again. As a result, speculates Romme, "the big fire of 1988 was to some extent inevitable."

With the park closed to visitors for a while at the height of the blaze, and with some towns and even the famous Old Faithful Lodge threatened with destruction, it was little wonder that politicians reacted as strongly as they did against the let-it-burn policy. Despite assertions from Secretary Hodel and others, however, the let-it-burn policy effectively remains in place, at least in the long term. This was the recommendation of a special commission convened to study the impact of the fire. The 10-person commission announced its recommendation on Dec. 15, 1988, by which time the fires and the emotions they had aroused had died down.

"The natural history of Yellowstone is a history of change, and it has often been violent change," commented Robert Barbee, the park's superintendent. "The Yellowstone Basin as we know it today was formed by fire and ice—by volcanoes and glaciers. We've been through just another severe round of fire. Our visitors will be able to watch the way nature repairs its wounds." [Roger Lewin]

In laboratory animals, dioxins and furans have proven to be very potent cancer-causing agents—even at microscopic doses. Less certain is the risk these chemicals pose to human beings. The Science Advisory Board of the U.S. Environmental Protection Agency (EPA) reported in late November that the best available scientific data suggest a daily dioxin dose of as little as 0.006 *picogram* (one trillionth of a gram) per kilogram of body weight increases the lifetime risk of developing cancer by one in a million. This is the level at which EPA usually considers regulating exposures. Moreover, United States Food and Drug Administration calculations indicate Americans typically consume about 170 times that amount of dioxin daily.

In December 1988, U.S. scientists with three federal agencies reported that they were coordinating a government investigation to be completed by April 1990. The inquiry was to assess the potential health risk of these paper contaminants and identify ways to reduce dioxin formation in the paper-bleaching process.

Lead pollution. In August 1988, the EPA proposed new rules to lower human exposure to lead in drinking water. The rules would require public drinking-water suppliers to neutralize acidic waters with alkaline additives. This would reduce the corrosiveness of water, which can leach lead from metal pipes and solder. In all, EPA Administrator Lee M. Thomas said, the new proposals would affect about 53,000 public water systems, lowering lead exposures for 138 million people.

Several scientific studies also identified new health effects of lead. On Jan. 9, 1989, for example, researchers at the University of Cincinnati in Ohio reported finding that even low-level exposures to lead could impair a preschool child's sense of balance. Children are most susceptible to this effect at the age of 2—when the nerves and muscles that will establish balance are maturing.

In June 1988, EPA scientist Joel Schwartz published data showing a strong relationship between blood-lead levels in men and elevated blood pressure. On March 15, 1989, he presented the results of follow-up studies that showed even comparatively low levels of lead in men were associated with an increased risk of heart disease.

The same month, a *toxicologist* (scientist who studies poisons) from the University of Rochester in New York presented data from tests on animals indicating that the elderly may face a high and previously unrecognized sensitivity to lead toxicity. In addition, according to Schwartz and two other researchers, a survey involving almost 3,000 U.S. women indicated that *osteoporosis*—bone loss that typically occurs in women after menopause, usually between the ages of 45 and 50—releases large quantities of lead that had been stored in bone. Released from bone into the blood, this lead is free to harm sensitive organs, such as the brain, liver, and kidneys.

Radon. A new EPA study of indoor radon levels, released on Sept. 12, 1988, offered evidence that *radon*—a naturally occurring radioactive gas—is an even more widespread hazard than had been suspected. The EPA's new analysis, conducted in seven states and on several Indian reservations, found unacceptably high levels of the gas—4 picocuries of radon per liter of air or higher—in one-third of the 11,000 homes surveyed. (A *picocurie* is one-trillionth of a *curie*, the unit for measuring the intensity of radioactivity.)

A similar earlier survey, reported by the EPA in 1987, had been conducted in 10 other states. It found that radon levels in one-fifth of the homes where air had been sampled exceeded this guideline.

Claiming EPA's 1988 data established radon as the nation's foremost natural health hazard, the U.S. Public Health Service issued an "advisory" recommending that all U.S. homes promptly be tested for the pollutant. On April 20, 1989, the EPA announced that it was strongly recommending similar radon testing of all public schools and corrective action—for example, increasing ventilation—where levels were too high.   [Janet Raloff]

In the Special Reports section, see Is EARTH OVERHEATING? In WORLD BOOK, see ENVIRONMENTAL POLLUTION.

Genetic Science

The first transplant of a "foreign" gene into the body of a human being took place in May 1989. Doctors at the National Cancer Institute in Bethesda, Md., inserted into the genes of a cancer patient copies of a bacterial gene to help monitor treatment of the patient's disease. See IMMUNOLOGY.

DNA image. The most detailed pictures ever taken of *deoxyribonucleic acid* (DNA)—the molecule of which genes are made—were reported in January 1989 by scientists at Lawrence Livermore National Laboratory and Lawrence Berkeley Laboratory, research facilities operated by the University of California. A *scanning tunneling microscope*, which can make out individual atoms, was used to create the images.

The microscope has a tiny needle that rides on a "cushion" of electrons to trace the surface of whatever molecule or other specimen is being looked at. The electrons tunnel, or jump, from the tip of the needle onto the specimen. As the needle rides up and down over "peaks" (atoms) and "valleys" (the spaces between atoms), a computer translates the motions into a three-dimensional picture.

Although molecules such as DNA can be seen with other types of powerful microscopes, the specimens must first undergo special preparation. This process tends to distort the molecules' true shapes. Because the steps involved in preparing material for the tunneling microscope are much less harsh, molecules can be viewed in a more natural state. With regard to DNA, this means that some of its interesting features, such as the "grooves"—the spaces between the coils of the corkscrew-shaped molecule—that are part of its normal structure, are preserved.

The California scientists got such good pictures of the DNA molecule that they were actually able to measure the width of the grooves and the distances between them. The researchers predicted that use of the scanning tunneling microscope will lead to important new insights in the study of other biologically important molecules, in addition to DNA.

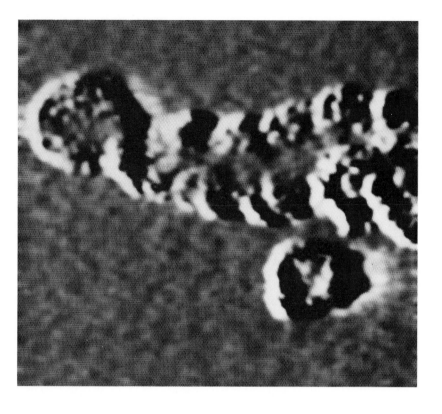

The first close-up images of unaltered deoxyribonucleic acid (DNA) that show the double helix were released in January 1989 by scientists at Lawrence Berkeley Laboratory and Lawrence Livermore National Laboratory, both in California. The pictures were made with a *scanning tunneling microscope*. This microscope produces details as small as an atom by means of a needle that rides over the surface of a substance on a "cushion" of electrons.

Genetic Science

Continued

Mapping human genes. The United States Department of Energy (DOE) and the National Institutes of Health (NIH) announced in autumn 1988 that they would work together on an ambitious project to decipher the *human genome*—all the DNA in a human cell. The agencies also agreed to issue periodic progress reports on the genome effort and to share information and facilities. In the Special Reports section, see CREATING THE ULTIMATE MAP OF OUR GENES.

Shortly after the announcement of the joint research effort, the NIH named James D. Watson, who shared the 1962 Nobel Prize for determining the structure of DNA, as associate director of its portion of the genome project. In the People in Science section, see JAMES D. WATSON.

Tastier supermarket tomatoes? A genetically engineered tomato that could be left on the vine longer than regular tomatoes before being shipped to grocery stores was reported in August 1988 by scientists in California and in England. Researchers at Calgene, In-

corporated, a biotechnology company in Davis, Calif., and at the University of Nottingham, England, identified the gene that causes tomatoes to soften. The gene codes for an *enzyme* (a protein that controls a biochemical reaction). This enzyme helps break down cell walls and is produced only when the fruit begins to ripen.

The scientists used genetic engineering techniques to create tomato plants with two copies of the softening gene—the normal gene that was already in the plant cells and a second, added gene. They inserted the extra gene into the cells of pieces of tomato stems growing in culture dishes. The extra gene was inserted "backwards" so that when it was copied by *ribonucleic acid* (RNA), a molecule similar to DNA, it would produce an RNA strand that was the exact opposite of the one created by the normal gene.

This technique was based on the fact that DNA is a double-stranded molecule resembling a twisted ladder. When a protein is needed, the section of DNA containing the gene that codes for the protein unzips so that an RNA "blueprint" can be made. The side of the DNA ladder containing the code for producing the protein, and normally used to make RNA, is called the "sense" strand; the other side is the "antisense" strand. Normally, the RNA made from the DNA is a sort of mirror image of the DNA sense strand. Following the coded instructions in the RNA blueprint, other kinds of RNA then assemble materials in the cell to create the protein.

In the case of the extra gene inserted into the tomato plant, the antisense strand of its DNA was copied by the RNA. This created antisense RNA. Because the normal gene created normal RNA and the reversed gene made antisense RNA, the two RNA strands joined together like the two halves of a zipper. When that occurred, the RNA strand from the original gene could not pass on its message for the manufacture of the softening enzyme. The action of the original gene was thus blocked. As a result, the tomato plants that grew from the pieces of stem produced far less of the enzyme that breaks down plant cells.

The new tomato could have great commercial value. Regular varieties of tomatoes cannot be left on the vine to ripen because they become too soft to ship without damage.

Antisense-RNA technology was still a fairly new and experimental technique in 1989. Researchers predicted that the procedure would have many applications in genetic engineering. It may be possible in the future to use antisense RNA to block the production of other specific substances in crops—such as caffeine in coffee beans.

Multiplying genes. A way of making millions or billions of copies of a single gene—even a gene thousands of years old—was announced in late 1988. It stems from new developments in a technique called the *polymerase chain reaction* (PCR).

Researchers at the Cetus Corporation in Emeryville, Calif., had developed the basic PCR procedure in 1985. The technique gets its name from an enzyme called a polymerase that plays a key part in the process of making copies of a gene. That process is called a chain reaction because, like a nuclear chain reaction, it keeps doubling in effect. A great many copies of a gene can be made this way in a few hours.

In the original procedure, the researchers had to know the sequence of nucleotides making up the beginning and end of the gene. They then had to create pieces of DNA called *primers* that would attach to the beginning and ending sequences of the gene to define the boundaries of the gene for the polymerase. Through a complex process of heating and cooling a solution containing the gene and the polymerase, a billion or more copies of the gene could be made.

PCR techniques developed in 1988 made the method simpler to carry out and increased its usefulness. In one variation, a primer need be prepared for only one end of a gene rather than both ends. Another variant of the procedure allows researchers to copy several adjacent genes at the same time.

One of the most important new uses of PCR is in the investigation of crimes. The technique can multiply the genes in a tiny tissue sample found at a crime scene—blood or hair, for example—making it much easier to carry out a DNA analysis of the specimen.

Error-prone AIDS virus. The virus that causes AIDS often makes mistakes when reproducing itself in the human body, scientists at several U.S. research centers reported in the fall of 1988. The scientists said that characteristic may account for the virus's ability to thwart and eventually destroy the body's immune system.

Like a number of other viruses, the AIDS virus uses an enzyme called *reverse transcriptase* to copy itself in the cells it invades. The enzyme varies somewhat in form and function from one type of virus to another.

According to the latest findings, the reverse transcriptase used by the AIDS virus is faulty. When reproducing the AIDS virus from materials in the cell, the enzyme makes mistakes 10 to 20 times more often than the copying enzymes used by other viruses. Moreover, while some versions of the enzyme are able to identify and correct their copying errors, the AIDS virus's enzyme has no such ability.

As a result of the enzyme's sloppiness, many copies of the virus have

Genetic Science

Continued

antigens (identifying molecules on the virus's surface) that differ from those of the original virus. Because of this, the immune system may recognize and attack the original virus but fail to detect the altered copies in time to prevent a fatal infection.

This theory is supported by hospital studies of AIDS patients. Researchers have found that patients often have several slightly different versions of the virus in their blood.

Genes and colon cancer. Further evidence that at least some cancers occur when genes that suppress uncontrolled cell growth are lost was reported in April 1989 by three teams of U.S. researchers. The scientists were from the Johns Hopkins University School of Medicine and the Johns Hopkins Medical Institutions, both in Baltimore, and the University of Utah Medical Center in Salt Lake City. They studied tumor-cell DNA from patients with *colorectal cancer* (cancer of the lower large intestine) and found that in nearly every tissue sample, parts of several chromosomes were missing.

Chromosomes are structures in the cell that carry the genes. There are two copies of each chromosome in a cell, one inherited from the mother and the other from the father. Every human cell has 23 chromosome pairs.

The scientists examined the chromosomes of both normal and cancerous tissues from 56 patients who had been operated on for colorectal cancer. They exposed the chromosomes to various radioactive *probes*—pieces of DNA that matched known genetic sequences within the chromosomes. If a particular sequence was present, the probe for that sequence would bind to it. If it was missing, there would be nowhere for the probe to bind.

After being exposed to the probes, the batches of DNA were placed on sheets of X-ray film. Wherever a probe had attached to a segment of a chromosome, the film was fogged by the probe's radioactivity.

The researchers then compared X-ray film of the tumor-cell DNA with film of the DNA from normal cells. They discovered that as many as 15

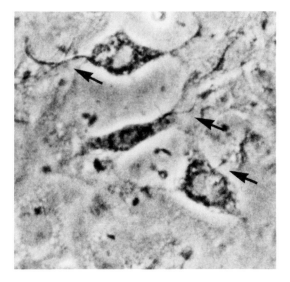

By transporting stray pieces of DNA from cells that have died into living cells, *above,* asbestos fibers (arrows) may cause cancer. Researchers at Mount Sinai Medical Center in New York City theorize that a DNA fragment picked up by an asbestos fiber, *right,* is carried into the nucleus of the cell and inserted into the cell's DNA, setting off uncontrolled growth of the cell.

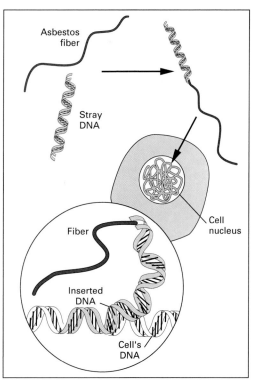

Asbestos fiber

Stray DNA

Cell nucleus

Fiber

Inserted DNA

Cell's DNA

pieces of chromosomes, present in healthy tissues, were missing in the cancerous tissues. The number of missing chromosome pieces varied widely from patient to patient.

The scientists followed the course of each patient's disease. They found that the more chromosome segments a patient was lacking, the more likely he or she was to suffer a recurrence of the cancer, and to die of it. They also discovered that a damaged chromosome 17 was one of the most common defects among the 56 patients whose DNA was analyzed.

In a related study, researchers at the same institutions, together with investigators from the M. D. Anderson Hospital and the Baylor College of Medicine—both in Houston—reported in April 1989 that they had discovered a specific genetic abnormality in colorectal tumor cells. The scientists found that a particular gene was missing on one copy of chromosome 17. The gene on the other copy of that chromosome was *mutated* (changed).

The researchers speculated that the protein for which that gene codes may be an important cancer-suppressing protein. Their findings also suggested that if just one copy of the gene is present and functioning properly, colorectal cancer will not develop. But if one gene is missing and the other is malfunctioning, runaway cell growth can occur.

Melanoma gene. Still another finding relating genetics to cancer was reported in May 1989 by scientists at the National Cancer Institute and several other U.S. research centers. The investigators announced that they had found two *markers* for a gene that makes people susceptible to melanoma, a deadly form of skin cancer. Markers are variations in DNA sequences that can be detected with the aid of special chemicals that cut chromosomes into many pieces. The researchers located the markers, which are on chromosome 1, by cutting apart the DNA of people in families with a history of melanoma. [David S. Haymer]

In WORLD BOOK, see AIDS; CANCER; CELL; GENETIC ENGINEERING; GENETICS.

Geology

Devastating earthquakes struck the Soviet Union's republics of Armenia, Azerbaijan, and Georgia in December 1988. The damage caused by the quakes, which occurred in an area where several plates that make up Earth's crust are colliding, was intensified by local soil conditions and faulty construction techniques. See Close-Up.

Ice ages, icecaps. During 1988 and 1989, researchers presented new evidence that may increase geologists' understanding of conditions during the most recent ice age, which began about 2 million years ago and ended about 10,000 years ago. During this ice age, there may have been as many as 18 periods of *glaciation* (glacier formation), separated by *interglacials* (periods between glaciations when the glaciers melted and shrank).

New information about the growth of icecaps in Europe during the most recent glaciation, which began about 112,000 years ago, was reported in March 1989 by palynologists at the University of Marseille in France. (*Palynologists* are paleontologists who study fossilized pollen.) The scientists based their work on studies of fossil pollen found in France. By studying the pollen, palynologists can learn which plants were present in the region surrounding the deposit in the past. Because the types of pollen found reflect both temperature and moisture conditions, fossil pollen can reveal important information about the climate as well.

The French pollen records provide clues to climatic conditions in eastern France, which lay between icecaps forming over Scandinavia and those forming in the Alps. The pollen deposits span a remarkably long period, from the last interglacial, which began about 128,000 years ago and ended about 112,000 years ago, to the present. Because most geologists believe that we are presently in an interglacial, they want to know how the last interglacial ended.

According to the French scientists, the pollen record indicates that the last interglacial ended with an abrupt temperature drop. At the same time, however, precipitation increased greatly.

Geology

Continued

The scientists found that 112,000 years ago, much of Europe was covered by dense forests, which grow during periods of increased precipitation. About 90,000 years ago, however, much of the forest gave way to grassland and shrubs, a sign of decreased precipitation. About 10,000 years later, the forests again dominated the landscape. In all, this cycle was repeated four times, until 18,000 years ago, when the icecaps covering Europe reached their maximum extent.

The scientists concluded from this evidence of alternating forests and grasslands that the European icecaps did not grow steadily. They believe that periods of precipitation and ice growth were followed by drier periods during which the ice sheet stabilized or shrank slightly, as temperatures rose. After each period of warmth, however, the icecaps grew larger.

Some scientists have argued that the growth of the icecaps in Europe and North America was the result of temperature changes in the Atlantic Ocean. The French scientists, however, contend that increased precipitation on land—reflected in the spread of the forests—was essential for the icecaps' growth.

Icecap melting. A shift in the amount of solar radiation reaching Earth may have been a major factor in accelerating the end of the last glaciation, according to research reported in August 1988. The study was conducted by COHMAP (Cooperative Holocene Mapping Project), a multidisciplinary group led by paleoclimatologist John E. Kutzbach of the University of Wisconsin at Madison. The *Holocene* is the current geologic epoch. It began about 12,000 years ago, when the last glaciers began to melt rapidly.

The amount of radiation reaching Earth's atmosphere varies with periodic shifts in Earth's orbit around the sun. One of these shifts, which follows a cycle lasting 18,000 years, involves the time of year when Earth is closest to the sun. This affects the extent of temperature differences between the seasons of the year. For example, today Earth is closest to the sun in early January.

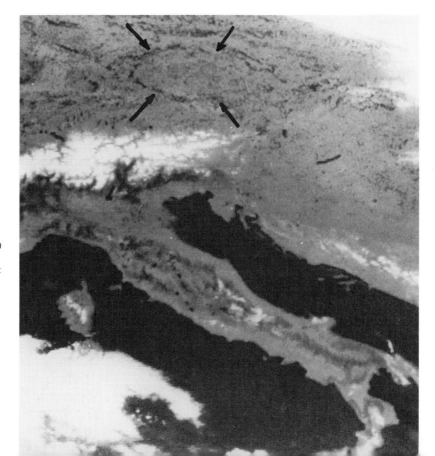

The discovery of what may be a huge meteor crater (arrows) covering much of western Czechoslovakia was reported in December 1988 by scientists at Boston University in Massachusetts who studied satellite photos. According to the scientists, the depression, which is 320 kilometers (200 miles) in diameter, could have been created 15 million years ago when a meteor 80 kilometers (50 miles) across slammed into Earth. Such an impact would have caused an explosion 1 million million times more powerful than the explosion of the atom bomb dropped on Hiroshima, Japan, in 1945.

Armenia's Killer Quakes

Two earthquakes within four minutes on Dec. 7, 1988, and aftershocks that continued for weeks killed 25,000 people, left 500,000 people homeless, and caused about $20 billion in damage in the Soviet Union's republic of Armenia. The quakes, which caused tremors across the region between the Black and Caspian seas, also affected the Soviet republics of Azerbaijan and Georgia. But the damage there was not nearly so severe.

The damage was the worst in and near the Armenian cities of Spitak, Kirovakan, and Leninakan. About half of Leninakan, the second largest city in Soviet Armenia with a population of 290,000, was destroyed. Spitak, a much smaller town, was nearly leveled.

Armenia is an earthquake-prone region, where several of Earth's tectonic plates are colliding. (Tectonic plates are huge sections of Earth's outer shell on which the continents and oceans ride.) Armenia sits within the Caucasus Mountains, part of a chain of mountains extending from Gibraltar eastward to the Himalaya.

This mountain chain provides dramatic evidence of a powerful geologic process that began about 50 million years ago. At that time, the African, Arabian, and Indian plates began colliding with the Eurasian plate. The impact caused the edges of the plates to crumple and rise, forming mountains.

The Caucasus Mountains, in particular, were created by the collision of the Arabian and Eurasian plates. Because the two plates are still moving together—at the rate of 3 centimeters (1⅙ inches) per year—the crust is under enormous pressure. The region is also riddled with *faults* (breaks in Earth's crust). Earthquakes always occur along faults.

The principal fault involved in the December earthquakes runs west-northwest from Spitak. Just outside the town, geologists found a slope about 2 meters (6½ feet) high and 8 kilometers (5 miles) long where the fault broke the surface during the quakes. Geologists believe the fault may extend an additional 7 kilometers (4⅓ miles). The *focus* of the main earthquake (the point along the fault where the earthquake began) was only about 10 kilometers (6 miles) below the surface. The *epicenter* of this quake (the point on the surface above the focus) was about 9 kilometers (5½ miles) from Spitak.

The fault at Spitak is a shallow *thrust fault*, created when a section of crust under great pressure is thrust over another section of crust. During the earthquake, the northeast side of the fault, on which Spitak sits, rode up and over the southwest side of the fault. Earthquakes along such faults, especially shallow thrust faults, are relatively rare. But earthquakes along these faults tend to be very damaging when they do occur in populated areas.

Although geologists have only incomplete earthquake records for the Armenian region, it appears that the area is actually less active than other regions along the zone where the tectonic plates are colliding. The records indicate that since the first reported quake in A.D. 863, the Armenian region has experienced at least 30 significant earthquakes, compared with thousands of significant earthquakes for the entire collision zone. The last major earthquake in Armenia struck Leninakan in 1926.

Study of the earthquake damage in Soviet Armenia revealed that the severity of damage depends on more than the severity of the quake. The damage to Spitak, Leninakan, and Kirovakan depended mainly on how close each city was to the epicenter of the earthquake and on the type of soil and rock beneath them. Spitak probably suffered the worst because of its nearness to the epicenter and its position along the ruptured fault. Damage in Kirovakan, 25 kilometers (15½ miles) east of the epicenter, was also extensive. But Kirovakan, like Spitak, sits in a river valley where thin soil overlies bedrock. This bedrock may have helped minimize the damage in Kirovakan.

In contrast, Leninakan, which was farther from the epicenter than Kirovakan, suffered more damage than Kirovakan. Geologists believe that was because Leninakan sits on the bed of an ancient lake. The loosely packed soil typical of such areas amplifies earthquake vibrations, increasing the damage.

The amount of damage in the three cities also depended upon the way the buildings were constructed, according to a team of United States geologists and earthquake engineers who visited Armenia. Most buildings made of stone consisting of soft volcanic rock were severely damaged or destroyed. Buildings made of prefabricated concrete floors loosely joined to concrete columns and beams collapsed completely. This was the most common type of modern building in Soviet Armenia. Even more deadly, these buildings collapsed into piles of rubble, leaving little open space where trapped people might survive. In contrast, buildings made of precast concrete panels and walls locked together stood up well to the shaking. [Eldridge M. Moores]

Devastation in Armenia
Shrouded bodies lie amid the rubble in Spitak, *left,* one of several towns in the Soviet Union's republic of Armenia devastated by two earthquakes on Dec. 7, 1988. Only damaged sections of an ancient cathedral in Leninakan, *below,* remain. The quakes and their aftershocks occurred in a geologically active region of the Soviet Union dominated by the Caucasus Mountains, *bottom left.* The epicenter of the main quake, *bottom right,* was only 9 kilometers (5½ miles) from Spitak.

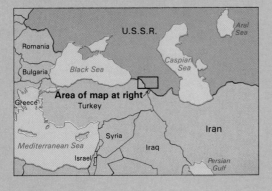

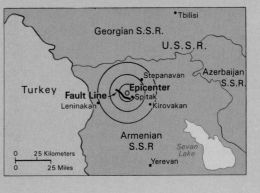

Geology
Continued

Large boulders littering Australia's Simpson Desert may have been dropped there by ice floes 100 million years ago, during the middle of the Cretaceous Period, according to research reported by scientists at the University of Adelaide in Australia. At that time, Australia was still attached to Antarctica and the Simpson Desert in central Australia was an inland sea. The research challenges the long-held belief that Earth was ice-free during the Cretaceous Period.

Nevertheless, the Northern Hemisphere experiences winter in January because it is tilted away from the sun and receives less sunlight. Earth is farthest away in early July, but the tilt of the Northern Hemisphere toward the sun results in warm summer temperatures. Because of this orbital pattern, the difference between average winter and summer temperatures is relatively small.

In their work, the scientists used both biological and geologic evidence, such as studies of pollen and water levels in ancient lakes, and computer models based on that evidence. They found that 18,000 years ago the Northern Hemisphere in winter was receiving about the same amount of solar radiation as it is today. But much of this radiation was reflected back into space by the extensive white icecaps that covered much of the Northern Hemisphere. As a result, the contrast between winter and summer temperatures was greater than that today.

By about 12,000 years ago, however, Earth's orbit had changed so that the Northern Hemisphere was receiving more solar radiation during the summer, when Earth was tilted toward the sun, than during the winter. The higher summer temperatures accelerated the melting of the icecaps, which had begun about 3,000 years earlier.

Breakup theory. The breakup of a huge ice sheet that covered much of what is now northern Scandinavia and the Soviet Union triggered the melting of the glaciers 15,000 years ago, according to research reported in November 1988. The Barents Shelf Ice Sheet, which also extended over the Barents Sea, covered an area larger than the United States. The icecap was relatively thin, however, compared with continental icecaps.

Marine geologists Glenn Jones and Lloyd Keigwin of Woods Hole Oceanographic Institution in Woods Hole, Mass., analyzed the ratio of two *isotopes* (forms) of oxygen in samples of ancient seawater to determine the age of the first major event in the melting of the glaciers. The samples were obtained from sediment cores taken from the Norwegian Sea.

The ratio of the two isotopes depends on water temperature and saltiness. The amount of one, called oxygen 18, in seawater increases when water temperatures drop or saltiness increases. The proportion of the isotope oxygen 16 increases when temperatures rise or saltiness decreases.

In samples dating from 15,000 years ago, the scientists found increased levels of oxygen 16. The scientists determined that this represented either a temperature increase of 5 Celsius degrees (9 Fahrenheit degrees) or a sudden influx of fresh water. Because such a dramatic temperature rise was unlikely, the scientists concluded that the increase resulted from fresh water pouring into the Norwegian Sea because of the breakup of the ice sheet.

The reason for the breakup is unclear. But the scientists speculated that the weight of the ice sheet caused the sea floor beneath it to sink, raising sea levels. As the water rose, the ice sheet was lifted off the sea floor, broke up, and melted.

According to the scientists, the disintegration of the ice sheet may have greatly reduced the amount of solar radiation reflected back into space and, thus, raised atmospheric temperatures. They said this may have triggered the melting of the icecaps covering Europe and North America.

Causes of ice ages. Mountain building may have triggered the beginning of the last ice age 2 million years ago in several ways, according to research reported in July 1988 by geologists Maureen Raymo, William Ruddiman, and Philip Froelich of the Lamont-Doherty Geological Observatory in Palisades, N.Y. In the mid-1980's, Ruddiman suggested that the rise of the Himalaya and the Rocky Mountains changed air circulation patterns in the atmosphere, which caused the ice age. In their new study, the Lamont scientists suggested another, less direct cause for the ice age—rock weathering and erosion.

When mountains are formed, more new rock is exposed to *weathering* (the breakup of rock due to physical and chemical processes). The atmospheric gas carbon dioxide (CO_2) plays a vital role in weathering. This gas is present in precipitation and reacts with chemical compounds in rocks, causing them to crack and break up. The chemical

Geology
Continued

reactions remove this CO_2 from the atmosphere.

The scientists theorized, therefore, that large-scale weathering would greatly lower the CO_2 content of the atmosphere. Since CO_2 traps heat in the atmosphere, a decline in atmospheric CO_2 would cause Earth to cool, creating conditions favorable for the formation of glaciers.

Extinction wave. The discovery of geologic evidence that a *tsunami* (huge tidal wave) struck the Gulf Coast region of what is now the United States about 66 million years ago was reported in July 1988. This provided additional support for the theory that an asteroid collided with Earth about that time, wiping out many animal species, including the dinosaurs. Evidence of a tsunami, perhaps more than 50 meters (160 feet) high, was reported by geologists at several universities.

The scientists discovered evidence of the tsunami in sedimentary rock that formed 66 million years ago on the floor of the gulf about 50 meters below the surface. Normally, rock from this depth consists of silt and mudstone, a sedimentary rock containing clay. In the Gulf Coast rock, however, the geologists found a layer of sandstone. One section of the sandstone contained debris, including fish teeth, shell fragments, and large clumps of mudstone up to 1 meter (3 feet 4 inches) across. The scientists also reported that the surface of the sandstone layer had ripples caused by waves.

They concluded that the sandstone represents an abrupt change in the sedimentary record of the region, which they attribute to a tsunami. They argued that such large clumps of mudstone could have been deposited only by very strong currents, such as those created by a tsunami.

The scientists calculated that the impact of an asteroid even 5,000 kilometers (3,100 miles) away could easily have produced the tsunami that struck the Gulf Coast. [William W. Hay]

In the Special Reports section, see Is Earth Overheating? and Who (or What) Killed the Giant Mammals? In World Book, see Geology; Ice Age.

Immunology

The first authorized transfer of a "foreign" gene into a human being was performed in May 1989. In an effort to assess the effectiveness of a treatment for cancer, researchers at the National Institutes of Health (NIH) in Bethesda, Md., introduced a gene from a bacterium into a gravely ill patient.

The patient, who volunteered for the procedure, was suffering from advanced melanoma, a severe form of skin cancer that spreads rapidly to other parts of the body. The NIH researchers injected the patient with a special type of white blood cells called *tumor-infiltrating lymphocytes* (TIL's). White blood cells are important disease-fighting elements of the immune system. The TIL's had been extracted from the patient's cancerous tissues.

The cells were first treated with a natural immune-system substance called *interleukin-2*, which increases the number of white blood cells. The more of these cells there are, the better is their ability to fight cancer. The researchers also inserted the bacterial gene into the TIL's.

The bacterial gene produces a protein that makes cells resistant to the antibiotic neomycin. The gene was placed in a harmless mouse virus, which was then allowed to infect the white blood cells. The virus carried the gene into the TIL's. The genetically altered TIL's were then administered to the patient.

The gene did not help the TIL's battle the patient's cancer. Rather, it simply made it easier for the researchers to track how effectively the TIL's fought the cancer.

After administering the TIL's and letting them do their work, the scientists extracted more tumor tissues from the patient and exposed them to neomycin. Cancer cells that had been infiltrated by the neomycin-resistant TIL's were not affected by the drug; the antibiotic, because of the high concentration used, killed other cancer cells from the tissue samples.

The researchers said they hoped their study would shed light on how TIL's attack cancer cells and why some cells escape destruction. Their objec-

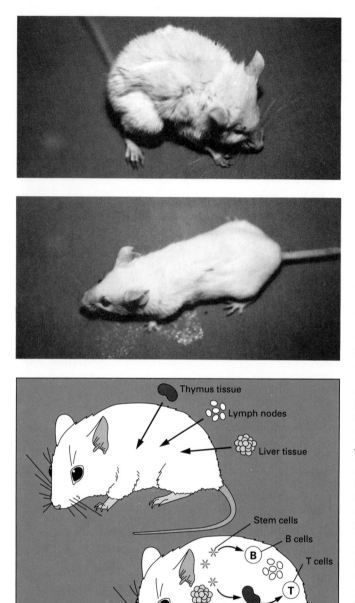

A type of mouse with no immune system of its own, *top,* was transformed into a mouse with a human immune system, *center,* by scientists at Stanford University in California. The researchers implanted human fetal thymus tissue, lymph nodes, and liver tissue into the mice, *above.* The liver tissue produced *stem cells,* from which all types of blood cells originate, including the white blood cells of the immune system. The implanted tissues changed the stem cells into immune-system cells called B cells and T cells.

tive is to find ways of increasing the cancer-fighting power of TIL's. The scientists said they were already experimenting with adding other genes—ones that produce cancer-fighting substances—to TIL's.

The NIH gene-transfer procedure actually marked the second time that a patient was given copies of a new gene. In the early 1980's, a California researcher conducted an unauthorized experiment in which he gave a patient copies of a gene designed to cure a blood disorder. The treatment failed, and the scientist was censured.

Human immune system in mice. The transplantation of functioning human immune systems into mice was reported by two California research teams in September 1988. The mice should have many important uses in medical science, such as enabling researchers to test treatments against a number of diseases and to study the effects of infectious microorganisms—including the AIDS virus—on the human immune system.

Both research groups—at the Medical Biology Institute in La Jolla and at Stanford University—started with a special strain of mice that are born without an immune system. The La Jolla scientists injected the mice with human B cells and T cells, white blood cells that are major components of the immune system. The cells reproduced in the mice's bodies and migrated throughout the animals' circulatory systems.

The Stanford researchers implanted human fetal liver tissues, thymus-gland tissues, and lymph nodes, into the mice. In the mice's bodies, the liver cells produced stem cells, which develop into the various kinds of blood cells. The implanted tissues converted the stem cells into B cells and T cells.

The mice with immune-system transplants by both research teams were fully protected against infectious disease. Ordinarily, mice of the strain used by the scientists die soon after birth unless they are kept in a sterile environment.

Rebuilding bone marrow. In other immune-system research, Stanford scientists reported in July 1988 that they had restored functioning bone marrow in normal mice whose marrow had been destroyed by radiation. Bone marrow is the source of blood cells in all adult mammals, including human beings.

The scientists grew mouse stem cells in the laboratory and injected them into the irradiated mice. The key to the procedure was using highly purified stem cells that were not mixed with any other kinds of cells. The investigators found that they could rebuild a mouse's bone marrow with as few as 80 to 100 such stem cells. With less pure batches of mouse cells, some 300,000 cells are ordinarily needed to restore destroyed bone marrow. The Stanford procedure may eventually simplify the regeneration of human bone marrow that has failed as a result of leukemia or radiation treatment for cancer.

Origin of the AIDS virus. There is little evidence to support the theory that the AIDS virus originated in African monkeys, according to a report in June 1988 by Japanese immunologists.

For several years, researchers had speculated that the AIDS virus evolved from the *simian immunodeficiency virus*

(SIV). SIV infects the green monkey, an animal found in west Africa. Up to 50 per cent of green monkeys have *antibodies* (infection-fighting proteins) against SIV in their blood.

Although the monkeys do not develop an AIDS-like disease—or any other illness—from the virus that infects them, scientists named the virus SIV because they thought it was similar in structure to the AIDS virus. The Japanese immunologists reported, however, that SIV is not like the AIDS virus. They found only one strain of SIV that is similar to the AIDS virus, and that was taken from Asian macaque monkeys born at two laboratories in the United States.

Investigators continued to search for ways to combat the AIDS virus. In one approach, they made copies of a receptor molecule on white blood cells, which the virus uses to enter the cells, to trap the virus. In the Special Reports section, see MAGIC BULLETS AGAINST DISEASE. [Paul Katz]

In WORLD BOOK, see AIDS; CANCER; IMMUNITY; VIRUS.

Materials Science

Materials science research in 1988 and 1989 was particularly active in two important areas—the development of *alloys* (metal mixtures) for the structures of aircraft and space vehicles, and research on materials for the electronic circuits of high-speed computers.

Aerospace alloy. Weldalite 049, an aluminum-lithium alloy under development at Martin Marietta Laboratories in Baltimore, moved rapidly toward commercial use during the year. Researchers from Martin Marietta and Reynolds Metals Company, the commercial producer of Weldalite 049 sheet and plate, were working together to develop the alloy for use on the United States government's planned heavy-lift booster rocket called the Advanced Launch System (ALS). Private contractors are to produce ALS designs by mid-1990.

Aluminum-lithium alloys are lighter and stiffer than other aluminum alloys used in aerospace devices. Compared with plastic composites now used to make aircraft bodies and wings, they are less expensive, easier to form into

complex shapes, and more resistant to damage.

The lithium in the alloys is responsible for the light weight and increased stiffness. The alloys also contain magnesium, copper, or both of these metals, which increase the alloy's strength.

For example, Weldalite 049, with a large amount of copper, has about twice the *yield strength* of the leading space alloy, whose main ingredients are aluminum and copper. Yield strength is a measure of a material's ability to return to its original shape after it has been bent.

Scientists believe that some aluminum-lithium alloys would be excellent materials for making the large tanks that contain the liquid hydrogen and oxygen used to power the space shuttle. These tanks must withstand very low temperatures—in the case of liquid hydrogen, $-258°C$ ($-432°F$.). At such temperatures, most materials become brittle. These aluminum-lithium alloys, however, have the unusual property of becoming stonger as the temperature is lowered.

How Many Motors Can Fit on the Head of a Pin?

If you could develop a motor smaller than a dust mote, tinier than a fly's foot, so miniscule that it could be seen clearly only under a microscope, what might you do with it?

That's what scientists are asking themselves—because now they've got such a motor. Thousands, in fact. And they're coming up with fascinating answers.

So far, the microbe-sized motors don't work very well. Their gears and rotors turn in a halting, jerky way, and they break after a few revolutions. But the fact that such tiny motors have been built at all is a major technological breakthrough. Before May 1988, in fact, nobody was sure such a thing was possible.

The first proof that it is indeed possible took place at the University of California at Berkeley in the early morning hours of May 27, 1988. In an engineering laboratory two graduate students, Long-Sheng Fan and Yu-Chong Tai, had been working late into the night. Squinting through a powerful microscope, they gently attached wires as thin as a spider web to electrodes leading to a rotor so tiny some 50,000 of them could fit into a thimble.

When the students sent a tiny surge of current through the wires, the microscopic rotor strained, then suddenly twitched into motion, rotating about half a turn. "And I jumped," Fan

said later. "I was terribly surprised—and terribly excited, too."

He should have been. For months, such prestigious organizations as AT&T Bell Laboratories, the Massachusetts Institute of Technology, and various laboratories in Japan, had been experimenting with microscopic levers, rotors, gears, and other machine parts that moved when prodded with a very fine wire. But the Berkeley device moved by itself when hit with a small electric current—a major leap forward. "Before, we had no proof a rotor that size would turn," says Richard Muller, the students' adviser. "Now we do. And now the future is closer."

When researchers in this field—called *microengineering*—look forward a decade or two, they see various kinds of dust-sized machines doing some amazing things. They envision, for instance, tiny surgical power saws programmed to begin operation only when they encounter cholesterol deposits in blood vessels. Injected by the thousands into the bloodstream, they would float quietly along until coming upon a fatty blockage in a blood vessel. Then, activated by their sensors and powered by a store of electricity, they would slice the life-threatening deposit off the vessel wall. The cut-up fragments would be flushed from the body in the urine—as would the used microsaws.

It sounds fanciful, and perhaps it is. But researchers like to point out that before the invention of transistors in the late 1940's, the

Experimental micromotors and other microscopic devices built in 1988 and 1989 included a rotor, *above,* developed at the University of California at Berkeley; gear-operated tongs, *above right,* constructed at AT&T Bell Laboratories; and a series of interlocking gears, *right,* also created at Bell Labs. The devices were made with the same techniques used to etch out microchips.

idea of pocket-sized calculators, radios, and TV sets seemed far-fetched, too.

Microengineering has its roots in the technology of making electronic microchips. The big difference is that the chips sit motionless as electrons shuffle around their tiny circuits; micromachines are designed to move.

The techniques used for making micromotors are similar to those used in making microchips. To make a chip, engineers use a computer to produce a detailed drawing of the chip's complete circuit. They then transfer the drawing to a photographic negative, reducing its size until the lines are too fine to see without a microscope. This shrunken negative is called a *mask*.

In the next step, a light is shined through the mask onto a thin layer of light-sensitive silicon, creating a pattern sensitive to an acidic etching solution. When washed with the acid, unexposed areas of the silicon are eaten away, leaving only the circuit. Once a pattern is created, such circuits can be formed by the thousands. And that's why a pocket calculator, complicated as it is, costs so little.

Microengineers build their tiny motors the same way: They carefully deposit whisper-thin layers of silicon and similar materials and etch away all but the main design. In that way, they can make motors by the thousands.

Engineers have fashioned a number of experimental microgadgets. For example, at Bell Laboratories in Holmdel, N.J., researchers have "whittled" gears with teeth the size of red blood cells, springlike "inchworms" that move forward by alternately stretching and compressing, and air turbines that spin at 24,000 revolutions per minute when air is blown at them through a hypodermic needle.

At this point, no one knows where this research will lead. Nevertheless, microengineers foresee some amazing developments:

■ Microscrubbers that could be dumped over a ship's side by the bucketfuls to scour barnacles off the hull.

■ Crawling, speck-sized robots that will check for cracks inside nuclear reactors.

■ Microsaws, much like the cholesterol cutter, designed to navigate the body's smallest pathways to perform incredibly precise surgery, including chopping up individual cancer cells.

■ Perhaps even microscopic "soldiers" that, in case of war, could infiltrate enemy positions by the tens of thousands to destroy weapons and equipment with acids or tiny explosive charges.

All this is sheer speculation, of course, but with the history of transistors as a guide, two things are almost certain: The pace of development will be breathtaking, and the results will be more exciting than we can imagine. [Robert Gannon]

Superconducting circuits. A technique that might be used to build computer-chip circuits of so-called high-temperature superconductors was announced in May 1989 by researchers at the American Telephone and Telegraph Company's Bell Laboratories in Murray Hill, N.J. A superconductor is a material that conducts electricity without resistance. Conventional superconductors must be cooled to very low temperatures. The only practical way to make them cold enough to superconduct is to bathe them in liquid helium, which has a boiling point of −269°C (−452°F.). But liquid helium is expensive to use. Materials that become superconducting at much higher temperatures are under development.

Many of these high-temperature superconductors can be cooled with liquid nitrogen, whose boiling point is −196°C (−321°F.). Liquid nitrogen is much less expensive to use than liquid helium. See PHYSICS, FLUIDS AND SOLIDS.

Manufacturers want to use superconducting materials for making computer chips to avoid the generation of heat. Heat is caused by resistance in conventional chip conductors such as aluminum. Excessive heat can cause melting and therefore limits the size of conductors and the spacing between electronic components that are built into chips. Eliminating heat in conductors would enable components to be squeezed closer together without a danger of melting. This would lead to faster computers by decreasing the time it takes for electrical signals to flow between components.

Bombarding a film. The Bell Labs researchers deposited a film of superconducting material about 1 ten-thousandth of a millimeter thick on a chip of silicon, the basic material of most computer chips, then bombarded the film with beams of charged atoms. The scientists guided the beams so that they struck the entire surface of the film except for one or more narrow strips. The atoms damaged the crystal structure of the areas they struck, so these areas could not superconduct. The only superconducting areas remaining were the strips, which could serve as "wires."   [Jay Myers]

In WORLD BOOK, see PHYSICS.

Medical Research

A new nonsurgical treatment in which a chemical related to ether, an anesthetic, is used to dissolve gallstones was reported by a group of physicians at the Mayo Clinic in Rochester, Minn., in March 1989.

The Mayo team reported that they had used the new technique to treat 75 patients with the most common type of gallstones, those formed from excess cholesterol. The researchers used a solvent called methyl-tert-butyl ether to dissolve the gallstones.

To prepare for treatment, the patients took iodine tablets with their evening meals for two days. The iodine was absorbed by the gall bladder, making the organ visible when viewed on a fluoroscope, an X-ray imaging device containing a fluorescent screen. The surgeons performed the procedure using a catheter, or narrow tube, that was inserted through the patients' right side. By watching the catheter's progress on the fluoroscope, the physicians were able to guide it into the gall bladder. The solvent was injected into the gall bladder through the catheter and immediately suctioned out, a procedure repeated four to six times per minute for an average of five hours.

At the end of treatment, more than 95 per cent of the stones had been dissolved in 72 patients. Seven patients had enough remaining stones or debris to cause symptoms, and 6 of them eventually required surgery to remove the gall bladder. Gallstones recurred in 4 patients in whom they had been completely dissolved.

The physicians concluded that while the removal of the gall bladder is still the only sure way to eliminate gallstones and prevent new ones from forming, treatment with the solvent may be a good alternative for patients who have medical conditions that make them poor candidates for surgery or for patients who do not want to undergo an operation. The doctors cautioned, however, that more studies are needed to determine the treatment's long-term effectiveness.

Partial livers. Results of the first transplants of portions of livers into patients without removing the patients' own livers were reported in December 1988 by a medical team at Erasmus University in Rotterdam, the Netherlands. Between October 1986 and April 1988, surgeons performed the operation on six patients who had life-threatening liver disease complicated by other medical conditions that made them poor candidates for conventional liver transplantation. Usually, the patient's diseased liver is removed and replaced by an intact liver.

The new procedure was a modification of an operation called *auxiliary liver transplantation*, in which a donor's entire liver is implanted in the patient but the patient's diseased liver is not removed. Researchers had theorized that auxiliary liver transplantation should be less risky than conventional transplantation because the operation is less complicated and takes less time. Also, the transplanted liver should not have to be the same size as the patient's. Finally, if the transplanted liver failed, the patient's diseased liver should be able to perform some liver functions.

But of the 50 patients who had undergone auxiliary liver transplantation before October 1986, only 2 survived for as long as one year. Some patients died because the transplanted liver was too large to fit easily in the abdominal cavity. Others died because the donor liver did not have enough blood vessels attached to provide an adequate blood supply or because blood clots developed in the attached veins.

The Erasmus medical team decided to try overcoming many of these problems by transplanting only one segment of a donor liver. Experiments had shown that a portion of a liver could increase in size enough to do the work of a normal liver, which includes breaking down nutrients, producing blood proteins, and filtering toxic materials from the bloodstream.

The Erasmus surgeons first removed the segment of a donor liver that contains the largest of the liver's four lobes and to which the organ's major blood vessels are attached. They placed the liver segment below the patient's own liver. To provide an adequate blood supply to the transplanted organ they attached veins and arteries from the partial liver to the patient's own blood vessels. After surgery, patients were given drugs to prevent the formation of blood clots.

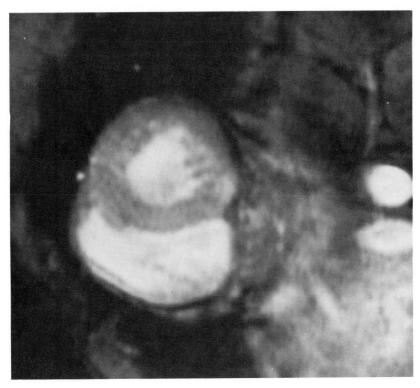

This frame from a moving picture of a beating heart (viewed from above looking toward the feet) was made with a form of magnetic resonance imaging (MRI), a noninvasive technique that uses magnets and radio signals to "see" inside the body. Researchers at the University of California, San Francisco, developed the moving picture technique, called Cine-MRI, which takes 30 to 40 images per heartbeat. A computer converts the MRI images to a motion picture of the beating heart. Such movies may help doctors diagnose heart diseases.

Medical
Research
Continued

The patients received follow-up examinations. X rays indicated that the patients' original livers soon began to waste away, while the transplanted partial livers began to grow. Four of the patients had *hepatitis*, an inflammation of the liver, before the operation, and after surgery, all four developed hepatitis in the new liver segment. All recovered, however, and by December 1988 all six patients had nearly normal liver function. On the basis of their experience, the Erasmus researchers concluded that auxiliary partial liver transplantation could be useful for high-risk patients with life-threatening liver disease.

Understanding Alzheimer's proteins. Biomedical researchers in 1988 and 1989 made substantial progress in defining the role of the β-*amyloid* protein, a major component of the plaque that accumulates in the brains of victims of Alzheimer's disease and appears to interfere with brain function. Earlier, researchers had established that β-amyloid is made when a larger protein circulating in the blood is broken

down. The new findings may lead to ways of preventing the build-up of β-amyloid.

In July 1988, a group of scientists at the Salk Institute for Biological Studies in La Jolla, Calif., and the University of California at San Diego determined that the larger molecule is almost identical to a protein called *heparan sulfate proteoglycan* (HSPG). HSPG is found near *synapses* (the points at which nerve impulses are transmitted from one nerve to another). The researchers think that β-amyloid might be created when HSPG is broken down improperly. A build-up of β-amyloid at synapses might interfere with nerve impulse transmissions.

An abnormal version of the protein that breaks down into β-amyloid was found in the brains of Alzheimer's patients by a team of scientists from Case Western Reserve University School of Medicine in Cleveland and from Harvard Medical School in Boston. The researchers reported this in August.

The scientists isolated genetic mate-

New Ways to Lengthen Bones

Two devices are helping surgeons lengthen arm and leg bones shortened by accident, disease, or genetic abnormality. An expandable bone implant, *right,* is being used chiefly in children to replace cancerous bone that has been surgically removed. The device is a tube within a tube that can be lengthened quickly and relatively painlessly as the child grows. The second device is a brace that stretches bone, *below.* Pins inserted into opposite ends of the bone are attached to two rings outside the skin. The two rings are then connected to adjustable rods. The surgeon makes a relatively shallow incision around the outside of the bone between the rings. By stretching the rod, the surgeon can stretch the bone, which may grow as much as 1 centimeter ($\frac{2}{5}$ inch) every 10 days.

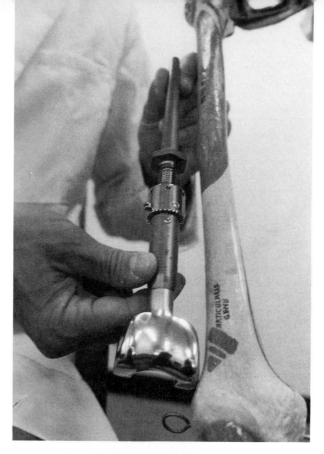

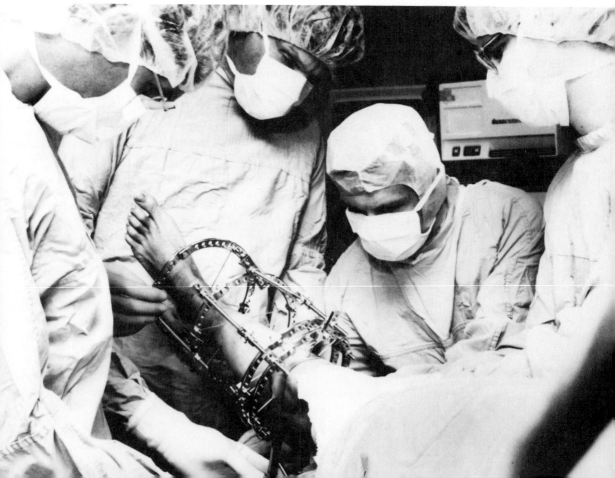

rial from the protein found in the brains of 11 people who had died of Alzheimer's disease. They also took genetic material from the brains of 7 people who had died of other causes and who had had no symptoms of Alzheimer's disease.

The researchers found that tissue from two regions of the brains of the Alzheimer's victims had nearly twice the amount of genetic material coding for the protein than did tissue from the normal brains. Moreover, they found that this "extra" genetic material differed slightly from the genetic material found in normal brains. The difference was that the material lacked genetic instructions to make enzymes that prevent the entire protein from being broken down. The researchers speculated that because this abnormal version of the protein lacks these enzymes, it may be broken down more easily into β-amyloid.

Growing new blood vessels. A method to stimulate and direct blood vessel growth in rats after surgery was reported in September 1988 by a team of experts from the National Heart, Lung and Blood Institute in Bethesda, Md.; a surgeon from the Children's Hospital National Medical Center, in Washington, D.C.; and a team of molecular biologists from the American Red Cross in Rockville, Md.

The researchers knew that a protein called *heparin-binding growth factor* (HBGF) triggers blood vessel growth in animals and that it also binds to gelatin, a material used to make surgical sponges, which are used to pack wounds. They reasoned that if HBGF were added to tiny fragments of gelatin sponges and implanted in the body, blood vessel growth would be stimulated near the sponges.

To test this hypothesis, they implanted HBGF-treated gelatin sponges in the necks and abdomens of one group of rats and implanted untreated gelatin sponges in the same places in a second group of rats. Two weeks later, they removed the sponges and studied blood vessel development in the area. They found new blood vessel growth within and surrounding the HBGF-treated sponges, but none in or around the untreated sponges. Moreover, HBGF-treated sponges placed between two organs caused new vessels to grow and connect the organs.

The researchers predicted that the technique might eventually be used to bring new vessels to such areas as arteries obstructed with atherosclerotic plaque, which can lead to a heart attack. It could also be used to speed wound healing and to provide a blood supply to transplanted organs.

Halting blood vessel growth. A new combination of drugs to inhibit the development of blood vessels was reported in March 1989 by a team of chemists and bioengineers from Children's Hospital in Boston and the University of Pennsylvania in Philadelphia. This research might be applied to the treatment of cancerous tumors by blocking vessels that supply the tumors. It might prevent blindness in diabetics by preventing excess blood vessel growth in eyes.

The researchers knew that the anticoagulant drug heparin, which limits blood clot formation, can, when combined with steroid drugs, slow the development of blood vessels in chick embryos. For this study, they tested the effectiveness of synthetic heparin substitutes in chick embryos. They found that one substitute, β-cyclodextrin tetradecasulfate, inhibited vessel growth when used with a steroid and promoted vessel growth when used alone.

For the test, the researchers implanted tiny pellets containing β-cyclodextrin tetradecasulfate in the corneas of rabbits' eyes. In the corneas of other rabbits, the scientists implanted three other types of pellets, one containing β-cyclodextrin tetradecasulfate along with a steroid, another containing only the steroid, and a third containing no active ingredients. They then put a biochemical that stimulates blood vessel formation into the rabbits' eyes.

When the researchers examined the rabbits' eyes 13 days later, they found that the new blood vessels in the eyes of rabbits treated with the steroid were less than half as long as those in the untreated eyes, but the eyes treated with the steroid and β-cyclodextrin tetradecasulfate were only 18 per cent as long. In the rabbit eyes treated with β-cyclodextrin tetradecasulfate alone, blood vessels were 164 per cent longer than those in the untreated eyes.

The researchers suggested that, when used in combination with steroids, β-cyclodextrin tetradecasulfate might be an effective way to prevent the growth of blood vessels that feed malignant tumors in cancer patients or the overgrowth of blood vessels in the eye that can cause blindness in people with diabetes.

Iron and cancer risk. A large amount of iron stored in the body can increase the risk of cancer in men, according to an October 1988 report of the results of a large study sponsored by the National Cancer Institute (NCI) in Bethesda, Md.

The NCI research team examined the relationship between iron levels and cancer risk among the 14,407 adult men and women participants in the National Health and Nutrition Examination Survey, which was begun in 1971. Participants in the study had undergone a test to determine how many molecules of *transferrin*, an iron-carrying protein, were actually carrying iron in their blood. The amount of iron bound to transferrin molecules indicated the extent of iron stored in each of the volunteers.

Between 1981 and 1984, 3,355 men who had participated were located and interviewed. Of these, 242 had developed cancer. The NCI research team found that the men who developed cancer had higher levels of iron than those who did not. Cancer risk among men with the highest iron levels was 40 per cent higher than among those with the lowest levels.

The NCI researchers also located and interviewed 5,367 women; of these, 203 had developed cancer. But, overall, their levels of iron were not significantly higher than those of the women who had not developed cancer.

The researchers also found that some types of cancer, particularly cancers of the colon, esophagus, bladder, and lung, appeared to be associated with high iron stores, while others, like stomach cancer, did not. Because iron stores increase proportionately with the amount of iron consumed in the diet, the researchers suggested that taking iron supplements may be unwise unless they are needed to combat anemia, a condition characterized by low levels of red blood cells.

Diet, exercise, and heart disease. Weight loss, whether achieved by diet or exercise, has a favorable effect on the level of fats in the bloodstream, which is linked to the development of heart disease. These findings were reported in November 1988 by a team of medical researchers from Stanford University in California, and the University of Washington in Seattle.

The researchers studied 131 male nonsmokers who weighed from 120 per cent to 160 per cent of their ideal body weight. At the beginning of the study, the researchers measured the men's blood pressures and their blood levels of cholesterol and triglycerides, fatty substances that in some cases encourage the development of heart disease.

The men were then randomly assigned to three groups. The first group was put on an exercise program and the second on a calorie-restricted diet. Both programs were designed to reduce body fat by one-third within nine months and then to stabilize the men's weight for the last three months of the study. The third group, the control group, was advised to continue their usual eating and exercise habits.

At the end of 12 months, the researchers computed the changes in the men's total body weight, fat weight, and lean-body weight. Compared to the control group, the dieters as a group had significant reductions in all three categories, and the exercisers had significant losses of total weight and fat weight, though not of lean-body weight.

Total levels of cholesterol did not change significantly in either the diet or exercise group when compared with the control group, however. But the first two groups had significantly higher blood levels of *high density lipoproteins*, compounds that appear to have a protective effect against heart disease. Similarly, both the diet group and the exercise group had significant reductions in their blood levels of triglycerides. The researchers concluded that dieting and exercising are equally effective in reducing the amount of body fat and helping to reduce the risk of heart disease.   [Beverly Merz]

In WORLD BOOK, see ALZHEIMER'S DISEASE; CANCER; GALL BLADDER; LIVER.

Meteorology

For much of the Midwestern United States, the drought and heat wave of 1988 was the worst such event since the Dust Bowl days of the 1930's, when a drought lasting seven years brought disaster to farmers in the Southwest and the Great Plains. By June 1988, in a belt stretching from Montana eastward to Ohio, the weather resembled that normally found in the deserts of the Southwestern states. Rain fell only infrequently from a few widely scattered thundershowers.

In many places, daytime temperatures climbed into the upper 30's Celsius (90's Fahrenheit) or higher, while relative humidities fell below 20 per cent for several weeks in a row. Crops withered in the field or never sprouted. Some relief finally came in early July with rain across the Midwest.

The drought conditions continued through the fall and into winter. The Climate Analysis Center of the National Oceanic and Atmospheric Administration (NOAA) reported that as of Feb. 9, 1989, moderate to severe drought still prevailed over 30 per cent of the land area of the United States. Many of the regions affected by the midwinter drought were the same ones most affected by the summer's severe drought.

La Niña. There did not appear to be a single cause for the persistent drought, which developed at different times in different portions of North America. In January 1989, however, atmospheric scientists Kevin Trenberth and Grant Branstator of the National Center for Atmospheric Research (NCAR) in Boulder, Colo., and Phillip Arkin of NOAA reported findings that appeared to determine one of the causes for the severe drought in the spring and summer of 1988. Their research established a link between the drought period and the *La Niña phenomenon*. La Niña is an unusually cold ocean-surface current that occurs over large areas of the equatorial Pacific Ocean an average of every four years. It is a counterpart of the better-known *El Niño phenomenon*.

El Niño is an unusually warm sea surface current. The two currents seem

A satellite photograph reveals the swirling clouds of Hurricane Gilbert centered over the Caribbean Sea in September 1988. This was the most intense hurricane ever recorded in the Western Hemisphere. Meteorologists reported that the eye of the hurricane was so narrow it resembled a monster tornado.

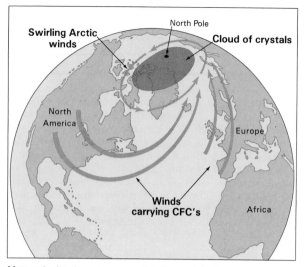

Meteorologists launch a research balloon, *right*, into the atmosphere over the Arctic to determine if ozone is declining there, as it is over Antarctica. Findings from a research expedition in January and February 1989 showed that, as in the Antarctic, a polar vortex, *above*, creates atmospheric conditions that help form polar stratospheric clouds. Winds carry chemicals known as CFC's from North America and Europe to the polar region, where they concentrate in cloud crystals and eventually break down ozone molecules.

In the diagram labels:
- North Pole
- Swirling Arctic winds
- Cloud of crystals
- North America
- Europe
- Winds carrying CFC's
- Africa

Meteorology

Continued

to alternate in cycles, though a La Niña had not been observed since 1975. The onset of the La Niña phenomenon between March and June 1988 was coupled with the appearance of an abnormally warm region of water to the southeast of Hawaii, creating unusually strong contrasts between warm and cold areas on the surface of the ocean. These differences in ocean surface temperatures, the researchers found, set in motion a chain of events that ultimately changed the flow of the winds in the upper atmosphere over North America.

Using computer simulations, they found that *storm tracks*, the paths followed by moisture-bearing low-pressure systems, were deflected to the north and west, away from the Midwestern United States. A mass of high-pressure air established itself over the Plains and the Midwest, blocking the development of spring and summer rainstorms and resulting in the drought. The computer simulation techniques developed by Trenberth and his colleagues in studying the La

Niña phenomenon may improve long-term weather forecasts and predictions of future climate.

Records in Alaska. Scientists were reminded again in 1989 of the complexity of the weather and the problems faced by those trying to analyze the factors that control Earth's climate. While scientists were still puzzling over the record 1988 summer heat, the state of Alaska was reporting record low temperatures. In early January 1989, a high-pressure air mass established itself over central Alaska, trapping a flow of exceptionally cold air from Siberia and the Chukchi Sea over the state. This sent temperatures plunging for about 2½ weeks. The coldest reported temperature was −60°C (−76°F.) at Tanana on January 27.

Arctic ozone. Atmospheric scientists from the United States and four other countries in January and February 1989, conducted the Airborne Arctic Stratospheric Expedition to determine if the ozone layer in the upper atmosphere over the Arctic has been damaged as it has in the upper atmosphere over Antarctica. *Ozone* is a gas molecule composed of three oxygen atoms. In the upper atmosphere, it prevents biologically harmful ultraviolet radiation from the sun from reaching Earth.

The expedition confirmed a decline of about 6 per cent in winter ozone concentrations over the Arctic since 1970. This decline is about three times greater than what scientists expected to find, but not nearly as dramatic as the decline observed over the Antarctic. In 1987, a scientific expedition to Antarctica detected an ozone decline as great as 60 per cent from previous levels. The decline was so widespread that scientists described it as an "ozone hole" over Antarctica.

Although no "ozone hole" was detected over the Arctic, expedition members found evidence of high concentrations of chlorine compounds. These compounds are the culprits suspected of causing the ozone decline.

Scientists believe that the source of these chlorine compounds is the industrial and commercial use of chemicals known as *chlorofluorocarbons* (CFC's). CFC's have a wide range of industrial and commercial applications, such as in cleaning solvents, refrigerants, and aerosol sprays.

They are good for such uses because they do not react with other chemicals. But CFC's also do not react with other gases in the atmosphere and so remain unchanged as they slowly rise into the upper atmosphere. Once they are in the upper atmosphere, ultraviolet radiation from the sun causes the breakup of CFC's, releasing atoms of chlorine. Each chlorine atom acts as a *catalyst* (a substance that speeds up chemical reactions while itself remaining unchanged) that converts ozone to ordinary oxygen.

The exact sequence of events leading to the destruction of ozone is complicated and is only beginning to be understood. It appears that a key role is played by *polar stratospheric clouds*, clouds that form in the stratosphere, 16 to 48 kilometers (10 to 30 miles) above Earth's surface. During the long polar night of winter, temperatures in this region of the atmosphere can fall to $-90°C$ ($-130°F$.), allowing clouds composed of minute crystals of ice and nitric acid to form. Chlorine com-

pounds concentrate in these crystals. When sunlight reaches the polar regions at the end of winter, large quantities of chlorine are released rapidly, resulting in a decrease in ozone.

The Arctic expedition observed polar stratospheric clouds, and researchers predicted that if the clouds persisted into spring, when the sun rises in the Arctic, significant damage could occur to the ozone layer in the Northern Hemisphere. Polar stratospheric clouds, however, are thinner and occur less frequently in the Arctic than in the Antarctic. So researchers expect less ozone destruction over the Arctic.

Climate change. Methane released from coal mining and from oil and gas fields accounts for about 30 per cent of the methane in Earth's atmosphere, according to a report in late 1988 by atmospheric chemists David Lowe and Stanley Tyler of NCAR. Methane, along with carbon dioxide and other gases, is a so-called *greenhouse gas* that traps heat from the sun. Some scientists fear that an increase in such gases could cause a climate change on Earth. Scientists believe that methane plays a major role in contributing to a long-term rise in average global temperature that has been detected.

The amount of methane in the atmosphere has doubled in the last 150 years, and scientists have been trying to determine the sources of the additional methane. Lowe and Tyler devised analytic techniques that made it possible to find individual sources of methane and estimate how much each contributes to the total amount in the atmosphere. The 30 per cent from coal mining and from oil and gas fields was a much larger contribution than previously thought.

Previously, scientists suspected that the main sources of methane were from the decay of organic materials in rice paddies after harvest and from intestinal gases in cattle as well as from the burning of fossil fuels. The new findings suggest that simply drilling holes into Earth's surface in search of such fossil fuels as coal, oil, and natural gas releases substantial amounts of methane.   [John T. Snow]

In the Special Reports section, see IS EARTH OVERHEATING? In WORLD BOOK, see METEOROLOGY; OZONE.

Neuroscience

The first operation in the United States to transplant fetal cells into a human brain was performed in November 1988 at the University of Colorado Health Science Center in Denver. Neuroscientists at the center implanted brain cells from an aborted fetus into the brain of a 52-year-old man with severe Parkinson's disease, a neurological disorder that causes tremors and muscle rigidity. On the basis of earlier experiments with rats, the researchers hoped that the fetal tissue would produce a brain chemical called *dopamine*, which is deficient in the brains of Parkinson's disease victims.

In May 1989, the director of the Colorado research team, neuroscientist Curt Freed, reported that the patient was doing well. Freed said the patient, who had suffered from Parkinson's disease for 20 years, was walking 50 per cent faster and taking less medication. Nevertheless, the neuroscientist said, the patient was far from cured. He added that any expectations that fetal brain-tissue implants will eliminate Parkinson's disease are "unrealistic."

Shortly after the Denver man was operated on, doctors at the Yale University School of Medicine in New Haven, Conn., performed the same procedure on two Parkinson's disease patients.

Fetal brain-tissue implants have been done since 1987 in China, Cuba, Great Britain, Mexico, and Sweden. But the use of aborted fetuses as a source of tissue for surgical procedures is extremely controversial. In March 1988, the Administration of President Ronald Reagan prohibited the use of fetal tissue in federally funded research until the moral, ethical, and religious issues involved can be sorted out. That ban was still in effect in 1989.

Brain-tissue implants and epilepsy. For the time being, most research on brain-tissue implants is being done with rats. In December 1988, neuroscientists Gyorgy Buzsaki and Fred Gage of the University of California at San Diego reported that implanted brain tissue reduced the number of epileptic seizures in experimental rats.

Using tissue from fetal rat brains, the

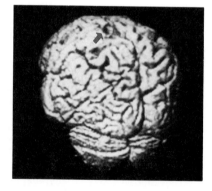

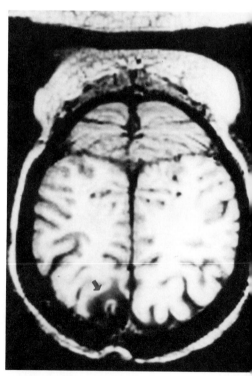

Using magnetic resonance imaging (MRI) and a computer graphics program, scientists at the University of Chicago developed a method of creating three-dimensional views of the brain surface to aid surgeons in locating abnormal tissue. An MRI cross section, *right,* shows the approximate location of damaged tissue (arrow) in the left side of a brain. But the new 3-D image, *above,* reveals to surgeons where this tissue is on the brain's surface (arrow).

researchers and their colleagues treated adult rats whose brains had been surgically altered to induce epileptic seizures. They found, in particular, that tissue taken from an area of the brain called the *locus coeruleus* significantly decreased the number of seizures when implanted into the adult rats' brains.

Epilepsy, which is characterized by electrical abnormalities in the brain and often by seizures and loss of consciousness, is the most common of all neurological disorders. Epilepsy affects some 2 million to 3 million people in the United States alone. The causes of most epilepsy are not known, though many cases are the result of brain injury. The experimental results reported by Buzsaki and Gage suggest that brain-tissue implants may offer a means of controlling this serious brain disorder.

The brain and species traits. In another study of transplanted brain tissue, reported in September 1988, neuroscientists in France related the outcome of experiments on how the developing brain determines particular kinds of behavior in various species. The researchers, at the Institute of Cellular and Molecular Biology in Nogent-sur-Marne, inserted quail brain tissue into chicken embryos.

Using tiny instruments and operating through holes cut in eggs, the investigators removed varying amounts of tissue from quail embryos. Actually, no brains had yet formed in the embryos, but the tissues were taken from the part of the embryo that would have become the brain. The tissues were then inserted into chicken embryos from which corresponding sections of tissue had been removed.

The scientists studied 20 chicks that survived the operation and hatched. They were particularly interested to see how the implanted brain tissue would influence the chicks' "crowing." Although crowing is normally done only by adult roosters, the researchers caused the chicks to make a crowing sound by giving them hormones.

The researchers found that some of the chicks that developed from the embryos crowed much like quails. Fifteen of the chicks, which had received relatively small amounts of quail brain tissue, crowed like normal chickens. But the other five chicks, with larger quail brain implants, behaved much differently. Three of those chicks made sounds that were distinctly quaillike; the remaining two sounded like a cross between a quail and a chicken.

Experiments such as this may help explain how genes in brain cells determine behavioral differences between species. More generally, such studies may lead to a better understanding of how immature brain cells develop to form a fully functioning brain.

The versatile cortex. The various parts of the *cerebral cortex* are not as rigidly specialized as had been thought, neuroscientists at the Massachusetts Institute of Technology (M.I.T.) in Cambridge reported in December 1988. The cerebral cortex is the outer layer of the brain, where reasoning and other advanced mental processes occur. The M.I.T. scientists said their animal experiments indicate that while the brain is still developing, areas of the cortex can take over functions that they do not normally perform.

The investigators studied the visual system in the brains of newborn ferrets, animals similar to weasels. They used ferrets in their research because the visual system of newborn ferrets is not as well developed as that of most other animals. This enabled the scientists to get a better look at how the developing brain establishes the neural connections needed for vision.

The scientists destroyed parts of the ferrets' *visual cortex*, the area of the cortex that is involved with vision. Ordinarily, *neurons* (nerve cells) in the *retina* (the lining at the back of the eye) send out fibers that connect with neurons in the visual cortex. With the vision centers destroyed, the nerve fibers from the retina migrated instead to a part of the cortex that in normal circumstances handles only *auditory* (hearing) information.

To help this "rewiring" process along, the researchers cut developing fibers in the auditory portion of the *thalamus*, a structure beneath the cortex that serves as a sort of "switching station" between sensory organs and the cortex. With the auditory fibers removed, space was created in the thalamus for the visual fibers, which

Neuroscience

were searching for a target in the brain.

Later, the researchers tested the ferrets' ability to see by presenting them with various kinds of visual stimulation. During the tests, instruments monitored the electrical activity in the animals' brains. With each visual stimulus, the instruments detected a response in the neurons of the auditory cortex and auditory thalamus. These cells responded as though they were part of the normal visual system.

This result suggests that there may be a number of fundamental "modules" in the cortex. Each module might be capable of becoming a processing center for vision or hearing—and perhaps for other kinds of sensory information as well—depending on the input it receives during the early development of the brain.

Site of biological clock. Researchers have known for years that mammals have a "clock" somewhere in their brains—a control center that regulates *circadian rhythms*. Circadian rhythms are the body's daily biological cycles, controlling such activities as sleep and wakefulness. In November 1988, neuroscientists at the University of Virginia in Charlottesville reported that the *suprachiasmatic nucleus* (SCN), a small cluster of cells in the middle of the brain that neuroscientists have long suspected of playing a role in daily rhythms, is the long-sought biological clock.

The investigators performed a series of tissue-transplant experiments with hamsters. Some of the animals were normal hamsters, which have a circadian cycle of 24 hours; the others were *mutant* (genetically altered) hamsters whose cycles were only 20 or 22 hours long.

The scientists first removed the SCN from the brains of the hamsters in both groups. They then implanted an SCN from a mutant hamster into the brain of each normal animal, and vice versa. When the hamsters had recovered from their operations, the circadian rhythms of the two groups were reversed: The normal hamsters had a daily cycle of 20 to 22 hours, and the mutants were on a 24-hour cycle.

The identification of the internal clock is an important stepping stone in understanding the basic, automatic mechanisms of brain function. It may also help in finding ways to relieve human sleep disorders.

A chemical basis for bulimia? Bulimia, a severe eating disorder seen most commonly in teen-age girls and young women, may not be strictly a psychological problem. Bulimia has been thought to stem from a lack of self-esteem or a desperate desire to be fashionably thin. In September 1988, however, neuroscientists at the National Institute of Mental Health in Bethesda, Md., and Duke University in Durham, N.C., reported that the bulimia patients they tested had a shortage of a chemical that controls feelings of hunger.

Bulimia is marked by uncontrollable eating binges, typically followed by self-induced vomiting or the use of laxatives. In many cases, patients report that they do not feel full after eating, regardless of how much food they have consumed.

The scientists examined the possibility that this inability to feel satisfied by food might be related to blood levels of *cholecystokinin* (CCK), a hormone released in the small intestine after eating. The hormone apparently signals the brain that enough food has been consumed to meet the body's immediate needs, and the individual then feels satisfied.

The researchers studied 14 bulimia patients. They found that the patients' blood levels of CCK after a meal were indeed significantly lower, compared with the levels of 10 volunteers who did not suffer from bulimia. In fact, the amount of CCK in the patients' blood was always lower than normal, regardless of when they had last eaten.

To investigate whether bulimia might respond to drug therapy, the scientists gave five of the patients an antidepressant medication. The drug raised the patients' CCK level and reduced their urge to continue eating after a meal. The researchers said further studies will be required before it can be stated with certainty that bulimia can be controlled with drugs. But their results strongly indicated that bulimia is a physical as well as a psychological disturbance. [George Adelman]

In WORLD BOOK, see BRAIN; NERVOUS SYSTEM.

Nobel Prizes

The Royal Academy of Sciences in Stockholm, Sweden, in October 1988, awarded the Nobel Prize in chemistry to three scientists from West Germany and the Nobel Prize in physics to three scientists from the United States. Also in October, the Karolinska Institute in Stockholm awarded the Nobel Prize for physiology or medicine to two U.S. biochemists and a British pharmacologist. The three recipients of each prize shared a cash award of about $390,000.

Chemistry. The Nobel Prize for chemistry went to Robert Huber of the Max Planck Institute for Biochemistry in Martinsried, West Germany; Johann Deisenhofer, formerly of the Martinsried institute and now of the Howard Hughes Medical Institute in Dallas; and Hartmut Michel of the Max Planck Institute for Biophysics in Frankfurt. The three were recognized for determining the structure of a bacterial protein that performs *photosynthesis*, the process by which green plants and certain bacteria use energy from sunlight to make carbohydrates for food energy.

Michel overcame the greatest technical difficulty of the project in 1982, when he isolated the photosynthesizing protein and made it into a crystal so that its structure could be studied. Deisenhofer and Huber then joined Michel in analyzing the crystallized protein with a technique called *X-ray crystallography*. By 1985, the three scientists had worked out the complete arrangement of the more than 10,000 atoms that make up the protein.

Their achievement led to increased understanding of the chemistry of photosynthesis. It also opened the possibility that scientists may someday harness the sun's energy with solar cells similar to plant cells.

Physics. The Nobel Prize for physics was awarded to Leon M. Lederman, director of the Fermi National Accelerator Laboratory in Batavia, Ill., and a former member of the SCIENCE YEAR Editorial Advisory Board; Melvin Schwartz, head of Digital Pathways Incorporated, a computer firm in Mountain View, Calif.; and Jack Steinberger of the European Laboratory for

Winners of the 1988 Nobel Prize in physics—for producing the first laboratory-made stream of subatomic particles called *neutrinos*—were three U.S. physicists, *clockwise from right,* a happy Leon M. Lederman of the Fermi National Accelerator Laboratory in Batavia, Ill.; Jack Steinberger of the European Laboratory for Particle Physics in Geneva, Switzerland; and Melvin Schwartz of Digital Pathways Incorporated in Mountain View, Calif.

Nobel Prizes

Particle Physics (CERN) in Geneva, Switzerland.

The three physicists were honored for work they performed in 1961 and 1962 at Columbia University in New York City. There, they became the first researchers to produce a stream of *neutrinos*, subatomic particles with no electric charge or measurable mass. They developed a technique for using neutrino streams much like X rays, firing the neutrinos at other subatomic particles to study the structure of those particles. The physicists also discovered a previously unknown neutrino, the *muon neutrino*, believed to be 1 of 12 basic building blocks of matter.

Physiology or medicine. The Nobel Prize for physiology or medicine was shared by Gertrude B. Elion and George H. Hitchings of Wellcome Research Laboratories in Research Triangle Park, N.C., and Sir James Black of King's College School of Medicine and Dentistry of the University of London.

In the 1940's, Elion and Hitchings found that cancer cells and disease-causing bacteria and viruses process genetic information in a manner different from that of healthy cells. That discovery enabled the two researchers to develop drugs that destroy diseased cells by interfering with their reproduction, without harming normal cells. The scientists created the first drugs used in cancer chemotherapy as well as antiviral drugs used to treat herpes.

Black discovered two important groups of drugs that work by blocking special areas called *receptor sites* on the surfaces of cells. One group of drugs, called *beta-blockers*, are used to treat heart disease and high blood pressure. They block the stimulating effects of the hormones *epinephrine* and *norepinephrine*, thus reducing the heart rate and easing the heart's workload. The other group of medications, *histamine H_2-receptor antagonists*, are used to treat digestive ulcers. They block the stomach's response to a body chemical called *histamine* that triggers secretion of acid. One of these drugs, which Black developed in 1975, is *cimetidine*, trade-named Tagamet. [Sara Dreyfuss]

In WORLD BOOK, see NOBEL PRIZES.

Nutrition

Nutrition studies in 1988 and 1989 yielded new information about dietary supplements and about the role of food in disease prevention.

Vitamin E may be safe to take in large quantities, according to a September 1988 report by scientists at Hoffman-La Roche, Incorporated, a drug manufacturer in Nutley, N.J. Health experts had worried about long-term toxic effects from high doses of vitamin E because many people take 100 to 400 international units (IU) of vitamin E per day. The recommended dietary allowance (RDA) is 15 IU. The drug company scientists reviewed six studies conducted since 1974 in which people took between 600 and 3,200 IU of vitamin E—40 to 213 times the RDA—for up to six months. The scientists found no significant side effects.

In other reports, researchers had noted such side effects as fatigue, diarrhea, and changes in thyroid hormone levels from increased levels of vitamin E. The Hoffman-La Roche investigators found, however, that these side effects occurred in extremely small studies or could be associated with factors other than vitamin E.

The only problem associated with vitamin E seems to occur in people taking medication that interferes with blood clotting. Vitamin E makes it even more difficult for blood to clot.

Vitamin E protects cells from harmful molecules called *free radicals* that can damage cell membranes. The free radicals can come from the cell or from the outside environment. Over time, cell damage may result in premature aging, heart disease, or cancer. Research indicates that it may be necessary to take more than 10 times the vitamin-E RDA to prevent cell damage.

Zinc and cholesterol levels. Zinc supplements may help lower blood levels of beneficial *high-density lipoproteins* (HDL), which remove a fatty substance called *cholesterol* from artery walls, reducing the risk of heart disease. This was the conclusion of a June 1988 report by nutritionists at the University of Wyoming in Laramie. Zinc is a mineral needed for important enzyme reactions in the body.

Drawing by D. Reilly; © 1989 The New Yorker Magazine, Inc.

Wellness Update: Thirty-year-old man starting on the twenty-five-thousand-pound oat-bran muffin he must consume over forty years in order to reduce significantly his risk of death from high cholesterol

Nutrition

Continued

The Wyoming scientists studied the effects of 50 to 75 milligrams (77 to 166 grains) of zinc per day (3½ to 5 times the RDA) on 22 volunteers over 12 weeks. Although there was no change in total cholesterol or in harmful *low-density lipoproteins* (LDL), which deliver cholesterol to blood vessels, beneficial HDL levels dropped in those taking the higher zinc doses. Those taking the lower zinc doses had lower HDL during the last week of the study than those not taking the supplement.

Previous studies also reported this adverse effect of zinc, but in those studies it occurred with much larger doses of the mineral: 10 or more times the RDA. Scientists assume that the harmful effect on HDL levels may be due to zinc interfering with copper absorption. Low levels of copper have been linked to cardiovascular disease.

Multivitamins and birth defects. Women who take vitamin supplements before and after they become pregnant have less risk of having a baby with birth defects than women who do not take vitamins, according to a December 1988 report. Medical epidemiologist Joseph Mulinare and his associates at the U.S. Centers for Disease Control in Atlanta, Ga., questioned mothers of more than 3,000 babies born between 1968 and 1980.

The researchers found that women who took multivitamins had a 60 per cent lower risk of having a child with a serious nervous-system disorder called a *neural tube defect* than those who did not take vitamins. Neural tube defects range from failure of the bones of the spinal column to close completely around the spinal cord, a condition called *spina bifida*, to a lethal condition known as *anencephaly* in which most of the brain is missing.

The researchers pointed out, however, that vitamin takers may follow healthier life styles in general than those who do not take vitamins. Further study is needed to determine whether vitamin supplements alone— or some other factor—is preventing birth defects.

Surgeon general's report. In July 1988, Surgeon General of the United

Nutrition

Continued

States C. Everett Koop issued the first *Surgeon General's Report on Nutrition and Health*. The report, which took four years to complete, summarized more than 2,500 scientific studies. It concluded that most nutritional problems in the United States result from nutrient excesses or imbalances caused by poor eating habits.

The report also established that diet affects the risk for chronic disease. Diets high in calories, fat, salt, sugar, and alcohol and low in fiber are linked with 5 of the 10 leading causes of death: coronary heart disease, cancer, stroke, diabetes, and *atherosclerosis* (progressive clogging of the arteries). In addition, three other causes of death (cirrhosis of the liver, accidents, and suicide) are associated with excessive alcohol intake. Together, these eight causes accounted for almost 1.5 of the 2.1 million deaths in the United States in 1987. Diet also affects the risk for high blood pressure, obesity, and dental problems.

The report recommended several changes in diet:

■ Cut down on fat intake, particularly *saturated fat*, the fat found in meat and dairy products.
■ Increase intake of fruits, vegetables, and grains.
■ Choose fish, poultry, lean meat, and low-fat dairy products.
■ Limit high-cholesterol and high-fat foods, sugar, and alcohol to keep weight down.
■ Reduce intake of sodium by choosing foods that are low in sodium and cut down on salt added to food.
■ Limit alcohol to no more than two drinks per day.

The report also recommended that people exercise regularly.

Other sections of the report addressed the nutritional concerns of particular age groups. Children should limit foods high in sugar to decrease the risk for tooth decay. Teen-aged girls and adult women should drink milk and eat other foods high in calcium. Children, teen-agers, and women of childbearing age should eat foods rich in iron.   [Jeanine Barone]

In WORLD BOOK, see NUTRITION.

Oceanography

One of the worst oil spills in history polluted the ocean off Alaska, spoiled beaches, and killed fish and marine mammals in March 1989. The oil spill resulted when an oil tanker, *Exxon Valdez*, ran aground on a reef in Prince William Sound. See ENVIRONMENT.

Warmer oceans. The oceans are growing warmer, according to a report released in April 1989. Because they store heat, the oceans play a key role in global climate. Accurate and extensive measurement of ocean temperatures is important for predicting climate change over long periods of time.

Oceanographer Alan E. Strong of the United States National Oceanic and Atmospheric Administration reported in April that sea surface temperatures measured from Earth-orbiting satellites between 1982 and 1988 revealed that the oceans are warming at a rate of about 0.1 Celsius degree (0.2 Fahrenheit degree) per year. Detailed study revealed gradually increasing sea surface temperatures in the Atlantic and Pacific oceans but insignificant changes in the Indian Ocean.

These results were based on monthly day and night satellite measurements of sea surface temperature. Data from ships and buoys collected during this same period showed a warming trend about half that detected from satellites.

Although ships and buoys have long provided sea surface temperature data, coverage has been limited to small parts of the global ocean, and, as a result, trends in temperature change become apparent only after a long period of time. Satellites, however, can cover far more area and make it possible for oceanographers to observe short-term trends. Sea surface temperature measurements from satellites are made with *infrared* (heat radiation) detectors. Satellites will provide the data needed to monitor global climate changes of the kind predicted by the *greenhouse effect*, the trapping of heat from the sun by gases in the atmosphere (in the Special Reports section, see IS EARTH OVERHEATING?).

Underwater plateau. Scientists in 1988 and 1989 were analyzing cores drilled from one of the world's largest

Student's Hunch Pays Off

A strange glow, *right,* was seen near a volcanic vent called a *black smoker* on the floor of the Pacific Ocean in July 1988 by scientists aboard the research submarine *Alvin.* They had been tipped off to the possibility of finding mysterious deep-sea light while investigating the Juan de Fuca Ridge off Vancouver Island, Canada, by Cindy Van Dover, *above,* a graduate student at Woods Hole Oceanographic Institution in Massachusetts. Van Dover had studied a species of eyeless shrimp that live around a black smoker in the Atlantic Ocean, *above right,* and found they have organs containing the light-sensitive chemical rhodopsin. Van Dover reasoned that there must be a source of light around black smokers for the shrimp to sense, and *Alvin*'s discovery appeared to confirm her theory.

Oceanography

underwater structures, the Kerguelen Plateau. Located in the remote subantarctic part of the Indian Ocean, the plateau is 2,500 kilometers (1,550 miles) long and resembles Argentina in size and shape. The cores were drilled by French and American oceanographers aboard the research drill ship *JOIDES Resolution* on the 20th cruise of the Ocean Drilling Program in spring 1988. The scientists were led by Roland Schlich of the Institute de Physique du Globe in Strasbourg, France; Sherwood W. Wise, Jr., of Florida State University in Tallahassee; and Amanda Palmer of Texas A&M University in College Station.

Oceanographers have begun to reconstruct the plateau's 97-million-year history using evidence from cores drilled from the sea floor at five different sites. The oldest material at the bottom of the cores was volcanic rock that had erupted as the plateau took shape and formed either above or very near sea level. These rocks provided clear evidence that the Kerguelen Plateau had once been above water during its earliest history. Additional evidence of its land phase came from fragments of fossil wood recovered from reddish-brown, soillike clays in the cores. Such clays are typically found in warm, moist climates.

Fossils found in the cores showed that the plateau was covered by the sea about 66 million to 97 million years ago. The fossils were found in layers of limestone containing pieces of marine creatures such as clams, sponges, and sea urchins, and even the tooth from what may have been a *mosasaur*, a giant swimming lizard.

Findings from the expedition indicated that over the next 65 million years, the plateau sank deeper beneath the sea, leaving behind beds of fine-grained chalk made up of the tiny skeletons of single-celled marine plants and animals. The plateau continued to sink during the next 1.6 million years until it reached its current depth of more than 1 kilometer (0.6 mile). During this same period, blooms of tiny marine algae and layers of rocks were carried by icebergs from Antarctica and deposited on the floor of the plateau. Cores containing this material provided scientists with evidence of a significant cooling period that began some 36 million years ago.

Old rocks. During the summer of 1988, scientists aboard the *JOIDES Resolution* retrieved the oldest marine rocks ever recovered by scientific ocean drilling. West German oceanographer Ulrich von Rad and U.S. oceanographers Bilal Haq of the National Science Foundation in Washington, D.C., and Suzanne O'Connell of Texas A&M University reported the recovery of the 220-million-year-old rocks in September 1988.

Scientists drilled on the Wombat and Exmouth plateaus off the northwest continental margin of Australia. They sought to recover rocks dating from the present to some 248 million years ago, when, scientists believe, a single ancient supercontinent called *Pangaea* began to break up.

According to the theory of *plate tectonics*, Earth's crust is made of gigantic plates that float on Earth's mantle. The movement of these plates causes continental drift and the formation of new sea floor along midocean ridges.

The Wombat and Exmouth plateaus are parts of the Australian continental margin, which was once bounded by the now-extinct Tethys Sea. The Tethys divided Pangaea, and over time the formation of new sea floor separated Pangaea into the continents of South America, Africa, Australia, India, and Antarctica. The movement of the massive plates underlying these continents erased the Tethys Sea. The northwest Australian continental margin is one of the few sites in the world where scientists can recover material from this ancient sea.

Plant and animal fossils found in the cores helped the oceanographers trace the separation of Australia and India, the destruction of the Tethys Sea, and the rise and submergence of the Wombat Plateau. They also found clues about sea level changes from samples of coral reefs, in mudstones from lagoons, and in clay and silt from deltas. Similar features occurred on other continental margins at about the same time, thus providing support for the idea that major changes in sea level take place at the same time around the world.   [Lauriston R. King]

In WORLD BOOK, see OCEAN.

Paleontology

Charges that an Indian paleontologist falsified numerous fossil discoveries in the Himalaya have threatened scientists' understanding of the paleontological and geologic history of that mountainous region in Asia. In April 1989, paleontologist John A. Talent of Macquarie University in Sydney, Australia, accused paleontologist Viswa Jit Gupta of Panjab University in Chandigarh, India, of a massive forgery of fossil data reported in hundreds of articles over the past 25 years. The data have greatly influenced geologic and paleontological research in the Himalaya. If Talent's charges are true, the case would be one of the biggest scandals in paleontological history.

For example, Talent contended that fossil *conodonts* (microscopic toothlike fossils) that Gupta reported finding in the Himalaya actually appear to have come from an area south of Buffalo, N.Y. Talent, who is a specialist on *ammonoids* (chambered shells of ancient squidlike animals), also charged that distinctive red-brown fossil ammonoids supposedly found in India actually came from Morocco. In fact, according to Talent, the fossils may have been purchased at a rock shop in Paris.

Gupta denied the charges. He accused Talent of "malicious bias" and "professional jealousy."

Dinosaurs in the dark. Dinosaur fossils found in Australia have cast doubt on the idea that darkness and cold—the result of the collision of a meteor with Earth—were important factors in the extinction of the dinosaurs 65 million years ago. Some scientists believe that such an impact threw up a huge cloud of dust that blocked much of the sun's heat and light.

The fossils were discovered in southeastern Australia by a team of paleontologists headed by P. V. Rich of Monash University in Melbourne, Australia. Found in rocks dating from the early Cretaceous Period, 105 million to 130 million years ago, the fossils represent at least six types of dinosaurs.

The fossils were found in a part of Australia that lay well within the Antarctic Circle during Cretaceous times,

Oldest known reptile
A 340-million-year-old fossil reptile, *below right,* found in Scotland is the oldest ever discovered. It provides evidence that reptiles have existed 40 million years longer than scientists had believed. A reconstruction of the fossil, *right,* which is 20.3 centimeters (8 inches) long, suggests that it resembled modern lizards.

Longest dinosaur?
Scientists working in New Mexico, *right,* uncover the tailbones of what may be the longest dinosaur ever found. The dinosaur, called *seismosaurus* (earth shaker lizard), lived about 144 million years ago. Using the tailbones to reconstruct the dinosaur's appearance, *below,* the scientists determined that seismosaurus was at least 33 meters (110 feet) long and weighed more than 83 metric tons (75 short tons). To find more of the dinosaur's bones, scientists are experimenting with ground-penetrating radar, *bottom.* Radio waves emitted by the radar pass below the surface and are reflected by objects underground. The scientists hope the reflections will reveal buried fossils.

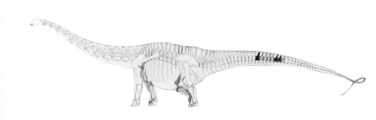

perhaps within a few hundred kilometers of the South Pole. This implies that the dinosaurs lived in an environment that had prolonged periods of darkness and cool temperatures. (Since the Cretaceous Period, the movement of the gigantic plates that make up Earth's outer shell has carried Australia northward.)

A geochemical analysis of minerals in which the fossils were discovered revealed that the average annual temperature may have been as low as −6°C (21°F.). It is possible that the dinosaurs migrated to warmer locations during the winter, as some modern Arctic animals, such as caribou, do today. The scientists noted, however, that several of the dinosaurs had very large eyes and well-developed *optic lobes* (areas of the brain involved in vision). Impressions of the optic lobes were found on the interiors of the skulls. Both features suggest that the dinosaurs were able to see in low levels of light.

Dinosaur egg. The discovery of the only known dinosaur egg from the Upper Jurassic Period—160 million years ago—was reported in March 1989. The Jurassic was a time when dinosaurs were most numerous and diverse. The egg was found by a team of scientists headed by paleontologist Karl Hirsch of the University of Colorado in Boulder.

The investigators are unsure what type of dinosaur laid the egg. A CT (computerized tomographic) scan of the egg, which is filled with sediment, suggested that it may also contain a dinosaur embryo.

Oldest insect. The discovery of the oldest known fossil insect was reported in November 1988 by a team of paleontologists led by Conrad C. Labandeira of the University of Chicago. The fossil insect, which belonged to a primitive group of insects called bristletails, was found in rock from the Lower Devonian Period, about 390 million years old, in Quebec, Canada. The fossil is 15 million years older than that of any other known insect. The specimen is also the oldest fossil of a land-dwelling animal ever found in North America.

The fossil insect has external mouthparts that seem to be adapted for piercing and chewing soft plant mate-

Paleontology
Continued

rial. Fossils of primitive plants were found with the insect. According to the scientists, the insect's similarity to modern insects suggests that insects were already well established 390 million years ago. If so, the scientists theorized, animals emerged on land earlier than previously believed and at the same time that the first land plants appeared.

Predators take sides. Some of the earliest predators on Earth apparently had special preferences when it came to prey, according to paleontologists Loren E. Babcock and Richard Robison of the University of Kansas in Lawrence. In February 1989, they reported on a study of fossils of trilobites that had been bitten and survived. The trilobites, an extinct group of marine arthropods distantly related to modern horseshoe crabs, lived during the middle part of the Cambrian Period, about 540 million years ago.

The paleontologists found that the trilobites' predator, which is unknown, apparently preferred to attack the trilobites on their right side. Up to about three times as many of the fossil trilobites show bite marks on their right side as on their left side.

Ancient amphibians. Several nearly complete skeletons of fossil amphibians found in 335-million-year-old rock in Iowa may increase scientists' knowledge of the earliest land animals. The discovery was reported in June 1988 by a team led by paleontologist John Bolt of the University of Chicago. The fossils are the oldest well-preserved land *vertebrates* (animals with backbones) ever found in North America.

The fossil amphibians, which represent previously unknown species, were from 1 to 1.5 meters (3 to 5 feet) long. Although they had well-developed legs and so were capable of walking on land, they apparently spent most of their time in the water. Bolt and his colleagues believe that one of the fossil amphibians may have belonged to a line of animals that led from amphibians to reptiles.   [Carlton E. Brett]

In the Special Reports section, see WHO (OR WHAT) KILLED THE GIANT MAMMALS? In WORLD BOOK, see DINOSAUR; INSECTS; TRILOBITE.

Physics, Fluids and Solids

The development of so-called *high-temperature superconductors* progressed steadily in 1988 and 1989 as did work on theories about how these superconductors work. A superconductor is a material that conducts electricity with no resistance when chilled to an extremely low temperature. The highest known *critical temperature* (temperature at which superconductivity begins) was $-250°C$ ($-418°F$.) until 1986, when scientists reported on the first of the materials that came to be known as high-temperature superconductors.

The first of these was a *ceramic* with a critical temperature of $-243°C$ ($-405°F$.). Ceramics are solids that are neither metals nor plastics. Dinnerware, for example, is made of ceramics. By contrast, most superconductors known before 1986 were metals or *alloys* (metal mixtures).

Since then, other researchers have developed ceramic materials with even higher critical temperatures. The highest such temperature is $-148°C$ ($-234°F$.) for a ceramic announced in early 1988 by scientists at the International Business Machines Corporation (IBM) Almaden Research Center in San Jose, Calif.

Theoreticians thwarted. Since 1957, physicists have had a theory to explain superconductivity in metals and alloys. This is the BCS theory, named after its developers, United States physicists John Bardeen, Leon N. Cooper, and J. Robert Schrieffer. The three scientists shared the 1972 Nobel Prize in physics for their work.

As of the summer of 1989, however, there was no theory to explain how ceramics superconduct. In fact, a discovery announced in January 1989 complicated the search for such a theory. This discovery concerned the nature of the current flowing through these materials.

In ordinary conductors such as metals, the carriers of electric current are individual *free electrons*, which are loosely bound to atoms and therefore can hop readily from atom to atom. In conventional superconductors, these electrons travel by twos in so-called *Cooper pairs*.

Studying Physics on a Roller Coaster

Each year, thousands of high school physics students and their teachers throughout the United States go to amusement parks to see and feel physics in action. In fact, amusement parks are such good physics teaching tools that the American Association of Physics Teachers in January 1988 commissioned a handbook called *Amusement Park Physics*. And one of the most thrilling amusement-park rides, the roller coaster, has proven to be one of the most valuable tools for demonstrating fundamental concepts of physics to high school students.

Concepts such as potential energy, kinetic energy, gravity, inertia, centripetal force, and weightlessness may seem difficult in the classroom. But they "come alive" on a roller-coaster ride.

Potential energy is stored energy. In a roller-coaster car it is the energy of height. As the car is lifted, it gains potential energy. *Kinetic energy* is energy of motion; the faster the roller-coaster car is moving, the more kinetic energy it has. The ups-and-downs of a roller-coaster ride involve the continuous interchange of potential energy and kinetic energy. After allowing for energy loss due to friction, height alone controls the top speed of a roller-coaster car as it reaches the bottom of an incline. The steepness of the drop determines how rapidly top speed is reached.

Gravity is responsible for converting potential energy to kinetic energy, making a car gather speed as it rolls down an incline. Gravity causes objects to have weight—yet the weight of the car and riders does not affect the speed. Gravity does pull down harder on heavier riders or fuller cars, but the heavier objects are harder to pull. The two effects balance, and the speed of the ride stays the same. This can be proven by an experiment timing two cars speeding down the incline. One car should have the lightest students on board; the other should carry the heaviest students.

Inertia makes any moving object travel in a straight line unless a force is applied to make it curve or change speed. The curved track of a roller coaster applies a *centripetal* (center-seeking) force to the car, preventing the car from traveling in a straight line and making it follow the track's curvature. This force can be applied either as a push from the outside of the curve (if, for example, the car is going around inside a loop) or a pull from the inside (if the car is going over the top of a hill), as long as it is directed toward the center of the curve.

A rider does not feel inertia but does feel centripetal force—in an odd way. The direction of this force seems to be pushing opposite to its actual direction. For example, when the roller coaster car goes through the "valley" between hills, both the car and the rider must change direction—from heading down to heading up. In this situation, the centripetal force pushes up through the seat against the rider's body, but the rider feels as if he or she is pushing down hard against the seat. In other words, the rider seems to become heavier.

The amount of centripetal force depends on both the speed of the car and the sharpness of the curve. The faster a car is moving, the more centripetal force it needs to stay on a curved track. And the tighter the curve, the more centripetal force is needed.

Many roller-coaster hills are curved so that a rider has moments of feeling "weightless." Weightlessness, an apparent absence of weight, is actually made possible by weight. To understand why this is so, imagine that an experimental car carrying loose sandbags instead of people streaks up a ramp and, near the top, stops

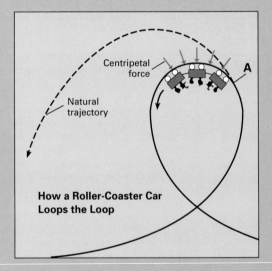

How a Roller-Coaster Car Loops the Loop

At every point on the roller coaster loop, just as at point A, inertia and gravity make a car "want" to break through the track and follow a natural *trajectory* (curved path). The track prevents this and, at the top of the loop, creates the *centripetal force* that makes the car follow a tighter path. The seats transmit this force to the riders and press down on them. The riders, however, feel as if they are being pressed up into their seats.

suddenly. As the car stops, the sandbags, having no seat belts, fly out of the car and plunge to the ground, following a natural *trajectory* (curved path) determined by the combination of the force of gravity—whose action gives the sandbags weight—and their speed.

Now imagine a similar experiment conducted with a roller coaster that is designed to closely resemble this natural trajectory. The roller-coaster car, however, does not stop near the top of the hill. Instead, it goes up and over the hill. This time, the bags will not fly out but will hover above the seats. The same thing happens to people. Even though safety-belted, roller-coaster riders speeding down a natural-trajectory slope tend to hover a bit above the seat—and thus feel weightless.

The natural trajectory also comes into play on looping roller coasters that turn the cars upside down at the tops of the loops. Riders must be going fast enough at the top so that the natural trajectory is significantly larger than the curve of the loop. Because the only way up is to exchange kinetic energy (speed) for potential energy (height), the cars must go very fast as they enter the bottom of the loop. This means that, at the bottom of the loop, the curve must not be so sharp that centripetal force reaches dangerous levels. Unfortunately, the first looping coasters, built of wood, had circular loops that, because of their shape, created dangerously large centripetal force at the bottom of the loop. These coasters, built in the 1890's at Coney Island in New York City and at Atlantic City, N.J., were quickly dismantled after riders complained of neck and back injuries.

But E. W. Green of New York City in 1901 patented the steel Loop-the-Loop, a loop with a teardroplike *clothoid* shape that solved the force problem. At the bottom of this loop, the curve is so gradual that, even though the cars are moving rapidly, centripetal force is not excessive. At the top, where the cars move relatively slowly, the curve is extremely sharp, generating enough centripetal force to keep the riders in their seats.

The Loop-the-Loop was a commercial failure because it could carry only four passengers at a time. But in 1976, Anton Schwarzkopf designed "The Revolution," a clothoid coaster that used conventional cars. This ride, at Magic Mountain in Valencia, Calif., became the first commercially successful looping coaster. By June 1989, there were 103 looping coasters, all built of steel and all using some variation of the clothoid shape.

If you get a chance to ride one of them, try to remember your physics as your car streaks toward the top of a loop and begins to turn upside down. The force—the centripetal force—is with you.   [Barbara Wolff]

In most high-temperature superconductors, however, the current is carried by pairs of *electron holes*. These are empty spaces around atoms in the material's crystal structure where electrons normally are situated. Under the influence of an electric field, an electron can jump from one hole to another. The hole the electron left behind can in turn be filled by a neighboring electron, which leaves another hole. As this process repeats itself, a hole, in effect, "travels" through the crystal. The original electron holes come from *doping*, replacing atoms in the crystal with atoms that have fewer electrons than the ones they replace.

All high-temperature superconductors known before January 1989 carry superconducting current by means of holes. That month, Japanese scientists at the University of Tokyo reported that they had discovered high-temperature superconducting materials in which electrons carry superconducting current. The researchers created these materials by doping certain substances with atoms that had more electrons than did the atoms they replaced. In March 1989, physicists at American Telephone and Telegraph Company (AT&T) Bell Laboratories in Murray Hill, N.J., announced another such superconductor.

An important result of these discoveries is that any explanation of superconductivity in high-temperature superconductors must describe current in terms of electrons as well as holes. Many physicists do not believe that this will be an insurmountable obstacle because electron holes behave much like positively charged particles. Electrons are negatively charged.

Creeping fields. A discovery announced in October 1988 may be a major obstacle on the road to the development of practical devices that use high-temperature superconductors, such as magnets. The movement of magnetic fields inside some of these materials may increase their electrical resistance.

The presence of moving magnetic fields can be shown by the *Meissner effect*, the rejection of a magnetic field by a superconductor that is cooled below its critical temperature. When a

Pieces of very cold superconducting material hang suspended below a magnet. This so-called suspension effect was discovered by physicist Palmer N. Peters at NASA's Space Sciences Laboratory in Huntsville, Ala., and reported in June 1988. Scientists had known for more than 50 years that another effect enables a superconductor to float above a magnet.

pellet of superconducting material that has been cooled below its critical temperature is held in the air a few millimeters above the magnet and then released, it will remain suspended in the air as long as it stays cold enough to be a superconductor.

The Meissner effect occurs because the magnetic field of the permanent magnet causes superconducting currents to flow on the surface of the pellet. These currents produce a magnetic field in the direction opposite that of the permanent magnet's field. The portion of the superconductor's field inside the superconductor has exactly the same strength as the portion of the magnet's field extending inside the superconductor. So the magnet's internal field is canceled out. But the magnet's external field exerts a repelling force on the superconducting current carriers (electrons or holes) flowing on the surface of the pellet, causing the pellet to remain suspended.

Not all superconductors react to external magnetic fields in the same way. Superconductors that are made of a single metal, such as lead or tin, expel magnetic fields entirely from their interiors. These are called *type I* superconductors.

By contrast, a *type II* superconductor does not entirely expel a magnetic field from its interior once the external field reaches a certain strength. Type II superconductors include the high-temperature ceramic superconductors, most alloys, and the metals niobium and vanadium.

The field inside a type II material becomes concentrated in various positions that depend upon the crystal structure of the particular superconductor. Certain irregularities in the shape of the superconductor's crystal structure and certain *impurities* (atoms that normally are not present in the material) can "pin down" these field concentrations.

Thus, a type II superconductor suspended in the air above a permanent magnet, when pushed and released, moves as if it were stuck in sand. The resistance to movement is caused by friction opposing changes in the position of the magnetic field concentrations inside the superconductor.

By contrast, a suspended type I superconductor does not resist movement in this way because it has no magnetic field in its interior. When it is pushed sideways, it moves freely. When the superconductor is released, it oscillates freely around a single position in the air.

In a metal or alloy type II superconductor, movement of these magnetic field concentrations—known as *flux creep*—creates some electrical resistance, but not enough to prevent these materials from being useful for a variety of superconducting applications. In some high-temperature materials, however, electrical resistance can become excessively high. This happens as the temperature is raised, but still kept well below the critical temperature. As the temperature increases, atoms in the superconducting material vibrate more and more rapidly, increasing flux creep. The moving field concentrations interfere with the electrons or holes forming the superconducting current, thereby raising resistance.

Physicist Peter L. Gammel and his colleagues at AT&T Bell Laboratories

reported in October 1988 that flux creep can be exceptionally strong in ceramic superconductors that are made up of the chemical elements yttrium, barium, copper, and oxygen. This discovery disappointed many researchers because these materials have shown the most promise of all the high-temperature superconductors that might be used in magnets. The discovery indicates that, for these materials to be useful in magnets, the materials would have to be chilled to temperatures lower than previously thought, or that engineers would have to settle for less powerful magnetic fields.

Several physicists have pointed out that a redesign of the crystal structure might overcome excessive flux creep in these materials. Altering the makeup of the impurities or changing the irregularies within the crystal might "entangle" the field concentrations, making the concentrations much less mobile.   [Alexander Hellemans]

In World Book, see Physics; Superconductivity.

Physics, Subatomic

The announcement in March 1989 that a nuclear fusion reaction had been set off at room temperature sparked a flurry of research in laboratories throughout the world, as scientists tried to confirm or disprove the experimental results that prompted the announcement. See Close-Up.

SSC site. The site for the Superconducting Super Collider (SSC), the largest and most powerful particle accelerator ever planned, was announced by the United States Department of Energy (DOE) in November 1988. The DOE chose a site near Waxahachie, Tex. The SSC is to circulate two beams of protons within a gigantic ring and direct the beams to collide head-on, producing subatomic particles. The results of these powerful collisions may broaden physicists' understanding of the forces that govern the universe.

Plans call for housing the SSC in an underground tunnel 85 kilometers (53 miles) in circumference surrounding Waxahachie. Inside, the beams will be accelerated to a combined energy of 40 trillion electron volts (TeV). (An elec-

tron volt [eV] is a tiny amount of energy. A 100-watt light bulb emits 625 billion billion eV in 1 second.) Physicist Roy F. Schwitters of Harvard University in Cambridge, Mass., was chosen to direct the laboratory. Physicist Helen T. Edwards of the Fermi National Accelerator Laboratory (Fermilab) near Chicago was placed in charge of design and construction.

The SSC could be operating by the late 1990's but first, supporters of the project must persuade the Congress of the United States to appropriate money to build the machine. The estimated construction cost is $6 billion, a figure that political observers say many in Congress may find difficult to justify in the face of the federal government's huge budget deficit.

Furthermore, researchers must develop designs for the thousands of magnets the machine would require to control the beams. The magnets would be unprecedented in size, magnetic strength, and precision of assembly.

No new particles yet. Meanwhile, hopes for particle physics in the United

Nuclear Fusion: from Stars to Jars?

The world was startled in March 1989 by the claim that an easy path had been found to the long-sought scientific goal of bringing the power of the sun down to Earth. For more than 40 years, scientists have been trying to produce useful amounts of energy as the sun and other stars produce it—by combining light atomic nuclei such as hydrogen into heavier ones in a reaction known as *nuclear fusion*.

This kind of reaction is the opposite of *nuclear fission*, the process that produces energy in atomic power plants. In a fission reaction, a heavy nucleus such as a uranium nucleus splits into two lighter ones.

The essential job of a fusion reactor would be to bunch nuclei so close together that they would fuse or join together. Atomic nuclei on Earth normally stay too far apart to fuse. Their protons have positive electric charges, and the mutual repulsion of like charges keeps the nuclei sepa-

rated. But inside stars, temperatures reach hundreds of millions of degrees. This makes atoms get close enough for fusion to occur.

In their efforts to produce fusion energy, researchers have relied on huge, expensive machines designed to produce, for brief instants, temperatures approaching those inside stars. But the startling report in March 1989 came from a pair of chemists in Utah who had labored for five years without research funds. Furthermore, the two chemists, B. Stanley Pons of the University of Utah and Martin Fleischmann of the University of Southampton, England, used a simple, tabletop device that has been common in chemical laboratories for more than 100 years.

The device was an *electrolytic cell*, a glass jar containing two electrodes that are connected to an electric power source such as a battery. When the jar is filled with water containing a small amount of a chemical that makes water a better conductor of electricity, a current flows. The current breaks up water molecules, which consist of two hydrogen atoms and one oxygen atom.

Normally, these atoms bubble away as hydrogen and oxygen gases. But some metals used as electrode materials can—like a sponge—soak up a great deal of hydrogen in the spaces between the metal atoms.

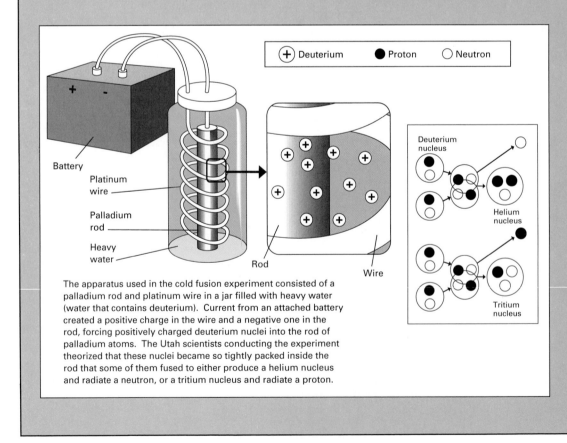

The apparatus used in the cold fusion experiment consisted of a palladium rod and platinum wire in a jar filled with heavy water (water that contains deuterium). Current from an attached battery created a positive charge in the wire and a negative one in the rod, forcing positively charged deuterium nuclei into the rod of palladium atoms. The Utah scientists conducting the experiment theorized that these nuclei became so tightly packed inside the rod that some of them fused to either produce a helium nucleus and radiate a neutron, or a tritium nucleus and radiate a proton.

For their experiment, Pons and Fleischmann used a positive electrode of platinum and a negative electrode made of the metal palladium, which is an excellent hydrogen "sponge." They filled the jar with a special type of water called heavy water.

Heavy water contains deuterium, an *isotope* (form) of hydrogen. This isotope is heavier than ordinary hydrogen because it has more particles in its nucleus. The nucleus of an ordinary hydrogen atom is made up of a single proton. A deuterium nucleus consists of one proton and one neutron. Deuterium is one of the best fuels for fusion.

After a few months of operation, the electrolytic cell began to generate more heat than could be accounted for by the electricity consumed. No known chemical reaction could produce this much energy.

Fleischmann and Pons claimed that the extra energy was a result of fusion. They said that the palladium electrode soaked up so much deuterium that deuterium nuclei came close enough to one another to fuse.

When deuterium nuclei fuse, two reactions occur, at roughly equal rates. One leaves a stable nucleus of helium-3 and a free neutron. The other leaves a nucleus of tritium (another hydrogen isotope) and a proton. Protons are quickly stopped by the negative electrode or the water, but neutrons are harder to stop. If fusion occurred in the Utah device, some neutrons would have been absorbed by deuterium atoms in the water, producing gamma rays. Most of them, however, would have escaped the cell.

Pons and Fleischmann detected both neutrons and gamma rays. Furthermore, an analysis of residues of the negative electrode revealed the presence of tritium, a product of fusion.

There was, however, one serious inconsistency in the results. The chemists detected much too little radiation or tritium to account for the energy generated. This suggested that though fusion might be taking place, it was not the source of the energy produced.

The apparatus was so simple that within a few weeks, there had been scores of attempts to duplicate the results. Most of these attempts failed, however. Some of the investigators suggested that fusion had not occurred and that Pons and Fleischmann had estimated the energy release incorrectly.

The verdict on whether or not fusion can occur in a jar is not yet in. It is most likely that "cold fusion" is either a mistake or a blind alley that will lead to no practical end. But in the spring of 1989, a great many normally skeptical scientists were cautiously optimistic over the prospects.   [Robert H. March]

States rest on two recently completed machines, Fermilab's Tevatron Collider and the Stanford Linear Collider (SLC) at the Stanford Linear Accelerator Center in California. The Tevatron hurls a proton beam against a beam of *antiprotons* (antimatter counterparts of protons) in head-on collisions that have a combined energy of 1.6 TeV per pair of particles. From June 1988 to May 1989, the Tevatron ran nearly continuously with at least 10 billion particles in each beam.

The scientific fruits of the Tevatron have been slow to ripen, however. The machine has produced higher levels of energy and statistical accuracy than its predecessor, the Super Proton Synchrotron collider at the European Laboratory for Particle Physics (CERN) near Geneva, Switzerland. But the scientists have not yet seen what they were hoping for—new kinds of fundamental particles.

Physicists are especially eager to find two new particles to fill gaps in their picture of matter. One of these, the *t-quark*, is the heaviest of six fundamental building blocks of protons and neutrons. The other is the *Higgs boson*, which plays a crucial role in the universe by allowing matter to stand still. Without the particle, all other particles would have no mass at all, and therefore would move perpetually at the speed of light.

So far, physicists working at the Tevatron have seen no hint of the Higgs boson. And all they can say about the t-quark is that, if it exists, it must be at least 75 times heavier than a proton.

Z^0's in the linear collider. Physicists using the SLC in April 1989 detected their first Z^0 particle after more than a year of trying. Within a month, they were observing several each day. This particle transmits one of the forces that operate inside atomic nuclei.

The SLC is a novel machine in which two particle beams, one of *electrons* and the other of *positrons* (antimatter counterparts of electrons) are allowed to collide only once.

It takes about 92 billion electron volts (GeV) of energy to make a Z^0. Researchers at proton-antiproton colliders have observed only a handful of these particles, but electron-positron machines should produce many more.

A linear accelerator that is about 3.2 kilometers (2 miles) long speeds an electron beam and a positron beam simultaneously, each to an energy of 50 GeV. At the exit end of the linear accelerator, magnets first steer electrons and positrons in opposite directions, then turn them back for a head-on rush to the final collision. To produce a usable number of collisions in a single try, SLC operators must carefully steer the two beams to a common focus only thousandths of a millimeter in diameter when the beams collide.

The SLC's linear design allows the machine to be much smaller than a conventional accelerator that boosted electron and positron beams to the SLC's beam energy. Conventional machines keep the beams moving in circular paths for hours, with a few particles colliding head-on each time around the machine. Electrons and positrons lose a great deal of energy as they travel in a circular path, so extra power must be supplied to keep the beams at their top energy. The smaller the circle, the more energy is lost at each turn. The SLC suffers only slightly from this energy-robbing effect, however, because its electrons and positrons swing only once around the track before they collide.

Other accelerators. In the summer of 1989, the Large Electron-Positron Collider (LEP) at CERN was scheduled to begin operation. LEP, a conventional stored-beam machine, was expected to operate initially at the same energy as the SLC and produce many more collisions per second, yielding hundreds of Z^0 particles per day.

Another nation joined the accelerator "club" in October 1988 when the Beijing Electron-Positron Collider went into operation in China. At 3.2 GeV, it is too low in energy to probe any new phenomena, but it should help to train a new generation of Chinese physicists.   [Robert H. March]

In the Special Reports section, see THE CASE OF THE DARK MATTER. In WORLD BOOK, see PARTICLE ACCELERATOR; PARTICLE PHYSICS; QUARK.

Psychology

A major research focus in psychology in 1988 and 1989 was on the interaction between body and mind, including the physical changes triggered by emotions and the relationships between personality type and certain illnesses.

Emotions and physical responses. Psychologists have long known that emotions are accompanied by specific physical changes in the *autonomic nervous system*, the part of the nervous system that controls such involuntary reactions as heart rate and blood flow. Moreover, people who put on facial expressions reflecting such emotions as fear, anger, sadness, and disgust experience bodily changes similar to those they would have if they really felt the emotion. Simulating anger or sadness, for example, increases the heart rate. Forming an expression of disgust lowers the heart rate. (This is not true of all emotions, however. Mimicking a happy expression, for example, does not produce the bodily responses associated with genuine happiness.)

The physical responses triggered by facial expressions seem to be inborn, rather than learned, according to psychologist Paul Ekman of the University of California at San Francisco. Ekman and his colleague Robert Levenson of the University of California at Berkeley reported in January 1989 at the meeting of the American Association for the Advancement of Science (AAAS) in San Francisco that people making faces have the same bodily reactions whether they come from the United States or from somewhere as culturally different as Sumatra, Indonesia.

Ekman and Levenson recorded the physical responses—including heart rate, skin temperature, and speed and depth of breathing—of 46 Sumatran men, aged 17 to 28, as they made specific facial expressions. They found the same pattern of bodily changes in Sumatrans as in Americans. "It is the first evidence of the universality of autonomic nervous system pattern," Ekman says.

The site of anxiety. The location of what may be the part of the human brain that experiences fear and anxiety was reported by researchers at Wash-

Psychology

Continued

ington University School of Medicine in St. Louis, Mo., in February 1989. Psychiatrist Eric M. Reiman and his colleagues used an imaging technique called *positron emission tomography* or PET scanning, which reveals the brain's chemical activity.

The researchers measured blood flow in the brains of eight healthy volunteers before, during, and after the volunteers received what they were told would be a painful electric shock. The volunteers were injected with water containing small amounts of radioactive oxygen, which then flowed through the bloodstream and collected in the most active parts of the brain. PET scanning detected the radiation given off by the oxygen. A computer image then displayed which parts of the brain contained the most radioactivity and therefore were most active when the volunteers were anxious about receiving the electric shock (which turned out to be mild rather than painful).

The researchers found that anxiety is associated with increased activity in two areas of the brain called the *temporal poles*. The temporal poles are the tips of two larger brain regions known as the *temporal lobes*, located on both sides of the head inside the temples just behind the eyes. This study marked the first time PET technology had been used to study the brain area involved with an emotion, and Reiman plans to go on to research other emotions.

Disease-prone personalities. As psychologists continue to identify links between the body and the mind, some believe that psychology may eventually play an important role in maintaining physical as well as mental health. British psychologist Hans J. Eysenck described some controversial findings about this possible mind-body link in August 1989 at the meeting of the American Psychological Association in Atlanta, Ga.

According to Eysenck, a simple psychological test may predict whether a person will develop cancer, heart disease, or neither. And if the test indicates that a person has a disease-prone personality, behavioral therapy may help protect the person against illness.

Eysenck collaborated with Ronald Grossarth-Maticek, a Yugoslav psychol-

Pigeons in a psychology experiment at the University of Iowa in Iowa City show the ability to distinguish among several classes of objects. The birds, which are rewarded with grain for pecking keys that represent the right answers, can correctly assign pictures of objects to various categories, such as "chair," "flower," or "automobile."

ogist who started his research in the early 1960's in Yugoslavia and now works in West Germany. Grossarth-Maticek began by measuring the personality traits, smoking and drinking habits, and physical health of a large random sample of people. Based on the personality tests, he predicted the illness each person would get, designating the volunteers as one of four types: type 1, cancer-prone; type 2, heart-disease-prone; and types 3 and 4, relatively healthy. He then followed the people over a 20-year period to find out what happened.

In general, according to Grossarth-Maticek's work, a cancer-prone person is unassertive and overly patient, tends to avoid conflict, has feelings of hopelessness, and cannot express unpleasant emotions. A person susceptible to heart disease tends to be easily angered, hostile, and aggressive.

Based on these traits, Grossarth-Maticek was able to predict death from cancer with 50 per cent accuracy—six times more accurate than a prediction based on cigarette smoking. His predictions of who would die from heart disease were nearly as good.

"These dramatic results," says Eysenck, "indicating a powerful role for personality and behavior in cancer and heart disease, lead to an all-important question: Can we prevent these deaths by changing people's personalities?"

Antidisease therapy. In an effort to find the answer, Eysenck and Grossarth-Maticek used simple behavioral therapy methods—including hypnosis, relaxation therapy, and *modeling* (showing patients how to change their behavior)—to change the volunteers' attitudes and habits. The two psychologists taught cancer- and heart disease-prone people to express their emotions more readily, to cope with stress, and to become more self-reliant.

One half of a group of 100 people allegedly having cancer-prone personalities received this behavioral therapy; the others received no therapy. Thirteen years later, 45 of the 50 people who received therapy were still alive. Only 19 of the 50 people who did not receive therapy survived. Similar results were achieved with 92 people said to be heart-disease prone: 37 of 46 who received therapy were alive 13 years

later, but only 17 of 46 survived without it.

The therapy consisted of 30 one-hour sessions, which Eysenck admits is lengthy and expensive. But in another study, the researchers used group therapy on 20 people who met on two or three occasions for a total of only six hours. "Here too," says Eysenck, "we found a marked difference in the number of people who died of cancer and coronary heart disease, again favoring the therapy group."

The two psychologists' claims have stirred much controversy. Many other studies have failed to find links between psychological traits and specific illnesses. In addition, scientists who reviewed Grossarth-Maticek's research found some flaws, such as inconsistencies in the number of people reportedly studied.

Many scientists agree, however, that if behavioral techniques are even half as effective against cancer and heart disease as Grossarth-Maticek and Eysenck found, the therapy would be highly beneficial. "If this research holds up under ongoing scrutiny," Eysenck says, "we will be entering a new era of health care and disease prevention."

Eyesight and IQ. The link between early visual abilities and later intelligence was also discussed at the January 1989 AAAS meeting. Psychologist Joseph F. Fagan III of Case Western Reserve University in Cleveland reported that tests of visual preferences in infants can help predict later intellectual development. The vision test consists, basically, of holding an infant in front of a "stage" to which different images are attached. The images, shown singly or in pairs, are objects of different shape, size, or color. An observer behind the stage watches the infant's eyes and records how long the child looks at each image as a measure of interest in that image.

More intelligent babies, Fagan found, show greater interest in new or novel images. Because discrimination and recognition memory are two of the abilities measured by intelligence tests later in life, Fagan's visual tests might function as a sort of intelligence test for infants.   [Robert J. Trotter]

In WORLD BOOK, see PSYCHOLOGY.

Public Health

The number of drug-related AIDS cases in the United States increased sharply in 1988. Of the 32,311 new cases of AIDS in the United States and its territories, 10,747—or about one-third—were linked to intravenous drug use. This was nearly double the 5,747 drug-related AIDS cases reported in 1987.

These findings were reported in March 1989 by *epidemiologists* (infectious disease specialists) at the federal Centers for Disease Control (CDC) in Atlanta, Ga. The increase in drug-linked cases indicates important shifts in how AIDS is spread and a need for new approaches to AIDS prevention.

AIDS (acquired immune deficiency syndrome) is a fatal disorder that affects the body's disease-fighting immune system. The virus that causes AIDS is most commonly spread by intimate sexual contact or by sharing hypodermic needles or syringes.

As part of public health monitoring of AIDS, state and local health departments collect information about new AIDS cases and forward it to the CDC.

The health departments gather the age, race, sex, and other basic information for each AIDS case. In addition, the local agencies attempt to identify the factors that put each patient at greater risk for AIDS, such as drug abuse or homosexual behavior.

Drug-related AIDS cases in 1988 involved three groups: (1) intravenous drug users; (2) their sex partners; and (3) children born to mothers infected with the AIDS virus either because of intravenous drug use or contact with an infected sex partner. Drug abuse or sexual relations with a drug user accounted for most cases of AIDS in women and heterosexual men. The 847 cases of AIDS in heterosexual partners of drug abusers accounted for 55 per cent of all the cases thought to involve the heterosexual spread of AIDS. Drug-linked AIDS cases occurred more commonly among blacks and Hispanics than among whites.

Compared with previous years, the 1988 findings showed how seriously the problem of intravenous drug abuse contributes to the spread of AIDS. This

Surgeon General of the United States C. Everett Koop leads Washington, D.C., schoolchildren in a no-smoking pledge. Koop, whose crusade against smoking along with his AIDS education efforts made him one of the best-known public-health officials in the nation's history, announced in May 1989 that he would retire on October 1.

Public Health

trend was even more dramatic in the Northeast, where the percentage of AIDS cases linked to drug use has been greater than in other regions of the United States. In the Northeast during 1988, drug-linked AIDS exceeded the number of all other AIDS cases.

The CDC epidemiologists noted that public health efforts need to focus on reducing the spread of the AIDS virus among drug users. They said that these efforts will be especially difficult among intravenous cocaine users, who inject drugs more often and share needles more frequently than do users of other drugs. Community-based prevention programs were urged by the epidemiologists to include AIDS education, counseling, and testing programs, especially in drug-treatment centers, jails and prisons, and public health-care facilities.

Homicide and handguns. Community regulations limiting the availability of handguns may reduce firearm-related homicides, according to a study reported in November 1988 by researchers at the University of Washington in Seattle and other institutions. Handguns and other firearms are involved in about 60 per cent of homicides in the United States, and gun-control policies have been strongly debated. Supporters of gun control claim that making firearms easy to get leads to more fatal shootings. Opponents of gun control argue that stricter regulations would have little effect on murder rates because people intent on killing would only work harder to obtain a gun or would kill by other means. One important reason for this debate has been the lack of sound scientific information about the relationship between firearm availability and homicide.

In a study designed to provide some of the missing information, the researchers compared homicide patterns in Seattle with those in Vancouver, Canada, from 1980 to 1986. These two cities, only 225 kilometers (140 miles) apart, have similar populations, economies, and other characteristics. Seattle, however, has lenient regulations concerning handgun ownership, while the laws are quite restrictive in Vancouver. In Seattle, the rate of gun ownership is more than three times the rate of ownership in Vancouver.

The researchers found that overall rates of nonfatal crimes, including burglary and robbery, were similar in both cities. In contrast, homicides involving handguns were nearly five times more likely in Seattle than in Vancouver. Rates of homicide by means other than firearms were the same in the two cities. These findings suggest to the researchers that restricting access to handguns might lower the homicide rate.

Health impact of disasters. The information collected in disaster settings may be crucial in deciding how to allocate public health resources. This conclusion was supported by experiences in the African nation of Sudan. In August 1988, floods caused by heavy rains in Khartoum, Sudan, killed at least 91 people and left approximately 750,000 people homeless. Health problems related to the flooding were assessed and reported by officials of the Sudanese Ministry of Health and representatives of the U.S. government.

After the flood, public health officials set up disease surveillance systems. They gathered epidemiologic information as quickly as possible to guide public health and medical relief efforts. Disease surveillance and epidemic monitoring systems used information from hospitals, clinics, and special surveys carried out by mobile field teams. Evaluation of more than 29,000 visits to health facilities indicated that diarrhea affected 31 per cent of the patients; malaria, 20 per cent; and respiratory problems, 17 per cent.

Mobile field teams examined 17,639 Sudanese children aged 1 to 5 years to assess their nutritional status. The teams found that 10 per cent of the children were severely undernourished and another 14 per cent were moderately undernourished. Measles outbreaks can result in high death rates in undernourished children. As a result, public health workers in Sudan decided to administer measles vaccine to approximately 40,000 unimmunized children between the ages of 6 months and 5 years.

The U.S. Public Health Service in late 1988 recommended that all American homes be tested for radon, an invisible, odorless radioactive gas. See ENVIRONMENT. [Richard A. Goodman]

In WORLD BOOK, see PUBLIC HEALTH.

Science Education

Science education reform in the United States gained new impetus from a study released on Sept. 22, 1988, by the National Assessment of Educational Progress (NAEP). The NAEP, created by the United States Congress to monitor student achievement, found the scientific knowledge of U.S. elementary and high school students "distressingly low," despite some recent improvement.

The NAEP report, called *The Science Report Card: Elements of Risk and Recovery*, was based on nationwide tests given in 1985 and 1986 to 17,000 students aged 9, 13, and 17, and to 34,932 students in grades 3, 7, and 11. According to *The Science Report Card*, nearly half of the 13-year-olds tested did not understand basic scientific concepts well enough to apply them. Among 17-year-olds, the study said, a majority of the students tested were "poorly equipped for informed citizenship and productive performance in the workplace." Only 7 per cent of that age group was prepared to do college-level science work.

Project 2061. Despite widespread agreement on the need to reform how science is taught, debate continued concerning the nature of the reform. The American Association for the Advancement of Science (AAAS), the world's largest federation of scientific organizations, sponsored a reform effort called Project 2061, with financial support from the Carnegie Corporation of New York and the Mellon Foundation. Project 2061, named for the year when Halley's Comet will return, is based on the idea that educators can and should determine what scientific concepts and skills are essential for every high school student to know.

Project 2061 began in 1985, the year of the comet's last approach to Earth. A panel of experts spent more than four years developing a detailed outline of essential scientific knowledge. In February 1989, the AAAS announced the beginning of the second phase of the project. The association selected six school districts, each of which will produce a model curriculum.

Science
Education
Continued

Science/Technology/Society. The Project 2061 approach was questioned by educators involved in the Science/ Technology/Society (S/T/S) effort, coordinated by Pennsylvania State University in University Park with support from the National Science Foundation, an independent federal agency that supports both scientific research and education.

The S/T/S movement focuses upon students as active partners in the education process. It encourages young people to become question-askers, information-seekers, decision-makers, and action-takers. Several states, including Arizona, California, Colorado, Iowa, Missouri, New York, Pennsylvania, and Utah, have initiated statewide efforts to introduce S/T/S.

The National Science Teachers Association (NSTA), with 50,000 members the world's largest organization dedicated to improving science teaching, actively encouraged both Project 2061 and S/T/S efforts. The group also undertook several initiatives of its own to encourage science education reform.

One NSTA project that attracted national attention was an effort to extend science courses over several years to replace the usual offering of one year each of biology, chemistry, and physics in high school.

Involvement of industry in science education continued to expand during 1988. The Triangle Coalition for Science and Technology Education, a three-way partnership involving education, science, and industry, promoted state and regional alliances to improve how science is taught. Colorado had one of the more advanced statewide alliances with a central staff, regular meetings, and an array of projects. Iowa Governor Terry E. Branstad initiated a similar program, financed by legislative appropriations and matching contributions from a variety of Iowa businesses and industries. In many states, the NSF provided funds (usually on a matching basis) to support partnerships between industry and education groups.   [Robert E. Yager]

In WORLD BOOK, see EDUCATION; SCIENCE PROJECTS.

Science
Student
Awards

Winners in the 48th annual Westinghouse Science Talent Search were announced on March 6, 1989, and winners of the 40th annual International Science and Engineering Fair were named on May 12. Science Service, a nonprofit organization in Washington, D.C., conducts both competitions.

Science Talent Search winners. The 40 finalists were chosen from 1,461 seniors from high schools throughout the United States. The top 10 finalists received scholarships totaling $140,000 provided by the Westinghouse Electric Corporation.

First place and a $20,000 scholarship went to 16-year-old Christopher McLean Skinner, a senior at Hall High School in Little Rock, Ark. Skinner analyzed a mathematical equation named after Diophantus, a Greek mathematician of the A.D. 200's often called "the father of algebra."

Second place and a $15,000 scholarship were awarded to Jordan S. Ellenberg, 17, of Winston Churchill High School in Potomac, Md., for a mathematics project in which he identified

sets of whole numbers that produce the same remainder when divided by a given number.

Third place and a $15,000 scholarship went to the youngest of the 40 finalists, 15-year-old Richard H. Christie of Penfield High School in Penfield, N.Y. Christie won for a study of interactions between the body's nervous and immune systems.

The winner of fourth place and a $10,000 scholarship was Stacy E. Benjamin, 16, of Francis Lewis High School in New York City, who studied how race influences people's perception of the severity of crimes.

Fifth place and a $10,000 scholarship were awarded to S. Celeste Posey, 17, of North Carolina School of Science and Mathematics in Durham, N.C., for a study of *deoxyribonucleic acid* (DNA), the material of which genes are made.

Sixth place and a $10,000 scholarship went to Allene M. Whitney, 17, of Capital High School in Helena, Mont., who developed a safety test for lakes contaminated by a type of blue-green algae that poisons fish and cattle.

Science Student Awards

Continued

Christopher
McLean Skinner

Jordan S. Ellenberg

Richard H. Christie

The seventh-place winner, who received a $7,500 scholarship, was Kevin N. Heller, 17, of Half Hollow Hills High School West in Dix Hills, N.Y., who investigated the effects of temperature on "jumping genes," genes that can change their position on the chromosomes of *maize* (Indian corn).

Eighth place and $7,500 went to Andrew W. Jackson, 18, of Roxbury Latin School in West Roxbury, Mass., who developed a new *spectrograph*, an instrument that spreads out light into a spectrum and records it for study.

Ninth place and $7,500 were awarded to Andrew J. Gerber, 16, of Midwood High School in New York City, who analyzed how certain drugs act on the brain.

Tenth place and $7,500 went to Divya Chander, 17, of Pascack Valley High School in Hillsdale, N.J., who studied how bacteria invade tissues.

Science fair winners. The 40th annual International Science and Engineering Fair took place May 7-13 in Pittsburgh, Pa. The 746 contestants were chosen from finalists at local science fairs in the United States and other countries.

Two, three, or four First Award winners were selected in each of 13 categories. The 33 First Award winners of $500 each were:

- Behavioral and social sciences. Candice A. Rideout, 18, Aldershot High School, Burlington, Canada; Heather M. Levi, 14, Northdale Junior High School, Coon Rapids, Minn.
- Biochemistry. Anuj Steve Narang, 17, Eastside High School, Gainesville, Fla.; Jennifer Ryder, 16, Edison/Computech High School, Fresno, Calif.
- Botany. Lori Ann Stec, 16, Detroit Country Day School, Birmingham, Mich.; Shen-horn Yen, 17, Affiliated Senior High School of National Taiwan Normal University, Taipei, Taiwan; Gar Ling Tse, 18, James B. Castle High School, Kaneohe, Hawaii.
- Chemistry. Tamara Koverman, 16, Montrose High School, Montrose, Colo.; Michael J. Stern, 18, Armand Hammer United World College, Montezuma, N. Mex.
- Computer science. Michael Hutchings, 17, Stuyvesant High School, New York City; Wendy M. Jones, 18, Renaissance High School, Detroit.

- Earth and space science. Heather Swartz, 17, Colville High School, Colville, Wash.; Matthew Roy Campbell, 16, Spartanburg High School, Spartanburg, S.C.
- Engineering. Chad Bouton, 18, Ames High School, Ames, Iowa; Melvin L. Holmquist, 18, Grand Rapids Senior High School, Grand Rapids, Minn.; Brygg Anders Ullmer, 15, Lexington High School, Lexington, S.C.; Amy J. Watson, 18, Xenia High School, Xenia, Ohio.
- Environmental sciences. Joseph Chi Hung Ho, 18, Williamson High School, Williamson, W. Va.; Gideon Yu, 17, University School of Nashville High School, Nashville, Tenn.; Keith C. Curtis, 16, Detroit Country Day School.
- Mathematics. Vamsi K. Mootha, 18, Monsignor Kelly High School, Beaumont, Tex.; Vladimir Teichberg, 17, Bronx High School of Science, New York City.
- Medicine and health. Amber N. Foster, 18, Winona Senior High School, Winona, Minn.; Avik Sumon Roy, 16, Keystone High School, San Antonio; Rhonda R. Schafer, 18, Wilton High School, Wilton, N. Dak.; Ricardo Emilio Rodriguez-Rosa, 17, Dr. Santiago Veve Calzada High School, Fajardo, Puerto Rico.
- Microbiology. Sourav K. Poddar, 17, Clear Lake High School, Houston; Sundar Natarajan, 17, Alhambra High School, Alhambra, Calif.; Rolf N. Barth, 17, Upper Arlington High School, Upper Arlington, Ohio.
- Physics. Shreyas S. Vasanawala, 16, Sidney Lanier High School, Montgomery, Ala.; William A. Cordova, 18, Alamogordo High School, N. Mex.
- Zoology. Ryan Mamoru Iwasaka, 16, H. P. Baldwin High School, Wailuku, Hawaii; Mark S. Monroe, 16, Ballard High School, Louisville, Ky.

Physics Olympiad. The 19th annual International Physics Olympiad took place June 23-July 2, 1988, in Bad Ischl, Austria. Seven gold, 22 silver, and 30 bronze medals were awarded. Three U.S. team members—Michael Edwards of the Kinkaid School in Houston, Ian Lovejoy of Lowell High School in San Francisco, and Matthew Stone of Portsmouth Abbey School in Portsmouth, R.I.—won silver medals in the competition. [Sara Dreyfuss]

Space Technology

The United States achieved success with both its manned space shuttle and unmanned rocket programs in 1988 and 1989, indicating that the National Aeronautics and Space Administration (NASA) had largely recovered from the shuttle *Challenger* accident in 1986 and other failures that followed. The Soviet Union, meanwhile, experienced a series of setbacks in both its manned space station and unmanned planetary program. The Soviet Union, however, successfully launched its first space shuttle in an unmanned test flight which demonstrated that Soviet space technology nearly equals that of the United States.

The European space program successfully launched 8 Ariane commercial missions carrying 14 satellites between June 1988 and June 1989. And the Chinese space program launched both a new weather satellite and a commercial payload for West Germany. Japan had another successful year by launching two missions during the same 12-month period. Israel joined the club of spacefaring nations by launching its first satellite on Sept. 19, 1988.

Return of the shuttle. After its Sept. 29, 1988, launch from the Kennedy Space Center in Cape Canaveral, Fla., the space shuttle *Discovery* made a near perfect flight with its five-member astronaut crew. On October 3, it ended with a successful landing at Edwards Air Force Base in California, buoying NASA's spirits and clearing the way for continued use of the shuttle for major U.S. space science missions. The 26th mission of the shuttle program, the flight came two years and eight months after a rupture in a solid rocket booster caused an explosion that destroyed *Challenger* and killed its seven-member crew on Jan. 28, 1986.

Although *Discovery* launched a satellite, the overriding objective of the flight was to test engineering changes to the shuttle and new NASA management and communications procedures. For example, the solid-fuel rocket boosters that powered *Discovery* were totally redesigned, and even though the shuttle's main liquid-fuel engines

The Soviet Union's first space shuttle, *Buran* (Snowstorm), successfully completes its unmanned test flight in November 1988, landing at the Baikonur Cosmodrome near the Aral Sea. The Soviet shuttle is nearly identical in design to U.S. shuttles, but is launched with liquid-fuel booster rockets rather than the solid-fuel boosters that launch the U.S. shuttles.

were not involved in the accident, they also had 35 major modifications.

Discovery carried in its payload bay a large *Tracking and Data Relay Satellite* (*TDRS*) attached to a large upper-stage booster. The *TDRS* satellite acts as a tracking station, relaying communications from shuttles and other satellites to a single ground station located at White Sands, N. Mex. The shuttle released *TDRS* in a low Earth orbit so that its booster could then be fired, lifting *TDRS* to a stationary *geosynchronous orbit*, which means that the satellite orbits 35,900 kilometers (22,300 miles) above Earth at exactly the same speed as Earth's rotation. This keeps it above the same point on Earth.

More shuttle flights. NASA had a second equally successful shuttle mission from Dec. 2 to 6, 1988, using the orbiter *Atlantis*. This flight carried a secret Defense Department payload. *Aviation Week & Space Technology* magazine reported that the payload was a large new Lacrosse reconnaissance satellite that uses radar instead of ordinary photography. Radar images of sites on Earth of interest to military intelligence can be obtained through heavy clouds and at night. Other satellites can photograph Earth only during daytime on cloudless days.

The shuttle *Discovery* was launched again on March 13, 1989. As on its earlier mission, *Discovery* was used to place another *Tracking and Data Relay Satellite* in orbit. The mission returned to Earth on March 18.

Magellan launched. The first planetary mission to be launched by the shuttle had been scheduled to lift off on April 28 on board the orbiter *Atlantis*. The launch was delayed, however, until May 4 because of a faulty fuel pump. The spacecraft—the *Magellan Venus Radar Mapper*—was attached to an upper-stage booster and was deployed from *Atlantis'* cargo bay. The first and second stages of the booster were then fired to place *Magellan* on a path to Venus, where it was scheduled to arrive in August 1990.

Unmanned launches. On September 5, a medium-sized Titan-2 booster was used to launch a U.S. Navy ocean surveillance satellite into orbit from Vandenberg Air Force Base in California. On May 10, the U.S. Air Force used a Titan 34D booster to launch two large communications satellites from Cape Canaveral.

Soviet space program. Although the Soviet Union continued an ambitious space program in 1988 and 1989, the program suffered several setbacks, including the total failure of two spacecraft sent to Mars. Nevertheless the Soviet Union achieved a stunning success with the launch of the first Soviet space shuttle on Nov. 15, 1988.

Unlike the United States, the Soviet Union decided to fly the first test of its space shuttle without a crew. The vehicle, named *Buran* (Snowstorm), completed three Earth orbits and made a computer-controlled landing at the Baikonur Cosmodrome.

The successful landing without cosmonauts on board was not the major achievement of the flight. Many U.S. and European airliners that routinely carry passengers can, and sometimes do, make fully automatic landings without the pilots touching the controls. Instead, the most noteworthy achievement was the Soviets' ability to integrate advanced new technology in several different disciplines such as heat protection, propulsion, and electrical power and the ability to design computers and software that could fly the winged vehicle through a reentry into Earth's atmosphere.

Although the *Buran* orbiter looks almost identical to the U.S. space shuttle, the rocket system that launched *Buran* was substantially different from that used by the United States. *Buran* rode piggyback on a Soviet Energia heavy lift booster, which can be used to launch payloads other than the shuttle. The Energia uses all liquid fuel, unlike the U.S. shuttle, which uses solid fuel in its strap-on booster rockets.

Space flight record. Soviet cosmonauts on the *Mir* space station set a record of more than a year in space. On Dec. 21, 1987, Soviet cosmonauts Vladimir Titov and Musa Manarov were launched to *Mir*, where they remained for 366 days, returning to Earth on Dec. 21, 1988. During their time in space, they were visited by a number of other cosmonauts.

On Aug. 29, 1988, the Soviets launched the *Soyuz TM-6* spacecraft to *Mir* with three cosmonauts to visit the

Space
Technology
Continued

long-duration crew. The *TM-6* cosmonauts included mission commander Vladimir Lyakhov, physician Valery Polyakov, and an Afghan air force pilot—Abdullah Ahad Mohmand. After a one-week stay on the station, Lyakhov and Mohmand climbed into a *Soyuz TM-5* spacecraft used by a previous crew and prepared for return to Earth on September 6. Polyakov remained on board to monitor the health of Titov and Manarov during the final stages of their flight.

When Lyakhov and Mohmand fired the descent engine of their *Soyuz*, however, it shut down prematurely. Later it began firing unexpectedly, and the crew had to turn it off to prevent a landing in China. The problems—which caused great concern about the astronauts' safety—were traced to computer software and errors by the cosmonauts. They landed safely on September 7.

The next crew to visit *Mir* was launched on November 26. It included French Air Force Brigade General Jean-Loup Chrétien. During that flight, Chrétien and a Soviet cosmonaut conducted a spacewalk outside the station to erect a small test structure designed by French engineers.

Space station problems. The *Mir* program, which had been going so well, began to encounter problems in April 1989. The Soviets had planned to launch two new 15-ton modules to expand the station. But design problems delayed their scheduled launch. The Soviets had also planned to launch a new crew to the station on April 19 but canceled that launch. The cancellation of any new flights to *Mir* disrupted Soviet intentions to keep the station permanently manned. All cosmonauts on *Mir* returned on April 27.

Aviation Week & Space Technology reported that the reason for the delay in future flights was a gradual decrease in the ability of the *Mir* station to generate electrical power with its large solar array panels. The Soviets decided to leave the station unmanned until mid-1989.   [Craig P. Covault]

See also ASTRONOMY, SOLAR SYSTEM. In WORLD BOOK, see SPACE TRAVEL.

Zoology

Why do some individual animals consistently produce more surviving offspring than other members of their species? In the case of certain birds, the answer seems to be that they limit the number of eggs they lay to what they can probably raise successfully. That finding was reported in November 1988 by zoologists at the Edward Grey Institute in Oxford, England.

The researchers made a nine-year study of a bird called the great tit, which lives in Africa, Asia, and Europe. Mated pairs of these birds lay as many as 13 eggs or as few as 5 eggs.

From 1959 to 1963 and from 1977 to 1980, the scientists studied 1,267 great-tit nests in a wooded area of Oxford, adding or removing three or four eggs from 483 of the nests. The nesting birds treated the foster eggs, and the young that hatched from them, the same as their own.

The scientists found that the birds laying the most eggs produced more young that survived than birds that laid fewer eggs even when eggs were taken away from their nests. For example, if a pair of birds started with 11 eggs but had 2 of them taken away, these birds still produced more surviving young than pairs that started with 9 or 10 eggs.

Too many baby mammals. Mammals often have more offspring than they can care for. The reason for that phenomenon, researchers at Cambridge University in England reported in January 1989, seems to be that pregnancy takes much less of a physical toll on a female mammal than does producing milk to feed the young. So females tend to breed with little regard for the amount of food available. But after giving birth, if food is in short supply, they allow the young to die.

The British scientists studied wild red deer on the Isle of Rhum, off the west coast of Scotland. This is a harsh environment where, in some years, heavy rains cut down the amount of grass available for the deer to eat.

From 1971 to 1987, they kept track of 283 female deer. Each year, the scientists noted whether a deer had a calf and, if so, whether the calf died

Saving Sea Turtles

Ila Loetscher of Padre Island, Texas, *above left,* hugs an Atlantic ridley turtle, the world's most endangered sea turtle, which she has spent more than 20 years trying to save. For her efforts, the National Wildlife Federation gave her a special award in 1988. The ridley's only remaining nesting ground is a beach in Mexico, where the turtles lay their eggs in the sand, *above.* In the late 1970's, the U.S. National Park Service became interested in Loetscher's campaign. Each year, the service gathers about 2,000 ridley eggs and flies them to Padre Island for incubation. When they are 1 year old, the baby turtles are released and allowed to make their way into the sea, *left.*

317

Zoology

Continued

Two California gray whales trapped by ice in the Arctic Ocean near Barrow, Alaska, in October 1988 surface through a breathing hole. For three weeks, the whales attracted international attention as Eskimos, scientists, and environmentalists monitored the animals' health and kept breathing holes open. Finally, on October 28, Soviet icebreakers cleared a path to the open sea, and the whales swam to freedom.

shortly after birth, survived less than a year, or lived past its first birthday.

To assess the fitness of the various mother deer, the researchers looked at how well a mother survived the winter and whether she gave birth the following year. They also recorded the birth date and weight of each new calf. They were then able to compare the effect of two situations on a mother's health: having a calf that died soon after it was born, or providing milk for a calf that survived.

Mothers that gave birth to young that died within three months seemed as healthy as deer that had not been pregnant for a year. But those that raised a calf for at least six months were less healthy and less likely to give birth the following year. Calves born the next year to those mothers tended to be smaller and to be born 10 days later than calves born to that mother the year before, and they had a 10 per cent lower chance of surviving. Also, these mothers suffered more during years when the grass was scarce.

The researchers concluded that it is

better—from the standpoint of perpetuating the species—for mammals to give birth even if there is a chance that they will be unable to provide for the newborn's survival. If it turns out that food is plentiful, a deer and her calf will probably both survive (though the mother is likely to be somewhat weakened by producing milk and nursing). If food is scarce, the calf can be allowed to die and the mother—none the worse for wear—can breed again the next year.

Fashioned by food. For at least one caterpillar, the saying "You are what you eat" really holds true, a California scientist reported in February 1989. Biologist Erick Greene of the University of California at Davis discovered that a moth caterpillar, *Nemoria arizonaria*, takes on the appearance of a twig or a cluster of flowers, depending on when it hatches and what it feeds on.

The *Nemoria* moth lives in Arizona, New Mexico, Texas, and northern Mexico. The adult moths produce two broods of offspring each year—one in the spring and one in the summer. The

Zoology

Continued

moth larvae, or caterpillars, feed on the flowers and leaves of oak trees. At hatching, the larvae of the two broods look alike, but they develop very differently after that.

Larvae born in the spring eat the oak flowers, called *catkins*, and they soon bear a close resemblance to the flowers. The caterpillars become fuzzy and yellow with two rows of rust-colored dots that look like catkin pollen sacs. This appearance makes it easy for the caterpillars to blend in with the flowers and avoid being eaten by birds.

In summer, when the other brood of larvae hatch, the flowers are gone. These caterpillars feed on oak leaves and develop smooth bodies with gray-green skin. The summer caterpillars, too, have natural camouflage; when they are motionless, they can be mistaken for twigs.

To learn what causes the two broods of caterpillars to develop so differently, Greene raised spring and summer *Nemoria* larvae in the laboratory. He exposed both groups of caterpillars to varying conditions that included cool or warm temperatures, 12½ or 14 hours of "daylight," and a diet of catkins or oak leaves.

Diet was the only variable affecting the caterpillars' development. Larvae from both broods that ate catkins took on the appearance of the flowers; those that ate leaves soon began to look like twigs.

Next, Greene fed another group of newly hatched spring and summer larvae diets consisting of catkins, leaves, or catkins mixed with leaves or leaf chemicals. Although the results of this experiment were not quite as clear-cut as those from the previous experiment, they still showed the strong effects of diet on the caterpillars' development.

The leaf chemicals that cause the caterpillars to assume the appearance of twigs are called *tannins*, Greene reported. During its evolutionary history, *Nemoria arizonaria* developed a bodily response to tannins that caused it to resemble a twig—a form that would best protect it from predators during the summer. In the absence of tannins, the larvae mimic catkins, the

best springtime camouflage. In the Special Reports section, see Practicing to Deceive.

Hunter becomes the hunted. To eat or be eaten? That is the key question facing all animals, but seldom is there any question about who eats whom. In October 1988, however, two South African zoologists reported on two sea-bottom communities in which predators and prey switched roles.

Amos Barkai of the University of Cape Town and Christopher McQuaid of Rhodes University in Grahamstown studied the underwater animals of two nearby islands—Marcus Island and Malgas Island—off the west coast of South Africa. The rocks on the sea floor around Marcus Island are covered with mussels and large marine snails called whelks, but few lobsters. Around Malgas Island, just 4 kilometers (2½ miles) away, rock lobsters predominate, with mussels and whelks as their chief food source. Only a few kinds of mussels and two species of whelks in that area avoid being eaten by the lobsters.

Barkai and McQuaid wanted to learn why the lobsters stay away from Marcus Island. They placed 1,000 rock lobsters into the waters off Marcus Island. Incredibly, the lobsters were quickly overwhelmed by large numbers of whelks and eaten. As soon as a lobster landed on a rock, a mass of whelks—more than 300, on the average—would attach themselves to the animal, weighing it down so it could not swim away. The whelks would devour the lobster in less than an hour.

Lobsters used to live off Marcus Island, but they vanished about 20 years ago. The disappearance of the lobsters may have been due to a reduction in the oxygen content of the island's waters at the time. Once the lobsters were gone, the whelks and mussels they ate thrived unchecked, so much so that the prey—the whelks—have become so numerous they can turn on their former predator, the lobster.

Birds aid honey seekers. In parts of Africa, according to tales that had long been told but never confirmed, people and birds have formed an unusual alliance. The birds act as scouts for honey gatherers and lead the way to beehives in return for a portion of the honeycomb. In March 1989, two biologists reported that this human-bird partnership is true.

The researchers—from the National Museum of Kenya in Nairobi and the Max Planck Institute in Seewiesen, West Germany—set out to investigate claims about the almost mythical bird, known as the greater honey guide. The honey guide reportedly points the way to nests and even indicates to honey gatherers how far away the hives are. For three years, the biologists lived among the Boran, a nomadic people in northern Kenya who reportedly depended on the honey guide's help.

The researchers observed a number of Boran honey-gathering forays. They related that the Boran call the birds for the hunt by whistling through clasped fists or snail shells. A nearby honey guide that hears the signal then flies off in search of a bees' nest. When it has found one, it alerts its human partners by darting close to them and calling persistently.

As soon as the honey guide is sure that it has everyone's attention, it heads toward the hive. After disappearing for about two minutes, the bird returns and perches a short distance away. When the Boran get close to the bird, it takes off again. In this way, the honey guide eventually leads its followers to the hive.

By following the birds, the Boran honey gatherers cut their search time by two-thirds, spending an average of about three hours—instead of nine—looking for a hive. The honey guide also benefits. By breaking up a bee colony, the Boran make the honeycomb more accessible to the birds so they can pick out the larvae and beeswax, both of which they eat. Without the honey gatherers' help, the scientists calculated, the birds would have been able to get at only 4 per cent of the 186 hives found during the three-year research project.

The scientists also noted that in parts of Kenya where people can purchase honey from beekeepers or food markets, the honey guide has ceased its guiding behavior. [Elizabeth J. Pennisi and Thomas R. Tobin]

In World Book, see Animal; Zoology.

Science You Can Use

In areas selected for their current interest, *Science Year* presents information that the reader as a consumer can use in making decisions—from buying products to caring for personal health and well-being.

Taking the Caffeine Out of Coffee

More and more, coffee drinkers are doing without the jolt that caffeine provides. Caffeine, a slightly bitter substance, is a stimulant found naturally in coffee, tea, cocoa, and kola nuts. It is added to some soft drinks and to more than 1,000 over-the-counter drugs.

Nearly 25 per cent of the 130 billion cups of coffee drunk in the United States each year are now decaffeinated. Jitters and sleepless nights are partly responsible for the move away from caffeine. But in recent years, worries about whether caffeine has long-term effects on health have also played an important role. Concerns about caffeine have also spilled over into the tea and soft drink markets. As a result of the concern over caffeine, between 1962 and 1986, the percentage of coffee drinkers who regularly drink decaffeinated coffee rose from 4 to 17 per cent. Even more people switch from regular to decaffeinated coffee in the afternoon or evening.

Although some caffeine remains in coffee or tea after the decaffeination process, the amount is extremely small—no more than 1 to 5 milligrams per cup. In general, more than 97 per cent of the caffeine is removed. Since regular coffee contains only about 1 per cent caffeine, that means that decaffeinated coffee is about 99.07 per cent caffeine free.

Caffeine is removed from coffee beans using two basic processes called the direct and indirect methods. The direct process is the simplest, cheapest decaffeination method. Regardless of the solvent used, first the *green* (unroasted) coffee beans are moistened with steam—which draws the caffeine toward the surface of the bean. The beans may then be flushed with one of four solvents: methylene chloride, ethyl acetate, coffee oils, or liquid carbon dioxide. The caffeine dissolves easily in the solvent and thus is extracted from the beans. The solvent then contains about 97 per cent of the caffeine that was in the beans. If the solvent is methylene chloride, any remaining in the beans is removed by steaming the beans again. This causes the methylene chloride, which has a lower boiling point than water, to evaporate. The beans are then ready for drying, roasting, and grinding.

If ethyl acetate, a compound found naturally in many fruits is used, the beans are not steamed a second time. Although some ethyl acetate remains in the beans, the level is lower than that found in such fruits as pears and apples and is generally considered safe.

The third solvent used in the direct process is coffee oils, compounds naturally present in coffee. The oils are obtained from used coffee grounds. Although the coffee oils extract the caffeine, they also remove some of the solids found in green coffee that give roasted coffee its flavor. However, the beans simultaneously absorb flavor elements from the oil, which helps offset the flavor lost.

The fourth solvent used in the direct process is liquid carbon dioxide. Carbon dioxide, which normally exists as a gas, becomes liquid under high pressure. The beans are steamed and moistened with water, then placed in a pressurized container and flushed with liquid carbon dioxide, which dissolves the caffeine. The beans are then dried. This drying process removes any liquid carbon dioxide residue left in the beans. The liquid carbon dioxide method is a fairly efficient decaffeination method because the caffeine can easily be separated from the liquid and the carbon dioxide recycled.

In the indirect process, water is used to soak the beans rather than steam. There are two indirect methods: *the Swiss water process*, which uses *activated charcoal* (charcoal from which most impurities have been removed), and a method that uses methylene chloride.

In the Swiss water process, the beans are soaked in hot water to draw off the caffeine, then drained. The drained water, which contains caffeine as well

How Coffee Beans are Decaffeinated

Coffee beans may be decaffeinated using one of two processes: direct and indirect. In the direct process, the *green* (unroasted) beans are flushed with one of four solvents: methylene chloride, ethyl acetate, coffee oils, or liquid carbon dioxide. In the indirect process, the green beans are soaked in water.

Direct process (using methylene chloride, ethyl acetate, or coffee oils)

The green beans are steamed to draw the caffeine to the surface.

The beans are then flushed with the solvent to extract the caffeine.

If methylene chloride is used, the beans are steamed again to remove chemical residue.

Direct process (using liquid carbon dioxide)

Beans are steamed and moistened with water to draw caffeine to the surface.

Beans are flushed with liquid carbon dioxide under pressure to remove the caffeine.

The beans are dried, which removes any liquid carbon dioxide residue.

Indirect process (Swiss water process)

Beans are soaked in hot water to extract the caffeine.

Beans are drained. Water is passed through charcoal filters to remove caffeine but not flavor elements.

The flavored water is then concentrated and used to coat the beans.

Indirect process (using methylene chloride)

Beans are soaked in water enriched with flavor elements from green beans to remove the caffeine.

Beans are drained. Water is mixed with methylene chloride, which dissolves the caffeine.

The water is heated to boil away the methylene chloride and caffeine.

The water, rich in flavor elements, is used to soak the next batch of beans.

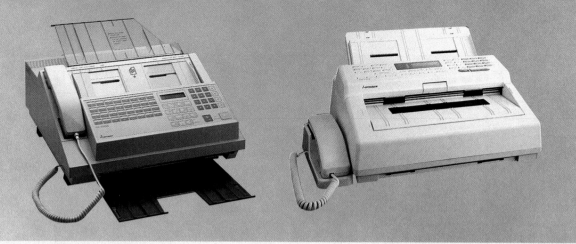

Facsimile transmission has become one of the fastest growing areas of modern communication technology. Commercial fax machines, *above left,* have become common in many business offices around the world. Machines for home use, *above right,* are beginning to gain popularity.

usually a CCD. The information is then read by photodiodes as in a movable scanner machine.

In both types of machines, the information about the reflections is broken down into *digital code* (a series of 1's and 0's) and transmitted as an audio frequency tone over telephone lines to the receiving fax machine. Most fax machines transmit the information in four-line segments.

The fax machine on the receiving end is notified of an incoming message by an electronic signal sent by the transmitting machine after telephone contact is established. A device in the receiving part of the machine reconverts the audio tone into the electronic digital code used to guide the operation of 1,728 tiny heating elements that extend across the width of the page. When an electric current passes through one of the heating elements, its temperature rises. Because the heating element is in contact with the heat-sensitive paper used to record messages, the hot element creates a black dot.

Each wire in the receiving part of the machine corresponds to a single photodiode in the transmitting machine. Thus, if the sensing device in the transmitting machine registers a dark spot at a particular point on the page, a wire in the receiving machine produces a dot at the corresponding location on the paper being printed. If the sensing device registers a light spot, the wire leaves the corresponding spot untouched. In this way, the page is reproduced line by line.

The *resolution* (clarity) of the reproduced image depends on how many dots there are: the greater the number of dots, the greater the clarity. Standard fax machines print 5,983 dots per square centimeter (38,600 per square inch).

Fax technology has come a long way since the first commercial machines were introduced in the 1960's. The first digital machines, called Group III models, hit the market in 1981. The fax boom really began with these machines. Their digital signals made them much faster and provided better resolution. Group III machines can transmit a page in 10 to 30 seconds. They account for 90 per cent of the approximately 2 million fax machines in use today worldwide.

Group III machines have other improvements as well. They have a computer chip memory that allows the storage of up to 100 pages of data and 150 telephone numbers. This enables users to send copies of a document, one after another, to more than one place.

Group III fax machines send and receive up to 4,800 *bits* per second. (A bit is a 1 or 0 in the digital code.) Group

III machines also feature another innovation called *error correction*. If there is light static or other distortion on the phone line, the machine can screen it out. If the distortion is heavy, however, the receiving machine can ask the transmitting machine to retransmit a portion of the data.

Less costly Group III machines, which easily fit atop a desk, are for users who send or receive only one to five documents a day. Although these machines transmit and receive documents at about the same speed as the more costly machines, they lack options, such as multipage document-feeding mechanisms that speed up processing. These machines, which carry a price tag of $1,200 to $2,000, can store up to about 20 telephone numbers but no other data. They also have a resolution of less than 5,983 dots per square centimeter.

Heavy-volume Group III fax machines, which are generally larger than low-volume models, can send or receive several hundred pages a day. The cost of the more sophisticated machines runs from $5,000 to $10,000. But because the facsimile market is so competitive, experts expect prices to fall about 20 per cent annually.

In these models, options abound, such as the ability to use plain paper instead of the more costly heat-sensitive paper. The image is created by a *thermal transfer process*. In this process, the heating elements in the receiving part of the fax machine are in contact with a heat-sensitive ribbon. When the ribbon is heated by the heat elements, it deposits ink onto the paper, creating a black dot. The heat also fuses the dot to the paper. Other models use laser printers to create messages.

Plain paper printing is standard with the newest generation of fax machines—the Group IV machines. These machines have a resolution of 13,951 dots per square centimeter (90,000 per square inch) and can transmit a page in only three seconds. They can also transmit and receive in color. But Group IV machines are in their infancy. The cost often exceeds $10,000, and they require special phone lines available in only a few areas.

For owners of personal computers (PC's) who want fax capabilities, *PC fax boards* are an option. A PC fax board is a computer board that plugs into the central processing unit of a personal computer and is operated with accompanying software. Fax boards, which cost from $400 to $1,000, allow users to send material to and receive material from other PC fax boards as well as from conventional fax machines. But a PC fax system does not transmit messages from paper copy the way a fax machine does. A separate document scanner device must be used to transmit messages on paper. A PC fax system can, however, print messages on a computer printer.

One advantage of most PC fax systems is that they have more memory than a conventional fax machine. But because a PC fax board can only transmit the type of data that can be stored in the computer's memory, it is not a substitute for a fax machine.

Not everyone is thrilled with the facsimile phenomenon. For overnight delivery companies, the success of fax has meant steadily decreasing revenues. But overnight delivery companies offer services fax cannot. For example, they can send original documents as well as three-dimensional objects.

Smaller, cheaper fax machines may also be ushering in an era of personal faxing. One compact model that sells for about $700 doubles as a telephone. Another model is small enough to fit under the dashboard of a car. One of the surest measures of fax's success, however, is the rapid appearance in fax machines of the same stuff that clutters home mailboxes—junk fax from advertisers.   [Jennifer Christensen]

Getting a Reading on Blood Pressure Devices

Devices that enable people to monitor their blood pressure at home can play an important role in the treatment of *hypertension* (high blood pressure). In 1985, the National High Blood Pressure Education Coordinating Committee reported that home monitoring can help alleviate one of the biggest problems in the treatment of hypertension—the tendency for patients to abandon their prescribed treatment program. Although treatment has great long-term benefits, hypertension medication may have unpleasant side effects, such as headaches, nausea, and impotence. As a result, some patients feel little motivation to continue treatment. Blood pressure readings taken at home can provide visual feedback that demonstrates the effectiveness of the treatment.

Home-use devices, like the devices used in doctors' offices, measure the force that blood exerts against the walls of the arteries as it is pumped by the heart. The measurement of this force—your blood pressure—is expressed as two numbers, such as 120/80. The first number is the systolic pressure, which represents the force of blood pushed through the arteries as the heart beats. The second number is the diastolic pressure, which represents the force between beats. Blood pressure that is persistently equal to or greater than 140/90 is considered high.

Blood pressure is measured with a device called a *sphygmomanometer* (pronounced *sfig moh muh NAHM uh tuhr*) and with a stethoscope. The word sphygmomanometer comes from two Greek words: *sphygmo* (pulse) and *manós* (at intervals). There are three types of home-use sphygmomanometers: mercury, aneroid, and electronic models. All of them operate on the same basic principle.

A sphygmomanometer consists of an inflatable cuff that wraps around the upper arm just above the elbow; a rubber bulb and tubing to inflate the cuff; and a measuring device. Inflating the cuff compresses the main artery in the arm, temporarily stopping the flow of blood. Using a mercury or a gauge-type sphygmomanometer, the person taking the reading places a stethoscope on the inner arm over the artery just below the cuff, then slowly lets air out of the cuff. (In an electronic model, the stethoscope is built into the cuff.)

At first, there is no sound in the stethoscope. But as the cuff deflates and blood begins to flow through the artery again, the stethoscope picks up a rhythmic sound. The reading on the measuring device when the sound first is heard represents the systolic pressure—the greater pressure as the heart contracts, pushing blood through the artery. As more air escapes from the cuff and blood flows freely through the artery again, the sound grows fainter. The second reading, taken just before the sound disappears altogether, represents the diastolic pressure—the lower pressure as the heart rests between beats.

Home blood pressure devices range from very simple hand-operated devices costing about $20 to electronic units that are almost completely automatic and may cost more than $100. According to the American Heart Association, each of the three types—mercury, aneroid, and electronic—has advantages and disadvantages.

The mercury sphygmomanometer used in the home is identical to the mercury device used in doctors' offices. It has a long glass tube filled with mercury, which serves as a pressure gauge. The higher the blood pressure, the higher the column of mercury rises. (All blood pressure readings are expressed as equivalents of millimeters [mm] of mercury [Hg], no matter which kind of sphygmomanometer is used.)

The mercury sphygmomanometer is the least expensive, simplest, most reliable, and most accurate blood pressure monitor. In fact, it is used to *calibrate* (adjust the accuracy of) other types of

How Blood Pressure Is Measured

Blood pressure is measured with a sphygmomanometer, a device consisting of an inflatable cuff and a measuring gauge. The cuff, strapped around the arm just above the elbow, is inflated to cut off the blood flow through the main artery in the arm. Then, air is slowly released.

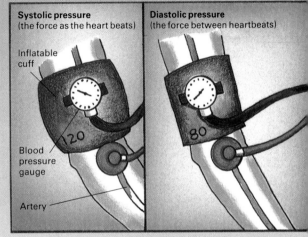

Systolic pressure (the force as the heart beats)

Inflatable cuff

Blood pressure gauge

Artery

Diastolic pressure (the force between heartbeats)

blood pressure monitors. But mercury sphygmomanometers can be awkward to carry and set up. The column of mercury must be perfectly upright, and the scale must be read at eye level.

Aneroid monitors are easier to carry and do not contain mercury—a potentially toxic substance. They register pressure on a circular gauge with an indicator needle whose movement varies with air pressure in a small metal chamber behind the gauge. But aneroid models are fairly delicate, more complicated, and less accurate than mercury devices. Their accuracy must be checked at least once a year against a mercury sphygmomanometer.

Both the mercury and aneroid devices require a certain level of manual dexterity. Users must attach and pump up the cuff, position the stethoscope, and deflate the cuff using only one hand. Some models have a stethoscope already attached to the cuff. Instead of featuring the usual Velcro-like fasteners, some models have cuffs with a sliding bar that helps the user loop the cuff around the arm and pull it tight,

thus making attaching the cuff easier.

Electronic models are the easiest type of device to use. With some models, the patient simply positions the cuff properly, presses a button to automatically inflate the cuff, and watches the blood pressure reading appear on a digital display. Electronic monitors do not require the user to listen for the sound of blood moving through the artery. Some electronic monitors automatically sense the surges of blood through the artery. Others have a built-in microphone that registers the rhythmic sound. Such features make the measuring process easier for people with hearing impairments.

Some electronic models also inflate the cuff automatically. That feature can be an advantage for people with arthritis or other problems who find it difficult to squeeze the rubber bulb on mercury and aneroid models.

But electronic models also are expensive, and making sure the microphone or other device is positioned over the artery can be difficult. Because electronic models tend to be less accu-

When the pressure in the artery is equal to the pressure in the cuff, blood begins to flow again. A stethoscope placed over the main artery detects a rhythmic sound as the flow begins. The reading on the gauge at this time represents the systolic pressure, the force that the blood exerts on the artery walls when the heart beats, *above left.* As the cuff deflates and the blood flows freely, the sound grows increasingly fainter. A reading taken just before the sound can no longer be heard, *above,* represents the diastolic pressure, the force exerted on artery walls between heartbeats.

Blood Pressure Devices

Type of device	Advantages	Disadvantages
Mercury	■ Most accurate type of device ■ Least expensive type of device ■ Most reliable type of device	■ Awkward to carry and set up ■ Gauge may be difficult to read ■ Requires some manual dexterity to attach and inflate the cuff ■ Requires normal hearing for accurate reading ■ May break and release mercury, a toxic substance
Aneroid	■ Easy to carry ■ Gauge easier to read than a mercury column ■ Very reliable	■ Less accurate than a mercury device ■ Not as sturdy as a mercury device ■ Requires some manual dexterity to attach and inflate the cuff ■ Requires normal hearing for accurate reading
Electronic	■ Easiest type of device to use ■ Sound detected by electronic sensors; useful for people with hearing problems ■ Models that automatically inflate the cuff help people with dexterity problems	■ Most expensive type of device ■ Least accurate type of device ■ Body movements or room noises may cause inaccurate readings

rate than either mercury or aneroid monitors, their accuracy should be checked more than once a year, according to the American Heart Association. Consumers should also be aware that body movements or room noises can cause inaccurate readings on some electronic monitors.

Medical experts suggest that consumers keep several other points in mind when buying and using a blood pressure device:

■ Make sure that the monitor comes with clear, simple, specific instructions.

■ If you decide on an aneroid or electronic monitor, consider buying it from a local medical-supply house or distributor that performs calibrations. People with home monitors may also have their devices calibrated at their doctor's office.

■ Make sure that the blood pressure cuff fits your arm properly. Because cuffs come in different sizes, an im-proper fit can result in an inaccurate reading.

■ Consult with your doctor to make sure that you are using the monitor properly.

■ Remember that blood pressure changes from minute to minute with different body positions, physical activity, and emotions. If you have a series of unusual readings, however, see your doctor—and take the device along so that your technique and the device's accuracy can be checked.

■ Remember that home monitors are not intended for self-diagnosis or treatment. One—or even several—high readings do not necessarily mean that you have hypertension.

■ Above all, remember that a home device is not a substitute for regular care by your doctor. Don't change your treatment program based on readings from a home monitor. The readings may be inaccurate. [Michael Woods]

330

Cooking with Microwaves

Dinner is on the table: soup just waiting for a garnish of parsley; juicy pot roast; potatoes—ready for a pat of butter. The vegetables are perfect—still slightly crispy when you bite into them. But even better, the whole meal took little more than an hour to cook. The secret, as any connoisseur of the quick kitchen meal will tell you, is a microwave oven, one of the most popular kitchen appliances in use today. By 1988, an estimated two-thirds of all households in the United States had at least one microwave oven.

Put virtually any food in a microwave oven, press the start button, and in minutes—or seconds—you're ready to eat. Gravy boils, popcorn explodes, and butter melts before your eyes. Yet the inside of the oven—unlike a conventional gas or electric oven—remains cool to the touch.

How is it all done? The answer lies in high-frequency radio waves called *microwaves*. Microwaves have many uses. They detect speeding cars and keep track of airplanes. They relay long-distance telephone calls and television programs via satellite. And they can also cook food at least four times faster than conventional gas or electric ovens. The principle behind all these uses of microwaves is based on one of the best-kept secrets of World War II—radar.

Microwaves are created by an electronic vacuum tube called a *magnetron*, a device developed for use in radar systems during World War II. During a lab test of the magnetron in 1945, an engineer at the Raytheon Company got too close to the device and a candy bar he had in his pocket melted. The idea of microwave cooking was born, and in 1955 the first consumer microwave oven was introduced.

Microwave ovens are much more efficient than gas or electric ovens. To cook a casserole in a conventional oven, the gas burner or electric coil must first heat the air in the oven, then the air must heat the pot before the pot can cook the food. Only about 6 per cent of the heat energy produced by a gas oven—14 per cent of the heat produced by an electric oven—actually reaches the food. The remainder is lost heating everything else around the food. With microwave cooking, which produces heat directly inside food, more than 50 per cent of the energy produced reaches the food.

Microwaves are not *heat* but short *radio waves* that vary in length from 1 millimeter (0.0394 inch) to 30.5 centimeters (12 inches). Part of the electromagnetic spectrum, they are shorter than ordinary radio waves but longer than infrared light waves.

The magnetron in a microwave oven uses electric current and magnetic fields to generate microwaves that *oscillate* (change the direction of their electromagnetic field) 2.45 million times per second. The oscillating microwaves travel from the magnetron via a tiny antenna to a hollow metal tube called a wave guide.

Before the microwaves enter the oven, however, they pass from the wave guide through a set of metal fan blades called a *stirrer*. As the blades in the stirrer turn, they disperse the microwaves relatively evenly throughout the oven. This action prevents one part of a roast, for example, from being struck by a higher concentration of microwaves—and thus overcooking—at the expense of another part, which would be undercooked.

Most microwave ovens let you set a cooking level: high, medium, low, or defrost. But a magnetron's power can't be controlled; it's either creating microwaves or it's not. To lower the heating power, electronic circuitry turns the magnetron on and off. For the medium setting, it's turned on and off for an equal amount of time during the heating cycle. During the low and defrost settings, it's off more than it's on. (The magnetron is always on during the high setting.)

Once inside the oven, the microwaves bounce off the metal walls until they enter the food. Only molecules of water can absorb microwaves. The water molecules in the outer layers of food absorb the microwaves and begin to "vibrate." This motion generates heat in the water molecules, which bump into other molecules nearby and set them vibrating. This heats the outer 2.5 to 4 centimeters (1 to 1.5 inches) of the food, and the heat is transferred to the inner portions of the food.

Contrary to popular belief, microwave ovens do not cook food from the inside out. The microwaves are absorbed before they can penetrate deeper than about 4 centimeters. That is why most microwaved foods must stand for a time after cooking and before being served. This allows the deeper or thicker parts of the dish not directly bombarded by microwaves to heat by *conduction* (the movement of heat through a material). As one molecule strikes another, the motion of the molecules—and therefore the heat—is carried deeper into the food.

Foods cooked in a microwave come out pale, partly because of the shorter cooking time. By browning a cake we are, after all, burning it slightly. Microwaved beef doesn't turn an eye-appealing dark brown because its surface temperature remains relatively low. The surface temperature of beef cooked in a conventional oven may reach 170°C (338°F.). This high temperature causes *oxymyglobin*, a bright red pigment in muscle, to break down and turn brown. The surface temperature of microwaved beef, however, never exceeds 100°C (212°F.). This temperature is not high enough to completely break down the oxymyglobin in the beef.

Because glass, ceramics, paper, and most plastics do not absorb microwaves, these materials can be used as cookware in the oven. Metal cookware, in contrast, reflects microwaves—that's why metal is used to line the inside of the oven—and so shields food from the microwaves, preventing it from being heated. In preventing the food from absorbing microwaves, the metal cookware can also cause an excessive build-up of microwaves in the oven, producing sparks that can short-circuit the appliance.

Cooking time in a microwave oven depends on a number of factors. One obvious factor is the food's original temperature. A less obvious factor is the amount of food being cooked. For example, you can bake a potato in a conventional oven in about 50 minutes. Add two, four, or six more potatoes to the oven and the baking time is basically the same. But there are only so many microwaves—and thus, only so much energy—entering a microwave oven. You can microwave a potato in 3 to 5 minutes. But increase the number of potatoes, and you must increase the cooking time. The liquid portions of dishes also cook faster than the drier portions. In addition, some foods, such as those high in fats and sugar, absorb heat from the vibrating water molecules faster than other foods. That means bacon cooks somewhat faster than vegetables.

Another factor is the thickness or thinness of the food. For example, the thinner sections of the food—such as the soup at the edges of a bowl—cook faster than the middle, because the microwaves can reach farther into—or even all the way through—the thinner sections. Stirring food periodically helps distribute the heat more evenly. In addition, cutting or molding food into uniform, regularly shaped pieces that absorb microwaves everywhere at about the same rate helps food cook more evenly.

Rotating foods can also help all parts of a dish get a relatively equal share of microwaves. With some ovens, you must reach in and turn the food every once in a while. Others come with an automatic turntable.

Wait. *Reach in* and turn the food? Isn't that a bit dangerous with all those microwaves bouncing around? It could be—if the microwaves were still present. But all microwave ovens have elaborate safety features.

Ever since microwave ovens were first introduced for the home in 1955, their safety has been questioned. If a microwave can cook a hot dog in seconds, consumer advocates asked, what could it do to the chef? There have been two areas of concern—leakage and direct exposure.

Leakage occurs when microwaves escape during the normal operation of

How Microwaves Cook

The energy used to cook food in a microwave oven is not heat, but high-frequency radio waves. Microwaves cook food fast because they produce heat directly inside the food.

Microwaves are generated by an electric current and magnetic fields in a magnetron, an electronic vacuum tube, *right.* A tiny antenna sends the microwaves to a wave guide, a hollow metal tube. Before entering the oven, the microwaves pass through the rapidly turning metal blades of a stirrer, which disperses the microwaves more evenly throughout the oven.

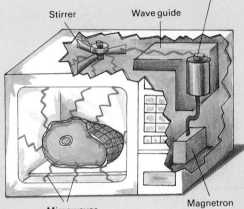

Stirrer Wave guide Antenna

Microwaves Magnetron

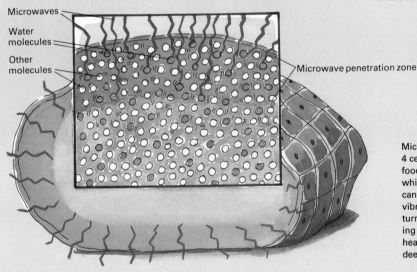

Microwaves

Water molecules

Other molecules

Microwave penetration zone

Microwaves penetrate up to about 4 centimeters (1.5 inches) into food. They cause water molecules, which are the only substance that can absorb microwaves, to begin vibrating. The water molecules, in turn, strike other molecules, causing them to vibrate. This generates heat, and the heat is transferred deep into the food.

the oven. Microwaves can't escape through the sides, rear, top, or bottom of the oven because the cavity is sealed in metal. Also, the front-door window contains a metal mesh. The hundreds of tiny holes in the mesh let you see inside the oven. But the diameter of the holes is smaller than the diameter of the microwaves and so the microwaves cannot pass through. Some microwaves do escape through the door seal, however.

To keep leakage there to a minimum, the door is equipped with a plastic frame. The frame diverts the microwaves and bounces them back into the oven cavity.

Federal standards limit the radiation leakage from the door to a maximum of $5/_{1,000}$ of a watt per square centimeter near the surface of the oven. That's $1/_{8,000}$ of the energy released by a 40-watt light bulb, an extremely low amount of radiation. But is it harmless? Most scientists believe it is, but the effects of long-term low-level microwave radiation have been debated for decades—and are still being researched today.

Direct exposure to microwave energy is, of course, dangerous. But open the door to a microwave oven while it's running, and the unit turns off instantly. The door contains up to three switches that must be closed in order for the oven to turn on. If you're still uneasy about exposure to microwave radiation, just follow this rule: Keep your distance from the oven while it's in use.   [William J. Hawkins]

333

Sorting Out the Averages

You may read in the newspaper that the average number of cars per household in your state is 2.6. Another story may state that the median price of houses in your area reached $110,000 last year. Still another article may report that the most common number of children per family in your town is 2.

All of the numbers in these newspaper reports are what statisticians call *measures of central tendency*. The statisticians use such measures when they want a single number to represent—or be typical of—a group of numbers. All of the measures are sometimes confusingly called *averages*, but their real names are *mean*, *median*, and *mode*. They all have their uses, and sometimes one is more useful than another.

The *mean*, for example, is what most of us probably think of when we hear the word *average*. Imagine a set of test scores from a small class of eighth-grade students: 45, 45, 50, 55, 60, 65, 90, 90, and 90. If we want to know how well the class as a whole did on the test, we can calculate the *mean* or *arithmetical average*. This is done by adding up all the scores and dividing by 9, the total number of scores. Thus, the mean equals 65.6 (45+45+50+55+60+65+90+90+90—or 590—divided by 9, and rounded off).

Per capita (Latin for *by the head*) numbers are calculated in the same way. We determine the total for all and divide by the number of people. For example, per capita income in the United States is the country's total income (including salaries, profits, and interest) for a year divided by the total number of people in the United States.

The mean does not have to be an actual number in the group we are working with. No student in our eighth-grade class scored 65.6 on the test, and unless the teacher awarded partial credit for partially correct answers, 65.6 would not even be a possible score. This is how a statistician may conclude that the average number of cars per household in your state is 2.6, even though there is no such thing as 0.6 of a car.

What does the mean tell us? It tells us what each individual would be like if all were the same. This enables us to make predictions. That is, if we know the average performance of one small group within a larger group—such as one eighth-grade class in a school—we can predict the performance of similar groups—such as other eighth-grade classes in that school.

The *median* is another measure of central tendency. The median is the halfway point in a group of numbers. We calculate the median by ranking the numbers from the smallest to the largest and then finding the number that is in the middle of the list. In the case of the eighth-graders, there are nine scores and so the median is the fifth number—60. Half the test scores are below 60; half are above.

With the eighth-graders' scores, the mean and the median are close together—65.6 and 60—so both probably are good measures of how the entire class is doing. The median is a better measure than the mean, however, when several very high or low numbers in the group distort the mean. For example, consider this group of numbers—the cost of houses in a one-block area: $25,000, $30,000, $30,000, $40,000, $45,000, $50,000, $55,000, $60,000, and $250,000. The mean—or average—price of the nine houses is $68,333, and yet eight of them cost less than that. In this case, the mean clearly is a meaningless measure and the median price—$45,000—gives a better picture of the cost of the houses on the block.

The third measure, the *mode*, is the number that occurs most frequently in a group. In the case of the houses, the mode is $30,000, because two houses cost that much; in the case of the students' grades, the mode is 90, since three students scored 90 and no more than two students received any other single grade.

Knowing that there are clusters of numerical facts—in this case, house prices or test scores—may be useful. The mode can be misleading, however. Although it tells us the most common number in a group, that number may be much higher or much lower than most of the other numbers. If, for example, two more houses costing $250,000 were built on the block, the mode would be $250,000—which would give a very distorted picture of prices. And in the case of the students, the mode suggests that the class as a whole performed well on the test, when, in fact, most of the students did not. A teacher looking at both the mode and the mean or median, however, would determine that three bright students have pulled up the class average and that some students need special attention.

Because these three statistics—the mean, the median, and the mode—react differently to changes in distribution, statisticians may decide to use different ones to produce different results.

By citing different kinds of averages, statisticians can use the same pool of numbers to produce very different impressions. In the case of the eighth-grade class, if the teacher wanted to suggest that the class was doing well, he could report the mode—which is 90. But if the school's principal wanted to suggest that the students were not doing well, she could cite the mean—which is 65.6. And if the parents of the student who scored 65 were upset with their child's score, they could determine that at least their eighth-grader scored above the median. [Donald W. Swanton]

Figuring the Averages

There are three types of averages: the mode, median, and mean. Used to figure the average price of a house on this block, they can produce very different impressions. The *mode* (most common price) is $25,000, though three of the five houses cost more than that. The *mean* (arithmetical average) is $81,000, though none of the houses are that price and four of the houses cost less than that. The *median* (halfway point) is $45,000, showing that half of the houses cost more than that and half of them less.

Mode $25,000
   (most common price)

Mean $81,000
   (arithmetical average)

Median $45,000
   (halfway point)

People in Science

Scientific research must be directed and overseen. This section details the lives of two leading scientists who have turned their attentions from the laboratory to the administrative end of science, directing the overall activities of some of the greatest research institutions in the world.

The codiscoverer of the structure of DNA is still hard at work—directing a famous laboratory and coordinating a huge gene-mapping project.

James D. Watson

BY PETER R. LIMBURG

James Dewey Watson—Nobel Prize winner, molecular biology pioneer, research director—is a busy man, not to mention one of the most famous scientists in the world. Watson is best known as the codiscoverer, with British biologist Francis Crick, of the structure of deoxyribonucleic acid (DNA), the stuff of which genes are made. But he accomplished that almost 40 years ago, and a lot has happened in his life since then.

Today, Watson is juggling the demands of two very important jobs. He is director of the prestigious Cold Spring Harbor Laboratory on Long Island, New York, a leading center of research in the fields of genetics and molecular biology and on cancer. And since the fall of 1988, he has also been a director of the human genome project. The goal of that ambitious nationwide undertaking, financed by the federal government, is to identify all of the 50,000 to 100,000 human genes. In the Special Reports section, see CREATING THE ULTIMATE MAP OF OUR GENES.

Watson has been, by turns, a researcher and a teacher, but for some time now he has been mainly an administrator. He says he does not miss doing his own research, because he is closely involved with the work being done by Cold Spring Harbor's staff of more than 100 molecular biologists. Similarly, he has no desire to return to the classroom, though he has made several major contributions to science

Watson goes over some paperwork in his office at the Cold Spring Harbor Laboratory on Long Island, New York. He has been director of this renowned center for research in genetics and molecular biology since 1968.

in his book was that the way molecules behave depends on their structure. Therefore, he said, the key to the genes and their uncanny ability to duplicate themselves during cell division must lie in the structure of their molecules. Schrödinger's ideas later inspired Watson to try to solve the structure of the DNA molecule.

Jim graduated from the University of Chicago in 1947 at the age of 19. With an eye toward landing a job as curator of birds at the American Museum of Natural History in New York City, he had earned a bachelor's degree in zoology. But, meanwhile, he became intrigued with the idea of unraveling the mystery of the genes. So he enrolled in graduate studies in zoology at Indiana University in Bloomington.

One of the faculty members there was a brilliant microbiologist, Salvador Luria, who became one of the major formative influences on Watson's scientific career. Luria's research specialty was *bacteriophages*—viruses that infect bacteria. Luria thought that studying how the viruses reproduce themselves inside bacteria might shed light on how genes function. Soon, Watson was also concentrating on bacteriophages.

In 1950, Watson, barely 22 years old, received his doctoral degree. With Luria's help, he obtained a grant from Merck & Company, Incorporated, a large pharmaceutical company, to study bacteriophages at the University of Copenhagen under Herman Kalckar, a

Danish biochemist. Kalckar, preoccupied with personal problems, gave Watson little to do, but in the spring of 1951 he took the young research fellow with him to a scientific conference in Naples, Italy. There, Watson attended a lecture by a visiting British scientist, Maurice Wilkins of King's College in London, who was showing *X-ray diffraction* photos he had made of crystallized DNA molecules. X-ray diffraction photos are made when X rays sent through a crystal encounter atoms in the substance. The pattern the diffracted X rays make is recorded on a photographic plate, and this is analyzed to determine the molecular structure of the substance. This technique can be used on any substance that can form crystals, which have a regular, orderly arrangement of atoms.

DNA was first extracted from the nuclei of cells in the late 1800's, but for decades scientists had debated its function. In 1951, most researchers still believed that genes were made of protein, which is also abundant in chromosomes. But Wilkins and a growing number of other scientists were convinced that DNA was the molecule of which genes are made. Among those sharing this minority view was Watson, who by this time was becoming much more interested in DNA than in bacteriophages. He realized that if DNA could crystallize, it must have a regular structure. Furthermore, that structure could almost certainly be determined—preferably by him. For such an important discovery, he could expect to win the Nobel Prize. Excited, Watson hoped that Wilkins might want him as a research assistant, but Wilkins was not interested.

On the way back to Copenhagen, Watson learned that Linus Pauling of the California Institute of Technology (Caltech), one of the world's foremost chemists, had unraveled the molecular structure of keratin, the protein of which hair and fingernails are made. Pauling called the structure the *alpha helix* because it spiraled like a corkscrew. Watson, and many other scientists, began to wonder whether DNA might also be a helix. In Watson's words, the idea of a helical structure for DNA "was in the air" at that time.

Watson decided that if he was going to determine the structure of DNA, he would have to learn how to study X-ray diffraction photos. In the fall of 1951, he managed to get a research position at the famous Cavendish Laboratory at Cambridge University in England. The laboratory's director, Sir William Lawrence Bragg, had won the Nobel Prize in 1915 for his pioneering work in X-ray diffraction.

It was at Cambridge that Watson met Francis Crick, who became his collaborator in the search for the structure of DNA. At the time he met Watson, Crick was still working on a doctorate in biology, studying the molecular structure of the blood component hemoglobin by X-ray diffraction. Although he was 35 and Watson a brash, cocky 23, the two men took an immediate liking to each other.

Watson and Crick were both bright, quick-minded, and insatiably curious. Both had a self-deprecating sense of humor and were

Watson and an assistant look at blueprints for a neuroscience center that was under construction in 1989 at the Cold Spring Harbor Laboratory. Watson predicts that neuroscience will be one of the most active research arenas in coming years, and he wants Cold Spring Harbor to be a major player.

regarded by friends and co-workers as eccentric but amusing. They meshed so well that they frequently finished each other's sentences. Although the two were assigned to different professors, they spent so much time together that they were soon given a small office by themselves so that they could talk without disturbing the other researchers. Crick taught Watson the basics of X-ray crystallography. Watson, in turn, got Crick interested in the DNA puzzle.

A great deal was known about DNA by this time. Scientists knew that it was an acid, that it was found in the nuclei of all cells, and that it was a very large molecule. They had also learned that it was composed of sugars and phosphate groups, linked in long chains, plus nitrogen-containing compounds called *bases*. Scientists had even identified the bases: adenine (A), cytosine (C), guanine (G), and thymine (T). But they did not know how all these components fitted together to form a functioning DNA molecule. Nor were they certain what that function was. Almost all biologists believed that the DNA was just a kind of framework or backbone on which the genes, made of protein, sat.

In a way, Watson and Crick should not have been searching for the structure of DNA at all. Neither had been authorized to study DNA, and neither was truly qualified: Both men were weak in chemistry, and Watson was also weak in mathematics. To top it off, Maurice Wilkins, a friend of Crick's, had a prior claim on the research.

Wilkins was trying to work out the structure of DNA by interpret-

ing X-ray diffraction photographs. This was a difficult task requiring very precise measurements of greatly enlarged pictures and endless mathematical calculations of the angles at which atoms of various elements form bonds with each other. Wilkins, moreover, had run into a roadblock. His laboratory had hired a brilliant crystallographer, Rosalind Franklin, to assist him, but relations between the two had deteriorated. Soon they were barely speaking to each other.

Meanwhile, Watson and Crick had concluded on the basis of Franklin's research and their own X-ray diffraction analyses that DNA was almost certainly a helix, and that building models of the molecule's possible configurations was the way to solve the puzzle. They had several fundamental questions to solve, however. How many sugar-phosphate chains were there? Were the chains in the center of the molecule or on the outside? How did the bases form bonds? And were the bases linked to each other?

Hoping to gain some insights into those questions, Watson attended a seminar at which Franklin presented her X-ray crystallography findings, but he neglected to take notes. Relying on his scanty and imperfect recollections of Franklin's talk, he and Crick built a "Tinkertoy" model of the DNA molecule with balls, representing atoms, joined by sticks and wires. The model had three sugar-phosphate chains in the middle, like backbones. The bases were tacked awkwardly onto the outside. A lot of fudging had been required to make the parts fit at all, and the model threatened to fall

Watson shares a moment with his wife, Elizabeth, who stopped by his office for a brief visit.

apart at any moment. It clearly was not the right solution. To make matters worse, Bragg learned of their failure and forbade them to do any further work on DNA.

A year passed. During that time, Pauling had turned his attention to DNA. As fate would have it, Pauling's son Peter had come to Cambridge for graduate studies and was sharing an office with Watson. On a December day in 1952, Peter Pauling entered the office grinning broadly, holding a letter from his father. In the letter, Linus Pauling announced that he had worked out a structure for DNA. Watson was in despair. But Pauling had given no details of his ideas, and Crick reasoned that if he and Watson worked out the structure independently and published their findings at the same time as Pauling, they would still get credit.

A few weeks later, Peter received another letter from his father. This time, the renowned chemist had included details of his DNA model. Pauling said the DNA molecule was a three-chain helix with the sugar-phosphate backbones in the center—the same basic structure that Watson and Crick had tried and given up on a year earlier. A look at Pauling's sketches showed Watson that Pauling had made a basic mistake in his chemical bonds and that his model, too, was unworkable. Still, there was a chance that Pauling would soon realize his error and be back in the running.

Watson by this time was doubly determined to resume working on

DNA. Encountering Bragg one morning, he made the case that with Wilkins and Franklin still at odds with each other, he and Crick stood the best chance of beating Pauling. Bragg, enthused by the prospect of his laboratory's getting credit for solving the structure of DNA, gave Watson the go-ahead to concentrate on the problem.

Watson and Crick were soon building new models. They tried again to construct a helix with the backbones in the center but were forced to conclude that such an arrangement would not work.

Starting over once more, they fashioned another helix, this one with two backbones on the outside of the molecule. The twin spirals of the separated sugar-phosphate chains had such a pleasing symmetry that the two scientists thought they must be on the right track. New measurements from Franklin confirmed that the partially completed model agreed perfectly with DNA X-ray analyses.

The question of how the bases bonded together was still unsolved, however. Watson thought they might join in like pairs—A to A, C to C, and so on—but on close inspection that theory did not hold up.

One day after lunch, Watson cleared the top of his desk and began cutting model DNA bases out of cardboard. Though crude, the pieces were roughly correct in shape and scale. As he pushed them around in various arrangements, Watson suddenly noticed that an A-T pair was identical in shape and size to a C-G pair. Excitedly, he asked a colleague, an expert in crystallography, to look at the pairings and tell him if the molecular bonds between them were feasible. The other scientist said he could see nothing wrong with them.

When Crick arrived, he examined Watson's solution and declared that it must be correct. Furthermore, as they both quickly realized, the A-T, C-G pairings explained the amazing ability of genes to reproduce themselves. When the double helix separates into two individual strands during cell division, they reasoned, this simple pairing arrangement enables each strand to reconstruct the original molecule unerringly from raw materials in the cell. An A on one strand will always attract a T, a T will attract an A, and so on.

Watson and Crick completed their model with A-T and C-G base pairs. Everything fitted beautifully. For several days, the two scientists checked and rechecked their creation and could find nothing wrong with it. Besides, they told each other, the model was simply too pretty not to be true.

Wilkins and Franklin agreed, as did every other scientist who came to view the model. The structure of DNA had been solved. In April 1953, the British scientific journal *Nature* published a paper describing Watson and Crick's discovery. The concept it presented—the self-reproducing double helix—became the basis for modern genetics and the exciting developments of genetic engineering.

Watson, Crick, and Wilkins shared the Nobel Prize for physiology or medicine in 1962 for their work on DNA. Watson thinks Franklin also deserved the prize, but she had died of cancer in 1958.

On the grounds of the National Institutes of Health (NIH) in Bethesda, Md., Watson chats with Elke Jordan, director of the NIH Office of Human Genome Research. Watson spends part of every workweek commuting to the Washington, D.C., area to carry out his duties as associate director of the NIH project to map the human genome, all the genes in a human cell.

Meanwhile, Watson had left research for the classroom, accepting a teaching position in 1956 at Harvard University in Cambridge, Mass. As a teacher, Watson was often accused of mumbling. Yet his classes were always full, and many of his students found his lectures inspiring. He also earned high praise from his graduate students for giving them full credit for the research they performed under his supervision.

In 1968, Watson married Elizabeth Lewis, a 19-year-old junior at Radcliffe College. They met in his Harvard laboratory, where she was working as an assistant.

That same year, Watson made the best-seller lists with *The Double Helix*, a personal account of how he and Crick discovered the structure of DNA. As soon as it was published, *The Double Helix* aroused a storm of criticism in the scientific community—not least of all from Crick and Wilkins. This was not surprising, since Watson portrayed many of his former colleagues as eccentrics and buffoons. He was actually harder on himself than on anyone else in the book, but this was small comfort to their outraged feelings. Despite the outcry, Watson felt that *The Double Helix* was a major contribution to

At the NIH's National Institute of Child Health and Human Development, Watson confers with geneticist Igor Dawid. New knowledge gained from mapping human genes should help scientists understand how human beings develop from a fertilized egg to a fully grown adult.

popular science writing because it told how science is really done: not by selfless idealists working solely for the cause of knowledge, but by ambitious, competitive human beings who frequently make mistakes and who sometimes act petty and nasty.

There was yet another big event in Watson's life in 1968: He was named director of the Cold Spring Harbor Laboratory, where he had spent his summers as a graduate student doing research on bacteriophages. Cold Spring Harbor, founded in 1890 on the site of an old whaling station, had become one of the most respected centers for scientific research in the world. It was one of the birthplaces of molecular biology and modern genetic science. With its easygoing, unstructured atmosphere in which researchers were left alone to pursue their own projects, the laboratory had become a magnet for top scientific talent. The institution also had gained renown as a forum for the exchange of ideas. Each year, the laboratory hosted courses and symposiums that were attended by scientists from around the world.

Watson inherited a formidable job, for the laboratory was in dire financial straits. Previous directors, trying to make do with a shrinking budget, had let the facilities deteriorate in order to have enough money for research. Run-down and chronically short of cash, the lab was threatened with closing.

Watson turned out to be just the tonic the laboratory needed. He

After a long day of meetings at the NIH, Watson takes a rare moment to joke and relax before catching a plane back to New York and his other job as director of Cold Spring Harbor Laboratory.

proved to be an amazingly effective fund-raiser, and under his direction new research facilities were built and the seedy older buildings fixed up or torn down and replaced. For eight years, Watson divided his time between Harvard and Cold Spring Harbor, spending his summers at the laboratory and commuting from Cambridge on weekends during the rest of the year. In 1976, he resigned from Harvard to devote his full attention to the lab, and under his direction it has continued to flourish and grow.

Watson has always been a believer in unfettered dialogue, and he has never shunned controversy. In the 1970's, he took part in what was perhaps that decade's most important scientific debate—over the potential hazards of the new *recombinant-DNA technology*, the basis of genetic engineering. Recombinant-DNA technology involves taking a gene (or genes) from one organism and inserting it into the DNA of another organism. The purpose is to use the second organism to produce large quantities of a desired protein. Critics of genetic engineering, as well as a number of cautious biologists, warned that recombinant-DNA experiments—most of which were being done with bacteria or viruses—might create deadly new germs.

In 1976, the NIH established strict guidelines for government-sponsored recombinant-DNA research, including the use of expensive, specially designed laboratories to confine genetically engineered bacteria and viruses. Many scientists considered the guidelines unnecessarily restrictive, and Watson was soon at the forefront of those agitating for their relaxation. In a series of articles in scientific journals and consumer publications, he pointed out that genetically altered microorganisms are so weakened that they would almost certainly not survive outside the laboratory and that, in nature, bacteria are constantly exchanging pieces of DNA with one another.

Watson also pointed out that recombinant-DNA technology could yield such benefits as vaccines and unlimited supplies of pharmaceutic drugs. In 1979, the NIH relaxed its guidelines.

Today, Watson is speaking out in favor of the human gene-mapping project. He is convinced that the massive undertaking will more than make up for its cost by yielding the most fundamental knowledge possible about our genes and how they control human life. That knowledge should help researchers find cures for many diseases in which faulty genes play a part, including heart disease and cancer. "If we can get to the genetic bases of diseases, we'll have major breakthroughs," Watson says.

The genome project will undoubtedly make it possible to screen DNA to identify individuals who are at risk for developing genetically caused diseases. Many of those people may someday be helped with gene therapy—receiving normal versions of their defective genes.

Genetic screening could be misused, however. Would employers, for example, discriminate against applicants whose genes make them vulnerable to certain diseases? Might unscrupulous individuals use knowledge of their rivals' genetic flaws to destroy those persons' careers?

Watson is quick to acknowledge the ethical issues posed by the genome project, but he is hopeful that society will rise to the challenge. He thinks that genetic screening should be done *only* with the consent of the individual and that a person's genetic profile should not be released to anyone, including the government or law enforcement agencies, without that person's authorization. (He would make an exception to that rule in the investigation of violent crimes, where genetic information can often establish guilt or innocence.) He believes that society will take steps to prevent any wrong-headed use of genetic knowledge.

Watson is clearly excited about the gene-mapping project. Exciting, in fact, is a word he uses often when talking about science and the frontiers of research . He predicts that the study of the human brain will be one of the hottest areas of research in coming years. Accordingly, a state-of-the-art neuroscience building was under construction in 1989 at the Cold Spring Harbor Laboratory.

His tireless labors in the vineyards of science have brought Watson many top honors in addition to the Nobel Prize. In 1974, he received a medal of achievement from the National Academy of Sciences, and in 1977 he was honored with America's highest civilian award, the Presidential Medal of Freedom.

Watson and his wife, Elizabeth—now an architectural historian—have two teen-aged sons. In contrast to his highly visible public self, Watson prefers to keep his private self hidden from view, but he will admit to a few of his favorite pastimes. He enjoys listening to classical music, he reads avidly, and he exercises by playing tennis. And whenever he can find the time, he still likes watching birds.

This theoretical physicist oversees research at two major institutions and still devotes time to the problem of scientific illiteracy.

Walter E. Massey

BY JOHN CAMPER

Walter E. Massey has two big jobs. He is vice president for research at the University of Chicago, one of America's leading research universities, with 57 Nobel Prize winners among its current and former faculty members and students. He also oversees the Argonne National Laboratory in suburban Chicago, one of the centers of United States research on peaceful uses of atomic energy. Massey used to be known as one of the top black scientists in the United States. Today, however, this theoretical physicist and leading figure in the world of scientific research is known simply as one of the top scientists in the United States.

This is no small achievement for someone who grew up in the Deep South in the 1940's and early 1950's, when black people were not even allowed to use the same rest rooms or drinking fountains as white people. Then, schools were segregated—by law—and Massey's all-black school in Hattiesburg, Miss., was far inferior to the local whites-only school, with fewer course offerings and inadequate facilities. Massey left high school in his sophomore year. He went on to obtain a doctorate in physics without graduating from high school, though in 1981 the school board in Hattiesburg awarded him an honorary high school diploma.

In addition to his two main jobs, Massey is chairman of the board of a not-for-profit corporation that develops products based on research at Argonne and the university. He is also chairman and immediate past president of the 138,000-member American Association for the Advancement of Science (AAAS), the world's largest federation of scientific and engineering societies. In addition, he serves on the boards of Amoco Corporation, Brown University, the Museum of Science and Industry in Chicago, First National Bank of Chicago, Motorola Corporation, and Tribune Company. He holds, at last count, eight honorary degrees.

All that without graduating from high school? Massey certainly was capable of finishing high school, but because of a chance occurrence, he didn't have to. In the spring of 1954, a few weeks before the Supreme Court of the United States outlawed racial segregation in public schools in the landmark ruling on *Brown v. Board of Education of Topeka*, 15-year-old Walter happened to take a test for a scholarship program funded by the Ford Foundation to identify black high school students capable of doing college work.

"The idea was that there might be students who would be better off going to college than spending their time in an environment where they were not being challenged," Massey recalls during an interview in his modestly appointed office at the University of Chicago. His mother, Essie, an elementary-school teacher in Hattiesburg, had agreed to drive some high school students to Jackson, Miss., to take the qualifying examination on a Saturday morning, and Walter decided to go along.

"She said, 'Well, why don't you take the test as long as we're going up there?' So I took it—on a lark, frankly," says Massey. A few months later, he was offered a scholarship to Morehouse College, a highly regarded all-black institution in Atlanta, Ga.

Massey was excited about going to Morehouse and glad to leave the confinement of small-town, segregated life in Mississippi. "But I was scared, too," he remembers. "I wasn't sure I was ready for college."

Massey's high school had not offered the same level of courses as white schools. By the end of his sophomore year, Massey had taken no mathematics above the level of beginning algebra. He had never studied chemistry and had never heard of physics. But his school did have a dedicated faculty who tried as best they could to overcome the built-in shortcomings of a segregated school system.

Entering Morehouse in the fall of 1954 was a rude awakening for Massey. "I had no idea what I was going to do at Morehouse," he recalls. "I didn't know how college worked." After two weeks on campus, he was so lonely and frightened he called his mother and his father, Almar, a laborer in a chemical factory, and asked them to drive to Atlanta and take him home. In retrospect, says Massey, he's glad they refused.

Ironically, for a student who would go on to become a physicist, Massey initially got good grades in every subject except physics. In fact, he almost flunked physics in his first semester, partly because he

The author:
John Camper is a reporter for the *Chicago Tribune.*

Walter Massey and his secretary at the University of Chicago, Janice Nash Stroud, review his schedule of appointments and conferences. As vice president for research at the university, Massey has seen the focus of his scientific career shift from theoretical physics to administering scientific research.

had never taken a course in trigonometry, a branch of mathematics that's necessary for performing routine calculations in physics. So he taught himself trigonometry in his spare time.

Massey received his bachelor's degree in physics and mathematics in 1958 and stayed on at Morehouse for a year, teaching physics to freshmen and sophomores. From Morehouse, he had planned to take a job as a mathematician at the U.S. government's missile and weapons testing site at White Sands, N. Mex., but that year of teaching gave Massey a taste for the academic life he was never to lose. So he went to Howard University in Washington, D.C., another predominantly black school, to do graduate work in physics.

Dissatisfied with the level of teaching at Howard, Massey soon transferred to Washington University in St. Louis, Mo. He almost didn't make it through. In his fourth year of graduate school, he ran into a problem that threatened to prevent him from completing his doctoral research project, which involved calculating the forces between atoms of liquid helium.

"I don't remember exactly what the problem was, but it made the project extremely difficult to bring to a conclusion," he says. "I didn't think I was ever going to solve it. I became very frustrated. This happens to practically every graduate student. They hit a point where they believe the project will never be finished and the whole thing is just not worth it.

"I went to my thesis adviser and told him I thought I should quit. My mother had died around that time, and I was emotionally overwrought. I just sat in his office and cried. Well, I don't remember exactly what he said, but he said all the right things and he talked me out of it. If I had left then, I don't know where I would have ended up."

Massey received his doctorate in 1966 and took a job the same year as a theoretical physicist at Argonne, the laboratory he would later

At Argonne National Laboratory near Chicago, Massey meets with a scientist working on the Advanced Photon Accelerator project, a device that is expected to produce the brightest beam of high-energy X rays ever available for research. Massey oversees research at Argonne, a research laboratory operated by the University of Chicago for the U.S. government.

run. Argonne is one of seven national laboratories set up by the federal government after World War II (1939-1945). The laboratories grew out of the Manhattan Project, which developed the atomic bomb. Some of these national laboratories developed new and more powerful weapons, but Argonne specialized in peaceful uses of atomic energy and in studying the effects of nuclear radiation on plant and animal life.

Massey's highly theoretical research involved the interaction of atomic particles at very low temperatures. Massey chose to study the extremely complex atomic interactions in liquid helium, one of the few substances that remains liquid at *absolute zero* (the lowest temperature possible at $-273.15°C$ [$-459.67°F$.]).

Theoretical physics tends to attract scientists who prefer to work by themselves, hunched over a computer working out equations. Massey was no exception. "I was not a tinkerer in high school," he says. "I liked to read and to figure out problems. The thing I liked best about theoretical physics was that it was something you could do by yourself. That's why I went into theoretical physics rather than experimental physics, which requires you to be in a lab, often working with large groups."

Equally important, theoretical physics was a field practically free of racial prejudice. A theory stands or falls on its own, whether developed by a black or a white person. "It is a field in which your ability is judged on the basis of how well you can master the field," Massey says. "There's not as much room for interpretation of your work as there is in sociology or even in psychology."

But in the racially and politically turbulent 1960's, Massey began to feel he was not taking an active part in the events of those days and was evading his responsibility to help other blacks gain access to higher education. So in 1968, he took a job as assistant professor of physics at the University of Illinois in Urbana-Champaign.

Massey got more involvement than he had bargained for. "The first night I was there," he says, "I received a call from someone saying they'd like me to come down to the city jail because 264 black students had been arrested during a protest, and they wanted black faculty to come down and support them."

As was not uncommon in the United States in the 1960's, black students had been protesting what they felt was racial discrimination by the university and the local police and townspeople. Massey went to the jail to help smooth things over. Afterward, he became actively involved in efforts to bring black students and faculty into the mainstream of academic life.

Massey founded and became the first president of an association for the university's 11 black faculty members (out of a total faculty of about 2,000). He advised the Black Students Association, served on a committee to work out a curriculum with an emphasis on black history and literature, and was on another committee to search for a director of that curriculum. In addition, Massey tutored and counseled black science students and helped recruit black high school students for the university.

Massey stayed at the University of Illinois for two years. "People were trying, they really were," he says, "but you were just called upon to do everything. Over the years, the University of Illinois has done a very good job at improving conditions for black students, but I can't say we had a lot of success during the two years I was there."

So when Massey was offered a job in 1970 as associate professor of physics at Brown University, an Ivy League school in Providence, R.I., he quickly accepted. With fewer than 7,000 students, Brown was about one-fifth the size of the University of Illinois, and Massey felt he could have a greater impact on a smaller university. Brown had proportionately more black faculty and students than the University of Illinois, and the city of Providence seemed more racially tolerant than Urbana-Champaign.

At Brown, Massey attacked a problem he had also encountered at the University of Illinois. "Many of the black students," he says, "were simply not prepared to handle science and math courses. I thought we ought to be addressing the problem at an earlier stage, not waiting until they got to college." Massey set up and directed the Inner City Teachers of Science, a program in which Brown students who were studying to be teachers went into high schools in inner-city Providence to familiarize themselves with urban school problems and work with science teachers.

Massey acknowledges that his program had mixed success. Only a handful of Brown graduates went on to become inner-city schoolteachers, and the program waned as student idealism began to fade in the mid-1970's. The greatest achievement of the program, he believes, was in making established teachers more receptive to the kinds of new ideas the Brown students brought into their classrooms.

While at Brown, Massey became increasingly interested in the work of administering a university. In 1974, he received a nine-month fellowship from the American Council on Education to study academic administration at the University of California in Santa Cruz. The following year, he became dean of Brown's undergraduate college, the chief faculty administrator in charge of curriculum development and student affairs. Massey continued teaching graduate students, but he had less time for his own physics research.

The provost of nearby Yale University in New Haven, Conn., Hanna Holborn Gray, was impressed by what she heard and saw of Massey's administrative skills. In 1979, the year after she became president of the University of Chicago, Gray asked Massey to move to Chicago to manage Argonne, which the university operates for the U.S. Department of Energy. Gray also offered Massey an appointment as professor of physics at the university.

"One of the great achievements of the University of Chicago was to be able to lure Walter from Brown," says Gray. "I can't say enough good about him as a colleague and contributor. He has an engaging style, a wonderful sense of humor, great clarity of intelligence, and he's a good listener."

In 1982, Massey was given the additional title of vice president for research at the university. Massey continued to have authority over Argonne, but he turned over day-to-day management of the laboratory to a new director, Alan Schriesheim, in 1984. Massey now has offices at both the university and the laboratory and spends one or two days a week at Argonne.

With 3,900 employees and a $300-million annual budget, Argonne is a major center of basic and applied research. Its scientists have studied such problems as the development of solar energy, the disposal of nuclear waste, and the design of advanced nuclear reactors.

Under Massey, Argonne continued to play a role in developing new technology, but, until 1985, a roadblock stood in the way of transferring that technology to the marketplace to benefit consumers. Before 1985, federal patent laws blocked the transfer of research done at national laboratories to the private sector.

The U.S. government was making a large investment in the research efforts of the national laboratories, Massey noted, but there

was little to show for it in the way of product spin-offs. The problem was that federal law defined national laboratory research as public property, available to everyone. But no private company would finance a research project at Argonne without the guarantee of an exclusive right to market products resulting from that research.

In 1985, however, Congress removed the prohibitions against transferring technology to the private sector, and Massey was instrumental in forming the first joint effort by a national laboratory and a university to transfer new technology to the marketplace. In the same year, with Schriesheim and others, Massey established the Argonne National Laboratory-University of Chicago Development Corporation (ARCH) to license products based on research at both the laboratory and the university.

Some scientists at the two institutions, according to Massey, resisted the idea. They were concerned that their ability to pursue basic research in an open environment might be compromised if too much emphasis were placed on possible commercialization of the results of that research.

Massey managed, in most cases, to convince the scientists that such concerns were unwarranted. "He probably is as fine a resolver of differing positions as anyone I ever met in my life," says Steven Lazarus, associate dean of the University of Chicago Business School and president of ARCH. "He has raised it to an art form. He's a guy who takes the best of a number of people's ideas and weaves them together into something strong. And he does it in such a way that everyone gets on board."

So far, ARCH has not been a big money-maker, according to Lazarus. The corporation has sold six product licenses for a total of about $250,000, not quite enough to cover expenses. But if one of the products should become commercially viable, he says, it could

Massey says the situation in science education today is different from that in 1957, when America embarked on a crash program to train more scientists after the Soviet Union launched *Sputnik 1*, the first artificial satellite. "Then we were primarily concerned with educating some exceptionally bright people," he says. "Now we're concerned with educating a broader group, and that's harder. We have to increase the number of minorities and women in science, if only because there aren't enough white males to do the job. At the time of *Sputnik*, you could design courses for the very good schools, but this time we really have to tackle the problem of inadequate schooling at a much broader level."

Massey has taken a particular interest in the AAAS Office of Opportunities in Science, which sponsors workshops in urban churches and community organizations to introduce black and Hispanic young people and their parents to careers in science. Massey speaks about twice a month to community, political, and scientific groups, making a persuasive case that young people should be encouraged to study science.

"You can't lose by studying science," he tells them. "No matter what you decide to do later in life, this kind of preparation will always be of value to you. What you learn as part of studying science and mathematics will give you a much broader base from which to do many other things." And a career in science, Massey adds, promises plenty of job opportunities, a good income, and security.

One of the most difficult barriers to overcome, Massey says, is the belief that scientists are all geniuses or oddballs who cannot relate to normal people. But scientists like to have fun, too. Massey's own life style bears that out.

He and his wife, Shirley, ski in New Mexico and Utah, ride their bicycles along Chicago's lakefront, play tennis, dine frequently in ethnic restaurants, and regularly attend concerts of the Chicago Symphony Orchestra. (He is a trustee of the Orchestral Association.) Massey also enjoys jazz and blues. A regular jogger until sidelined by a knee injury, Massey now does aerobic walking. His leisure reading ranges from history to science fiction; three of his favorite writers are Joseph Heller, Kurt Vonnegut, and Salman Rushdie.

Although Massey travels throughout the world for scientific conferences, he and his wife also travel abroad for pleasure: Their next trip will be to Greece. They often fly to Santa Fe, N. Mex., where their son Keith, 28, builds adobe houses. Their other son, Eric, 18, is a high school student.

"Scientists are normal people," Massey tells his audiences. "They have children. They play tennis.

"Science is fun, and it's 'do-able.' It's something that will really engage you and give you a great deal of satisfaction. Don't be afraid of it. It's not as intimidating as you might think.

"You can do it. *I've* done it. *I'm* not remarkable."

World Book Supplement

Revised articles reprinted from the 1989 edition of *The World Book Encyclopedia.*

© Catherine Ursillo, Photo Researchers

Fossils, such as these dinosaur skeletons, help museum visitors visualize ancient species. Scientists study fossils to learn about the development and ways of life of prehistoric organisms.

Fossil

Fossil is the mark or remains of a plant or animal that lived thousands or millions of years ago. Some fossils are leaves, shells, or skeletons that were preserved after a plant or animal died. Others are tracks or trails left by moving animals.

Most fossils are found in *sedimentary rocks.* These fossils formed from plant or animal remains that were quickly buried in *sediments*—the mud or sand that collects at the bottom of rivers, lakes, swamps, and oceans. After thousands of years, the weight of upper layers of sediment pressing down on the lower layers turned them into rock (see **Sedimentary rock**). A few fossils are whole plants or animals that have been preserved in ice, tar, or hardened sap.

The oldest fossils are microscopic traces of bacteria that scientists believe lived about $3\frac{1}{2}$ billion years ago. The oldest animal fossils are remains of *invertebrates* (animals without a backbone) estimated to be about 700 million years old. The oldest fossils of *vertebrates* (animals with a backbone) are fossil fish about 500 million years old.

Steven M. Stanley, the contributor of this article, is Professor of Earth and Planetary Sciences at The Johns Hopkins University. He has written several books on paleontology.

Fossils are more common and easier to find than many people realize. For example, fossils are plentiful in nearly every state in the United States. Even so, scientists believe that only a small portion of the countless plants and animals that have lived on earth have been preserved as fossils. Many species are thought to have lived and died without leaving any trace whatsoever in the fossil record.

Although the fossil record is incomplete, many important groups of animals and plants have left fossil remains. These fossils help scientists discover what forms of life existed at various periods in the past and how these prehistoric species lived. Fossils also indicate how life on earth has gradually changed over time. This article explains how fossils provide information on ancient life. For a description of animals of the past, see **Prehistoric animal;** for a description of early human beings, see **Prehistoric people.**

How fossils reveal the past

In the distant past, when most fossils formed, the world was different from today. Plants and animals that have long since vanished inhabited the waters and land. A region now covered with high mountains may have been the floor of an ancient sea. Where a lush tropical forest thrived millions of years ago, there may now be a cool, dry plain. Even the continents have drifted far from the positions they occupied hundreds of millions of years ago. No human beings were present to record these changes. But *paleontologists* (scientists who study prehistoric life) have pieced together much of the story of the earth's past by examining its fossil record.

Understanding ancient plants and animals. By studying fossils, paleontologists can learn a great deal about the appearance and ways of life of prehistoric organisms. One way paleontologists learn about a fossil animal or plant is by comparing it to living species. In many cases the comparisons show that the fossil species has close living relatives. Similarities and differences between the fossil species and its living relatives can provide important information. For example, fossils show that *Homo erectus*—a species that lived from $1\frac{1}{2}$ million to 300,000 years ago—was an ancient ancestor of modern human beings. Its fossilized pelvis, leg, and foot bones are similar in structure to modern human bones. Paleontologists know that the bones of modern humans are designed for walking upright. From this evidence, they have determined that *Homo erectus* also walked upright (see **Homo erectus**).

Fossil plants and animals that do not have close living relatives are more difficult to understand. One way to learn how they lived is to compare their fossils to unrelated living species that have similarly shaped structures. For example, fossils show that about 210 million to 63 million years ago there lived a group of reptiles with one long, slender finger extending from each front limb. This bone structure does not resemble that of any living reptile. It appears, however, similar to the wings of modern birds. Since modern birds use their wings for flying, paleontologists conclude that these ancient creatures also flew. Paleontologists call them *pterosaurs,* which means *winged lizards.*

The conditions under which fossil creatures died and were buried can also reveal how they lived. Paleontologists have found fossil nests of partially grown baby dinosaurs. These fossils indicate that certain species of dinosaurs fed and cared for their young in nests, much as today's birds do.

Fossils of tracks, trails, or burrows—called *trace fossils*—provide information on the behavior of prehistoric animals. Groups of dinosaur tracks, for example, suggest that some species of dinosaurs traveled in herds. Other trace fossils show that primitive worms lived in simple tubes dug in the sea floor.

Tracing the development of life. The fossil record provides important evidence of the history of life. Fossils indicate that over hundreds of millions of years life on earth has *evolved* (developed gradually) from simple, one-celled bacteria and algae into a tremendous variety of complex organisms. Fossils also indicate that certain species changed dramatically, giving rise to entirely new forms of life.

The location of fossils in the *strata* (layers) of sedimentary rock can show how living things increased in complexity through time. As sediment was deposited, new layers settled on top of older ones. When the sediment turned to stone, these layers were preserved in the order in which they were laid down. In undisturbed strata, fossils in the lower—and thus older—layers are more primitive than those in the younger strata found nearer the surface.

The fossils preserved in the strata of the Grand Canyon in Arizona provide a good example of the increasing complexity of living things. Strata near the bottom are about 1 billion years old and contain only primitive fossil algae. Strata dating from 600 million to 500 million years ago contain fossils of invertebrates, including those of extinct sea animals called *trilobites.* Remains of fish first appear in strata about 400 million years old. Some of the upper strata, which formed between 330 million and 260 million years ago, contain tracks of such early land animals as amphibians and small reptiles.

Certain fossils indicate that particular groups of plants or animals evolved from others. These *transition fossils* combine characteristics of two major groups. For example, fossil skeletons of *Ichthyostega,* a creature that lived about 360 million years ago, provide evidence that amphibians evolved from fish. Paleontologists classify

Donald Baird

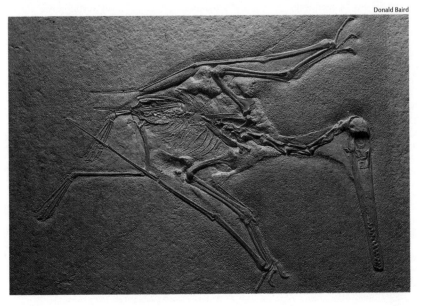

A fossil *Pterodactylus,* a type of pterosaur, provides information on the animal's behavior. The long, slender finger bones, which are similar to birds' wings, indicate that *Pterodactylus* flew. Its tapered snout and sharp teeth suggest that it fed on worms and other burrowing creatures, plucking them out of the earth as some modern birds do.

Tracing the history of life   In the Grand Canyon, many *strata* (layers) of sedimentary rock are exposed, *left.* Fossils in the strata show how living things increased in complexity over time. The oldest strata in the diagram at the right contain only simple fossil algae. Primitive sea animals—trilobites and brachiopods—appear in the next oldest strata. Younger strata, by contrast, contain fossils of more complex organisms, including traces of plants, fish, and reptiles.

Tom Algire, FPG

World Book diagram by Paul D. Turnbaugh

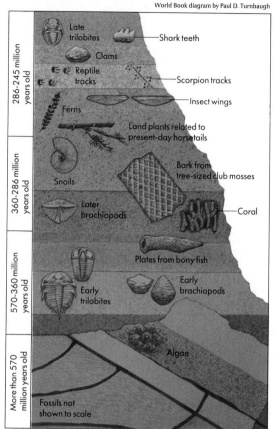

Ichthyostega as one of the first amphibians because it had legs and lungs, enabling it to live on land. *Ichthyostega's* leg bones, however, were similar to the fin bones of fish. It also had fishlike teeth and a broad, finned tail for swimming. Fossils indicate that later amphibians lost these fishlike traits and became better adapted to life on land.

Fossils also show how groups of plants and animals became more diverse after they originated. Fossil leaves and pollen grains of the first flowering plants date from the early Cretaceous Period, sometime after 138 million years ago. These fossils record only a small number of species. Fossils from the mid-Cretaceous, about 90 million years ago, include a wide variety of flowering plants from many different environments.

Recording changes in the earth. Paleontologists use fossils to determine how the earth's climate and landscape have changed over millions of years. For instance, they have found fossils of tropical palm trees in Wyoming, an area that has a cool climate today. These fossils indicate that the climate in that area has cooled. Paleontologists have found fossil oysters in Kansas and other areas that are far inland today. Such fossils reveal that a shallow sea once spread over these areas.

Fossils also provide evidence supporting the theory of *continental drift*—the idea that the positions of the continents have changed over hundreds of millions of years. Paleontologists have found similar kinds of fossil dinosaurs on all of the modern continents. It is unlikely that similar species could have evolved on separate continents. As a result, most earth scientists believe that when the dinosaurs first appeared—about 240 million years ago—nearly all the earth's land mass was united as

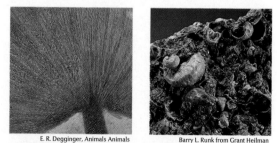

E. R. Degginger, Animals Animals

Barry L. Runk from Grant Heilman

Fossils reveal ancient environments. A fossil palm, *left,* suggests that Wyoming once had a tropical climate. Fossil oysters, *right,* indicate that a sea once covered part of Texas.

a single supercontinent. In contrast, fossils of mammals show complex differences from continent to continent. This indicates that after about 200 million years ago, when mammals were beginning to develop and spread, the supercontinent was breaking apart. The continents were drifting slowly to the positions they occupy today. See **Continental drift.**

How fossils form

The great majority of plants and animals die and decay without leaving any trace in the fossil record. Bacteria and other microorganisms break down such soft tissues as leaves or flesh. As a result, these tissues rarely leave fossil records. Even most hard parts, such as bones, teeth, shells, or wood, are eventually worn away by moving water or dissolved by chemicals. But when plant or animal remains have been buried in sediment, they may become fossilized. These remains are occasionally preserved without much change. Most, however, are altered after burial. Many disappear completely, but still leave a fossil record in the sediment.

Fossils may be preserved in several ways. The main processes of fossilization are (1) the formation of impressions, molds, and casts; (2) carbonization; and (3) the action of minerals.

Formation of impressions, molds, and casts. Some fossils consist of the preserved form or outline of animal or plant remains. Impressions, also called *prints* or *imprints,* are shallow fossil depressions in rock. They form when thin plant or animal parts are buried in sediment and then decay. After the sediment has turned to stone, only the outline of the plant or animal is preserved. Many impressions consist of small grooves left by the bones of fish or the thick-walled veins found inside leaves. Sometimes even delicate soft parts, such as feathers or leaves, are preserved as impressions.

Molds form after hard parts have been buried in mud, clay, or other material that turns to stone. Later, water dissolves the buried hard part, leaving a mold—a hollow space in the shape of the original hard part—inside the rock. A cast forms when water containing dissolved minerals and other fine particles later drains through a mold. The water deposits these substances, which eventually fill the mold, forming a copy of the original hard part. Many seashells are preserved as molds or casts.

Carbonization results when decaying tissues leave behind traces of carbon. Living tissues are made up of compounds of carbon and other chemical elements. As decaying tissues are broken down into their chemical parts, most of the chemicals disappear. In carbonization, a thin, black film of carbon remains in the shape of the organism. Plants, fish, and soft-bodied creatures have been preserved in precise detail by carbonization.

The action of minerals. Many plants and animals became fossilized after water that contained minerals soaked into the pores of the original hard parts. This action is called *petrifaction.* In many such fossils, some or all of the original material remains, but it has been strengthened and preserved by the minerals. This process is called *permineralization.* The huge tree trunks in the Petrified Forest of Arizona were preserved by permineralization.

In other cases, the minerals in the water totally re-

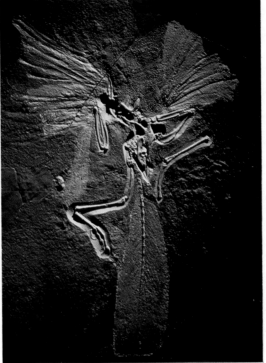

American Museum of Natural History

An impression of an archaeopteryx began to form when the bird was buried in soft silt. The silt turned to limestone, preserving the delicate outlines of the bird's wing and tail feathers.

American Museum of Natural History   Runk/Schoenberger from Grant Heilman

A mold preserved the three-dimensional form of a trilobite after its body decayed.

A carbonized fossil of a fern consists of traces of carbon in the shape of the leaf.

placed the original plant or animal part. This process, called *replacement,* involves two events that happen at the same time: The water dissolves the compounds that make up the original material, while the minerals are deposited in their place. Replacement can duplicate even microscopic details of the original hard part.

Other processes. Occasionally, animal and plant structures are fossilized with little or no change. In *mummification,* an animal's skin and other tissues are preserved by drying or by the action of chemicals. Mummification may occur when a dead animal is buried

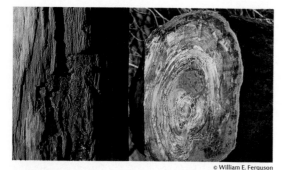

© William E. Ferguson

Petrified wood formed after dissolved minerals were deposited in the pores of dead tree trunks. The structure of the wood, including bark and growth rings, is visible in these specimens.

in a dry place, such as a desert, or in asphalt or some other oily substance.

Some processes fossilize whole animals. Insects sometimes are preserved whole in *amber,* the hardened sap of ancient pines or other trees. Such insects were trapped in the sticky sap and then sealed when it turned to amber. In Alaska and in Siberia, a region in northern Asia, woolly mammoths thousands of years old have been found frozen in the ground. Their hair, skin, flesh,

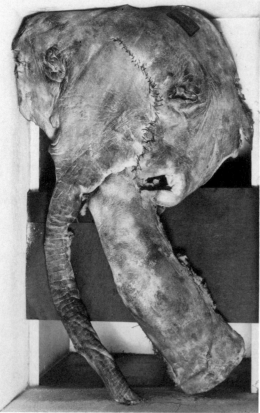

American Museum of Natural History

A baby woolly mammoth was unearthed from the frozen ground in Alaska. Scientists can learn a great deal from such frozen fossils because much of their tissue is preserved intact.

and internal organs have been preserved as they were when the mammoths died.

Studying fossils

Discovering fossils. Fossils can be found wherever sedimentary rocks are exposed. In moist regions, these rocks are usually buried under a layer of soil and plant life, but they become exposed by water erosion in river valleys. Sedimentary layers also become uncovered during highway construction and other building projects. In deserts and other arid regions, erosion exposes sedimentary rocks over broad areas. And oil-well drilling often brings up fossil-bearing sedimentary rocks from deep within the earth.

Paleontologists search in specific areas for particular types of fossils. In North America, for example, most fossil mammals are found west of the Mississippi River. Paleontologists hunt for fossil ancestors of human beings in eastern and southern Africa. Canada and Australia have deposits of well-preserved ancient marine invertebrates.

Collecting fossils. Different fossils require different collecting techniques. Fossils of shells, teeth, and bones preserved in soft sand or mud are easiest to collect. Paleontologists can dig out these fossils with a trowel or shovel or remove them by hand. Fossils preserved in hard rock are most easily found and collected when they have become exposed by natural *weathering.* Weathering refers to the chemical and physical processes that break down rock at the surface of the earth. Fossils that are more resistant to weathering than the surrounding rocks stand out on exposed rocky surfaces. Most such fossils can be collected by breaking loose the rock with a chisel, hammer, or pick. Paleontologists collect fossils that are hidden in solid rock by breaking the rock with a sledge hammer or a hammer and chisel. Rocks containing fossils often break along the surfaces of the fossils.

Fragile fossils must be protected before they are broken out of rock. Paleontologists wrap the exposed parts of such fossils in layers of cloth soaked with wet plaster. After the plaster hardens, the fossils can be safely chipped from the rock and transported to a laboratory, where the plaster is removed.

In the laboratory, paleontologists use electric grinding tools, fine picks, or even needles to remove any remaining rock. Fossils enclosed in limestone may be soaked in a weak acid solution, which dissolves the limestone but not the fossil. Paleontologists may decide to leave a fossil attractively exposed but still partly hidden in the rock.

Working with fragments. Many fossils are collected in fragments, which must be assembled like pieces of a jigsaw puzzle. In general, the first time a fossil species is reconstructed in this manner, the fragments must represent the complete specimen. Later reconstructions can be made from incomplete fragments by comparing them to the complete fossil and replacing the missing parts with artificial materials.

Vertebrate fossils can be reconstructed as *free mounts,* in which the skeleton seems to stand by itself. Paleontologists first make a small model of the finished skeleton. They then construct a framework of steel, plastic, or other strong material to support the skeleton. Fi-

© William E. Ferguson

Removing fossils from rock requires patience and the proper tools. The fossil collectors in the photo above employ hammers and chisels to chip huge dinosaur bones from an exposed rock wall. In the laboratory, *right,* a technician uses a small, handheld jackhammer called an *air scribe* to remove rock from fragile fossil fragments.

Albert Dickson

nally, they fasten the bones to the outside of the framework to hide it.

Classifying fossils. Like living plants and animals, fossil species are classified according to how closely related they are to one another. In general, scientists determine how closely related various species are by comparing their many biological features (see **Classification, Scientific**). For fossil groups, these features are primarily the shapes of hard parts, such as shells, teeth, and skeletons, because these are the features that are preserved. For example, paleontologists may look at skull shape and tooth size when determining the different species of saber-toothed cat.

Dating fossils. Through many years of research, paleontologists have come to understand the order in which most kinds of fossils occur in the geological record. When a fossil species is first discovered, it is usually found along with other species. If paleontologists know the position of the other species in the history of life, they can determine the position of the new species. This type of dating only indicates whether one fossil is older or younger than another fossil. It does not provide a fossil's age in years.

Paleontologists determine how old a fossil is by measuring the *radioactive isotopes* in the rocks that contain the fossil. Radioactive isotopes are forms of chemical elements that break down, or *decay,* to form other materials. Scientists know the rates of decay of various radioactive isotopes. By comparing the amount of a radioactive isotope in a rock to the amount of the material produced by its decay, scientists can calculate how long the decay has been taking place. This length of time represents the age of the rock and the fossils it contains.   Steven M. Stanley

Related articles in *World Book* include:

Andrews, Roy Chapman	Earth
Ant (picture: Fossils of ants)	Evolution
	Geology
Anthropology (picture)	Insect (picture: Fossil
Coal (picture:	imprint of a dragonfly)
Fossil ferns)	Osborn (Henry F.)
Cuvier, Baron	Paleontology
Dinosaur	Plant (Early plants)

Rock (Organic sediments)
Teilhard de Chardin, Pierre

Tree (Fossil trees; picture)

Outline

I. How fossils reveal the past
 A. Understanding ancient plants and animals
 B. Tracing the development of life
 C. Recording changes in the earth

II. How fossils form
 A. Formation of impressions, molds, and casts
 B. Carbonization
 C. The action of minerals
 D. Other processes

III. Studying fossils
 A. Discovering fossils
 B. Collecting fossils
 C. Working with fragments
 D. Classifying fossils
 E. Dating fossils

Questions

How are fossils formed by permineralization?
How do paleontologists remove fossils from rocks?
What are the oldest fossils?
How do fossils support the theory of continental drift?
What are trace fossils?
How do paleontologists date fossils?
Why do most fossils consist of preserved hard parts?
What is a free mount?
What do fossils reveal about the evolution of living things?
What features do paleontologists use in classifying fossil species?

Additional resources

Level I
Gallant, Roy A. *Fossils.* Watts, 1985.
Lauber, Patricia. *Dinosaurs Walked Here: And Other Stories Fossils Tell.* Bradbury, 1987.
Rhodes, Frank H., and others. *Fossils: A Guide to Prehistoric Life.* Golden Press, 1962.

Level II
Arduini, Paolo, and Teruzzi, Giorgio. *Simon & Schuster's Guide to Fossils.* Simon & Schuster, 1986.
Fortey, Richard A. *Fossils: The Key to the Past.* Van Nostrand, 1982.
MacFall, Russell P., and Wollin, J. C. *Fossils for Amateurs: A Guide to Collecting and Preparing Invertebrate Fossils.* 2nd ed. Van Nostrand, 1983.
Simpson, George G. *Fossils and the History of Life.* Scientific American Books, 1983.

Maps have many uses. For example, geologists, *top,* study maps of the earth's surface to find likely deposits of oil. A student may use a world map to learn where different countries are, *above left.* A navigator on an ocean freighter, *above right,* plots a course on a map called a *nautical chart.*

Map

Map is a drawn or printed representation of the earth or any other heavenly body. Most maps show part or all of the earth's surface. But maps also may show other planets, the moon, or the positions of stars in space. Most maps are flat, though some have raised surfaces. A globe is a map in the shape of a ball.

Maps express information through lines, colors, shapes, and other symbols. These symbols stand for such features as rivers, roads, and cities. The features represented on a map are greatly reduced in size. An inch (2.5 centimeters) on a map, for example, might represent a distance of 100 miles (160 kilometers).

We use maps to locate places, measure distances, plan trips, and find our way. Pilots of ships and airplanes use maps to navigate. Maps may also give us information about a place, such as its climate, population, and transportation routes. They can also show such patterns as where people live and how they use the land. We also use maps to make comparisons and draw conclusions. Geologists, for example, study maps of the earth's structure to help locate natural resources.

People probably made crude maps even before the development of written language some 5,500 years ago. Through the years, people have explored more of the world, adding new information to maps. Scientific discoveries have made maps more accurate. Today, most maps are based on photographs taken from the air. *Cartography* is the making and study of maps. Someone who makes or studies maps is a *cartographer.*

Types of maps

There are many kinds of maps. The most familiar types are (1) *general reference maps,* (2) *mobility maps,* (3) *thematic maps,* and (4) *inventory maps.*

General reference maps identify and locate a variety of geographic features. Such maps may include land features, bodies of water, political boundaries, cities and towns, roads, and many other elements. People use general reference maps to locate specific places and to observe their location in relation to other places. The maps of states, countries, and continents in atlases are examples of general reference maps. Maps that emphasize the boundaries of counties, states, countries, or other political units are called *political maps.* Maps that emphasize the location of such features of the earth's surface as mountains, rivers, and lakes are called *physical maps* or *terrain maps.*

Mobility maps are designed to help people find their way from one place to another. There are mobility maps for travel on land, on water, or in the air. A map used to navigate a ship or an airplane is called a *chart.*

Road maps are the most familiar kind of mobility map. Road maps represent different categories of roads, such as divided highways, four-lane roads, and scenic routes. They also show the cities, towns, state parks, and other places connected by those roads. Travelers use road maps to plan trips and follow lengthy routes.

Street maps are similar to road maps. But street maps show a much smaller area in much greater detail. People use street maps to find specific addresses and to plan and follow short routes.

Transit maps show the routes of buses, subways, and other systems of *mass transit* (public transportation in cities). Transit maps help people reach their destination by means of public transportation.

Aeronautical charts are maps used to navigate airplanes. Many pilots of small, low-flying aircraft plan and follow a course by using VFR (*v*isual *f*light *r*ules) charts. VFR charts show such landmarks as bridges, highways, railroad tracks, rivers, and towns. They also show the location of airports and the heights of mountains and

Map   371

other obstructions. Other pilots of low-flying planes—and all crews of high-flying aircraft—use IFR (*instrument flight rules*) charts, which are designed for radio navigation. IFR charts locate transmitters that beam very high frequency radio signals, which help airplane crews determine their position and course.

Nautical charts are maps used to navigate ships and boats. Nautical charts show water depths, lighthouses, buoys, islands, and such dangers as coral reefs and underwater mountains that come near the surface. They also locate the source of radio signals that navigators use to determine their course and position.

Thematic maps show the distribution of a particular feature such as population, rainfall, or a natural resource. They are used to study overall patterns. A thematic map might show, for example, where petroleum is produced in North America or how the average yearly rainfall varies from one part of Canada to another.

Many thematic maps express quantities by means of symbols or colors. For example, the *Population* map in the **Mexico** article in *World Book* uses tiny dots, each of which represents 25,000 people. The number of dots in an area shows how heavily settled that area is. The *Population density* map in the **Maryland** article, by contrast, uses color. In this map, shades of orange indicate four levels of population density.

Some thematic maps express quantities by using lines that pass through points of equal value. General terms for such lines include *isograms, isolines,* and *isarithms.*

Specific types of isograms have special names. On a weather map, for example, lines called *isobars* connect places that have the same air pressure (see **Isobar**). Isograms may also indicate temperatures, precipitation, and other measurements. On *topographic maps,* which show surface features of the land, isograms called *contour lines* are used to depict areas of equal elevation.

Some thematic maps use variations in size and shape to express quantities. A map of the international petroleum trade might indicate a large flow of oil with thick arrows and a small flow of oil with thin arrows.

Inventory maps, like thematic maps, concentrate on a specific feature. But unlike thematic maps, which show distributional patterns, inventory maps show the precise location of the specific feature. A map showing every building in a community is an example.

Reading a map

Using a map requires certain skills. To read a map, it is necessary to understand *map legends, scale, geographic grids,* and *map indexes.*

Map legends list and explain the symbols and colors on a map. Some map symbols resemble or suggest the features they represent. For example, a tree-shaped symbol may stand for a forest or an orchard. But many symbols have no resemblance to what they represent, as when a circle stands for a city. In addition, the same symbol may represent different features on different maps. A circle, for instance, may represent 20 mobile

Types of maps

Of the many types of maps, the most familiar are (1) general reference, (2) mobility, (3) thematic, and (4) inventory maps.

General reference maps, such as the one at the top left, show various geographic features. This example includes both land and political features.

Mobility maps, like the road map at the top right, help us find our way from one place to another.

Thematic maps, such as the population density map at the bottom left, show distribution patterns for a specific feature. In this map, darker colors indicate more populated areas.

Inventory maps, like the land use map at the bottom right, show the location of specific features. This map shows the location of forestlands in dark green, of croplands in light green, and of urban lands in tan.

WORLD BOOK maps

General reference map

Road map

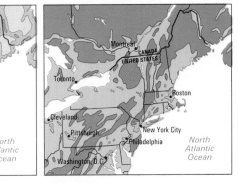

Population density map

Land use map

How to read a map

The illustrations on this page and the next demonstrate skills that are needed to read a map. They show how to use map legends and indexes, and they explain geographic grids and map scales.

Map legends A map legend explains what the symbols and colors on a map represent. The illustration below shows the complete legend and part of the political map from the **Washington** article. The white ovals have been added to the map to point out some of the features explained in the legend.

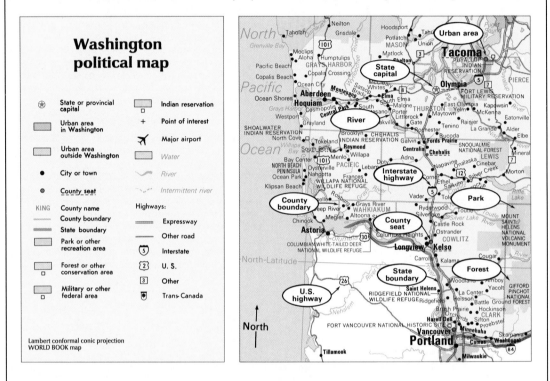

Washington political map

✪ State or provincial capital	▨ Indian reservation
▨ Urban area in Washington	+ Point of interest
▨ Urban area outside Washington	✈ Major airport
● City or town	▨ Water
◉ County seat	River
KING County name	Intermittent river
County boundary	Highways:
State boundary	Expressway
▨ Park or other recreation area	Other road
▨ Forest or other conservation area	⑤ Interstate
▨ Military or other federal area	② U.S.
	③ Other
	◈ Trans-Canada

Lambert conformal conic projection
WORLD BOOK map

Map indexes A map index helps us locate places. The example below, again taken from the **Washington** article, shows how to locate Walla Walla, Wash. The Walla Walla index entry is followed by the letter I and the number 14. This tells us that Walla Walla is found where row I and column 14 cross.

Washington map index (partial)

University Place*	20,381.	F	8
Urban	.C		7
Usk	.D		16
Utsalady	.F		2
Vader	406.	H	7
Valley	.D		15
Valley Ridge*	17,961.	E	8
Valleyford	.F		16
Vancouver	42,834°.	J	7
Vantage	.G		11
Van Zandt	.C		8
Vashon	.I		2
Vashon Heights	.I		2
Vaughn	.I		1
Veradale	7,256.	E	16
Verlot	.D		9
Wahkiacus	.I		10
Waitsburg	1,035.	I	14
Waldron	.C		7
Walla Walla	25,618.	I	14
Walla Walla East*	3,285.	I	14
Wallula	.I		13
Wapato	3,307.	H	11
Warden	1,479.	G	13
Washougal	3,834.	J	8
Washtucna	266.	G	14
Waterville	908°.	E	11
Wauconda	.C		13
Waukon	.F		15

Wenatchee	17,237°.	F	11
West Clarkston- [Highland]*	3,683.	H	16
West Federal Way*	16,872.	E	8
West Pasco*	5,729.	I	13
West Richland	2,938.	I	13
West Wenatchee*	2,187.	F	11
Westport	1,954.	G	5
Wheeler	.G		13
White Center [-Shorewood]*	19,362.	E	8
White Salmon	1,853.	I	9
White Swan	.H		10
Whites	.G		6
Wickersham	.C		8
Wilbur	1,122.	E	14
Wilkeson	321.	K	3
Willapa	.H		6
Wilson Creek	222.	F	13
Winchester	.F		12
Winlock	1,052.	H	7
Winona	.G		15
Winslow	2,196.	H	2
Winthrop	413.	C	11
Winton	.H		10
Wishram	.J		10
Withrow	.E		12
Woodinville	.H		3
Woodland	2,341.	J	7
Woodway*	832.	E	8
Yacolt	544.	J	8
Yakima	49,826°.	H	11
Yarrow Point	1,064.	H	3
Yelm	1,294.	G	7
Zenith [-Saltwater]*	8,982.	E	8
Zillah	1,599.	H	11

Map 373

Geographic grids   Geographic grids are networks of lines on a map that enable us to find and describe locations. The most common geographic grid uses east-west lines called *parallels,* or *lines of latitude,* and north-south lines called *meridians,* or *lines of longitude.* This network is known as the *graticule.*

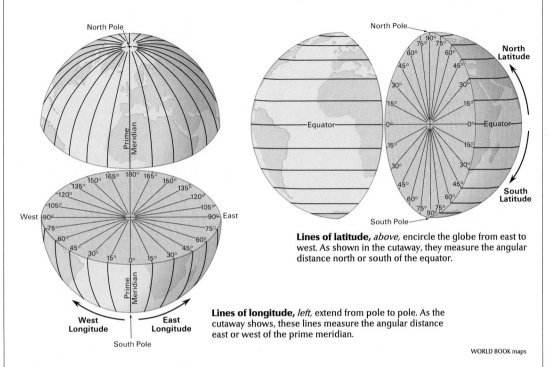

Lines of latitude, *above,* encircle the globe from east to west. As shown in the cutaway, they measure the angular distance north or south of the equator.

Lines of longitude, *left,* extend from pole to pole. As the cutaway shows, these lines measure the angular distance east or west of the prime meridian.

WORLD BOOK maps

Map scales   A map's scale shows the relationship between the distances on the map and on the earth's surface. The photos below show how to use a scale that marks off distances along a line.

Next place the paper along the map's scale, with the left mark at 0. If, as in this case, the scale is shorter than the distance, mark on the paper the end point of the scale and distance it represents—500 miles in this example.

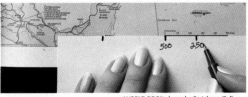

WORLD BOOK photos by Steinkamp/Ballogg

To find the distance between two points, such as Chicago and Montreal, first mark a piece of paper to show the distance between the two points on the map.

Then place the 500-mile mark at 0. The mark that represents Montreal is at about 250 on the scale. Thus, Chicago and Montreal lie about 500 plus 250, or 750, miles apart.

homes on one map and a petroleum deposit on another. It is important to read the map legend to find out exactly what the symbols mean.

Most maps are printed to show north at the top. Many map legends include an arrow that indicates which direction is north.

Scale. A map's scale shows the relationship between distances on the map and the corresponding distances on the earth's surface. Many maps show scale by marking off distances on a straight line. Each mark represents a certain number of miles or kilometers.

Other maps indicate scale in words and figures. For example, the scale might appear as "1 inch:15 statute miles." In other words, a distance of 1 inch on the map represents a distance of 15 miles on the earth's surface.

Another common method of expressing scale is by a *representative fraction,* such as "1:100,000" or "$\frac{1}{100,000}$." This means that a single unit of length on the map represents 100,000 of those units on the earth's surface. A centimeter on the map, for example, would represent 100,000 centimeters—1 kilometer—on the surface of the earth.

The amount of detail that a map can show depends on the scale chosen. A *large-scale* map would be chosen to show an area in great detail. Such a map has a large size relative to the area represented. It might have a scale in which 1 inch represents $\frac{1}{10}$ mile. A *small-scale* map, on the other hand, has a small size relative to the area represented and must leave out much detail. On such a map, 1 inch might represent 100 miles.

Geographic grids are networks of lines on maps that help us find and describe locations. The most common geographic grid uses east-west lines called *parallels* and north-south lines called *meridians.* The network of parallels and meridians is known as the *graticule.*

Parallels are lines that encircle the globe from east to west. The equator is the parallel that lies exactly halfway between the North Pole and the South Pole. Parallels are used to measure latitude—that is, the angular distance from the equator toward either pole. Latitude is measured in degrees of a circle. Any point on the equator has a latitude of zero degrees, written 0°. The North Pole has a latitude of 90° north and the South Pole a latitude of 90° south. Every other point on the earth has a latitude somewhere between 0° and 90°. Parallels are sometimes called *lines of latitude.* See **Equator; Latitude.**

Meridians are lines that extend halfway around the globe from the North Pole to the South Pole. By international agreement, mapmakers begin counting meridians from the line that passes through Greenwich, England, a borough of London. The Greenwich meridian is also known as the *prime meridian.* Meridians are used to measure longitude—that is, the angular distance east or west of the prime meridian. Like latitude, longitude is measured in degrees of a circle. Meridians, which are sometimes called *lines of longitude,* run from 0° at Greenwich to 180°. The 180° meridian lies halfway around the world from the prime meridian. Between the prime meridian and the 180° meridian are lines of west longitude (west of the prime meridian) and lines of east longitude (east of the prime meridian). See **Greenwich meridian; Longitude; Meridian.**

Longitude and latitude can be used to pinpoint any place on earth. For example, only one place can lie at 30° north latitude and 90° west longitude. An examination of a map of the United States reveals that this place is New Orleans, La.

Map indexes help us locate places on a map. A map index lists the features shown on a map in alphabetical order. In many atlases, each entry in the index is listed with its longitude and latitude. We can then use the longitude and latitude to find that feature on a map.

Many maps are divided into horizontal rows and vertical columns by an index grid. In most cases, letters along the sides of the map label the horizontal rows. Numbers across the top and bottom of the map label the vertical columns. Each entry in the map index is followed by a letter and a number corresponding to a row and a column on the map. The feature will be found where that row and column cross.

Map projections

Any system for transferring parallels and meridians from a globe onto a flat map is called a *projection.* Map-

Map projections

A map projection is a system for transferring the surface of the globe to a flat map. The maps at the bottom of the following panels show three common types of projections: cylindrical, conic, and azimuthal. The diagrams at the top of the panels show the relationship between the surface of the globe and that of the map.

Cylindrical projection

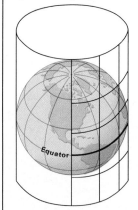

Cylindrical projections can be visualized by imagining a paper cylinder wrapped around an illuminated globe. The lines of the graticule would be projected onto the cylinder. The resulting map is free from distortion along the one or two lines where the cylinder touches the globe. But because the meridians do not meet at the poles, cylindrical projections seriously stretch regions near the poles.

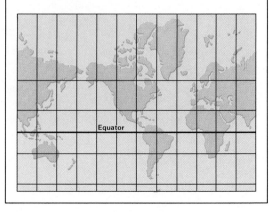

Map 375

makers create projections according to mathematical formulas, often with the aid of computers.

It is impossible to project a sphere, such as the earth's surface, onto a flat surface with complete accuracy. Every flat map has inaccuracies in scale that result from shrinking the globe in some places and stretching it in others to flatten it.

Some maps *distort* (show inaccurately) distances. On such maps, equal land areas may not appear of equal size. Many maps distort angles, resulting in misshapen seas and continents. Nearly all maps have one or two points or lines where there is no distortion. These are called *standard points* or *standard lines.* As we move away from them, the distortion of scale increases in a predictable way.

A map projection may be classified according to which properties of the globe it distorts least. *Equal-area projections* represent the sizes of regions in correct relation to one another but distort shapes. *Conformal projections* show angles and directions at any point accurately but distort size relationships. A map cannot be both equal-area and conformal, but many maps are neither. There is no name for this third category of projections classified by distortion.

A second way of classifying projections is according to the geometrical shape of the surface onto which the projection is drawn. Many maps are—in theory—projections onto a cylinder, a cone, or a plane.

Cylindrical projections are projections of the globe onto a cylinder. Although constructed by mathematical formulas, such projections can be visualized by imagining a paper cylinder wrapped around an illuminated globe. Lines from the globe would be projected onto the cylinder, which would then be slit and unrolled. The resulting map has one or two lines that are free from distortion. They occur where the cylinder touches the globe. On a cylindrical projection, all meridians will appear parallel on the map. The meridians thus fail to meet at the poles. As a result, such a map seriously stretches regions near the poles. Greenland, for example, will appear wider than South America, though it is actually much narrower.

The most famous cylindrical projection is the *Mercator projection.* This conformal projection is useful to navigators because a straight line drawn between any two points on the map provides a route that can be followed without changing compass direction.

Conic projections are projections of a globe onto a cone. To visualize a conic projection, imagine a paper cone with its open end resting over part of an illuminated globe. Lines from the globe would be projected onto the cone, which would then be slit and unrolled. If the point of the cone lies directly above one of the poles, the meridians are projected as straight lines radiating from the pole. The parallels appear as portions of a circle.

Conic projection

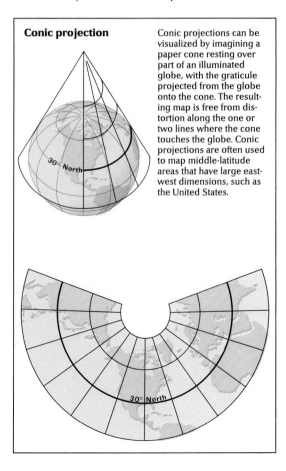

Conic projections can be visualized by imagining a paper cone resting over part of an illuminated globe, with the graticule projected from the globe onto the cone. The resulting map is free from distortion along the one or two lines where the cone touches the globe. Conic projections are often used to map middle-latitude areas that have large east-west dimensions, such as the United States.

Azimuthal projection

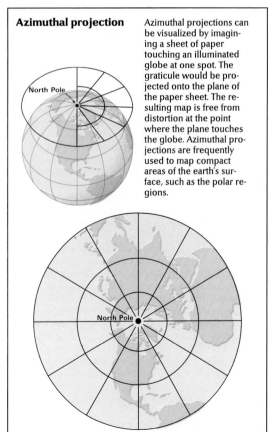

Azimuthal projections can be visualized by imagining a sheet of paper touching an illuminated globe at one spot. The graticule would be projected onto the plane of the paper sheet. The resulting map is free from distortion at the point where the plane touches the globe. Azimuthal projections are frequently used to map compact areas of the earth's surface, such as the polar regions.

One or two lines free from distortion occur where the cone touches the surface of the globe. With its point over a pole, the cone touches the globe at the middle latitudes. Therefore, such conic projections are commonly used to map middle-latitude areas with large east-west dimensions, such as the United States and the Soviet Union. Some conic projections combine slices from several cones to increase accuracy.

Azimuthal projections are projections of a globe onto a plane. To visualize an azimuthal projection, imagine a sheet of paper touching an illuminated globe at one spot. The lines of the globe would be projected onto the sheet. The point on the map projection where the plane touches the globe is free from distortion. Cartographers can also draw azimuthal projections in which the plane theoretically slices through the globe. On these projections, the circular line where the plane intersects the globe is free from distortion.

Azimuthal projections are used most commonly to map compact areas of the earth's surface, such as the polar regions. One type of azimuthal projection, called a *gnomonic projection,* shows the shortest distance between any two points on the earth as a straight line. This distance is known as a *great-circle route* (see **Great-circle route**). Gnomonic projections are especially useful for planning intercontinental flights.

Other projections. Several useful projections are not based on the cylinder, cone, or plane. For example, projections that are oval in shape fall into a different category. Equal-area oval projections have little distortion along the equator and along the meridian that runs through their center. Mapmakers can achieve even less distortion by splitting the oval into several arching shapes.

How maps are made

Experts from many fields gather the information that cartographers need. The cartographer then transforms this information into a meaningful visual representation. In general, mapmaking follows these steps: (1) observation and measurement, (2) planning and design, (3) drawing and reproduction, and (4) revision.

Observation and measurement. A variety of experts obtain the information shown on maps. The *geodesist* provides precise measurements of the earth's size and shape. The *surveyor* works out the location and boundaries of places by measuring distances, angles, and elevations. The *photogrammetrist* obtains measurements from aerial photographs. Some of the other specialists who contribute information include census takers, geographers, geologists, and meteorologists.

The production of new maps based on aerial photographs and other original surveys is called *base mapping.* Most maps made by base mapping are topographic maps that are large in scale and include much detail. They become the basis for many other maps made by the process of *compilation mapping.* Compilation mapping involves selecting information from large-scale maps and displaying it on a map at a smaller scale. Cartographers may also *compile* (collect) information from censuses and other sources for presentation on the finished map.

Planning and design. In planning a map, the cartographer considers the map's purpose and its likely users.

This information helps the cartographer decide which map projection and scale to use and which information to highlight or eliminate. The map's design helps communicate information effectively. In designing a map, the cartographer selects suitable symbols, writes titles and labels, and chooses lettering. In many cases, a graphic artist helps the cartographer design a map.

Drawing and reproduction. Maps may be drawn in several ways. Cartographers sometimes draw a map directly on paper or plastic drafting film. More commonly, however, they use a technique called *scribing.* In scribing, the mapmaker uses special tools to cut away the colored surface coating on a sheet of clear plastic. Lines and areas of the clear plastic are thereby exposed. These lines and areas correspond to lines and areas to be printed in ink on the map. Scribing produces maps with sharp, fine lines that would be difficult to achieve by the direct drawing method.

Cartographers today increasingly use computers to draw maps. A device called a *plotter,* which attaches to a computer, produces maps by scribing or by drawing with pen and ink. Computers can also use a beam of light from a laser to plot maps by exposing areas of photographic film. In addition, computers can scan base maps, aerial photographs, or actual physical surfaces and then use the data to print a map.

Cartographers often supervise the reproduction of maps so that the correct colors and symbols appear in the proper place on the final map. Most paper maps are printed from printing plates.

Additional steps are needed to produce maps that have a raised surface. These maps include *raised relief maps,* which have elevated surfaces to represent hills

Chicago Aerial Survey, Inc.

A cartographer scribes a map by cutting away the colored surface coating from a sheet of plastic. The scribed sheet is then used to make a printing plate. The clear areas on the sheet correspond to the areas that will print in ink on the finished map.

Map   377

NASA

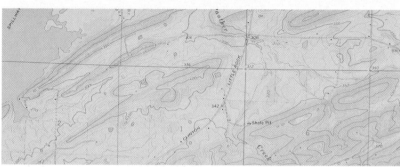

U.S. Geological Survey

Contour mapping begins with aerial photography. This photograph, *top,* shows the landscape around Hamlet, Ark., including hills and part of a lake, *upper left.* A machine called a *stereoplanigraph* traces the contours of the landscape from the photo onto a sheet of paper. The resulting contour map, *bottom,* shows elevations at regular intervals.

and mountains, and *tactual maps,* which have raised symbols that blind people can read by touch. To make such maps, cartographers first build a three-dimensional model of the map's raised surface, using plaster or a similar material. Next, the map's symbols and letter-

Chicago Aerial Survey, Inc.

A pen-and-ink plotter, *above,* uses information stored in a computer to draw contour lines on a topographic map. Other plotters can scribe maps according to computer data. Computer-linked plotters have become increasingly common.

ing are printed on a flat plastic sheet. The plastic sheet is then softened by heating, molded to the shape of the three-dimensional model, and hardened.

Revision. Cartographers must revise maps to keep them up to date. For example, changes in the population of cities, the shape of waterways, or the area of forests may require revisions on maps. Aerial photographs are commonly used to survey changes that have occurred since the map was last revised.

History

Ancient maps. The oldest existing map appears on a clay tablet made in Babylonia (now part of Iraq) around 2500 B.C. This map seems to show a settlement in a mountain-lined river valley. The Babylonians had a lasting influence on mapmaking. They developed the system of dividing a circle into 360 equal parts called degrees. We use this system to measure latitude and longitude.

The Egyptians made maps as early as 1300 B.C. They developed techniques of surveying, probably to remap property boundaries each year after the Nile River flooded its banks.

The Greeks made great advances in geometry and surveying, and they developed systems of map projection. The Greeks also speculated about the size and shape of the earth. Many of them believed it was a sphere. The Greek mathematician Eratosthenes calculated the circumference of the earth with remarkable accuracy around 250 B.C.

The most influential mapmaker of ancient times was probably Claudius Ptolemy, a Greek astronomer and geographer who worked in Alexandria, Egypt, around A.D. 150. Ptolemy brought together what was known about the world in his eight-volume *Geography.* It included maps and a list of about 8,000 places along with their latitude and longitude. Ptolemy also provided instructions for various systems of map projection.

Maps in the Middle Ages. Little scientific progress occurred in European mapmaking during most of the Middle Ages, the period that lasted from about 400 to the late 1400's. During the 1300's, however, European mapmakers began producing *portolan charts,* a group of maps notable for their accuracy. These navigation aids showed the coastline of the Mediterranean Sea and nearby regions in great detail. Lines across the map helped sailors determine compass directions.

During the Middle Ages, progress in mapmaking occurred mainly in the Arab world and China. Arab scholars developed methods of determining latitude and longitude after Ptolemy's *Geography* was translated into Arabic in the 800's. The earliest known printed map appeared in a Chinese encyclopedia around 1155, more than 300 years before printed maps were produced in Europe.

Advances in European cartography followed several developments of the 1400's. First, the translation of Ptolemy's works into Latin led to the rediscovery of his methods of map projection and of locating places systematically. Second, the invention of the printing press in the mid-1400's made maps more widely available. Many identical copies could be produced by printing maps instead of copying them by hand. Third, an age of exploration opened in the late 1400's, which increased knowledge of the world and interest in mapmaking.

By the late 1400's, educated Europeans had accepted the idea that the world is round. In 1492, the year that Christopher Columbus discovered the New World, a German merchant and navigator named Martin Behaim produced a globe that recorded the world as Europeans knew it before Columbus' voyage. Behaim's globe lacked the Americas, of course, and it depicted the Atlantic Ocean as much smaller than it actually is. By the early 1500's, mapmakers had begun including the New World on their maps. The name *America* first appeared

Harvard Semitic Museum

The oldest map known is a clay tablet found in Iraq. Made about 2500 B.C., it probably shows a settlement in a valley.

on a map produced in 1507 by a German cartographer, Martin Waldseemüller.

In 1569, Flemish geographer Gerardus Mercator published the first map based on his Mercator projection, which was of great value to sailors. The first collection of maps made specifically to be combined into an atlas was produced by the Flemish mapmaker Abraham Ortelius in 1570.

Scientific activity during the 1500's, 1600's, and 1700's produced new instruments and techniques that made measurements of location and elevation more accurate. Jean-Domenique Cassini, an astronomer at the Paris Observatory, began the detailed and accurate mapping of France's *topography* (surface features) in the late 1600's. That work continued for more than 100 years. In England, the astronomer Edmond Halley published a map of

From Ptolemy's *Geography,* published in Ulm by Leinhart Holle, 1482, Library of Congress

A map of the world formed part of Ptolemy's eight-book *Geography.* Ptolemy was a Greek geographer and astronomer who lived about A.D. 150. Few people knew about his maps until they were printed in an atlas in the late 1400's. The map at the left is from an edition of *Geography* published in 1482.

Map   379

the trade winds in 1686, which is considered the first *meteorological* (weather) map. Halley's map of the earth's magnetic fields in 1700 was the first published map that used isograms to connect points of equal value.

Mapping the New World. During the 1600's and 1700's, the colonization of the New World created a need for many new maps. The Spanish surveyed and mapped land under their control. In 1612, the English adventurer Captain John Smith published a map of Virginia's coastline. Smith also made the first English map of New England. During the early 1600's, the French explorer Samuel de Champlain mapped the region from Maryland to the St. Lawrence River in Canada.

Surveying was an important activity in the American Colonies. Surveyors Joshua Fry and Peter Jefferson published a map of the region from Virginia to the Great Lakes in 1751. In 1755, John Mitchell, a Virginia colonist, published his *Map of the British and French Dominions in America.* A copy of this map was used to mark the boundaries of the United States of America after the Revolutionary War ended in 1783.

As the pioneers moved westward during the 1800's, explorers and army engineers mapped trails and surveyed government lands. The United States government eventually established two agencies with responsibility for detailed, large-scale mapping. The Survey of the Coast—now the National Ocean Survey—was founded in 1807. The U.S. Geological Survey was officially created in 1879.

The development of thematic mapping. By the 1800's, the systematic collection of data through censuses had become common. Cartographers then created thematic maps to display and study this wealth of new information. The British cartographer Henry D. Harness advanced thematic mapping with several maps of Ireland published in 1837. Those maps used tones to indicate population density, black circles of different sizes to show the populations of cities, and lines of different thickness to represent traffic flow.

In 1855, John Snow, an English physician, dramatically demonstrated the value of thematic mapping for scientific research. On a map of London neighborhoods, Snow used a dot to represent each person who had died of cholera during an epidemic that year. A large number of dots clustered around a water pump on Broad Street helped locate the source of the infection.

Mapmaking and modern technology. During the 1900's, improvements in printing and photography have made it cheaper and easier to produce maps. Maps became more widespread as a result. The development of the airplane during the early 1900's made aeronautical charts necessary. Airplanes also made it possible to photograph large areas from the air.

Since the mid-1900's, the use of computers in mapmaking has increased greatly. Computers store, sort, and arrange data for mapping. They create map projections and control plotters that draw or scribe maps. The computer may even draw the map directly on its display monitor.

Space exploration also has contributed many devices to mapmaking and has furthered the mapping of moons, other planets, and the vast reaches of space. Artificial satellites carry *remote sensing devices* that send a variety of signals back to earth. These signals can be used in mapping landforms, mineral deposits, patterns of vegetation growth, environmental pollution, and other subjects.   Judy M. Olson

Related articles in *World Book.* See the maps with the state, province, country, and continent articles. See also the following articles:

Airplane (Flight navigation)	Mercator, Gerardus
Atlas	Meridian
Azimuth	Navigation
Colonial life in America	Photogrammetry
(map: "The Duke's Plan	Plane table
of 1661")	Radar (Pulse radar;
Geodesy	picture: Radar mapping)
Geography	Surveying
Globe	Topography
Greenwich meridian	Weather (Making a
International date line	weather map; map)
Isobar	World, History of the
Isotherm	(picture: An atlas
Latitude	printed in 1547)
Longitude	

Outline

I. **Types of maps**
   A. General reference maps
   B. Mobility maps
   C. Thematic maps
   D. Inventory maps
II. **Reading a map**
   A. Map legends
   B. Scale
   C. Geographic grids
   D. Map indexes
III. **Map projections**
   A. Cylindrical projections
   B. Conic projections
   C. Azimuthal projections
   D. Other projections
IV. **How maps are made**
   A. Observation and measurement
   B. Planning and design
   C. Drawing and reproduction
   D. Revision
V. **History**

Questions

How do general reference maps differ from thematic maps?
What does a map's scale show?
What three developments of the 1400's advanced European mapmaking?
Why do all flat maps have inaccuracies in scale?
Which parallel lies exactly halfway between the North Pole and the South Pole?
What information do geodesists, surveyors, and photogrammetrists obtain for mapmakers?
What is a *map projection*?
How are computers used in mapmaking?
What does a *gnomonic projection* show?
How did air travel affect mapmaking during the early 1900's?

Additional resources

Level I
Baynes, John. *How Maps Are Made.* Facts on File, 1987.
Carey, Helen H. *How to Use Maps and Globes.* Watts, 1983.

Level II
Blandford, Percy W. *Maps & Compasses: A User's Handbook.* TAB, 1984.
Greenhood, David. *Mapping.* Rev. ed. Univ. of Chicago Press, 1964.
Robinson, Arthur H., and others. *Elements of Cartography.* 5th ed. Wiley, 1984.
Wilford, John N. *The Mapmakers.* Knopf, 1981. A history of maps from the earliest to the present day.

© Henry Ausloos, Animals Animals   © Jane Shaw, Bruce Coleman Inc.

Ecology is the study of living things and how they interact with one another and with the nonliving elements of their environment. Ecologists study these relationships wherever life is found—from the savannas of Africa, *above left,* to the coral reefs of the tropical oceans, *above right.*

Ecology

Ecology, *EE KAHL uh jee,* is the branch of science that deals with the relationships living things have to each other and to their environment. Scientists who study these relationships are called *ecologists.*

The world includes a tremendous variety of living things, from complex plants and animals to simpler organisms, such as fungi, amebas, and bacteria. But whether large or small, simple or complex, no organism lives alone. Each depends in some way upon other living and nonliving things in its surroundings. For example, a moose must have certain plants for food. If the plants in its environment were destroyed, the moose would have to move to another area or starve to death. In turn, plants depend upon such animals as moose for the *nutrients* (nourishing substances) they need to live. Animal wastes and the decay of dead animals and plants provide many of the nutrients plants need.

The study of ecology increases our understanding of the world and its life. This is important because our survival and well-being depend on ecological relationships throughout the world. Even changes in distant parts of the world and its atmosphere affect us and our environment.

Although ecology is considered a branch of biology, ecologists use knowledge from many disciplines, including chemistry, physics, mathematics, and computer science. They also rely on such fields as climatology, geology, meteorology, and oceanography to learn about air, land, and water environments and their interactions. This multidisciplinary approach helps ecologists understand how the physical environment affects living things. It also aids them in assessing the impact of environmental problems, such as acid rain or the greenhouse effect (see **Acid rain; Greenhouse effect**).

Ecologists study the organization of the natural world on three main levels: (1) populations, (2) communities, and (3) ecosystems. They analyze the structures, activities, and changes that take place within and among these levels. Ecologists normally work out of doors, studying the operations of the natural world. They often conduct field work in isolated areas, such as islands, where the relationships among the plants and animals may be simpler and easier to understand. For example, the ecology of Isle Royale, an island in Lake Superior, has been extensively studied. Many ecological studies focus on solving practical problems. For example, ecologists search for ways to curb the harmful effects of air and water pollution on living things.

Populations

A population is a group of the same species that lives in an area at the same time. For example, all the moose on Isle Royale make up a population, as do all the spruce trees. Ecologists determine and analyze the number and growth of populations.

Factors that control populations. The size of any particular population depends upon the interaction of two basic forces. One is the rate at which the population would grow under the best possible conditions. The second is the combined effect of all the less-than-ideal environmental factors that limit growth. Such limiting factors may include low food supply, predators, competition with organisms of the same or different species, climate, and disease.

The largest size of a particular population that can be supported by a particular environment has been called the environment's *carrying capacity* for that species. Real populations normally are much smaller than their environment's carrying capacity for them because of the effects of adverse weather, a poor breeding season, hunting by predators, or other factors.

Factors that change populations. Population levels of a species can change considerably over time. Sometimes these changes result from natural events. For example, a change in rainfall may cause some populations to increase and others to decrease. Or the introduction of a new disease can severely decrease the population of a particular plant or animal species. In other cases, the changes may result from human activities. For instance, power plants and automobiles release acidic gases into the atmosphere, where they may mix with clouds and fall to earth as acid rain. In some regions that receive large amounts of acid rain, fish populations have declined dramatically.

Communities

A community is a group of animal and plant populations living together in the same environment. Wolves, moose, beavers, and spruce and birch trees are some of the populations that make up the forest community of Isle Royale. Ecologists study the roles different species play in their communities. They also study the different types of communities, and how they change. Some communities, such as an isolated forest or meadow, can be identified easily. But others are more difficult to define.

A community of plants and animals that covers a large geographical area is called a *biome.* The boundaries of different biomes are determined mainly by climate. The major biomes in the world include deserts, forests, grasslands, tundra, and several types of aquatic biomes. See **Biome.**

The role of a species in its community is called its *ecological niche.* A niche consists of all the factors that relate to a species' existence. It includes such factors as what the species eats or uses for energy; what predators it has; the amounts of heat, light, or moisture it needs; and the conditions under which it reproduces. Ecologists have long noted that many species occupy a highly specialized niche in a given community. Various explanations have been proposed for this. Some ecologists feel that it results from competition—that if two species try to "fill" the same "niche," then competition for limited resources will force one of the species out of the community. Other ecologists maintain that a species that occupies a highly specialized niche does so because of the rigid physiological demands of that particular role in the community. In other words, only one species occupies the niche not because it has out-competed other species, but because it is the only member of the community physiologically capable of playing that role.

Changes in communities occur over time in a process called *ecological succession.* This process occurs as a series of slow, generally orderly changes in the number and kinds of organisms that live in an area take place. Differences in the intensity of sunlight, protection from wind, and changes in the soil may alter the kinds of organisms that live in an area. These changes may also alter the number of populations that make up the community. Then, as the number and kinds of species change, the physical and chemical characteristics of the area undergo further changes. Eventually, the area may reach a relatively stable condition called the *climax community,* which may last hundreds or even thousands of years. However, the forces of nature ultimately cause even climax communities to change.

Ecologists distinguish two types of succession—primary and secondary. In *primary succession,* organisms begin to inhabit an area that had no life, such as a new island formed by a volcanic eruption. *Secondary succession* takes place after an existing community suffers a major disruption—for example, after a climax forest community is destroyed by fire. In this example, a meadow community of wild flowers and grasses will grow first, followed by a community of shrubs. Finally trees will reappear, and the area will eventually become a forest again (see **Forest** [Forest succession]).

Ecosystems

An ecosystem is the most complex level of organization in nature. It is made up of a community and its *abiotic* (nonliving or physical) environment, including climate, soil, water, air, nutrients, and energy. Ecologists who try to link together the many different physical and biological activities in an environment are called *systems ecologists.* Their studies often focus on the flow of energy and the cycling of materials through an ecosystem. Sometimes they use powerful computers to help understand the data obtained from field research.

Energy flow. Ecologists categorize the elements that make up or affect an ecosystem into six main parts, based on the flow of energy and nutrients through the system: (1) the sun, (2) abiotic substances, (3) primary producers, (4) primary consumers, (5) secondary consumers, and (6) decomposers. A simplified ecosystem is diagramed in this article.

The sun provides the energy that *primary producers* need to make food. Primary producers consist mainly of green plants, such as grass and trees, which make food by the process of photosynthesis (see **Photosynthesis**). Plants also need *abiotic substances,* such as phosphorus and water, to grow. *Primary consumers* include mice, rabbits, grasshoppers, and other plant-eating animals. Foxes, skunks, and other *secondary consumers*—or predators—eat animals. *Decomposers,* such as bacteria and fungi, break down dead plants and animals into simple nutrients. The nutrients go back into the soil and are used again by plants.

The series of stages energy goes through in the form of food is called a *food chain.* A simple food chain would be one in which grass is the primary producer. A primary consumer, such as a rabbit, eats the grass. The rabbit, in turn, may be eaten by a secondary consumer, such as a fox or a hawk. Decomposing bacteria break down the uneaten remains of dead grass, rabbits, foxes, and hawks, as well as the body wastes produced by the animals in the food chain. One of the food chains on Isle Royale has trees as the primary producers, moose as the primary consumers, and wolves as the secondary consumers.

Most ecosystems have a variety of producers, consumers, and decomposers, which form an overlapping network of food chains called a *food web.* Food webs seem especially complex in many tropical and oceanic ecosystems.

Some species eat many things, but others have very specific food requirements. Some primary consumers, for example, eat only one type of plant. If that plant species disappears from the ecosystem, so does the animal that eats it.

Energy moves through an ecosystem in a series of transformations. First, primary producers change the light energy of the sun into chemical energy that is stored in plant *protoplasm* (cell material). The energy stored in plants is then transferred to other organisms in the form of food. Primary consumers change it to a different kind of chemical energy and store it in their body cells. This energy changes again when the secondary consumer eats the primary consumer.

Most organisms have a low *ecological efficiency.* This means they are able to convert only a small fraction of the available energy into stored chemical energy. For example, green plants can change only about 0.1 to 1 per cent of the solar energy that reaches them into plant protoplasm. Most of the remaining energy is burned up during plant growth and escapes into the environment as heat. Similarly, *herbivores* (plant-eating animals) and *carnivores* (meat-eating animals) convert into their own body cells only about 10 to 20 per cent of the energy produced by their food.

Because so much energy escapes as heat at each step of the food chain, all ecosystems develop a *pyramid of energy.* Plants (primary producers) form the base of this pyramid. Herbivores (primary consumers) make up the next step, and carnivores (secondary consumers) form the top. The pyramid reflects the fact that more energy passes through the plants of the ecosystem than

through the herbivores, and even less energy flows through the carnivores. In many land ecosystems, the pyramid of energy results in a *pyramid of biomass.* This simply means that the combined *biomass* (weight) of the plants is greater than the combined weight of the herbivores, which in turn exceeds the total weight of the carnivores.

Ecologists have collected information on a pyramid of biomass on Isle Royale. They studied the relationship in the pyramid among plants, moose, and wolves. In one study, ecologists found that it takes 762 pounds (346 kilograms) of plant food to support 59 pounds (27 kilograms) of moose. This is the amount of moose needed to support 1 pound (0.45 kilogram) of wolf.

Cycling of materials. All living things are composed of certain chemical elements and compounds. Chief among these are water, carbon, hydrogen, nitrogen, oxygen, phosphorus, and sulfur. All of these materials cycle through ecosystems again and again.

The cycling of phosphorus provides an example of this process. All organisms require phosphorus. Plants take up phosphorus compounds from the soil, and animals get phosphorus from the plants or other animals they eat. Decomposers return phosphorus to the soil after plants and animals die.

In natural, undisturbed ecosystems, the amount of phosphorus remains fairly constant. But when an

WORLD BOOK diagram by George Suyeoka

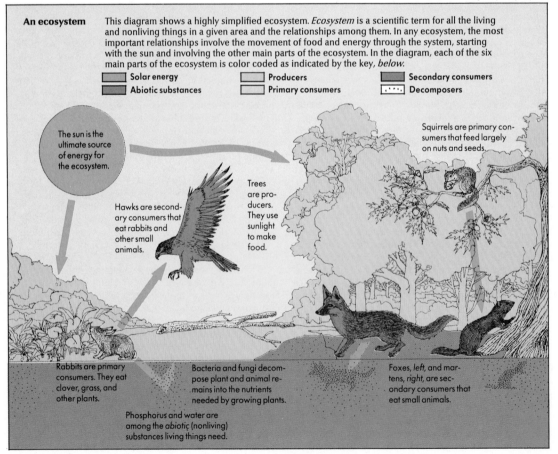

An ecosystem This diagram shows a highly simplified ecosystem. *Ecosystem* is a scientific term for all the living and nonliving things in a given area and the relationships among them. In any ecosystem, the most important relationships involve the movement of food and energy through the system, starting with the sun and involving the other main parts of the ecosystem. In the diagram, each of the six main parts of the ecosystem is color coded as indicated by the key, *below.*

Solar energy   Producers   Secondary consumers
Abiotic substances   Primary consumers   Decomposers

The sun is the ultimate source of energy for the ecosystem.

Squirrels are primary consumers that feed largely on nuts and seeds.

Trees are producers. They use sunlight to make food.

Hawks are secondary consumers that eat rabbits and other small animals.

Rabbits are primary consumers. They eat clover, grass, and other plants.

Bacteria and fungi decompose plant and animal remains into the nutrients needed by growing plants.

Foxes, *left,* and martens, *right,* are secondary consumers that eat small animals.

Phosphorus and water are among the *abiotic* (nonliving) substances living things need.

ecosystem is disturbed by human activity, the phosphorus often "leaks out," reducing the ability of the ecosystem to support plants. One way people alter the phosphorus cycle is by replacing forests with farmland. Without the protection of the forests, phosphorus is eroded from the soil and swept away into rivers and lakes. There, it often causes undesirable excess growth of algae. Eventually, the phosphorus becomes locked in sediments at the bottom of lakes or the sea. Because of this loss of phosphorus, farmers must use costly fertilizers to put the element back into the soil.

Changes in ecosystems occur daily, seasonally, and, as in the case of ecological succession, over periods of many years. Sometimes changes take place severely and abruptly, as when a fire sweeps through a forest or a hurricane batters a seashore. But most of the day-to-day changes, especially in the nutrient cycles, are so subtle that ecosystems tend to appear stable. This apparent stability among plants and animals and their environment has been called the "balance of nature." In the past, this concept of balanced, largely unchanging ecosystems was thought to be especially descriptive of climax communities. But these earlier views were based on short-term studies. Now that ecologists have had an opportunity to study ecosystems over longer periods, they have had to alter some of their ideas.

Conclusions based on population studies from Isle Royale point out some of this change in thinking. For a long time, Isle Royale had neither moose nor wolf populations. Then, the first moose swam to the island in about 1900. By 1930, ecologists estimated that the moose population had reached about 3,000. There was evidence that the moose were eating a large proportion of the plants on the island. In 1933, the moose began to die of starvation. Ecologists had predicted this decline because they understood the food relationship between the moose and plants.

The moose population increased again between 1948 and 1950. But about this time, wolves made their way to the island. As they killed the moose for food, the wolf population grew. Eventually, an apparently stable balance of about 600 moose and 20 wolves became established. Ecologists pointed to Isle Royale as an example of the way in which predators can control prey and thus contribute to the development of stability in ecosystems.

But beginning in the mid-1960's, the moose and wolf populations began to fluctuate. The apparently stable system, in which predators controlled their prey, turned out to be more complex. Ecologists now recognize that the original predator control theory was based on incomplete data. During the 1950's, when it looked as if wolves were controlling the moose, the winters were characterized by an unusual pattern of deep snows followed by rain and then a hard freeze. This resulted in snow with a hard crust. Wolves could run easily on the surface of this snow, but the heavier bodied moose broke through the crust. The moose could not, therefore, easily escape from wolves, nor could they effectively use their sharp, powerful hooves to defend themselves. Under these conditions, the wolves could easily kill moose.

Around 1965, winters on Isle Royale returned to normal, and the wolves caught fewer moose. By the early 1980's, the moose population had again become very large, even though the wolf population had also grown. Then the wolf population began to decline, despite the abundance of moose. By the late 1980's, ecologists feared that wolves might disappear completely from Isle Royale. All of these population changes forced ecologists to reevaluate their thinking about how predators and prey control one another's populations. Ecologists now recognize that although wolves and moose certainly can influence the size of each other's populations, they can completely determine one another's population size only under unusual circumstances.

Further ecological studies indicate that changes in the availability of food plants and nutrients may be as important in regulating the moose population as are the wolves. As for the wolves of Isle Royale, it appears that in-breeding and diseases—not lack of moose—are behind the die-off of the population. Thus, it seems that predator-prey models of population control probably are oversimplifications, and that what looks like a stable, balanced situation may in fact derive from the interaction of various changeable forces. Natural systems are filled with compensating mechanisms that help stabilize nature. Hence populations often need to be understood from the perspective of the entire ecosystem.

Applied ecology

Applied ecology is the use of ecological studies to achieve practical goals. These studies help us to preserve and manage natural resources and to protect the environment. Applied ecologists work with scientists from many different fields to try to solve problems that concern the health and well-being of all people.

Many ecologists are concerned about the rate at which people are depleting such nonrenewable resources as coal, gas, and oil, and about the pollution caused by their extensive use. Many ecologists believe that if the human population continues to grow, such problems as depletion of fuels, air and water pollution, deforestation, congestion, poverty, and the disruption of climate will also worsen.

Many people believe that the studies and activities of ecologists conflict with people's economic interests. But ecologists believe that ecological knowledge is essential for long-term economic well-being. They point out that the maintenance of natural ecosystems provides many benefits to society. For example, if air and water supplies are clean, people will be healthier, and medical costs will decrease. Ecologists believe it is important for all people to learn about ecology and the environment, so that human beings can live in greater harmony with the rest of the world.   Charles A. S. Hall

Related articles in *World Book* include:

Acclimatization	Environmental pollution
Adaptation	Habitat
Air pollution	Limnology
Animal	Phenology
Balance of nature	Plant
Conservation	Recycling
Environment	Water pollution

See also *Ecology* in the Research Guide/Index, Volume 22, for a *Reading and Study Guide.*

A *World Book* science project

The balance of nature

This project is designed to show that living things provide each other with substances necessary for life, and that a proper balance between plants and animals is needed to maintain life. By doing these experiments, you should be able to show how living things depend on one another. The plants supply food and oxygen for the animals. Wastes from the animals keep the plants alive.

Materials

Get 24 snails and 24 Elodea plants from a variety store or pet shop. Other materials for this project include seven 1-quart (0.9-liter) Mason jars with lids and screw caps, adhesive tape, fine sand, water and a water pitcher, and a small, bound notebook.

WORLD BOOK photo by Ralph Brunke

Procedures

Put about 1 inch (2.5 centimeters) of sand in each jar. Pour water into each jar until it is about 2 inches (5 centimeters) from the top. Fasten a numbered strip of tape to each jar. Place the exact number of snails and plants in each jar as shown. Push the plant roots into the sand. Screw the caps on the jars. Place the jars where they will get plenty of light, but little or no direct sun. A north window is ideal. Do not open the jars.

Observing the experiments

Check the condition of the snails and plants in each jar in the morning and in the evening. Record your observations in a notebook. Information should include the date and time of observation, the number of living and dead snails and plants, and the clearness of the water. Dirty water shows that conditions in the jar are becoming unsuitable for life. The jar where the plants and snails live longest will come closest to being in balance.

Put sand in jar.

Pour water in slowly.

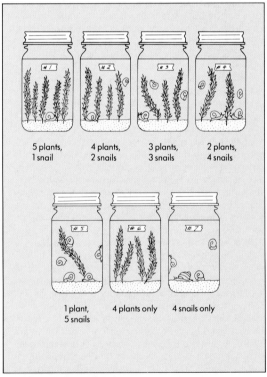

5 plants, 1 snail   4 plants, 2 snails   3 plants, 3 snails   2 plants, 4 snails

1 plant, 5 snails   4 plants only   4 snails only

Number each jar.

Put in plants and snails.

Further experiments

Perform other experiments to reach a more perfect balance between plants and animals. Larger containers, such as gallon jars, may be used. In one experiment, put goldfish with snails and plants. In another, use different kinds of water plants. Or, vary the amount or kind of light. For example, cover the jars with colored cellophane or use fluorescent lights.

Screw cap on jar.

WORLD BOOK illustrations by Zorica Dabich

Put jar near north window.

Here are your

1990 SCIENCE YEAR
Cross-Reference Tabs

For insertion in your WORLD BOOK

Each year, SCIENCE YEAR, THE WORLD BOOK ANNUAL SCIENCE SUPPLEMENT, adds a valuable dimension to your WORLD BOOK set. The Cross-Reference Tab System is designed especially to help students and parents alike link SCIENCE YEAR's major articles to the related WORLD BOOK articles that they update.

How to Use These Tabs

The top Tab on this page is ARCHAEOLOGY. Turn to the A volume of your WORLD BOOK and find the page with the ARCHAEOLOGY article on it. Affix the ARCHAEOLOGY Tab to that page.

Do the same with the remaining Tabs, and your new SCIENCE YEAR will be linked to your WORLD BOOK set.

Index

This index covers the contents of the 1990, 1989, and 1988 editions of SCIENCE YEAR, The World Book Science Annual.

Each index entry gives the edition year and a page number—for example, 90-143. The first number, 90, indicates the edition year, and the second number, 143, is the page number on which the desired information begins.

There are two types of entries in the index.

In the first type, the index entry (in **boldface**) is followed immediately by numbers:
 Botany, 90-235, 89-237, 88-238
This means that SCIENCE YEAR has an article titled Botany, and that in the 1990 edition the article begins on page 235. In the 1989 edition, the article begins on page 237, and in the 1988 edition it is on page 238.

In the second type of entry, the boldface title is followed by a clue word instead of by numbers:
 Chromosome: gene mapping, Special Report, 90-162; genetic science, 89-265

This means that there is no SCIENCE YEAR article titled Chromosome, but that information about this topic can be found in a Special Report in the 1990 edition on page 162. There is also information on this topic in the Genetic Science article of the 1989 edition on page 265.

When the clue word is "il.," the reference is to an illustration only:
 Glyptodon: il., 90-15
This means there is an illustration of this animal in the 1990 SCIENCE YEAR, on page 15.

The various "See" and "See also" cross-references in the index direct the reader to other entries within the index:
 Horticulture. See **Agriculture; Botany;** and **Plant.**
This means that for the location of information on horticulture—look under the boldface index entries
 Agriculture, Botany, and **Plant.**

Index

A

Abell 370: astronomy, 89-225; dark matter, Special Report, 90-119
Absolute zero: physics, 88-299; states of matter, Special Report, 88-188; superconductivity, Special Report, 89-106
Absorption lines: astronomy, 89-228; il., 89-204
Accelerator. See Particle accelerator.
Accelerator mass spectrometry: archaeology, Close-Up, 90-223
Accutane: drugs, 89-252
Acetylsalicylic acid: plant defenses, Special Report, 89-130
Acid rain: environment, 89-263, 88-264
Acne: Consumer Science, 88-334; drugs, 89-252
Acquired Immune Deficiency Syndrome. See AIDS.
Adaptation: mimicry, Special Report, 90-83
Addiction: public health, 89-309; Special Report, 88-117
Advanced Launch System (ALS): materials science, 90-277
Aeronautical engineering: aircraft design, Special Report, 88-171
Aflatoxin: agriculture, 90-212
Aggressive mimicry: mimicry, Special Report, 90-71
Agriculture, 90-212, 89-212, 88-212; Anasazi, Special Report, 89-32; archaeology, 90-219, 88-218; Biosphere II, Special Report, 89-144;books, 90-233; camel, Special Report, 88-58; environment, 88-266; global warming, Special Report, 90-128. See also Botany; Climate.
Agroforestry: Organization for Tropical Studies, Special Report, 90-184
AIDS: computer drug design, Special Report, 89-141; drugs, 88-251; genetic science, 90-268; immunology, 90-277, 89-273, 88-274; magic bullets, Special Report, 90-196; medical research, 88-276; Pasteur Institute, Special Report, 89-179; public health, 90-309, 89-309, 88-308; Special Report, 89-155
Air pollution. See Pollution.
Air pressure: wind shear, Special Report, 90-147
Air-traffic transponder: electronics, 88-259
Aircraft: wind shear, Special Report, 90-144
Aircraft design: Special Report, 88-171
Alar: agriculture, 90-213
Alcohol addiction: addiction, Special Report, 88-118
Algae: environment, 89-263; Great Barrier Reef, Special Report, 89-16
Alkaloid: plant defenses, Special Report, 89-121
Alligator: Everglades, Special Report, 88-16
Alloy: materials science, 90-277

Alpha particle: indoor air pollution, Special Report, 88-145
ALS. See Amyotrophic lateral sclerosis.
ALU (arithmetic-logic unit): computer chips, Special Report, 88-206
Aluminum-air batteries: energy, 88-260
Aluminum-lithium alloy: materials science, 90-277
Alvarez, Luis W.: deaths, 90-248
Alzheimer's disease: genetic science, 88-267; medical research, 90-281; neuroscience, 89-289, 88-289
American Association for the Advancement of Science (AAAS): Massey, Walter E., 90-352; science education, 90-311
Ames, Bruce N.: People in Science, 88-339
Amino acids: computer drug design, Special Report, 89-136; chemistry, 88-241; genetic science, 89-264
Amphetamine: addiction, Special Report, 88-120
Amphibian: paleontology, 90-299; zoology, 88-320
Amyotrophic lateral sclerosis (ALS): Hawking, Stephen W., 89-341; neuroscience, 89-288
Anasazi Indians: archaeology, 88-220; Special Report, 89-26
Andromeda nebula: dating methods, Special Report, 89-207; giant telescopes, Special Report, 90-88
Aneroid monitor: Consumer Science, 90-329
Animal: Biosphere II, Special Report, 89-144; mimicry, Special Report, 90-68; ozone hole, Special Report, 89-88; Pleistocene extinctions, Special Report, 90-10; white-tailed deer, Special Report, 89-91; Wilson, Edward, 89-357. See also Zoology.
Ant: Wilson, Edward, 89-357
Antarctica: environment, 89-261; glacier, Special Report, 88-70; meteorology, 89-285; oceanography, 88-294; ozone hole, Special Report, 89-78
Anthropology, 90-215, 89-215, 88-215; books, 88-235
Antibiotic: chemistry, 89-240; drugs, 88-252; Pasteur Institute, Special Report, 89-176
Antibody: AIDS, Special Report, 89-157; computer drug design, Special Report, 89-139; magic bullets, Special Report, 90-188
Antigen: AIDS, Special Report, 89-157; genetic science, 90-269; magic bullets, Special Report, 90-188
Antihistamine: Pasteur Institute, Special Report, 89-177
Antimatter: physics, 88-302; states of matter, Special Report, 88-193
Antiparticle: states of matter, Special Report, 88-193
Antitoxin: Pasteur Institute, Special Report, 89-173
Anxiety: drugs, 88-253; psychology, 90-306
Ape: anthropology, 88-217

Aphid: plant defenses, Special Report, 89-121
Appetite: chemistry, 88-240
Apple: agriculture, 90-213
Arc: astronomy, 89-225, 88-225; dark matter, Special Report, 90-119
Archaeology, New World, 90-217, 89-219, 88-218; Anasazi, Special Report, 89-26
Archaeology, Old World, 90-220, 89-221, 88-221; books, 89-235; Caesarea, Special Report, 90-40; Paleolithic art, Special Report, 88-42; Pleistocene extinctions, Special Report, 90-21
Archaeopteryx: dinosaur, Special Report, 89-57; paleontology, 89-300, 88-296
Arctic: ozone hole, Special Report, 89-85
Argonne National Laboratory: Massey, Walter E., 90-352
Arithmetical average: Consumer Science, 90-335
Armenia: geology, Close-Up, 90-272
Art: dinosaur artist, Special Report, 89-62. See also Prehistoric art.
Arthritis: anthropology, 90-216; computer drug design, Special Report, 89-141
Asbestos: environment, 89-263; indoor air pollution, Special Report, 88-149
Aspirin: medical research, Close-Up, 89-280; public health, 89-310
Assassin bug: mimicry, Special Report, 90-71; plant defenses, Special Report, 89-129
Asteroid: dinosaur, Special Report, 89-59; geology, 89-272; paleontology, 88-298
Astronomy: books, 90-233, 89-235, 88-235
Astronomy, Extragalactic, 90-225; 89-225, 88-225; dark matter, Special Report, 90-114; dating methods, Special Report, 89-205; Hawking, Stephen W., 89-341; physics, 88-302
Astronomy, Galactic, 90-228, 89-230, 88-229; giant telescopes, Special Report, 90-84. See also Galaxy; Star.
Astronomy, Solar System, 90-230, 89-232, 88-232; Uranus, Special Report, 88-101
Atlantis (space shuttle): space technology, 90-315
Atmosphere: astronomy, 90-231; Biosphere II, Special Report, 89-144; Close-Up, 88-265; giant telescopes, Special Report, 90-89; global warming, Special Report, 90-130; oceanography, 88-295; ozone hole, Special Report, 89-78. See also Pollution.
Atom: computer drug design, Special Report, 89-134; dark matter, Special Report, 90-120; physics, 89-302, 88-304; states of matter, Special Report, 88-184; superconductivity, Special Report, 89-106
Australopithecus: anthropology, 90-215, 88-215
Autism: immunology, 88-275

Automobile: energy, 89-258
Auxin: botany, 90-237
Average: Consumer Science, 90-334
Aviation: aircraft design, Special Report, 88-171; wind shear, Special Report, 90-144
Axion: dark matter, Special Report, 90-125

B

B12, Vitamin: nutrition, 88-293
B cell: immunology, 88-275; magic bullets, Special Report, 90-188
Babylonia: archaeology, 90-221
Bacillus. See Bacteria.
Bacteria: agriculture, 89-213, 88-212; Biosphere II, Special Report, 89-147; computer drug design, Special Report, 89-139; dentistry, 88-251; genetic science, 89-268; magic bullets, Special Report, 90-187; Pasteur Institute, Special Report, 89-173. See also **Salmonella.**
Bactrian camel: camel, Special Report, 88-60
Bar code: Consumer Science, 89-330
Barbiturate: addiction, Special Report, 88-119
Base: cancer genes, Special Report, 88-159; gene mapping, Special Report, 90-163; molecular biology, 88-285; Watson, James D., 90-344
Batesian mimicry: mimicry, Special Report, 90-74
Bath (England): Roman Bath, Special Report, 88-83
Bathypelagic zone: midwater, Special Report, 90-28
Battery: energy, 90-259, 88-260
BCS theory: physics, 90-299, 89-301; superconductivity, Special Report, 89-113
Bee: agriculture, 89-212; Wilson, Edward, 89-362
Beetle: World Book Supplement, 88-381
Behavior: neuroscience, 90-289; Wilson, Edward, 89-366
Benthic boundary layer: midwater, Special Report, 90-28
Berm: Caesarea, Special Report, 90-54
Beta-amyloid protein: medical research, 90-281
Beta decay: physics, 89-303, 88-304
Big bang theory: dark matter, Special Report, 90-123; Hawking, Stephen W., 89-345; states of matter, Special Report, 88-192
Big crunch theory: dark matter, Special Report, 90-126
Binary code: computer chips, Special Report, 88-200
Binary star: galactic astronomy, 90-229, 89-231, 88-229
Binding site: computer drug design, Special Report, 89-134
Biochemical scissors: gene mapping, Special Report, 90-165; magic bullets, Special Report, 90-195
Biodegradation: agriculture, 88-214;

waste disposal, Special Report, 90-60
Biofeedback: psychology, 89-308
Biogeography: Wilson, Edward, 89-361
Biological rhythms: neuroscience, 90-290; Special Report, 88-27
Biology: Biosphere II, Special Report, 89-143; books, 90-233, 89-235, 88-235; midwater, Special Report, 90-26; mimicry, Special Report, 90-68; Pasteur Institute, Special Report, 89-181; Wilson, Edward, 89-357; World Book Supplement, 88-366. See also **Animal; Botany; Cell; Ecoloogy Molecular biology; Plant; Zoology.**
Bioluminescence: midwater, Special Report, 90-36
Biomass: Organization for Tropical Studies, Special Report, 90-184
Biosphere II: Special Report, 89-143
Bipedalism: anthropology, 90-215
Biphasic schedule: biological rhythms, Special Report, 88-32
Bird: dinosaur, Special Report, 89-57; ecology, 89-253; environment, 88-264; Everglades, Special Report, 88-16; mimicry, Special Report, 90-76; paleontology, 89-300; plant defenses, Special Report, 89-129; zoology, 90-316, 89-319
Birth defects: drugs, 89-252; nutrition, 90-293
Black, Sir James: Nobel Prizes, 90-292
Black Death: archaeology, 89-224
Black hole: astronomy, 90-227, 228; dark matter, Special Report, 90-121; Hawking, Stephen W., 89-341
Black scientists: Massey, Walter E., 90-352
Black smoker: deep-sea drilling, Special Report, 88-139; il., 90-296
Black widow pulsar: astronomy, 90-229
Blast zone: Mount St. Helens, Special Report, 90-101
Blindness: neuroscience, 88-290
Blood: chemistry, 89-242; medical research, 88-276; neuroscience, 88-288; nutrition, 88-292
Blood pressure monitor: Consumer Science, 90-328
Blood transfusion: medicine, 88-282
Blood vessels: chemistry, 89-242; medical research, 90-283
Bond, James: deaths, 90-248
Bone, Fossil: dinosaur, Special Report, 89-44; dinosaur artist, Special Report, 89-62
Bone marrow: drugs, 88-252; immunology, 90-276; medicine, 88-280
Books of Science, 90-233, 89-235, 88-235
Boson: dark matter, Special Report, 90-124
Botany, 90-235, 89-237, 88-238; books, 90-233. See also **Agriculture; Plant.**
Bottom-up theory: dark matter, Special Report, 90-126
Brain: addiction, Special Report, 88-

117; anthropology, 88-218; ils., 89-277, 278; medical research, 90-281; medicine, 88-281; psychology, 90-306, 89-307; Wilson, Edward, 89-369. See also **Neuroscience; Psychology.**
Brain tissue transplant: medical research, 88-276; neuroscience, 90-288, 89-286, 88-288
Breast cancer: drugs, 90-252; il., 89-273; medical research, 89-283
Breeding: white-tailed deer, Special Report, 89-92; zoology, 89-317
Broadcasting, Television: TV technology, Special Report, 90-204
Brood parasitism: zoology, 89-319, 88-317
Brown dwarf star: astronomy, 90-230, 89-232
Bubonic plague: archaeology, 89-224
Bulimia: neuroscience, 90-290
Buran (space shuttle): space technology, 90-315
Burial site: archaeology, 90-220, 89-219; Close-Up, 90-218
Burk, Dean: deaths, 90-248
Bus, Computer: computer hardware, 90-245
Butterfly: mimicry, Special Report, 90-68; plant defenses, Special Report, 89-128
Byte: computer chips, Special Report, 88-201
Byzantine Period: Caesarea, Special Report, 90-54

C

CAD-CAM system: dentistry, 90-250
Caesarea: Special Report, 90-40
Caesarean section: medicine, 88-280
Caffeine: Consumer Science, 90-322
Calcium: dentistry, 88-250; nutrition, 88-292
Calculator: computer chips, Special Report, 88-200
Camel: Special Report, 88-58
Camera. See Photography; Video systems.
Cancer: AIDS, Special Report, 89-156; Ames, Bruce N., 88-339; cancer genes, Special Report, 88-157; chemistry, 89-241; computer drug design, Special Report, 89-141; drugs, 90-252; environment, 90-265, 89-262; genetic science, 90-269; immunology, 90-275, 89-273, 88-274; indoor air pollution, Special Report, 88-143; magic bullets, Special Report, 90-186; medical research, 90-284, 88-276; nutrition, 89-294; psychology, 90-308
Cannibalism: archaeology, 88-221
Canola oil: agriculture, 90-214
Cap: dentistry, 90-250
Car phone: Consumer Science, 89-322
Carbon dioxide: Biosphere II, Special Report, 89-144; botany, 89-238; Close-Up, 88-271; Consumer Science, 90-322; dating methods, Special Report, 89-200; geology, 90-274; global warming, Special

Index

Report, 90-130; Organization for Tropical Studies, Special Report, 90-178; ozone hole, Special Report, 89-89

Carbon 14. See **Radiocarbon dating.**

Carbon monoxide: astronomy, 88-226; indoor air pollution, Special Report, 88-151

Caterpillar: mimicry, Special Report, 90-70; zoology, 90-318

Cave art. See **Prehistoric art.**

Cave lion: il., 90-15

Cavities: dentistry, 88-250

CD. See **Compact disc.**

CD-ROM: computer hardware, 89-244; computer software, 89-247

Cell: AIDS, Special Report, 89-156; cancer genes, Special Report, 88-157; computer drug design, Special Report, 89-134; gene mapping, Special Report, 90-162

Cell-targeted therapy: magic bullets, Special Report, 90-186

Cellular phone: Consumer Science, 89-322

Celts: archaeology, 89-223

Cenozoic: dating methods, Special Report, 89-199

Center of gravity: aircraft design, Special Report, 88-177

Central tendency: Consumer Science, 90-334

Centripetal force: physics, Close-Up, 90-300

Ceramics (superconductors): materials science, 89-275; Nobel Prizes, 89-291; physics, 90-299, 89-301, 88-301; superconductivity, Special Report, 89-113

Cerebral cortex: neuroscience, 90-289

Challenger: space technology, 89-314, 88-313

Charge-coupled device (CCD): Consumer Science, 90-325; giant telescopes, Special Report, 90-90

Chemistry, 90-239, 89-239, 88-240; agriculture, 88-214; Nobel Prizes, 90-291, 89-290, 88-290; World Book Supplement, 88-372

Chemotherapy: drugs, 90-252; magic bullets, Special Report, 90-188; medical research, 89-283

Chernobyl: energy, 88-261

Childbirth: medicine, 88-280

Chimu (people): archaeology, 90-219

Chip, Computer. See **Microchip.**

Chlordane: environment, 88-266

Chlorine monoxide: environment, 90-262; ozone hole, Special Report, 89-82

Chlorofluorocarbons (CFC's): Close-Up, 88-265; environment, 90-262, 89-261; global warming, Special Report, 90-142; meteorology, 90-287; ozone hole, Special Report, 89-83

Cholecystokinen (CCK): neuroscience, 90-290

Cholesterol: drugs, 89-251; medical research, 89-282, 88-279; nutrition, 90-292, 89-291, 88-292

Christie, Richard H.: science student awards, 90-312

Chromosome: cancer genes, Special Report, 88-159; gene mapping, Special Report, 90-162; genetic science, 90-269, 89-265, 88-267; molecular biology, 88-288

Chron: geology, 89-270

Chronobiology: biological rhythms, Special Report, 88-30

Circadian rhythms: biological rhythms, Special Report, 88-28; neuroscience, 90-290

Citrus tree: plant defenses, Special Report, 89-121

Clearcutting: Mount St. Helens, Special Report, 90-113

Cliff dwelling: Anasazi, Special Report, 89-27

Cliff swallow: zoology, 89-319

Climate: dinosaur, Special Report, 89-58; ecology, 90-254, 89-253; geology, 90-270; global warming, Special Report, 90-128; meteorology, 90-287, 89-285; oceanography, 90-294; Organization for Tropical Studies, Special Report, 90-178; Pleistocene extinctions, Special Report, 90-18. See also **Weather.**

Cloning: agriculture, 89-213; Biosphere II, Special Report, 89-152; gene mapping, Special Report, 90-168; magic bullets, Special Report, 90-190

Clovis culture: archaeology, 90-217; Pleistocene extinctions, Special Report, 90-21

Cluster: astronomy, 90-229; dark matter, Special Report, 90-114

Cobalt 56: astronomy, Close-Up, 89-227

Cocaine: addiction, Special Report, 88-119; neuroscience, 89-286

Cockroach: chemistry, 88-241

Codabar: Consumer Science, 89-330

Coelenterate: midwater, Special Report, 90-27

Coffee: Consumer Science, 90-322

Cold fusion: Close-Up, 90-304

Collegenase: dentistry, 89-250

Collider. See **Superconducting Super Collider (SSC).**

Colon cancer: genetic science, 90-269

Color television: TV technology, Special Report, 90-205

Columbus, Christopher: archaeology, 89-219

Columbus Project: giant telescopes, Special Report, 90-96

Comet: astronomy, 89-232

Commercial broadcasting: TV technology, Special Report, 90-204

Communication: Wilson, Edward, 89-359

Communications satellite: Consumer Science, 89-324; space technology, 90-315, 89-316

Community, Animal: midwater, Special Report, 90-28

Compact disc (CD): computer hardware, 89-244; electronics, 89-256, 88-256. See also **CD-ROM.**

Compaq Computer: computer hardware, 89-243, 88-244

Compressed air energy storage: energy, 90-259

Computer: Biosphere II, Special Report, 89-147; books, 89-235; computer drug design, Special Report, 89-133; Consumer Science, 90-327, 89-330; Hawking, Stephen W., 89-353; Massey, Walter E., 90-360

Computer chip. See **Microchip.**

Computer hardware, 90-242, 89-243, 88-244; superconductivity, Special Report, 89-106. See also **Microchip.**

Computer software, 90-245, 89-245, 88-246; agriculture, 89-214; aircraft design, Special Report, 88-177

Computer virus: Close-Up, 89-246; computer software, 90-245

Computerized tomography (CT): medicine, 88-281

Concrete: Caesarea, Special Report, 90-46

Condor: environment, 88-266

Conductor: Superconductivity, Special Report, 89-106

Conservation: ecology, 89-254; Organization for Tropical Studies, Special Report, 90-178. See also **Ecology; Environment; Pollution.**

Construction: Caesarea, Special Report, 90-49

Continental margin: deep-sea drilling, Special Report, 88-141

Controlled burning: environment, Close-Up, 90-264

Cooper pairs: physics, 90-301, 89-301; superconductivity, Special Report, 89-114

Copepod: midwater, Special Report, 90-33

Coral reef: Biosphere II, Special Report, 89-150; ecology, 89-254; Great Barrier Reef, Special Report, 89-12

Corn: agriculture, 90-212

Coronary artery disease. See **Heart attack; Heart disease.**

Cosmic rays: dating methods, Special Report, 89-200

Cosmology: dark matter, Special Report, 90-123; Hawking, Stephen W., 89-342; states of matter, Special Report, 88-192

Crab spider: mimicry, Special Report, 90-68

Crack: addiction, Special Report, 88-120

Credit card: Close-Up, 88-258

Cretaceous Period: dinosaur, Special Report, 89-46; paleontology, 90-297, 88-298

Critical density: dark matter, Special Report, 90-123

Critical temperature: energy, 88-260; Nobel Prizes, 89-290; physics, 90-299, 89-301, 88-299; superconductivity, Special Report, 89-106

Cro-Magnon Man: Paleolithic art, Special Report, 88-42

Crown: dentistry, 90-250

Crystal: agriculture, 88-212; chemistry, 88-244; Close-Up,

Index

Index

71; global warming, Special Report, 90-133; Great Barrier Reef, Special Report, 89-13; Paleolithic art, Special Report, 88-43; Pleistocene extinctions, Special Report, 90-10
Ice volcano: astronomy, 90-232
Icecap: geology, 90-271; glacier, Special Report, 88-70; oceanography, 88-294
Immune system. See **Immunology.**
Immunology, 90-275, 89-273, 88-274; AIDS, Special Report, 89-155; computer drug design, Special Report, 89-140; magic bullets, Special Report, 90-186; medical research, 88-279; Nobel Prizes, 89-291; ozone hole, Special Report, 89-78; Pasteur Institute, Special Report, 89-168
Improved definition TV (IDTV): TV technology, Special Report, 90-208
Inca: archaeology, 90-219
Incineration: waste disposal, Special Report, 90-58
Indian, American: Anasazi, Special Report, 89-26; archaeology, 89-219; medical research, 89-278; Special Report, 89-93
Indoor air pollution: Special Report, 88-143; environment, 88-264
Inertia: physics, Close-Up, 90-300
Inflammation: computer drug design, Special Report, 89-141
Inflationary theory: dark matter, Special Report, 90-123
Infrared galaxy: astronomy, 88-226
Infrared light: astronomy, 90-228; giant telescopes, Special Report, 90-90
Inner City Teachers of Science: Massey, Walter E., 90-357
Insect: AIDS, Special Report, 89-159; chemistry, 88-240; ecology, 89-254, 88-253; mimicry, Special Report, 90-74; plant defenses, Special Report, 89-119; Wilson, Edward, 89-357
Insecticide. See **Pesticide.**
Integrated circuit: computer chips, Special Report, 88-203
Intelligence: neuroscience, 89-289; psychology, 89-308, 89-307
Interferon: magic bullets, Special Report, 90-194
Interglacial period: geology, 90-270
Interleukin: immunology, 90-275; medical research, 88-279
Interstellar space: astronomy, 89-233
Intrinsic brightness: dating methods, Special Report, 89-207
Iridium: chemistry, 89-242; dinosaur, Special Report, 89-59
Iron: medical research, 90-284
Island: Great Barrier Reef, Special Report, 89-14
Isotope: astronomy, 88-233; dating methods, Special Report, 89-200

J

Jellyfish: midwater, Special Report, 90-27

Jet lag: biological rhythms, Special Report, 88-33
Jet stream: global warming, Special Report, 90-133
Johnson-Sea-Link (submersible): midwater, Special Report, 90-32
JOIDES Resolution (ship): deep-sea drilling, Special Report, 88-130; oceanography, 90-296, 89-295, 88-294
Joint, Hip: anthropology, 90-215
Joint Airport Weather Studies (JAWS): wind shear, Special Report, 90-155
June grass: botany, Close-Up, 90-236
Junk DNA: gene mapping, Special Report, 90-163
Jupiter: astronomy, 89-233
Jurassic Period: dinosaur, Special Report, 89-46; paleontology, 90-298

K

Kaposi's sarcoma: AIDS, Special Report, 89-156
Keck telescope: giant telescopes, Special Report, 90-93
Killer bees: agriculture, 89-212
Killer cell: magic bullets, Special Report, 90-194
Kilobyte: computer chips, Special Report, 88-206
Kinetic energy: physics, Close-Up, 90-300

L

Lake Nios: Close-Up, 88-271; geology, 88-269
Lake Okeechobee: Everglades, Special Report, 88-12
Landfill: waste disposal, Special Report, 90-58
Language: neuroscience, 89-289
La Niña: global warming, Special Report, 90-133; meteorology, 90-286
Lapita culture: archaeology, 90-222
Laptop computer: computer hardware, 90-242
Large Magellanic Cloud: astronomy, Close-Up, 89-226; physics, 88-302
La Selva Biological Station: Organization for Tropical Studies, Special Report, 90-174
Laser: il., 89-239; physics, 89-302; tunneling, Special Report, 89-191
Laser printer: computer hardware, 90-243
Latex: plant defenses, Special Report, 89-120
Lead: dating methods, Special Report, 89-200; environment, 90-265, 89-263
Lead poisoning: oceanography, 88-295
Lederman, Leon M.: Nobel Prizes, 90-291
Lens: giant telescopes, Special Report, 90-86; Massey, Walter E., 90-360

Let-it-burn policy: environment, Close-Up, 90-264
Lidar: wind shear, Special Report, 90-157
Life: dating methods, Special Report, 89-205; ozone hole, Special Report, 89-78. See also **Biology.**
Lift: wind shear, Special Report, 90-151
Light: astronomy, 90-228; dark matter, Special Report, 90-116; dating methods, Special Report, 89-205; giant telescopes, Special Report, 90-84; midwater, Special Report, 90-33; physics, 89-302
Light radar: wind shear, Special Report, 90-157
Light-year: dating methods, Special Report, 89-205
Lightning: meteorology, 89-283
Limbic system: addiction, Special Report, 88-120
Limestone: Great Barrier Reef, Special Report, 89-13
Linguistics: Close-Up, 88-217
Lipid: medical research, 88-276
Liquid: states of matter, Special Report, 88-184
Liquid helium: materials science, 89-275; physics, 88-299; Nobel Prizes, 89-291; superconductivity, Special Report, 89-107
Liquid nitrogen: materials science, 89-275; physics, 88-299; superconductivity, Special Report, 89-107
Lithosphere: geology, 89-269, 88-273
Liver: chemistry, 90-241, 88-240; medical research, 90-280
Lobster: zoology, 90-320, 88-318
Lorenz, Konrad Z.: deaths, 90-248
Lou Gehrig's disease. See **Amyotrophic lateral sclerosis.**
Lovastatin: drugs, 89-251
Love: psychology, 88-306
Low definition: TV technology, Special Report, 90-200
Low-density lipoproteins (LDL): nutrition, 90-293
Lung cancer: environment, 89-262; indoor air pollution, Special Report, 88-143
Lyme disease: white-tailed deer, Special Report, 89-92
Lymphokine: medical research, 88-279

M

Macrophage: AIDS, Special Report, 89-157
Magellan Venus Radar Mapper: space technology, 90-315
Magic bullets: Special Report, 90-186
Magma: Mount St. Helens, Special Report, 90-101; oceanography, 89-296
Magnetic field: astronomy, 88-232; deep-sea drilling, Special Report, 88-140; geology, 89-269, 88-270; physics, 90-301; superconductivity,

392

Special Report, 89-108; zoology, 88-316

Magnetic resonance imaging (MRI): il., 90-281; superconductivity, Special Report, 89-116

Magnetosphere: astronomy, 88-232

Magnetron: Consumer Science, 90-331

Maiasaura: dinosaur, Special Report, 89-56; paleontology, 89-297

Malaria: immunology, 89-274

Mammal: Pleistocene extinctions, Special Report, 90-10; zoology, 90-316

Mammoth: il., 90-15; Pleistocene extinctions, Special Report, 90-24

Manganese: nutrition, 88-292

Manic depression: genetic science, 88-266; neuroscience, 88-289

Mantle: geology, 89-269

Map: geology, 89-272; World Book Supplement, 90-370

Mapping, Gene: See **Gene mapping.**

Marijuana: addiction, Special Report, 88-125

Marine archaeology: Caesarea, Special Report, 90-40

Marker, Genetic: gene mapping, Special Report, 90-168; genetic science, 90-270, 89-265; neuroscience, 88-289

Mars: astronomy, 90-231; il., 89-380

Mass: astronomy, 90-227, 229; Close-Up, 88-236; dark matter, Special Report, 90-116; Hawking, Stephen W., 89-346; physics, 89-303

Mass spectrometer: astronomy, 89-233

Massey, Walter E.: People in Science, 90-352

Mastodon: Pleistocene extinctions, Special Report, 90-20

Materials science, 90-277, 89-275

Mathematics: books, 90-233; Hawking, Stephen W., 89-341; psychology, 88-306

Matter: astronomy, 90-229; dark matter, Special Report, 90-114; physics, 90-305; states of matter, Special Report, 88-184

Maya: archaeology, 89-221

Mean: Consumer Science, 90-334

Measurement: chemistry, 89-242; Consumer Science, 89-328

Median: Consumer Science, 90-334

Medical research, 90-280, 89-277, 88-276; computer drug design, Special Report, 89-182; magic bullets, Special Report, 90-186; Nobel Prizes, 90-292; Pasteur Institute, Special Report, 89-168. See also **AIDS.**

Medical waste: waste disposal, Special Report, 90-57

Medicine, 88-280; biological rhythms, Special Report, 88-37; Nobel Prizes, 89-291, 88-291. See also **Disease; Public health.**

Megabyte: computer chips, Special Report, 88-206

Melanoma: genetic science, 90-270; immunology, 89-274

Memory (computer): computer chips, Special Report, 88-206

Meniscus mirror: giant telescopes, Special Report, 90-95

Menopause: nutrition, 88-293

Mercury sphygmomanometer: Consumer Science, 90-328

Mesa Verde: Anasazi, Special Report, 89-26

Mesolithic: archaeology, 88-221; Close-Up, 88-217

Mesopelagic zone: midwater, Special Report, 90-28

Mesozoic: dating methods, Special Report, 89-199

Metabolism: Great Barrier Reef, Special Report, 89-21; medical research, 89-278

Metamorphosis: plant defenses, Special Report, 89-123

Metastasis: cancer genes, Special Report, 88-159; immunology, 89-274; magic bullets, Special Report, 90-188

Meteorite: dating methods, Special Report, 89-205; paleontology, 88-298

Meteorology, 90-285, 89-283, 88-282. See also **Climate; Weather.**

Methadone: addiction, Special Report, 88-126

Methane: astronomy, 90-231; global warming, Special Report, 90-141; meteorology, 90-287

Michel, Hartmut: Nobel Prizes, 90-291

Microburst: meteorology, 89-285; wind shear, Special Report, 90-146

Microchip: Close-Up, 88-258; computer chips, Special Report, 88-199; computer hardware, 90-242, 89-243, 88-244; Consumer Science, 88-322; electronics, 88-256; materials science, 90-279; superconductivity, Special Report, 89-116; TV technology, Special Report, 90-208

Microengineering: Close-Up, 90-278

Microprocessor. See **Microchip.**

Microscopic motor: Close-Up, 90-278

Microwave oven: Consumer Science, 90-331

Microwave radiation: Consumer Science, 88-328; states of matter, Special Report, 88-197

Midwater: Special Report, 90-26

Milk: agriculture, 88-212; Consumer Science, 89-325

Milky Way: astronomy, 90-228, 89-230, 88-229; dating methods, Special Report, 89-208

Millisecond pulsar: astronomy, 90-229

Mimicry: midwater, Special Report, 90-37; plant defenses, Special Report, 89-130; Special Report, 90-68; zoology, 90-318

Mir space station: il., 89-384; space technology, 90-315, 89-315, 88-315

Mirror: giant telescopes, Special Report, 90-84

Moche tomb: Close-Up, 90-218

Mode: Consumer Science, 90-334

Molecular biology, 88-285; gene mapping, Special Report, 90-163; magic bullets, Special Report, 90-186; Watson, James D., 90-338

Molecular graphics: computer drug design, Special Report, 89-136

Molecular probe: cancer genes, Special Report, 88-168

Molecule: computer drug design, 89-136; medical research, 88-276; Nobel Prizes, 88-290; states of matter, Special Report, 88-184

Mollusk: zoology, 88-316

Monarch butterfly: mimicry, Special Report, 90-72; plant defenses, Special Report, 89-129

Monoclonal antibody: magic bullets, Special Report, 90-189

Mononucleosis: immunology, 88-275

Moon: chemistry, 89-243; dating methods, Special Report, 89-205; Uranus, Special Report, 88-101

Morphine: addiction, Special Report, 88-119

Mosquito: immunology, 89-274

Motor, Microscopic: Close-Up, 90-278

Mount Saint Helens: Special Report, 90-98

Mountain: geology, 90-274; tunneling, Special Report, 89-186

Mouse: genetic science, 89-264; immunology, 90-276

MS-DOS system: computer software, 88-246

Mu neutrino: physics, 89-303

Mulching: agriculture, 88-214

Müllerian mimicry: mimicry, Special Report, 90-74

Multiple Mirror Telescope: giant telescopes, Special Report, 90-89

Multiple vitamin: nutrition, 90-293

Mutagen: Ames, Bruce N., 88-340

Mutation: AIDS, Special Report, 89-156; anthropology, 89-216; cancer genes, Special Report, 88-162; mimicry, Special Report, 90-80; molecular biology, 88-287

Mutual eclipse: astronomy, 89-234

Mycobacteria: public health, 88-308

N

Narcotic: addiction, Special Report, 88-119

National Aeronautics and Space Administration (NASA): environment, 89-261; Organization for Tropical Studies, Special Report, 90-184; ozone hole; Special Report, 89-80

National parks: ecology, 88-254; environment, Close-Up, 90-264; Everglades, Special Report, 88-11

National Science Foundation: Organization for Tropical Studies, Special Report, 90-182

Native horse: il., 90-15

Natural history: books, 90-233, 89-236, 88-237

Natural selection. See **Evolution.**

Neanderthal man: anthropology, 89-217

Index

air pollution, Special Report, 88-155; Mount St. Helens, Special Report, 90-98; Organization for Tropical Studies, Special Report, 90-172; mimicry, Special Report, 90-68; plant defenses, Special Report, 89-119; Wilson, Edward, 89-361. See also **Botany.**

Plaque: Consumer Science, 88-331; dentistry, 90-250, 88-250

Plasma (physics): states of matter, Special Report, 88-190

Plastics: waste disposal, Special Report, 90-65

Plate tectonics: astronomy, 89-234; deep-sea drilling, Special Report, 88-130; geology, 90-272, 89-269, 88-269; oceanography, 90-296

Pleistocene Epoch: archaeology, 90-217; Pleistocene extinctions, Special Report, 90-10

Plume: oceanography, 88-294

Pluto: astronomy, 90-231; il., 89-233

Pneumonia: AIDS, Special Report, 89-156

Poison. See **Pesticide; Toxin.**

Polar wander: geology, 89-269

Pollen studies: Anasazi, Special Report, 89-33; geology, 90-270

Pollen tube: botany, 90-235

Pollution: agriculture, 88-214; Everglades, Special Report, 88-21; global warming, Special Report, 90-142; Great Barrier Reef, Special Report, 89-23; indoor air pollution, Special Report, 88-143; meteorology, 88-282; oceanography, 88-295; ozone hole, Special Report, 89-83; waste disposal, Special Report, 90-59; zoology, 88-317. See also **Ecology; Environment.**

Polymer: astronomy, 89-232; chemistry, 90-241

Population, Animal: ecology, 90-256; Organization for Tropical Studies, Special Report, 90-179; white-tailed deer, Special Report, 89-92; Wilson, Edward, 89-361

Population, Human: ecology, 88-256

Portable VCR: electronics, 90-257

Positive charge. See **Electricity.**

Positive ion: states of matter, Special Report, 88-190

Positron: physics, 90-305, 89-305, 88-302

Positron emission tomography (PET): neuroscience, 89-289; psychology, 90-307, 89-307

Postscript: computer software, 90-247

Potato: plant defenses, Special Report, 89-121

Potential energy: physics, Close-Up, 90-300

Poultry: agriculture, 90-213; Consumer Science, 89-325

Precambrian: dating methods, Special Report, 89-199

Predator: mimicry, Special Report, 90-70; zoology, 90-320

Pregnancy: medicine, 88-280

Prehistoric art: archaeology, 88-218;

Paleolithic art, Special Report, 88-42; Pleistocene extinctions, Special Report, 90-131

Pre-Columbian civilization: Close-Up, 90-218

Prehistoric people: anthropology, 89-215, 88-215; archaeology, 90-217, 89-220; Paleolithic art, Special Report, 88-42

Prevailing wind: wind shear, Special Report, 90-147

Primary mirror: giant telescopes, Special Report, 90-87

***Principia* (Newton):** Close-Up, 88-236

Program. See **Computer software.**

Project 2061: science education, 90-311

Projection-TV: TV technology, Special Report, 90-208

Protective adaptation: mimicry, Special Report, 90-83

Protein: Ames, Bruce N., 88-341; cancer genes, Special Report, 88-159; computer drug design, Special Report, 89-134; medical research, 90-281; neuroscience, 88-289

Proteinase inhibitor: plant defenses, Special Report, 89-123

Protoavis: dinosaur, Special Report, 89-58; paleontology, 88-296

Proton-antiproton collider: physics, 90-305

***Pseudomonas*:** agriculture, 88-212; drugs, 88-252; immunology, 89-273

Psychoactive drug: addiction, Special Report, 88-118

Psychology, 90-306, 89-307, 88-305; dentistry, 90-250. See also **Brain.**

Public health, 90-309, 89-309, 88-308; indoor air pollution, Special Report, 88-143

Pueblo Indians: Anasazi, Special Report, 89-26; archaeology, 88-220

Pulsar: astronomy, 90-225, 229, 89-231

Pygmy: anthropology, 88-218

Pyramid: archaeology, 89-223

Pyroclastic flows: Mount St. Helens, Special Report, 90-104

Q

Quantum mechanics: Hawking, Stephen W., 89-348

Quark: physics, 90-305, 89-305, 88-303; states of matter, Special Report, 88-192

Quasar: astronomy, 90-225, 89-227, 88-226; giant telescopes, Special Report, 90-84; ils., 89-204, 88-227

R

Rabies: Pasteur Institute, Special Report, 89-172

Races, Human: drugs, 90-251

Radar: aircraft design, Special Report, 88-178; geology, 88-272; wind shear, Special Report, 90-153

Radiation: archaeology, Close-Up, 90-223; Consumer Science, 90-333; dark matter, Special Report, 90-120;

dating methods, Special Report, 89-200; geology, 90-271; indoor air pollution, Special Report, 88-145

Radio galaxy: astronomy, 90-225

Radio telescope: dark matter, Special Report, 90-119

Radioactive waste: waste disposal, Special Report, 90-58

Radioactivity. See **Radiation.**

Radiocarbon dating: Anasazi, Special Report, 89-28; archaeology, Close-Up, 90-223; Caesarea, Special Report, 90-46; dating methods, Special Report, 89-200; Pleistocene extinctions, Special Report, 90-13

Radon: environment, 90-266, 89-262, 88-264; indoor air pollution, Special Report, 88-143

Railroad: tunneling, Special Report, 89-186

Rain forest: Biosphere II, Special Report, 89-143; ecology, 88-254; global warming, Special Report, 90-141; Organization for Tropical Studies, Special Report, 90-172

RAM (random-access memory) chip: computer chips, Special Report, 88-206

Rare earth: superconductivity, Special Report, 89-113

Receptor: addiction, Special Report, 88-120; AIDS, Special Report, 89-157; immunology, 89-273; magic bullets, Special Report, 90-194

Recycling: waste disposal, Special Report, 90-62

Red giant star: astronomy, 88-230; dating methods, Special Report, 89-208

Red shift: astronomy, 89-225; dark matter, Special Report, 90-116; dating methods, Special Report, 89-207

Reflecting telescope: giant telescopes, Special Report, 90-87

Reforestation: Mount St. Helens, Special Report, 90-113; Organization for Tropical Studies, Special Report, 90-178

Refracting telescope: giant telescopes, Special Report, 90-86

Relative dating: dating methods, Special Report, 89-199

Relativity, Theory of: Hawking, Stephen W., 89-347

Remission: magic bullets, Special Report, 90-190

Remotely Operated Vehicle (ROV): midwater, Special Report, 90-27

Renin: computer drug design, Special Report, 89-141

Reproduction: botany, 90-235; zoology, 90-316

Reptile: dinosaur, Special Report, 89-45; paleontology, 89-297

Resin: plant defenses, Special Report, 89-120

Resistance, Electrical: physics, 88-298; superconductivity, Special Report, 89-106

Restriction enzyme: gene mapping, Special Report, 90-165; genetics, 89-266; molecular biology, 88-285

Index

Retin-A: drugs, 89-253
Retinoblastoma: cancer genes, Special Report, 88-166
Reverse transcriptase: AIDS, Special Report, 89-157; genetic science, 90-269
Rhinovirus: computer drug design, Special Report, 89-140
Rhizobacteria: agriculture, 89-213
Ribonucleic acid. See RNA.
Rice: agriculture, 90-212, 88-213
Richter, Curt Paul: deaths, 90-249
Ride Report: space technology, 89-314
Ridley sea turtle: il., 90-317
RNA (ribonucleic acid): AIDS, Special Report, 89-157; astronomy, 88-234; botany, 90-237; gene mapping, Special Report, 90-163; genetic science, 90-267, 89-264. See also Cell; DNA; Virus.
Roads: Anasazi, Special Report, 89-36
Robot: midwater, Special Report, 90-27
Rock: oceanography, 89-296; tunneling, Special Report, 89-182. See also Geology.
Roller coaster: physics, Close-Up, 90-300
ROM (read-only memory) chip: computer chips, Special Report, 88-206
Roman Bath: Special Report, 88-83
Rome, Ancient: archaeology, 90-222; Caesarea, Special Report, 90-40
Root: botany, 89-237, 88-239
Rotational poles: geology, 89-269, 88-272
Rubidium dating: dating methods, Special Report, 89-205
Rubisco: botany, 88-239
Rumen: white-tailed deer, Special Report, 89-96

S

Saber-toothed cat: il., 90-15
Sahara rivers: geology, 88-272
Salicylic acid: botany, 89-237
Saliva: dentistry, 89-250, 88-251
Salmonella: Anasazi, Special Report, 89-39; Consumer Science, 89-325
Salmonellosis. See Salmonella.
San Andreas Fault: geology, 88-269
Sanitary landfill: waste disposal, Special Report, 90-58
Satellite, Communications. See Communications satellite.
Saturated fat: nutrition, 89-293
Savanna: Biosphere II, Special Report, 89-143
Scan line: TV technology, Special Report, 90-201
Scanning tunneling microscope (STM): chemistry, 88-242; genetic science, 90-266; il., 89-242
Schizophrenia: neuroscience, 88-288
Schwartz, Melvin: Nobel Prizes, 90-291
Science, History of: books, 90-233, 89-235

Science education, 90-311, 89-311, 88-310; Massey, Walter E., 90-361; Organization for Tropical Studies, Special Report, 90-179; science high schools, 88-351
Science student awards, 90-312, 89-313, 88-312
Science/Technology/Society (S/T/S): science education, 90-312, 89-311
Scorch zone: Mount St. Helens, Special Report, 90-101
Scrubber: waste disposal, Special Report, 90-61
Sea wall: Caesarea, Special Report, 90-44
Seal (animal): ecology, 90-256; zoology, 90-93
Seasonal affective disorder (SAD): biological rhythms, Special Report, 88-37
Seasonal dry forest: Organization for Tropical Studies, Special Report, 90-179
Seat-belt laws: public health, 88-309
Security system: Consumer Science, 88-328
Sedimentary rock: dating methods, Special Report, 89-198
Segmented mirror: giant telescopes, Special Report, 90-93
Segrè, Emilio F.: deaths, 90-249
Seismology. See Earthquake; Geology.
Seizure: neuroscience, 90-289
Semiconductor: computer chips, Special Report, 88-203; electronics, 88-256
Serotonin: addiction, Special Report, 88-121
Sex determination: genetic science, 89-267; Wilson, Edward, 89-363
Shiftwork: biological rhythms, Special Report, 88-35
Shock-wave therapy: medical research, 89-281
Shroud of Turin: Close-Up, 90-223
Siamese twins: il., 89-278
Silicon: chemistry, 88-244; computer chips, Special Report, 88-199
Silk moth: mimicry, Special Report, 90-77
Silurian: dating methods, Special Report, 89-199
Simian immunodeficiency virus (SIV): immunology, 90-277
Simplesse: nutrition, Close-Up, 89-292
Sink (habitat): ecology, 90-256
Siphonophore: il., 90-26
Skin: Consumer Science, 88-334; drugs, 89-253
Skin cancer: AIDS, Special Report, 89-156; immunology, 89-274; nutrition, 89-294; ozone hole, Special Report, 89-78
Skin patch: drugs, 90-251
Skinner, Christopher McLean: science student awards, 90-312
Skylab space station: il., 89-384
Sleep: biological rhythms, Special Report, 88-32
Sleep-learning: psychology, 89-308

Slurry shield: tunneling, Special Report, 89-189
Smart card: Close-Up, 88-258
Smoking: addiction, Special Report, 88-125; dentistry, 89-250; environment, 89-262; medical research, 89-277; public health, 89-309, 88-309
Snowpack: Mount St. Helens, Special Report, 90-107
Snowshoe hare: ecology, 90-254
Sociobiology: Wilson, Edward, 89-357
Software. See Computer software.
Solar energy: energy, 90-261, 89-258; global warming, Special Report, 90-137; geology, 90-271; Massey, Walter E., 90-360
Solar nebula: astronomy, 89-233; Close-Up, 89-227
Solar System. See Astronomy, Solar System.
Solids. See Physics, Fluids and Solids.
Somatotropin: agriculture, 88-212
Sonar: deep-sea drilling, Special Report, 88-135; geology, 89-272; neuroscience, 88-290
Sound waves: wind shear, Special Report, 90-154
Source (habitat): ecology, 90-256
South Pole: ozone hole, Special Report, 89-81
Space alloy: materials science, 90-277
Space shuttle: space technology, 90-314, 89-314, 88-313
Space station: il., 89-384; space technology, 90-315, 89-315
Space technology, 90-314, 89-314, 88-313; astronomy, 90-232; Biosphere II, Special Report, 89-153; books, 89-236; chemistry, 89-243; materials science, 90-277; Uranus, Special Report, 88-101; World Book Supplement, 89-373
Spectrometer. See Spectroscopy.
Spectroscopic Survey Telescope (SST): giant telescopes, Special Report, 90-96
Spectroscopy: dating methods, Special Report, 89-207; ozone hole, Special Report, 89-80; Uranus, Special Report, 88-104
Spectrum: astronomy, 90-231; dark matter, Special Report, 90-116
Speech synthesizer: Hawking, Stephen W., 89-353
Sphygmomanometer: Consumer Science, 90-328
Spider: mimicry, Special Report, 90-68
Spiral galaxy: dark matter, Special Report, 90-118
Spirit Lake: Mount St. Helens, Special Report, 90-108
Squall line: meteorology, 88-285
Stanford Linear Collider (SLC): physics, 90-305, 89-305
Star: astronomy, 90-225, 228, 89-230, 88-225; dark matter, Special Report, 90-114; dating methods, Special

Report, 89-205; giant telescopes, Special Report, 90-84; Hawking, Stephen W., 89-346. See also **Galaxy.**
Starfish: Great Barrier Reef, Special Report, 89-12
States of matter: Special Report, 88-184
Statistics: Consumer Science, 90-334
Stealth airplane: aircraft design, Special Report, 88-178
Steinberger, Jack: Nobel Prizes, 90-291
Steroid drugs: computer drug design, Special Report, 89-141; drugs, 89-252
Still-video camera (SVC): electronics, 90-257
Stimulant: addiction, Special Report, 88-119
Stone Age: anthropology, 89-218
Storm: oceanography, 89-295
Storm tracks: meteorology, 90-286
Stratosphere: Close-Up, 88-265; environment, 90-262; ozone hole, Special Report, 89-79
Stratum: dating methods, Special Report, 89-198
Stroke: medical research, Close-Up, 89-280; nutrition, 88-292
Strong force: Hawking, Stephen W., 89-350
Style: botany, 90-235
Submersible: midwater, Special Report, 90-27
Succession, Ecological: Mount St. Helens, Special Report, 90-109
Sumer: archaeology, 88-222
Sun: astronomy, 88-234; ozone hole, Special Report, 89-78; states of matter, Special Report, 88-190
Sunraycer: energy, 89-258
Sunspot: astronomy, 88-234; ecology, 90-254
Supercluster: astronomy, 89-228; dark matter, Special Report, 90-116
Superconducting Super Collider (SSC): physics, 90-303, 89-306, 88-301; superconductivity, Special Report, 89-116
Superconductivity: computer chips, Special Report, 88-209; energy, 88-260; Massey, Walter E., 90-360; materials science, 90-279, 89-275; Nobel Prizes, 89-290; physics, 90-299, 89-301, 88-298, 303; Special Report, 89-106; states of matter, Special Report, 88-188
Supercontinent: oceanography, 90-296
Superfluidity: states of matter, Special Report, 88-188
Supernova: astronomy, 90-225, 89-226; Close-Up, 88-228; dark matter, Special Report, 90-122; dating methods, Special Report, 89-209; giant telescopes, Special Report, 90-97; il., 88-231; physics, 88-302
Supersymmetry: dark matter, Special Report, 90-124
Swallowtail butterfly: mimicry, Special Report, 90-76

Swiss water process: Consumer Science, 90-322
Synapse: addiction, Special Report, 88-120
Systolic pressure: Consumer Science, 90-328

T

T cells: drugs, 88-252; magic bullets, Special Report, 90-186
Tail wind: wind shear, Special Report, 90-151
Tannin: plant defenses, Special Report, 89-123
Tasaday: Close-Up, 88-217
Taste: mimicry, Special Report, 90-74
Teaching, Science. See **Science education.**
Technology: books, 90-233, 88-237
Tectonics. See **Plate tectonics.**
Teeth, Fossil: anthropology, 90-216; dinosaur, Special Report, 89-44
Telephone: Consumer Science, 89-322
Telescope: dating methods, Special Report, 89-207; giant telescopes, Special Report, 90-84
Television technology: Special Report, 90-198. See also **Video systems.**
Temperature: agriculture, 88-212; energy, 88-260; geology, 90-274; meteorology, 90-287; oceanography, 90-294; physics, 88-299; states of matter, Special Report, 88-187. See also **Climate.**
Temperature, Global average: global warming, Special Report, 90-128
Temporal pole: psychology, 90-307
Tephra: Mount St. Helens, Special Report, 90-104
Terminus: glacier, Special Report, 88-71
Termite: Biosphere II, Special Report, 89-150; environment, 88-266; Wilson, Edward, 89-362
Testosterone: zoology, 89-317
Tetracycline: dentistry, 89-250
Tevatron Collider: physics, 90-305, 88-304
Thalamas: neuroscience, 90-289
Thermal barrier: aircraft design, Special Report, 88-181
Thermal transfer process: Consumer Science, 90-327
Thermodynamics: Hawking, Stephen W., 89-349
Thermoluminescence: anthropology, 89-215
Thistle: plant defenses, Special Report, 89-120
Thorium: dating methods, Special Report, 89-200; indoor air pollution, Special Report, 88-145
3-D video: electronics, 89-257; TV technology, Special Report, 90-209
Thrust-fault: geology, Close-Up, 90-272
Thunderstorm: meteorology, 89-283, 285; 88-282

Tidal wave: geology, 90-275
Tilapia: Biosphere II, Special Report, 89-152
Tobacco: addiction, Special Report, 88-125; plant defenses, Special Report, 89-121, 128
Tobacco smoke. See **Smoking.**
Tomato: genetic science, 90-267; plant defenses, Special Report, 89-122
Tomb. See **Burial site.**
Tool, Prehistoric: anthropology, 90-215; archaeology, 90-219, 88-218
Toothbrush: Consumer Science, 88-331
Top-down theory: dark matter, Special Report, 90-126
Tornado: wind shear, Special Report, 90-147
Toxic fumes: indoor air pollution, Special Report, 88-151
Toxic waste: waste disposal, Special Report, 90-61
Toxin: Ames, Bruce N., 88-346; immunology, 89-273; magic bullets, Special Report, 90-192; neuroscience, 89-288; plant defenses, Special Report, 89-120
Trajectory: physics, Close-Up, 90-300
Tranquilizer: addiction, Special Report, 88-119; drugs, 88-253
Transfer RNA: genetic science, 89-265
Transferrin: medical research, 90-284
Transistor: computer chips, Special Report, 88-203; superconductivity, Special Report, 89-111; TV technology, Special Report, 90-205
Transition temperature. See **Critical temperature.**
Transplantation, immune-system: immunology, 90-276
Transplantation surgery: chemistry, 90-241; neuroscience, 90-288, 88-288; medical research, 90-280
Transportation: superconductivity, Special Report, 89-116
Trash: waste disposal, Special Report, 90-56
Tree: Mount St. Helens, Special Report, 90-101; Organization for Tropical Studies, Special Report, 90-184
Tree-ring dating: Anasazi, Special Report, 89-28
Triangle Coalition for Science and Technology Education: science education, 90-312
Triassic Period: dating methods, Special Report, 89-199; dinosaur, Special Report, 89-45; paleontology, 88-296
Trichome: plant defenses, Special Report, 89-120
Trilobite: paleontology, 89-298
Trireme: archaeology, 90-221
Tritium: physics, 89-304
Tropical biology: Biosphere II, Special Report, 89-147; Organization for Tropical Studies, Special Report, 90-172

Index

Acknowledgments

The publishers of *Science Year* gratefully acknowledge the courtesy of the following artists, photographers, publishers, institutions, agencies, and corporations for the illustrations in this volume. Credits should read from top to bottom, left to right on their respective pages. All entries marked with an asterisk (*) denote illustrations created exclusively for *Science Year*. All maps, charts, and diagrams were prepared by the *Science Year* staff unless otherwise noted.

Cover E. S. Ross

4	John Dawson; E. S. Ross; © European Southern Observatory
5	Chris Palm*; © Gary Braasch
8	© Henry Groskinsky; Bob Hersey*; Woods Hole Oceanographic Institution
9	© Gary Braasch; © Ovak Arslanian; © Michael Fogden, Organization of Tropical Studies
10–14	John Dawson
16	Natural History Museum of Los Angeles County
17	UPI/Bettmann Newsphotos; Rouffignac Cave, Dordogne, France (© Jean Vertut); Trudy Rogers*
19	R. G. Larson from Illinois State Museum; R. G. Larson*; Illinois State Museum; Illinois State Museum
22	John Dawson; Denver Museum of Natural History; Denver Museum of Natural History
26	© Lou Lehmann, Can-Dive Services Ltd.
28	Oceaneering International, Inc.
29	© Can-Dive Services Ltd.; © Bruce Robison, Monterey Bay Aquarium Research Institute
30	Tony Gibbons*
35	Woods Hole Oceanographic Institution; Woods Hole Oceanographic Institution; © Pamela Blades-Eckelbarger
37	© Mars Youngbluth, Harbor Branch Oceanographic Institution
40	Bob Hersey*
45	Bill Curtsinger © National Geographic Society
47	Bob Hersey*
48	Bill Curtsinger © National Geographic Society
50–52	Bob Hersey*
56	© Rich Frishman
59	Joe Rogers*
60	Joe Rogers*; Joe Rogers*; Tymstra, Greenpeace
63	Joe Rogers*; Waste Management, Inc.
64	Greg Pease, Wheelabrator Environmental Systems, Inc.
65	Dennis A. Waters, Wheelabrator Environmental Systems, Inc.
66	Joe Rogers*; Waste Management, Inc.
68	E. S. Ross
71	© Norman Myers, Bruce Coleman Inc.
72	© Zig Leszczynski, Animals Animals; Steinhart Aquarium from Photo Researchers
73	© Allan Power, Bruce Coleman Inc.; © Allan Power, Photo Researchers
74	Steinhart Aquarium
75	© Stephen J. Krasemann, DRK Photo
76–79	E. S. Ross
81	James E. Lloyd
82	E. R. Degginger; Lincoln P. Brower
84–86	Joe Van Severen*
87	John Crerar Library, University of Chicago; © Palomar Observatory
88	© Roger Ressmeyer; © 1983 California Institute of Technology; © Palomar Observatory
90	© Roger Ressmeyer
91	Joe Van Severen*; © European Southern Observatory; Itek Optical Systems; Joe Van Severen*
92	© European Southern Observatory
94	© Roger Ressmeyer
98	Bill Eppridge, *Sports Illustrated;* © John Marshall; © Gary Braasch
102	Don Wilson*
103	© Gary Braasch; © Roger Werths, *Longview Daily News* from Woodfin Camp, Inc.
105	© John Marshall
106	Photos: © Gary Braasch; © John Marshall; © Gary Braasch—art: Tom Herzberg*
110	Don Wilson*; © Gary Braasch; © Gary Braasch
111	© John Marshall; Weyerhaeuser

112	© Keith Gunnar, West Stock; © John Marshall; © Gary Braasch
115	Chris Palm*
116	Joel R. Primack
117	Chris Palm*
118	National Optical Astronomy Observatories
120–122	Chris Palm*
129	JAK Graphics*
130	© Jim Richardson, West Light
131	E. R. Degginger; © Ted Cordingley, Nawrocki Stock Photo
132	JAK Graphics*
134	© Henry Groskinsky; National Center for Atmospheric Research
136	JAK Graphics*
138	JAK Graphics*; © Doug Wilson from Marilyn Gartman
139	© Wilson Goodrich from Marilyn Gartman
140	Photri from Marilyn Gartman; © Dan Guravich, Photo Researchers; © Lee Balterman from Marilyn Gartman
144	© Wendy Schreiber, National Center for Atmospheric Research/National Science Foundation; © Mark Perlstein; © Ovak Arslanian
148	Howard Berelson*; © Stuart Cohen, Stock, Boston
149	Art: Howard Berelson*—photo: Theodore Fujita
150–152	Howard Berelson*
153	© Jim Wilson, National Center for Atmospheric Research/National Science Foundation
155	© Roger Ressmeyer
156	Ovak Arslanian
158	© Michael Lange, Woodfin Camp, Inc.
161	Roberta Polfus*
162	Roberta Polfus*; © Pete Saloutos, The Stock Market; Patricia N. Farnsworth; Patricia N. Farnsworth
164–166	Roberta Polfus*
169	Roberta Polfus*; Roberta Polfus*; © Lennart Nilsson from *A Child Is Born;* © Howard Sochurek, The Stock Market
173	© Gary Braasch
175	Walter H. Hodge, Organization of Tropical Studies
176	© Michael Fogden, Organization of Tropical Studies; © Gregory G. Dimijian, M.D.; © H. Silvester, Photo Researchers
177	© R. L. Chazdon
180	© Gregory G. Dimijian, M.D.
181	© Gary Braasch
182–184	Donald Stone, Organization of Tropical Studies
186–196	Art: Guy Wolek*; Rick Incrocci*
198	Granger Collection; Shooting Star; Enyart, Shooting Star; Shooting Star; © Andy Hernandez, Picture Group; Don Wilson*
201	Don Wilson*; Advanced TV Research Program, Massachusetts Institute of Technology; Advanced TV Research Program, Massachusetts Institute of Technology
202	Don Wilson*
203	Art: Don Wilson*—photos: © Gerry Davis, Phototake
206	David Sarnoff Research Center; RCA; Steven Spicer*
207	© Hank Morgan; *World Book* photo; SONY Corporation; SONY Corporation; © Hank Morgan; Don Wilson*
210	C. Y. Huany, Lockheed Missiles and Space Company; Martin Marietta Corporation
211	© 1988 The Walt Disney Company; U. S. Department of Agriculture; Bowling Green State University
212	Martin Marietta Corporation
214	U. S. Department of Agriculture
216	Drawing by Sidney Harris; © 1988 The New Yorker Magazine, Inc.
217	Archeo-Tec
218	Ned Seidler © National Geographic Society; Bill Ballenberg © National Geographic Society
219	Martha Cooper © National Geographic Society
221	AP/Wide World

World Book Encyclopedia, Inc., provides high-quality educational and reference products for the family and school. They include The World Book Medical Encyclopedia, a 1,040-page fully illustrated family health reference; The World Book of Space Exploration, a two-volume review of the major developments in space since man first walked on the moon; and the Student Information Finder and How to Study Video, a fast-paced video presentation of key study skills with information students need to succeed in school. For further information, write WORLD BOOK ENCYCLOPEDIA, INC., P.O. Box 3576, Chicago, IL 60654.